How Asia Votes

How Asia Votes

John Fuh-sheng Hsieh
University of South Carolina

David Newman
National University of Singapore

CHATHAM HOUSE PUBLISHERS
SEVEN BRIDGES PRESS, LLC
NEW YORK · LONDON

Seven Bridges Press, LLC
135 Fifth Avenue, New York, NY 10010

Copyright © 2002 by Chatham House Publishers of Seven Bridges Press, LLC

All rights reserved. No part of this publication may be reproduced, stored in a retrieval system, or transmitted in any form or by any means, electronic, mechanical, photocopying, recording, or otherwise, without the prior permission of the publisher.

Publisher: Ted Bolen
Managing Editor: Katharine Miller
Cover Design: Stefan Killen Design
Cover Art: PhotoDisc, Inc.
Copyediting and Composition: Melissa A. Martin
Printing and Binding: Victor Graphics, Inc.

Library of Congress Cataloging-in-Publication Data
How Asia votes / edited by John Fuh-sheng Hsieh and David Newman.
    p. cm.
   Includes bibliographical references (p.) and index.
   ISBN 1-889119-41-5
   1. Elections—Asia—Case studies. 2. Voting—Asia—Case studies.
I. Hsieh, John Fuh-sheng, 1951– . II. Newman, David, 1956 Oct. 25– .
   JQ38 .H69 2002
   324.95—dc21

                         2001001104

Manufactured in the United States of Ameica
10 9 8 7 6 5 4 3 2 1

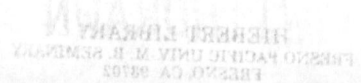

In memory of

William H. Riker

Contents

Tables and Figures	ix
Acknowledgments	xi

JOHN FUH-SHENG HSIEH AND DAVID NEWMAN
Introduction
Elections in the Asia-Pacific: A Decade of Change — 1

EMERSON M.S. NIOU
1. Village Elections: Roots of Democratization in China — 18

JOHN FUH-SHENG HSIEH
2. Continuity and Change in Taiwan's Electoral Politics — 32

DAVID NEWMAN
3. Hong Kong: A Decade of Change — 50

LO SHIU HING
4. Macau's Political Evolution and Prospects — 76

MICHAEL F. THIES
5. Changing How the Japanese Vote: The Promise and Pitfalls of the 1994 Electoral Reform — 92

CHAN WOOK PARK
6. Elections in Democratizing Korea — 118

STEVEN ROOD
7. Elections as Complicated and Important Events in the Philippines — 147

JEFFREY C. GALLUP
8. Cambodia: A Shaky Start for Democracy ... 165

SURIN MAISRIKROD
9. Political Reform and the New Thai Electoral System: Old Habits Die Hard? ... 187

JAMES UNG-HO CHIN
10. Malaysia: The Barisan National Supremacy ... 210

DIANE K. MAUZY
11. Electoral Innovation and One-Party Dominance in Singapore ... 234

DONALD E. WEATHERBEE
12. Indonesia: Electoral Politics in a Newly Emerging Democracy ... 255

Index ... 283

About the Contributors ... 291

Tables and Figures

TABLE I.1	Political Rights in the Asia-Pacific	2
TABLE I.2	Electoral Systems	4
TABLE I.3	Hypothetical Taiwanese Voter Preferences	5
TABLE I.4	Borda Count Results	6
TABLE I.5	Elections Held in Asian Democracies as of Mid-2000	15
TABLE 1.1	Survey of Village Election Methods in China	25
TABLE 1.2	Overall Distribution of the Quality of the Implementation of Village Elections	26
TABLE 1.3	Distribution of the Quality of the Implementation of Village Elections by Province	27
TABLE 1.4	The Quality of Village Election Implementation: Weighted Score and Rankings	28
TABLE 1.5	Election Quality and Village Power Center	29
TABLE 2.1	Vote Shares of the Various Political Parties in the Legislative Yuan Elections, 1969–98	37
TABLE 2.2	The Distribution of Seats in the Legislative Yuan	44
TABLE 3.1	Growth in the Hong Kong Electorate	54
TABLE 3.2	(S)election Methods of Government Officials in Hong Kong	58
TABLE 3.3	Changes in the Composition of the Hong Kong Legislature over Time	59
TABLE 3.4	Hong Kong Party Representation in Legco by Constituency in 1991, 1995, Provisional, and 1998 Legislatures	60
TABLE 3.5	Comparison of the 1991, 1995, and 1998 Geographic Constituency Elections in Hong Kong	62
TABLE 4.1	The Composition of Macau's Legislative Assembly, 1976–2009	77
TABLE 4.2	Voter Turnout in Macau's Legislative Assembly Direct Elections, 1976–96	81
TABLE 4.3	Results of Macau's 1992 Legislative Assembly Direct Elections	83
TABLE 4.4	Results of Macau's 1996 Legislative Assembly Direct Elections	85
TABLE 5.1	Japan's Lower House Electoral Rules: Before and After Reform	95
TABLE 5.2	Party Strength in Japan's House of Representatives, 1990 and 1993	98
TABLE 5.3	Party Strength in Japan's House of Representatives, 1996 and 2000	100
TABLE 5.4	Party Strength in Japan's House of Councillors	101
TABLE 6.1	Korea's National Assembly Election Results, 1988	122
TABLE 6.2	Korea's National Assembly Election Results, 1992	123
TABLE 6.3	Korea's National Assembly Election Results, 1996	124

TABLE 6.4	Korea's National Assembly Election Results, 2000	125
TABLE 6.5	Indices of Disproportionality and Party System Characteristics	132
TABLE 7.1	Sequence of Philippine Elections from 1992 to 1998	148
TABLE 7.2	Low Public Trust in Philippine Political Parties	154
TABLE 7.3	Shifting Party Affiliations after the 1998 Elections in the House of Representatives of the Philippines	155
TABLE 8.1	Results of the 1993 Cambodian Elections	168
TABLE 8.2	Results of the 1998 Cambodian Elections	179
TABLE 10.1	Malaysian Parliamentary Election Results, 1974–99	226
TABLE 11.1	The 1959 Election in Singapore: Seats Won	236
TABLE 12.1	Results of the 1955 Indonesian General Election	258
TABLE 12.2	New Order Election Results in Indonesia: Party Percentage of Vote and DPR Seats Won	261
TABLE 12.3	Provincial Representation in the 1999 Indonesian General Election	267
TABLE 12.4	Parties Contesting the 1999 Indonesian Election	272
TABLE 12.5	1999 Indonesian National Election Results	275
FIGURE 1.1	Ballot Design for the Transferable Vote Method	23
FIGURE 2.1	The Distribution of Voters on the National Identity Issue, 1992–99	39
FIGURE 2.2	Voters' Own Positions and Their Perceptions of the Various Parties' Positions on the National Identity Issue	40
FIGURE 2.3	The Distribution of Voters on the Reform versus Stability Issue, 1992–99	41
FIGURE 2.4	Voters' Own Positions and Their Perceptions of the Various Parties' Positions on the Reform versus Stability Issue	42
FIGURE 5.1	Japan's Party System, 1955–90	97
FIGURE 5.2	Japan's Party System, 1990–2000	99
FIGURE 5.3	Change in Japanese Voter Turnout, 1946–2000	110
FIGURE 7.1	Filipinos' Satisfaction with the Way Democracy Works, 1991–2000	149
FIGURE 7.2	Filipinos' Belief in Free and Fair Elections at the Precinct Level, 1984–98	160
FIGURE 7.3	Filipinos' Net Performance Ratings of President Joseph E. Estrada by Socioeconomic Class, 1990–2000	162

Acknowledgments

IN ASIAN FASHION, we believe that it is right and proper to acknowledge first our intellectual debt to our teachers. As such, we date the beginning of this project to our days, now more than twenty years past, as graduate students in the political science department at the University of Rochester. We thank Richard Niemi, Bing Powell, Bill Riker, and Bruce Bueno de Mesquita for stirring our interest in politics generally and in comparative and electoral studies more specifically. Bill is particularly missed.

We would like to thank the contributors. They were all forthcoming in agreeing to participate, and later they were all patient in responding to our numerous requests for revisions, ever-changing deadlines, and inquiries.

In addition, we would like to thank Melanie Manion, Alvin Rabushka, Andrew Nathan, Alfred Wilhelm, Peter Ordeshook, and Emerson Niou for commenting on and giving suggestions to our chapters.

In Taiwan, John Hsieh is grateful to the Opinion Research Taiwan and the Election Study Center of National Chengchi University for providing survey data and a fruitful research environment. In particular, John would like to thank I-hua Huang, Yih-yan Chen, Teh-fu Huang, Yung-tai Hung, I-chou Liu, and many other colleagues and research assistants at the center for their encouragement and assistance over the years. Tse-hsin Chen and Chi-min Chen have also been very helpful in collecting data from a variety of other sources. In the United States, John would like to thank the Department of Government and International Studies and the Center for Asian Studies at the University of South Carolina for providing valuable logistic support. Chun-ju Chen spent many days formatting the chapters in this volume. We owe her a great deal.

In Hong Kong, David Newman would like to thank David Phillips and Brian Bridges for their collegiality and support over the years, Li Pang-kwong for responding to persistent data requests, and Law Wing-sang for his insights into Hong Kong politics and personalities. In Singapore, David would like to thank the National University of Singapore's Public Policy Programme and its director,

Ong Jin-hui, for providing a supportive research environment for completing this book, as well as Mukul Asher, Tom Snyder, and Jay Walder for their friendship and Emil Bolongaita and Raja Nor Azwa for reading several of the chapters. Our appreciation is also extended to the Hoover Institution, Stanford University, for permission to reprint excerpts from "Hong Kong under Chinese Rule: The First Year," Essays in Public Policy, No. 90, 1998.

While our intellectual debts are considerable, we remain responsible for the final volume, and any errors are ours alone.

INTRODUCTION

Elections in the Asia-Pacific: A Decade of Change

by John Fuh-sheng Hsieh and David Newman

THE ASIA-PACIFIC REGION has experienced remarkable and unprecedented political change since the mid-1980s. In 1986 a popular revolution brought down the Marcos regime and reestablished democracy in the Philippines. At about the same time, the Nationalist government in Taiwan decided to launch a series of political reforms, which eventually led to democratic transition there. In 1987 South Korean President Chun Doo Hwan reached a compromise with the opposition, paving the way for the establishment of the democratic Sixth Republic. A similar process took place in Thailand, where, after a brief interlude of military intervention in 1991–92, the principle of civilian control over the government seemed to have taken root in the 1990s. As the decade came to a close, even Indonesia had successfully completed its first open and competitive election in decades.

In addition to Japan and those newly emerging third-wave democracies (Huntington 1991), a certain degree of liberalization, if not democratization, has also taken place in most of the countries in the region, including such communist countries as China and Vietnam (see table I.1). Elections, which are an integral part of democratic governance, have spread to quite a few countries in the Asia-Pacific.[1] Malaysia and Singapore have held elections since the 1950s, and Cambodia, Hong Kong, and Macau have experimented with electoral politics. Even in China, although there is still no direct popular election at the national level, the relatively competitive nature of village elections has attracted a lot of attention. One measure of the liberalization that has occurred in the region is the change in the Freedom House "political rights index." As shown in table I.1, of the ten countries surveyed in this volume, five have improved their five-year (1994–99) average "political rights index" rankings compared to the prior five-year period (1989–94). China, Japan, and South Korea experienced no change, and only Singapore and Indonesia experienced a decline. And, as the decade ended, Indonesia appeared poised to reverse this decline following the overthrow of Suharto.

Table I.1 Political Rights in the Asia-Pacific

Territory[a]	1999 Gastil Political Rights Index[b]	Average 1989 to 1994 Gastil Political Rights Index[b]	Average 1994 to 1999 Gastil Political Rights Index[b]
Cambodia	6.0	6.0	5.8
China	7.0	7.0	7.0
Indonesia	6.0	6.0	6.8
Japan	1.0	1.2	1.2
Korea, South	2.0	2.0	2.0
Malaysia	5.0	4.8	4.2
Philippines	2.0	2.8	2.2
Singapore	5.0	4.2	4.8
Taiwan	2.0	3.8	2.4
Thailand	2.0	3.2	2.8

Source: Freedom House 2000.

a. No figures are available for Hong Kong and Macau because the index is only calculated for countries.
b. The index ranges from 1 (best) to 7 (worst), referring to the degree of political rights in a country.

All these changes may have something to do with the socioeconomic development in this part of the world. Indeed, in terms of economic development, East Asia has been the fastest growing area in the world in the past several decades. Following rapid economic development, civil society emerges in many countries, demanding that the government loosen its control over the people. In the meantime, the influx of so-called Western influence also reshapes the traditional cultures in the region, and democratic values gradually take root. In countries such as Japan, the Philippines, Malaysia, and Singapore, foreign influence has taken a more direct form by setting up democratic institutions in those countries (Dahl 1971; Huntington 1991; Hsieh 2000).

Indeed, to fully understand the political dynamics in the Asia-Pacific region, electoral politics cannot be overlooked. Moreover, given their different historical, cultural, and socioeconomic backgrounds, it is interesting to contrast how Asians and Westerners behave in elections. The intention of this book is to fill the gap in the current literature by providing the reader with an overall understanding of elections in the Asia-Pacific, including both the institutional and behavioral aspects of electoral politics. The territories covered here include not only the old and new democracies such as Japan, South Korea, Taiwan, the Philippines, and Thailand, but also those that have experienced elections over the years: Malaysia, Singapore, Hong Kong, Macau, Cambodia, and Indonesia.[2] Also, given the attention that has been paid to the village elections in China, that country is included even though it does not hold direct national elections.

ELECTORAL SYSTEMS

On the institutional side, various electoral systems have been adopted by Asia-Pacific countries (see table I.2, p. 4). As has been argued repeatedly by voting theorists, the choice of voting system can alter the selection made by the electorate even though the preferences of the electorate are held fixed (Riker 1982a). Using Taiwan's 2000 presidential election as an example demonstrates this finding vividly.[3]

In this election, there were three major candidates: Lien Chan of the ruling Kuomintang (Nationalist Party, KMT), Chen Shui-bian of the Democratic Progressive Party (DPP), and James Soong, a KMT-turned-independent. With 39 percent of the popular vote, Chen defeated Soong and Lien, who received 37 percent and 23 percent, respectively. But by adding the 1 percent vote received by two other minor candidates to Chen's vote and assuming that each voter has a preference ordering for the set of candidates—ranging from most preferred to least preferred—table I.3 (p. 5) shows a hypothetical situation that illustrates our point. As can be seen from the table, for 40 percent of the voters, Chen was the first choice for president, while 37 percent preferred Soong and 23 percent preferred Lien. In a first-past-the-post, plurality voting scheme, Chen wins the presidency with 40 percent of the vote.

Does Chen have a unique claim to the presidency? While he was elected under a "fair" and democratic election scheme, is this the only outcome possible given the preferences of the voters? The French electoral system, also referred to as a double-ballot system, requires that a candidate receive at least a majority (one vote more than 50 percent) in order to be selected. If no candidate receives a majority of the vote, then the two candidates receiving the most votes compete in a "second round." Obviously, in the absence of a tie, one of the two must receive a majority in the second round and is selected.[4]

If Taiwan were to utilize the French voting scheme in its 2000 presidential election, Soong, Chen, and Lien would initially all compete against one another, and then, because Soong and Chen receive the most votes in round one, they would then proceed to round two. In round two, Soong and Chen would compete against one another, and although Lien does not compete, his supporters still vote—this time for their second choices. Of the 23 percent of the electorate originally voting for Lien, roughly 60 percent vote for Soong and 40 percent vote for Chen. The result is that Soong receives 51 percent of the vote (37 percent plus 14 percent) and Chen receives 49 percent of the vote. Soong is elected president in a fair, democratic election.[5] Thus a change in the rules can change the outcome even though the preferences of the voters remain fixed.

Table I.2 Electoral Systems

Territory	National Legislature (Lower House)				President
	Name	Seats	Electoral System[a]	Term (Years)	Popular Election; Term (Years)
Cambodia	National Assembly	122	PR (LR)	5	No
China	National People's Congress	2979	Not directly elected	5	No
Hong Kong	Legislative Council	60	20 by PR (LR); 30 by functional constituencies and 10 by an Election Committee (FPTP/BLOCK)	2	No
Indonesia	House of People's Representatives	500	462 by PR (LR); 38 appointed as representatives of the army	5	No
Japan	House of Representatives	500	Mixed 300 by FPTP; 200 by PR (d'Hondt)	4	No
Korea	National Assembly	299	Mixed 253 by FPTP; 46 by PR (LR)	4	Yes; 4
Macau	Legislative Assembly	23	8 by PR (d'Hondt); 8 by indirect election; 7 appointed	4	No
Malaysia	House of Representatives	192	FPTP	5	No
Philippines	House of Representatives	221	Mixed 80 percent by FPTP; 20 percent by PR	3	Yes; 6
Singapore	Parliament	90	83 by FPTP/Block; up to 15 appointed	5	Yes; 6
Taiwan	Legislative Yuan	225	Mixed 176 by SNTV; 41 national representatives and 8 overseas representatives by PR (LR)	3	Yes; 4
Thailand[b]	House of Representatives	393	Block	4	No

Sources: Keesing's Record of World Events 1998; Inter-Parliamentary Union; various chapters in this volume.

a. PR = proportional representation; FPTP = first-past-the-post; LR = largest remainder; SNTV = single nontransferable vote.
b. In 1997 a mixed system was adopted as a result of the constitutional reform. Under the new system, of the 500 members of the House of Representatives, 400 are elected by FPTP and the remaining 100 by PR.

Table I.3 Hypothetical Taiwanese Voter Preferences

	Chen Voters (40%)	Soong Voters (37%)	Lien Voters (14%)	Lien Voters (9%)
First Choice	Chen	Soong	Lien	Lien
Second Choice	Lien	Lien	Soong	Chen
Third Choice	Soong	Chen	Chen	Soong

While it might not be too surprising that a change in the rules could alter the outcome between Soong and Chen given the relatively small difference in the level of support they enjoyed, it would be a more significant concern if a set of fair democratic rules could select Mr. Lien as president. One criticism of the plurality voting system and the double-ballot election scheme is that neither considers the complete preference ordering of the voters. For instance, the plurality voting system does not consider any information about the voters' preferences other than the most preferred choice. The double-ballot election scheme considers the voters' first choice in the first round, and possibly a lower preference in the second round. Some voting schemes consider the voters' complete preference orderings.

The Borda count allows each voter to assign votes relative to the strength of his or her preferences. For instance, if there were three alternatives, as in table I.3, a voter would assign two votes to a first choice, one vote to a second choice, and no votes to a last choice. In Taiwan's 2000 presidential election, Soong's supporters would each cast two votes for Soong, one vote for Lien, and no votes for Chen. Chen's supporters would each cast two votes for Chen, one vote for Lien, and no votes for Soong. The Lien voters would each cast two votes for Lien, then roughly 60 percent of them would also cast one vote each for Soong and roughly 40 percent would cast one vote each for Chen. Assuming that there are only one hundred voters, the result, as shown in table I.4 (p. 6), is that Mr. Lien would have been elected in a fair and democratic election.

Although the Borda count has rarely been used in the real world, particularly for national elections, there are quite a few other types of electoral rules that have been applied to different parts of the globe. In the Anglo-American world, the first-past-the-post, plurality system in single-member districts (SMDs)[6] has been the norm. In the Asia-Pacific, most of the countries that have experienced strong Anglo-American influences, such as the Philippines and Malaysia, have also opted for such a system. In the mixed systems adopted by South Korea and Japan, the SMD plurality system is used for more than a majority of seats. The same is true of the new Thai system adopted in 1997. For the direct presidential election in South Korea, Taiwan, and the Philippines, such a rule has also been adopted.

A variant of the French double-ballot system is the Australian alternative vote. Under such a system, the voters are asked to order their preferences among

Table I.4 Borda Count Results

Candidates	Calculation of Votes	Total Votes
Lien	(23 x 2) + 40 + 37	123
Chen	(40 x 2) + 9	89
Soong	(37 x 2) + 14	88

all the candidates. If any candidate gains more than 50 percent of the first-preference vote, he or she is elected; otherwise, the second preferences of the voters who voted for the candidate with the least votes will be distributed to other candidates. If any candidate thus wins more than 50 percent of the vote, he or she is elected; otherwise, the previous procedure is repeated until a winner emerges. Unlike the French system, the Australian voters need to go to the polls only once.

The Australian alternative vote can be applied to multimember districts where two or more seats are available from a single district. This has been dubbed *single transferable vote* (STV) and has been used in the Irish and Maltese parliamentary elections. For example, in a two-member district with four candidates and 10,000 voters, a quota of 3,334 votes is established as the minimum necessary to be elected. Perhaps one candidate is successful initially. If a candidate is successful, having received 4,000 votes, her excess votes are not discarded. Rather, they are allocated to the remaining candidates in proportion to each of the 4,000 voters' second choices. If none of the remaining candidates then has acquired the requisite number of votes set out as the quota, the candidate with the fewest votes is removed from the process, and his votes are allocated to those voters' second choices. The process is continued until a second candidate is selected.

A method somewhat different from STV, which is called *single nontransferable vote* (SNTV), has been adopted in Taiwan, prereform Japan, and South Korea in the earlier period. Unlike STV, under which voters can order their preferences among the candidates, voters under the SNTV system can vote for only one candidate in multimember districts, and the candidates who obtain more votes than others get elected.

In such countries as Thailand (prior to the 1997 constitutional reform) and Singapore, the electors may cast as many votes as the number of seats available in the multimember districts. This strict application of plurality rule in multimember districts is called *block vote*. If the votes cast by each person must number fewer than the seats available, the system is limited vote, of which SNTV is a special case.

In the parliamentary elections in many Western European and Latin American countries, voters essentially vote for the political parties in multimember districts, and the allocation of seats among the political parties is determined by the votes received by the parties.[7] Such a system is called *proportional representation* (PR), and its purpose is to ensure a high degree of proportionality, that is, correspondence between the ratio of seats won by each political party and the proportion of votes it receives. In the first-past-the-post, plurality system, for instance, such proportionality may not be easily achieved. In the 1983 election in the United Kingdom, the Conservatives won 42 percent of the vote but managed to obtain 61 percent of the seats, while the Liberal/Social Democratic Alliance, with 25 percent of the vote, gained less than four percent of the seats. This would not have happened if PR had been employed.[8] Among the Asia-Pacific territories, PR has been used in Cambodia and Indonesia and has been introduced to Japan, South Korea, Taiwan, and Hong Kong to supplement the other rules that have been in place there.

In order to allocate the seats proportionally under PR, a variety of formulas can be chosen. One popular formula is the d'Hondt highest average system, which uses a series of divisors such as one, two, three, . . . to ensure that the average number of votes to win a seat is equivalent among all the political parties. First, the total vote obtained by each political party is divided by one, and the party with the highest "average" is awarded one seat. Then, the vote total of the party receiving the seat is divided by two, and this new "average" is compared to other parties' original vote totals. The party with the highest figure is given the second seat. At the following stage, if the party gaining the second seat is the same as the one securing the first seat, its original vote total is divided by three, and this new "average" is compared to other parties' vote totals. The party with the highest figure captures the third seat. If the party winning the second seat is different from the one acquiring the first seat, however, the second party's vote total is divided by two, and this new "average" is compared to the first party's "average" (already divided by two) and other parties' vote totals. The party with the highest "average" obtains the third seat. This process continues until all the seats are allocated. The PR part of Japan's new electoral system employs such a formula. In Macau, a slightly different formula is adopted. Instead of having one, two, three, . . . as divisors, it uses one, two, four, eight, . . . for calculating the "averages." Some Nordic countries use the Sainte-Laguë highest average system, in which the divisors are one and four-tenths, three, five, seven, ...

Another popular formula is the *largest remainder*. A quota (e.g., the total valid votes divided by the number of seats available in a district) is first determined. Each party's vote total is then divided by this quota, and the integer part of the quotient is the number of seats allocated to it. If there are remaining seats, the remainder of each party is compared, and the remaining seats go to the parties with the highest, the second highest, . . . remainder until all seats are allocated. This is the formula used in Hong Kong, Cambodia, Indonesia, Taiwan, and South Korea.[9]

As mentioned above, electoral rules matter, and different rules may result in the election of different candidates/parties. Moreover, electoral rules may also profoundly affect the political life in a society in a variety of ways. They will, for example, shape the party system, the electoral process, the internal dynamics within political parties, and so forth, to which we now turn.

Party Systems

In the modern world, political parties are an important part of the electoral process. In some countries, one party dominates the political scene to such an extent that all other parties are suppressed. This can be found in right- or left-wing totalitarian or authoritarian regimes. In democratic countries, one party such as the Liberal Democrat Party in Japan may continue to win the elections and to rule the country for a very long period of time. More frequently, there are several parties competing with one another. If there are obviously two major parties, it is a two-party system; otherwise, it is a multiparty system (Sartori 1976).[10]

In studies of electoral systems, there is a well-known proposition stating simply that, other things being equal, the SMD plurality voting will lead to a two-party system. William H. Riker dubbed this proposition Duverger's Law. A parallel proposition with regard to the PR system states that, under PR, a multiparty system is likely to emerge. This was called Duverger's Hypothesis by Riker (1982b). The reason that the former is considered a law and the latter a hypothesis is that the causal link between the SMD plurality system and the two-party system is very strong, almost universal except in cases where there is geographic concentration of minorities or a centralist party continues to win over the party at the extremes. Examples include Canada in the former case and the Congress Party in India in the latter (Riker 1982b).

More specifically, the reason SMD plurality voting brings about a two-party system involves strategic behavior by both the candidates/parties and the voters (Riker 1982b; Cox 1997). For example, in any given district, if one candidate is most likely to win, the best strategy for the other candidates is to coalesce so as to have some chance of defeating the likely winner. Gradually, two camps will emerge in the district, and if the cleavages (of class, religion, and so on) underpinning party competition are similar in almost all districts nationwide, it can be expected that a two-party system may develop in the country as a whole.

Similar logic influences voter choice. If a third-party supporter concludes that her most preferred candidate stands little or no chance of winning, then, in order not to waste her vote, she may opt for the lesser evil among the candidates of the two major parties. The votes may as a result be concentrated upon the two major parties. Hence, given the politicians' and voters' strategic behavior, a two-party system will emerge under the SMD plurality system.

Under the PR system, on the other hand, a minor party winning a small percentage of the vote may gain seats. Consequently, the incentive to engage in strategic behavior for both politicians and voters will be much less conspicuous. A multiparty system is thus quite likely. Nonetheless, although the PR system may not obstruct the survival of the third parties, it is unable to create those parties. Whether the third parties will be formed and gain a foothold depends very much upon the cleavages in the society. For a very long time in Austria, for instance, a two-party system was maintained even when PR was used (Riker 1982b).

For other proportional or semiproportional systems such as STV and SNTV, results similar to PR can be expected. Even the double-ballot system used in France may result in more than two political parties because what matters for the candidate in the first round is to remain viable in the second round, not necessarily in the top spot, and thus candidates and voters may not engage in the type of strategic behavior noted above in the first round.

Except in Japan, Taiwan, Malaysia, and Singapore, party systems in the Asia-Pacific are not fully institutionalized. Even in, say, Japan, the party system has undergone drastic changes in recent years. The fate of political parties in most of the countries in the region more often than not are tied to individual political leaders. This may have a lot to do with the brief history of competitive elections in those countries. The theory and the empirical evidence in the Western democracies may provide a clue to the evolution of party systems in the Asia-Pacific in the future.

ELECTION CAMPAIGNING AND VOTING BEHAVIOR

In addition to the number of political parties, electoral rules may influence campaigning and voter choices. Generally speaking, some rules are more likely to induce party-centered, and others candidate-centered, campaigning (Farrell 1996). Under the closed-list PR system, voters can choose only among the political parties; hence, political parties loom very large in campaigning. Except for a few political leaders, not much is heard about the individual candidates.

Under open-list PR systems, the voters are also able to vote for specific candidates, so candidates' names may become more conspicuous. In extreme cases—such as in Italy, prior to the recent electoral reform, or in Finland, where voters vote directly for the candidates, and the rank ordering on the party lists is determined essentially by the votes obtained by candidates—candidates become very visible in campaigning. Such preference voting within political parties often results in factional politics, among other things (Katz 1980).

Under the single-member district plurality system, electors cast votes for candidates; thus, candidates are certainly very important in the elections. Under normal circumstances, however, each party nominates only one candidate in a district so that candidates and parties are more or less synonymous. Thus both candidates and parties may play an important role in the electoral process.

The situation may be different under the SNTV system. Given the fact that under such a system, there may be fierce competition among several candidates nominated by the same political party in an electoral district, party label and issue position become less salient in election campaigning (Ramseyer and Rosenbluth 1997; see also chapters 2 and 5). Candidate-centered campaigning, however, is inevitable. A similar situation can also be expected under STV.

In some societies, particularly those where competitive elections are new, party systems may not be very well developed, and political parties may, to a large extent, be personality-based. Then the discussion of party-centered campaigning may not be meaningful. Voters may vote for a political party simply because they identify with the leader or leaders of the party. But in societies where political parties are well organized, voters may form partisan attachments as a cue to simplify their vote choices (Downs 1957). Indeed, in the study of advanced democracies, it is often found that partisan voting is more important than, say, candidate voting or issue voting. In a sense, party identification may be seen as a long-term stabilizing factor while candidate image and issue position are factors causing short-term fluctuations (Campbell et al. 1960).

In the countries covered in this book, candidates often play a very important role in election campaigning as well as in voters' choices. This may result from the short history of competitive elections and the type of electoral systems adopted in those countries—certainly a very different setting from that in Western democracies.

Structure of the Book

In editing a regional survey, it is challenging to determine the best approach to organizing the chapters. In the end, since there is no ideal structure, we have opted for a geographic organization focusing first on Northeast Asian and then Southeast Asian experience. The first four chapters could be grouped as "Greater China," but the common "Chinese" element would be overshadowed by the differences across the four societies.

Emerson Niou introduces the substantive chapters by examining the fascinating emergence of village elections in China. Since 1979, Chinese law has required more candidates for office than the number of seats to be filled and has allowed individuals to nominate others to contest for offices. While the party may still try to confirm nominations, these changes, coupled with the adoption of the *Organic Law of the Village Committee*, have encouraged a dramatic growth in local self governance and more accountable government. This chapter examines the various election schemes utilized at the village level in China. Perhaps most importantly, Professor Niou's study finds that the "quality" of the election system introduced is associated with the degree of autonomy granted to the elected officials.

John Fuh-sheng Hsieh examines electoral politics in Taiwan, showing that the basic structure underlying Taiwan's party politics is the national identity issue, which is quite different from that in most advanced democracies. Because most people subscribe to the status quo regarding the national identity issue, the ruling Kuomintang, seen as a status quo party, enjoys an advantage vis-à-vis other political parties. Indeed, the KMT is a rare case in which a ruling party during the authoritarian period is able to hold on to its governing position long after transition to democracy. As argued by Hsieh, Taiwan's party system has been stabilized in terms of competition between the traditional KMT camp and the traditional DPP camp. But within each camp, gradual fragmentation is also evident.

David Newman and Lo Shiu Hing explore two experiences concluding European colonial rule in Asia—Hong Kong and Macau, respectively. In Hong Kong, during the lead-up to China "reasserting" its sovereignty, the British made a belated effort to encourage electoral competition in the closing days of their administration. They encouraged elections, the emergence of local political figures, and the growth of political parties, in part, as potential defenses to offset the inevitable influence of the mainland in Hong Kong's political life. The political calendar of Hong Kong marked the end of the 1980s on 4 June 1989 in Tiananmen Square, and politics were born anew with more than one million Hong Kong people demonstrating in Victoria Park just eight years before the handover. The mainland's Hong Kong strategy throughout the 1990s was to trivialize the electoral process, the British reforms, and local prodemocracy politicians. Institutionally, the goal was to ensure that China had a fairly pliant legislature following the handover. Hong Kong's experience is a good example of how rules and institutional structures can influence actual electoral outcomes.

The experience of Portuguese rule in Macau was in some ways fundamentally different from that of the British in Hong Kong in that the Portuguese were reluctant rulers since the military coup in Portugal in 1974. In terms of the mechanics of elections and experiences leading up to their respective changes in sovereignty, however, the two former colonies were in many ways similar. Lo Shiu Hing traces the evolution of Macau's electoral system from the formation of the legislature in 1974 to the handover of sovereignty by Portugal to China in 1999. The legislature, once elected exclusively by fewer than 3,000 Portuguese residents of Macau, most recently attracted more than 75,000 voters, the vast majority of whom are Chinese. Both former colonies have evolved politically in response to newly enlarged electorates, a return to Chinese rule, and the emergence of political groups representing a wide variety of interests. Professor Lo concludes that the Macau experience has given rise to increasingly corrupt elections characterized by vote buying coupled with an expansion of patron-client politics. He concludes by speculating that these trends may foretell future developments in Hong Kong—Macau's neighbor to the east.

Michael Thies contrasts Japan's use of the single nontransferable vote in elections for the Lower House of the Diet from the end of World War II until 1993, with the current system of using single-member districts and proportional representation adopted in 1994. Professor Thies relates these rule changes to prospects of electoral success of the reformers and internal party organization, competition, and campaign strategies. He argues that the implications of the reforms will take time to work through the system but that the consequences of the reforms are predictable—more centralized political parties appealing to the public for support, less on the basis of candidate characteristics, as has been the case in the past, and more on policy differences between the parties.

Korea, like the Philippines, Taiwan, and Thailand, is an example of Huntington's third wave. Civilian demonstrations in the late 1980s and the formation of the Sixth Republic in 1988 has meant that Korea has experienced a full decade of democratic institutionalization capped by the election of Kim Dae Jung, the perennial opposition leader, as president in 1997. Chan Wook Park examines the highly candidate-centered, personalistic nature of Korean politics that is reinforced by strong regional identification. Moreover, Professor Park examines the effect of changes in the election rules, a reform initiative, on the electoral prospects of the various political contestants. Park concludes optimistically that Korea has successfully navigated its "democratic transition" and, while there is still room for additional reform, voters are increasingly likely to use elections as a mechanism for expressing preferences with respect to both policy and selection of leaders.

Following Korea, our focus shifts south and east.

After twenty-two years of Marcos rule, the Philippines has embraced elections with gusto. Elections for national or local offices were held every year from 1992 through 1998. A more regular pattern of holding four sets of elections over a six-year period has now been adopted. Dr. Steven Rood finds that these elections, while generally fair and open, are lacking in institutionalized political parties. Campaigning and political activity remain largely focused on personalities rather than on policy, with successful candidates often switching parties after the election. Moreover, more than a decade after the "people power revolution," the Philippines faces some lethargy in its democratic progress. This is highlighted by middle-class dissatisfaction with President Estrada—a nagging concern since the middle class has been an ardent supporter of democratic reform and elections since the revolution.

Of the ten countries surveyed in this volume, Cambodia is closest to being on the cusp of the democratic wave. If we narrowly view democracy as holding elections, Cambodia conducted two elections during the 1990s—one supervised internationally and one organized domestically. Both were conducted under threats of violence and intimidation, but in both cases the elections were generally viewed as successful and fair. Taking a somewhat broader view of democracy, what did *not* emerge in Cambodia during this period was a recognition that one potential outcome of an election was the opposition gaining control of government. For Hun Sen, the elections were a tool to placate the international community, not a domestic referendum on his regime. Jeffrey Gallup analyzes the Cambodian elections and the prospects of a civil society developing from these two elections.

Thailand has journeyed far along the democratic road during the course of the 1990s. As Surin Maisrikrod recounts, the country experienced a coup in 1991 and an effort by the military to impose its own candidate as prime minister in 1992. A backlash of protest and a petition to the king brought about democratic elections in 1992. Subsequent elections were held in 1995 and 1996. A Constitutional Drafting Assembly, established in 1996, ultimately restructured the role of the two legislative bodies and the mechanism of electing members. The reforms incorporated into the new constitution adopted in 1997, however, went even further. New constitutional provisions govern campaigning, prescribe educational requirements for election to either the Senate or House of Representatives, and even proscribe candidates for the Senate from campaigning. Dr. Surin Maisrikrod reviews these systemic changes and examines the role of parties and elections in Thailand in the 1990s.

Malaysia, like Singapore, Hong Kong, and several others, is a good example of an Asian nation where a particular regime manipulated election rules over time to ensure its continued success at the polls. Structural arrangements regarding the allocation of seats and crafting of boundaries have guaranteed that the ruling Barisan Nasional (BN), aligned with a set of coopted parties, wins at least a two-thirds majority. James Chin highlights the regional differences between peninsular Malaysia and the eastern Malaysian states of Sabah and Sarawak. He concludes with some conjectures on Malaysia's future given the recent efforts by the Malaysian opposition to unify in response to Prime Minister Mahathir's jailing of his former deputy, Anwar Ibrahim.

Diane Mauzy explains how Singapore, a moderately democratic state with a parliamentary system, an elected president, and regular, free, and honest elections, repeatedly reelects Lee Kuan Yew's People's Action Party (PAP) despite the fact that the party maintains a weak apparatus. Professor Mauzy focuses on several factors to explain the PAP's dominance including its control of parapolitical grassroots organizations, its maintenance of the first-past-the-post electoral system and compulsory voting, and its use of a series of constitutional innovations, such as the creation of multimember constituencies and nominated members of parliament. Moreover, forty years of sustained economic prosperity and clean government has not harmed the PAP.

Indonesia had held a relatively free and fair election in 1955, resulting in the formation of a fragile government. Soon afterwards, it was replaced by authoritarian rule. Not until June 1999 were Indonesians given another chance to vote in a democratic election. Given the shaky situation in Indonesia, the largest Muslim country in the world, the prospects for a well-functioning democracy remain uncertain. Donald Weatherbee provides a vivid account of the political development in Indonesia leading to the events in 1999.

CONCLUSION

As one reads this volume, one should not be surprised to encounter elections that vary considerably from one's own experience or to learn of election systems that may not be viewed as completely fair. It is important to keep in mind as we examine these twelve territories that a half dozen currently are or recently were one-party states. Two are newly free from colonial rule, and several, until recently, were dominated by the military. Cambodia is just emerging from civil war, and the Philippines emerged from the Marcos dictatorship in 1986. While many Asian countries are progressing toward some notion of democracy and elections, the quality of these elections varies widely.

Although the contributors to this volume were not asked specifically to address the quality of elections, the reader should remain alert to several dimensions of this issue. Broadly, this includes whether elections are free and fair. Specifically, many Asian countries have gerrymandered electoral boundaries to enhance the ruling party's electoral performance. Coupled with gerrymandering is the manipulation of electoral systems, or voting schemes, to reward governing parties. For instance, these characteristics can be found in Japan and Malaysia, which disproportionately reward rural voters with additional seats. One consequence of such action is that while the phrase "one person, one vote" is often bandied about, few countries seek to ensure that electoral districts are roughly the same size or that a voter's influence in determining the outcome of an election is roughly the same as that of other voters. Instead, district sizes vary considerably and the influence of a voter varies widely. For instance, in Hong Kong a corporate voter's single vote in a functional constituency can be as influential as several hundred individual voters in a geographical constituency.

Several countries seek to limit candidates testing their political support by imposing sizable financial bonds that are forfeited in the event that the candidate does not receive a minimum percentage of the vote. Such financial penalties potentially retard the development of new or minor parties. While the impact is uncertain in terms of quality, it is worth noting that several countries place limits on campaign advertising, expenditures, and activities. These limitations do not appear to prevent all instances of vote buying; such activities are widely commented on in several chapters in this volume. Vote buying takes on a particular art form in Singapore, where public housing residents who vote with the government receive priority renovations and additional amenities and those who defect to the opposition are relegated to the back of the queue.

Notably, since the ruling parties have successfully manipulated the electoral structures, there is less need to manipulate outcomes. Honest vote counting is pretty much the norm in Asia, with opposition parties generally accepting the legitimacy of the vote, if not the legitimacy of the voting method. In several countries, Singapore and Malaysia, for instance, the opposition is under no illusions regarding its prospects of unseating either the PAP or BN, the two ruling parties. Elections in these countries are referenda on the ruling party's administration and popularity, not decisions as to which party should govern.

Some countries, while advancing elections technically, have not readily embraced such constituent elements of democracy as freedom of expression, the right to organize or assemble, or the ability to publish. Several of the countries under study here still maintain draconian laws on assembly, constrain or control the press,

Table I.5 Elections Held in Asian Democracies as of Mid-2000

Territory	Presidential	Parliamentary
Cambodia		1993, 1998
Hong Kong		1991, 1995, 1998
Indonesia		1955, 1971, 1977, 1982, 1987, 1992, 1997, 1999
Japan		1946, 1947, 1949, 1952, 1955, 1958, 1960, 1963, 1967, 1969, 1972, 1976, 1979, 1980, 1983, 1986, 1990, 1993, 1996, 2000
Korea	1987, 1992, 1997	1948, 1950, 1954, 1958, 1960, 1963, 1967, 1971, 1973, 1978, 1981, 1985, 1988, 1992, 1996, 2000
Macau		1976, 1980, 1984, 1988, 1992, 1996
Malaysia		1959, 1964, 1969, 1974, 1978, 1982, 1986, 1990, 1995, 1999
Philippines	1946, 1949, 1953, 1957, 1961, 1965, 1969; 1981, 1986, 1992, 1998	1946, 1949, 1953, 1957, 1961, 1965, 1969, 1978, 1984, 1987, 1992, 1995, 1998
Singapore	1993, 1999	1955, 1959, 1963, 1968, 1972, 1976, 1980, 1984, 1988, 1991, 1997
Taiwan	1996, 2000	1947, 1969, 1972, 1975, 1980, 1983, 1986, 1989, 1992, 1995, 1998
Thailand		1933, 1937, 1938, 1946, 1948, 1952, 1957, 1969, 1975, 1976, 1979, 1983, 1986, 1988, 1992, 1995, 1996

Sources: Keesing's Record of World Events, various years; Gunn 1996, 160; various chapters in this volume.

Note: No direct popular election at the national level was held in China.

and intimidate the opposition and potential opposition through the use of the legal system. Though this topic is beyond the scope of this work, we believe that the appearance of elections in several of these countries has not yet altered many citizens' underlying tendency to avoid political activities and involvement.

Our optimistic conclusion, however, is that despite these deficiencies, elections are politically important in Asia. (For a summary of the elections held in these Asian territories, see table I.5.) In some countries they are mechanisms for selecting rulers and in others for legitimating rule. Perhaps more importantly for the future, the quality of elections appears to be improving and their role in society broadening. The 1990s closed with Asia looking very different than it did a decade earlier. The Philippines, Thailand, Taiwan, and Korea joined Japan as full-fledged democracies of reasonable quality. Indonesia and Cambodia stepped into the democratic breach, but it is still uncertain how these countries will fare. Malaysia and Singapore continue to hold to their increasingly distinctive form of one-party democracy, while China ambles toward a still tentative political reform at the local level. All in all, it has been an impressive ten years.

Notes

1. What constitutes a democracy is indeed a controversial issue. Here, we accept the procedural definition of democracy à la Joseph Schumpeter by thinking of democracy as "that institutional arrangement for arriving at political decisions in which individuals acquire the power to decide by means of a competitive struggle for the people's vote." (Schumpeter 1976, 269) For a dissenting view suggesting that elections are not an essential characteristic of democracy, see Mueller 1999.
2. The term *territory* is used to refer to the ten countries in this volume and Hong Kong and Macau—Special Administrative Regions of China. The terms *country* or *countries* are used to refer only to the ten sovereign states.
3. There are many examples similar to the one presented here. For instance, we are indebted to Bruce Bueno de Mesquita for drawing our attention to the United States 1992 presidential election as a case in point.
4. Most of the time in the French Fifth Republic, the double-ballot system in single-member districts has been used for both presidential and parliamentary elections. But the rules for who may compete in the runoff election if no candidate receives more than 50 percent of the vote in the first round are somewhat different in the presidential and National Assembly elections. In the former, only the top two candidates of the first round may enter the second round, and in the latter, any candidate who obtains more than 12.5 percent of the vote in the first round may compete later on.
5. In an interesting article, Christopher H. Achen argues that, indeed, Soong may defeat Chen if a double-ballot system is adopted. See Achen 2000.
6. In single-member districts, only one seat is available in each electoral district or constituency.
7. In a number of countries, voters may cast a ballot for specific candidates as well, but the allocation of seats among the political parties is determined essentially by the votes obtained by the parties.
8. An extreme example should clarify how these "discrepancies" between votes and seats can occur. Envision a 100-member legislature selected using single-member districts with just two parties competing. If party A received 51 percent of the vote in each district and party B received the remaining 49 percent of the vote in each district, party A would have won all 100 seats with just 51 percent of the total vote. In a PR system, party A would receive 51 seats and party B 49 seats. It is also worth pondering one implication of a PR system. Supporters of a PR system note, using the extreme first-past-the-post result above, that party B is essentially "locked" out of the legislature and that this is fundamentally unfair given that they received 49 percent of the vote. If the legislature employs a plurality voting scheme and the parties can maintain strict discipline, however, the result on any vote, on a policy on which the parties disagree, will be 51 to 49. Party B is essentially impotent despite being in the legislature.
9. For a detailed discussion of these formulas, see, for example, Taagepera and Shugart 1989.
10. A variety of methods may be used to count the number of political parties. A fashionable one is termed the Effective Number of Parties, which is defined as $1/\Sigma(p_i^2)$, where p_i refers to the proportion of seats or votes obtained by the *i*th party (Taagepera and Shugart 1989; Lijphart 1994).

REFERENCES

Achen, Christopher H. 2000. "Plurality Rule When Polling Is Forbidden: The Taiwan Presidential Election of 2000." Paper presented at the Conference on Taiwan Issues. Center for Asian Studies, University of South Carolina, Charleston. April.
Campbell, Angus, Philip E. Converse, Donald E. Stokes, and Warren E. Miller. 1960. *The American Voter*. New York: John Wiley.
Cox, Gary W. 1997. *Making Votes Count: Strategic Coordination in the World's Electoral Systems*. Cambridge, U.K.: Cambridge University Press.
Dahl, Robert A. 1971. *Polyarchy: Participation and Opposition*. New Haven, Conn.: Yale University Press.
Downs, Anthony. 1957. *An Economic Theory of Democracy*. New York: Harper and Row.
Farrell, David M. 1996. Campaign Strategies and Tactics. In *Comparing Democracies: Election and Voting in Global Perspective*, edited by Lawrence LeDuc, Richard G. Niemi, and Pippa Norris. Thousand Oaks, Calif.: Sage.
Freedom House. 2000. Annual Survey of Freedom Country Scores 1972–73 to 1998–99. http://freedomhouse.org/rankings.pdf.
Gunn, Geoffrey C. 1996. *Encountering Macau*: A Portuguese City-State on the Periphery of China, 1557–1999. Boulder, Colo.: Westview Press.
Hsieh, John Fuh-sheng. 2000. East Asian Culture and Democratic Transition: With Special Reference to the Case of Taiwan. *Journal of Asian and African Studies* 35:29–42.
Huntington, Samuel P. 1991. *The Third Wave: Democratization in the Late Twentieth Century*. Norman: University of Oklahoma Press.
Katz, Richard S. 1980. *A Theory of Parties and Electoral Systems*. Baltimore: Johns Hopkins University Press.
Keesing's Record of World Events. 1998. London: Longmans.
Lijphart, Arend. 1994. *Electoral Systems and Party Systems: A Study of Twenty-Seven Democracies, 1945–1990*. Oxford, U.K.: Oxford University Press.
Mueller, John E. 1999. *Capitalism, Democracy and Ralph's Pretty Good Grocery Store*. Princeton, N.J.: Princeton University Press.
Inter-Parliamentary Union. 1999. Parline Database. http://www.ipu.org/parline-e/parlinesearch.asp.
Ramseyer, J. Mark, and Frances McCall Rosenbluth. 1997. *Japan's Political Marketplace*. Cambridge, Mass.: Harvard University Press.
Riker, William H, 1982a. *Liberalism Against Populism: A Confrontation Between the Theory of Democracy and the Theory of Social Choice*. San Francisco: W.H. Freeman.
———. 1982b. The Two Party System and Duverger's Law: An Essay on the History of Political Science. *American Political Science Review* 76:753–66.
Sartori, Giovanni. 1976. *Parties and Party Systems: A Framework for Analysis*. Cambridge, U.K.: Cambridge University Press.
Schumpeter, Joseph A. 1976. *Capitalism, Socialism and Democracy*. New York: Harper and Row.
Taagepera, Rein, and Matthew Soberg Shugart. 1989. *Seats and Votes: The Effects and Determinants of Electoral Systems*. New Haven, Conn.: Yale University Press.

CHAPTER 1

Village Elections: Roots of Democratization in China

by Emerson M.S. Niou

CHINA'S PATH TOWARD DEMOCRACY started in 1912 when the Republic of China (ROC) was founded after the overthrow of the Qing Dynasty. The new government adopted several electoral laws, including the Electoral Law of the Senate and the Electoral Law of the House of Representatives of 1912, the Electoral Law of the President of 1913, the Electoral Law of the Legislative Chamber of 1914, the Electoral Rules of the Mayor of the Capital City of 1923 and the Rules for Implementation of Township Autonomy of 1928 (Ju 1987). The development of democracy in China, however, was interrupted shortly after the new republic was established by civil wars among warlords in the 1920s and by the Japanese invasion of China in the 1930s. Soon after China defeated Japan in 1945, a civil war between the Chinese Nationalist government and the Chinese Communists broke out. The People's Republic of China (PRC) was established in mainland China in 1949 after the Chinese Communists defeated the Nationalist government.

From 1949 to 1952, elections occurred in only a few cities where executive orders were issued by the city governments to elect the city's People's Congress Deputies (Ye 1993). The first electoral law, the Electoral Law of the National People's Congress and the Local People's Congresses at Different Levels, was enacted by the PRC in 1953.Because the nomination process was largely controlled by the Chinese Communist Party (CCP), however, and because the number of candidates allowed to compete must equal the number of seats to be filled, the elections under the 1953 electoral law were a mere formality (Ye 1993).

In what amounted to a literal reversal of the 1953 law, all elections at all levels of the People's Congress were suspended at the outset of the Cultural Revolution in the mid-1960s. Elections did not resume again in China until 1979 when the Chinese government passed the new Electoral Law of the National People's Congress and the Local People's Congresses at Different Levels. The 1979 law contained two major modifications of the 1953 law. First, whereas the 1953 electoral law restricted nomination authority to political organizations, the 1979 law extended to individuals the right to nominate candidates. Second, the 1979 electoral law stipulated that the number of candidates must be greater than the number of seats (Nathan 1985; Womack 1982). Because of those two important additions, the 1979 electoral law was procedurally more democratic than the 1953 law. Under the 1979 law, however, the CCP still monopolizes the final selection of candidates after they are nominated. Therefore, local People's Congress elections remain a political formality.

One of the most significant breakthroughs for democracy in China occurred with new legislation in 1987. Following more than a year of debate, the PRC's National People's Congress passed a provisional law on village committees, the Organic Law of the Village Committees.[1] According to the 1999 edition of the *Encyclopedia of Chinese Political Administrative Units*, there are about 730,000 villages in China. Given that 900 million people have household registration in rural China, the average population of a village is around 1,200. Within each village, there are several *villager groups*, each constituting about fifty to sixty households. The law stipulates that village committee members be directly elected by the villagers for terms of three years. These elections are significant because the popularly elected village committees are responsible for overseeing most of the day-to-day affairs of the village people. Although the Tiananmen Square incident in 1989 temporarily interrupted the momentum behind these democratic developments, this new democratic institutional arrangement survived criticism from conservatives within the Chinese Communist Party and has made a valuable contribution toward cultivating local self-governance (Wang et al. 1993; Manion 1996; Epstein 1996; Mi 1997; Shi 1999b). After directing the implementation of village elections for ten years, the Organic Law of the Village Committees was revised in November 1998. Several important democratic procedures, such as secret ballots, direct nomination and election, and more candidates than the seats to be filled, were added to the revised version of the electoral law for village committees. Village elections are disputably the only meaningful elections currently held on mainland China.

Studies of elections and democratization in rural China, thus far, have focused on the causes of the introduction of village elections (O'Brien 1994; Pei 1995; Kelliher 1997; Li and O'Brien 1999; Thurston 1998; Shi 1999b; O'Brien and Li 2000), the effects of Chinese culture and economic development on the prospects of democratization (Lawrence 1994; Oi 1996; Epstein 1996; O'Brien 1994; Thurston 1998; Shi 1999a), and the effects of elections on political officials' attitude toward governing (Manion 1996). No research, however, has focused on the mechanisms of different voting methods used in village elections. Furthermore, in spite of the fact that numerous international delegations have had the opportunity to observe village elections in different parts of China, a systematic understanding of the significant democratic attributes of these elections is still lacking.

Thus, without a comprehensive study of village elections in rural China, there is no way of determining how widespread, competitive, and democratic these elections are. In this chapter, I try to fill these gaps. To begin, I first provide a brief historical account of the establishment of the village committees and the politics behind the decision to implement direct elections in village politics.

Establishment of Village Committees as Self-Governing Organizations

During the People's Commune period, 1958–83, township governments were abolished and the commune committees assumed all economic and political power. Within each commune were several production brigades, and under each brigade were several production teams. The communes monopolized all resources, including food, capital, and commodity goods. Farmers were economically dependent on the commune. The economic reforms and de facto privatization in rural China introduced in 1978 drastically altered this relationship between farmers and communes. When production was no longer organized by people's communes but by individual farmers, the farmers regained autonomy of production and distribution of goods. Consequently, the People's Commune system in rural China gradually dissolved and lost its power (Burns 1988). But before township governments were formally restored to power in 1983, there was a period of political vacuum during which no political institution was responsible for administrating public affairs in rural China. In February 1980, peasants in Guozuo village, Pingnan township, Yizhou city, Guangxi Zhuangzu autonomous region, voluntarily established a village committee in order to maintain public security, resolve disputes, and provide public works in the villages (Mi 1998). As a way of curtailing a growing movement toward grassroots autonomy and in order to reestablish authority in rural areas, the Chinese central government immediately began to establish township governments to replace the people's communes and village committees to replace the production brigades. Article 111 of the 1982 Constitution of the People's Republic of China thus declares that village committees are self-governing bodies and that the chairman, deputy chairman, and members of the village committees are to be elected by local residents.

After the village committees were established, but prior to the passage of the 1987 Organic Law on the Village Committees, village committee members were generally appointed by the township government. Not surprisingly, in many villages, public meetings were rarely convened, and without mechanisms to hold village heads accountable for their actions, corruption in local affairs grew unchecked. Some villagers complained, "The officials come to the village merely to urge us to pay grain or money, or to force abortion. Some officials even have handcuffs or clubs with them, accompanied by the policemen. They come to the village to slaughter pigs, catch people, or confiscate houses" (Wang et al. 1995,

43). Some farmers reacted to regional abuses of power by sabotaging officials' property. In response to the deterioration of organizations and leadership at the rural grassroots level, the Legal Affairs Commission of the National People's Congress (NPC) and the Ministry of Civil Affairs (MAC) proposed to reform the village committees.

Peng Zhen, the former chairman of the NPC, played a significant role in introducing direct elections for village committee members; he introduced a bill that provided for their direct popular election. Because most members of the Standing Committee of the NPC strongly opposed Peng Zhen's bill, it was initially defeated at the committee level. Peng Zhen managed, however, to reintroduce the bill to the committee a few months before he retired from his position as NPC chairman. After a great deal of work, he finally persuaded the other members on the committee to embrace his idea of an elected village committee; the bill detailing the Organic Law in rural China finally passed into law on 24 November 1987 and formally took effect on 1 June 1988 (Wang et al. 1993; Li 1994; Bai 1995).

In the aftermath of the Tiananmen Square incident, the powerful Organization Department of the CCP, in conjunction with some provincial leaders, expressed its strong opposition to the introduction of direct elections in rural China. They charged that such efforts were "examples of peaceful evolution" and suggested abolishing the plan. At a critical moment, two senior leaders, Peng Zhen and Bo Yipo, openly opposed such allegations and defended the project of village-level elections. They even invited Song Ping, director of the Organization Department of the CCP and one of the most outspoken opponents of village elections, to Peng's home, where they personally rebuked his opposition and then pushed their case for village-level elections. As a consequence of their persistence, the democratic project survived the attack from the more conservative elements of the CCP (Bai 1995).

DIVERSITY OF VOTING METHODS

According to the Organic Law, each village committee consists of a committee chairman, one or two deputy chairmen, and a variable number of members; the size of the committee ranges from three to seven members.[2] Besides the principle of the direct election of candidates for all three positions by all eligible voters, the Organic Law does not provide any further guidance regarding voting procedures or methods.[3] To fill this void, provincial People's Congresses and local governments have taken the initiative in formulating local voting methods. Consequently, there exists a great deal of variation in the design of voting methods from province to province, county to county, and village to village. This section of the chapter provides a systematic introduction to the various voting methods used in village committee elections.

1. *Three simultaneously held elections.* Candidates on the ballot are divided into three different categories according to the positions for which they are nominated. No candidate can run for more than one position, and voters fill in ballots for all three positions simultaneously. If a candidate receives more than one half of the total votes cast, he/she wins the position.

According to some officials in charge of implementing village elections, this method has a serious flaw. They argue that because competent and talented candidates are a scarce commodity in many villages and because each candidate can only compete for one of the positions, to pit the two most qualified candidates against each other is a waste of human resources. To correct this problem, they favor the next method.

2. *Three sequentially held elections.* The election for the village committee chairman is held first, followed by the election for the deputy chairman, and finally, the election for the committee members. Candidates who fail to win the chairmanship can compete for deputy chairmanship in the second round of voting. Analogously, candidates who fail to win the deputy chairman position can then run for committee member positions. The advantage of this method is that it gives the candidates defeated in the previous elections a chance to run for the lower positions. In practice, however, this method poses great technical difficulties. In some villages, for example, it is difficult to have new ballots printed in time for the second or third round on election day. Thus, elections often require several days to complete. To reduce the cost of voting, some villages use the next method.

3. *Three simultaneously held elections, but candidates for higher-level positions are also listed as candidates for lower-level positions.* On the ballot, candidates for the committee chairman position are also listed as candidates for the deputy-chairman positions, and all the candidates for the deputy-chairman position are also candidates for the committee member positions. When counting votes, if a candidate does not win the committee chairman position, all the votes he receives for that position can be added to the votes he receives for the deputy-chairman position. The same principle applies when calculating a candidate's votes for the committee member position.

This method is potentially problematic for two reasons. First, if the winner of the committee chairman position also receives a large portion of the vote share for the deputy-chairman position, then it is likely that no candidate will receive more than 50 percent of the votes. Second, since candidates for the higher-level positions are also listed as candidates for the lower-level positions, this method gives local officials a loophole to limit the number of candidates in the elections, thus reducing the degree of competitiveness.

4. *The transferable vote method* (see figure 1.1 for a sample ballot). The transferable vote (TV) method is the most surprising discovery made in the present study of Chinese village elections. This procedure, which allows candidates to

Position \ Candidate	A	B	C	D	E	F	G
Committee Chairman							
Deputy Committee Chairman							
Committee Member							

Figure 1.1 Ballot Design for the Transferable Vote Method

compete for all three positions simultaneously, appears to be an electoral innovation unique to the Chinese experience. The ballot contains only the names of the candidates without specifying the positions for which they are running, and the candidates are simultaneously considered for all three positions. When voters cast their ballots, they specify the position that they want each candidate to fill. The candidate who receives more than one-half of the total votes for the position of committee chairman wins the chairmanship. Once the chairman is chosen, the votes cast for the losing candidates in the chairman race are then transferred to the race for the next position and added to their respective votes for that position. Thus, the total number of votes an individual receives for the position of deputy chairman is the sum of the votes earned by him for the committee chairmanship (assuming that he did not win that position) and the deputy chairmanship. Similarly, the total number of votes a candidate receives for the position of committee member is equal to the number of votes he receives for all three positions combined.

One advantage of the TV method, used in some counties in Liaoning province, is its simplicity. Candidates can compete for all positions simultaneously, and voters need only cast one ballot. But this voting method has at least two shortcomings. First, if there are more than two viable candidates for the committee chairmanship, it is likely that no candidate will receive more than 50 percent of the votes as required by election law. Then another election must be held. Second, even if this voting method can pull together the most talented group of villagers to constitute the village committee, there is no guarantee that they will not collude to exploit the whole village.

5. *The chairmanship method.* Prior to 1992 this method was used in areas of Tieling city (Liaoning province), Qinggang county (Heilongjiang province), and Xiangcheng and Xinzheng counties (Henan province) (Wang et al. 1993), and it is still used in some villages in Yuexi county, Anhui province (Xin 1998). Under this method, villagers elect the village committee chairman first. The newly elected chairman then nominates candidates for other committee positions. Another election is held to approve the nominees. In practice, however, in many villages, the

elected committee chairmen were allowed to appoint the other committee members, a unilateral move that violates the principle of popular elections of all village committee members stipulated in the Organic Law.

I propose a slight modification of this method to make it compliant with the Organic Law. First, villagers nominate only the candidates for the village committee chairman position. Second, a primary election is held to determine the top two vote-getters. Third, the two leading candidates for chairman each propose a slate of candidates for the other positions. Finally, in the general election, villagers vote for the team of candidates they prefer.

Several advantages accompany this method. First, since only two slates are on the ballot, one of the slates will win with certainty the majority vote. Second, because the committee chairman selects the rest of the committee members, it avoids internal strife and promotes efficiency within the committee. This method, however, could be potentially problematic if the committee is not properly checked and balanced by the village council.

How Democratic Are Village Elections in Rural China?

The first part of this chapter introduces and evaluates some commonly used voting methods used in Chinese village elections. An important follow-up question is this: How widespread in area and how democratic in procedure are village elections in China? Speculation and empirical findings vary widely. According to a survey conducted in 1993 and 1994, 49.8 percent of the villages nationwide had conducted competitive elections (Shi 1999a, 434). This statistic strikes one as being too high, since, according to the documents from the Ministry of Civil Affairs (see, for example, Wang et al. 1993), most of the provinces only started to conduct village elections in 1993 and, at the first stage, only selected counties were chosen as test sites within each province. Another survey of 478 villages in seven provinces (Anhui, Beijing suburbs, Fujian, Hebei, Jiangsu, Jiangxi, and Shandong) conducted in 1997 shows that 45 percent of the villages have ever held village committee elections, and at most 26 percent of the villages reported that candidates were selected by democratic procedures (O'Brien and Li 2000).

To get an estimate of how widespread and democratic Chinese village elections are, I took advantage of an opportunity to include some survey questions in a lottery contest questionnaire published in the December 1998 issue of a popular magazine, *Tribune of Villages and Townships*. The lottery contest was held to encourage its readers to study the newly promulgated Organic Law of Village Committee. To qualify for the drawing of prizes, which included nineteen televisions and sixteen DVD players donated by a television manufacturer, respondents had to correctly answer thirty questions related to the new Organic Law. The lottery received 13,665 respondents, from which 3,579 samples were drawn proportional to each province's total number of villages.[4] Of the 3,579 samples, 1,583 (44 percent) were from provincial, county, township, or

Table 1.1 Survey of Village Election Methods in China

1. In most recent years, have villagers in your village ever directly elected village committee members?

	Ever Directly Elected Village Committee Members	Appointed by Township Government	Appointed by Village Party Branch Secretary	Elected by Village Council
Number	2,753	358	102	366
(Percentage)	(76.92)	(10.00)	(2.85)	(10.23)

2. Did more than one candidate compete for the village committee chairman position?

	Yes	No
Number	2,183	570
(Percentage)	(79.30)	(20.70)

3. Do you remember what method was used to finalize the candidates for the general election?

	Primary Election	Village Council	Election Steering Committee	Village Party Committee	Township Government Branch	Joint Committee	Nomination Vote Method
Number	949	775	260	166	156	118	280
(Percentage)	(35.10)	(28.66)	(9.62)	(6.14)	(5.77)	(4.36)	(10.36)

4. In your opinion, was the election conducted faithfully?

	Very Well	Not So Good	Very Poorly
Number	1,466	1,044	242
(Percentage)	(53.27)	(37.94)	(8.79)

village officials; 1,777 (49.7 percent) were from farmers, labors, educators, or private entrepreneurs; the occupations of another 210 respondents were listed as "other"; and the remaining 27 respondents gave no answer to this question. Statistically, there exists no systematic difference between officials and the rest of the respondents in their answers. Because of the vast readership of the *Tribune of Villages and Townships*, this sampling scheme, although far from ideal, provides us a rough estimate of how well village elections have been implemented in China.

In the list of questions that I contributed to the questionnaire, respondents were asked whether in recent years villagers had ever directly elected village committee members. If the answer was yes, then they were asked whether there was more than one candidate running for the committee chairman position, what method was used to finalize the candidates, and whether they thought the elections were implemented faithfully. In table 1.1, I summarize the survey findings of these questions.

Table 1.2 Overall Distribution of the Quality of the Implementation of Village Elections

Implementation Quality	1 (Worst)	2	3	4 (Best)
Number	826	1,079	575	1,099
(Percentage)	(23.08)	(30.15)	(16.07)	(30.71)

To study the quality of the election implementation, I use the four survey questions to create a 4-point scale. If a village has held a direct, competitive election, if either a primary election (by villagers as a whole or by the village council) or a nominated vote method was used to finalize the candidates, and if the respondent felt the election was implemented faithfully, then the quality of the election is classified as the best, receiving 4 points on the scale. But if the respondent felt the election was implemented only satisfactorily, then election quality is assigned 3 points. If the respondent felt the election was not implemented faithfully, then election quality is assigned 2 points. If a village has held a direct and competitive election, but the candidates were nominated by the government officials or village party chief, then election quality is also assigned 2 points. If a village has held a direct election, but there was only one candidate for the committee chairman position, then quality is again assigned 2 points. If no direct election was ever held, then the quality of the election is the worst on the scale, receiving only 1 point. The distribution of this 4-point scale is summarized in table 1.2 (overall distribution) and table 1.3 (distribution by province).

To determine how well village elections have been implemented in different provinces, I constructed a quality index of elections by assigning 3 points to a province if a respondent ranks the province the highest on the quality scale, 2 points if a respondent considers the province's quality next to the best, 1 point if a respondent ranks the province third on the quality scale, and 0 if a respondent ranks the province the worst on the quality scale. The sum of these scores then is divided by the total number of respondents from the respective province. Table 1.4 (p. 28) shows that Jilin, Liaoning, Xinjiang, Fujian, and Sichuan are ranked as the top five, and Yunnan, Shanghai, Hainan, Anhui, and Guangxi are ranked as the bottom five.

According to the 1998 Organic Law, the village committee shall be accountable to the village assembly, which is composed of citizens eighteen years of age and older. In highly populated or widely dispersed villages, representatives may be elected to form a village council to discuss and decide the matters delegated to them by the village assembly. Also, Article 4 of the 1998 Organic Law clearly states, "The People's Government at the township, nationality township, and town levels shall give guidance, support, and assistance to the work of the village committees . . . [and] shall not intervene in matters that, according to existing law, lie within the jurisdiction of the self-governance of the village people." In

Table 1.3 Distribution of the Quality of the Implementation of Village Elections by Province

Province	1 [Worst]	2	3	4 [Best]	Row Total
Beijing	5 (8.2)	14 (23.0)	26 (42.6)	16 (26.2)	61 (1.7)
Tianjin	15 (25.4)	19 (32.2)	9 (15.3)	16 (27.1)	59 (1.7)
Hebei	49 (19.9)	26 (10.6)	76 (30.9)	95 (38.6)	246 (6.9)
Shanxi	51 (30.7)	47 (28.3)	30 (18.1)	38 (22.9)	166 (4.7)
Inner Mongolia	11 (15.5)	23 (32.4)	10 (14.1)	27 (38.0)	71 (2.0)
Liaoning	10 (11.4)	16 (18.2)	18 (20.5)	44 (50.0)	88 (2.5)
Jilin	4 (7.7)	13 (25.0)	4 (7.7)	31 (59.6)	52 (1.5)
Heilongjiang	6 (12.0)	18 (36.0)	9 (18.0)	17 (34.0)	50 (1.4)
Shanghai	7 (61.5)	24 (10.3)	4 (10.3)	4 (1.1)	39 (17.9)
Jiangsu	17 (11.0)	56 (36.1)	10 (6.5)	72 (46.5)	155 (4.4)
Jejiang	42 (20.1)	103 (49.3)	26 (12.4)	38 (18.2)	209 (5.9)
Anhui	69 (47.6)	36 (24.8)	17 (11.7)	23 (15.9)	145 (4.1)
Fujian	5 (6.3)	26 (32.5)	13 (16.3)	36 (45.0)	80 (2.3)
Jiangxi	19 (20.7)	37 (40.2)	7 (7.6)	29 (31.5)	92 (2.6)
Shandong	117 (26.2)	138 (30.9)	45 (10.1)	147 (32.9)	447 (12.7)
Henan	63 (25.4)	65 (26.2)	44 (17.7)	76 (30.6)	248 (6.9)
Hubei	45 (27.1)	65 (39.2)	18 (10.8)	38 (22.9)	166 (4.7)
Hunan	74 (30.3)	102 (41.8)	33 (13.5)	35 (14.3)	244 (6.9)
Guangxi	37 (49.3)	18 (24.0)	6 (8.0)	14 (18.7)	75 (2.1)
Hainan	22 (40.0)	18 (32.7)	9 (16.4)	6 (10.9)	55 (1.6)
Sichuan	33 (12.9)	58 (22.7)	57 (22.4)	107 (42.0)	255 (7.1)
Guizhou	7 (10.0)	25 (35.7)	6 (8.6)	32 (45.7)	70 (2.0)
Yunnan	23 (35.9)	24 (37.5)	4 (6.3)	13 (20.3)	64 (1.8)
Chongqing	8 (7.6)	44 (41.9)	17 (16.2)	36 (34.3)	105 (3.0)
Shaannxi	43 (26.5)	45 (27.8)	42 (25.9)	32 (19.8)	162 (4.5)
Gansu	26 (26.8)	25 (25.8)	13 (13.4)	33 (34.0)	97 (2.7)
Xinjiang	9 (17.3)	9 (17.3)	4 (7.7)	30 (57.7)	52 (1.5)
Total	826 (23.1)	1,079 (30.1)	575 (16.1)	1,099 (30.7)	3,579 (100.0)

other words, either the village assembly or the village council should have the ultimate decision-making power at the village level.

In practice, however, decision-making power at the village level may be vested in the township government, the Communist Party village branch office, or the joint conference of that office and the village committee. Each of these latter cases would directly violate of the spirit of village self-government. One question of particular interest is how the quality of village elections has affected the decision-

Table 1.4 The Quality of Village Election Implementation: Weighted Score and Rankings

Province	Weighted Score	Rank
Jilin	2.19	1
Liaoning	2.09	2
Xinjiang	2.06	3
Fujian	1.99	4
Sichuan	1.93	5
Guizhou	1.90	6
Hebei	1.89	7
Jiangsu	1.88	8
Beijing	1.87	9
Chongqing	1.78	10
Inner Mongolia	1.75	11
Heilongjiang	1.75	12
Gansu	1.55	13
Henan	1.54	14
Shandong	1.53	15
Jiangxi	1.50	16
Tianjin	1.45	17
Shaanxi	1.40	18
Shanxi	1.35	19
Hubei	1.31	20
Jejiang	1.29	21
Hunan	1.11	22
Yunnan	1.11	23
Shanghai	1.10	24
Hainan	0.98	25
Anhui	0.97	26
Guangxi	0.96	27

making power at the village level. If the election quality is high, does the township government or the secretary of the Communist Party village branch still retain a great deal of authority, or does the village committee or village council have more control over local affairs? To answer this question, I ran a simple cross-tabulation between the election quality and the organization that has the most influence over village affairs. In table 1.5, the Chi-square test shows that a clear correlation exists between these two variables. In villages with high quality of elections, the village council is more likely to have the final say on important village affairs. In villages with poor election quality, however, decision-making

Table 1.5 Election Quality and Village Power Center

Who has the final say in your village?	Election Quality—Number (Percentage)				Row Total
	1 [Worst]	2	3	4 [Best]	
Township Government	71 (8.8)	49 (4.6)	21 (3.7)	6 (0.6)	147 (4.2)
Village Party Chief	300 (37.3)	379 (35.9)	107 (19.0)	66 (6.4)	852 (24.6)
Joint Committee	183 (22.7)	273 (25.8)	147 (26.1)	189 (18.3)	792 (22.9)
Committee Chairman	56 (7.0)	56 (5.3)	32 (5.7)	17 (1.6)	161 (4.7)
Village Council	195 (24.2)	300 (26.4)	256 (45.5)	756 (73.1)	1,507 (43.6)
Column Total	806 (23.3)	1,057 (30.6)	563 (16.3)	1,034 (29.9)	3,459 (100.0)

Notes: Ordinal Measures of Association:
Gamma 0.476225
Somer's d 0.363901
tau-b 0.352995
Chi-square (12 d.f.) = 706.736594

authority for village affairs tends to reside in the hands of the township governments or the secretary of the Communist Party village branch.

Conclusion

Peng Zhen, former president of the National People's Congress in China, once said, "Once people can administer well the affairs of a village, they will gradually know how to administer affairs of a town and then of a county, and in this way, they will promote their ability to participate in state affairs through step-by-step training" (Peng 1991). This chapter shows that more than ten years after the passage of the provisional Organic Law of the Village Committee in 1987, the roots of democratization are growing strong in many provinces and that the quality of elections correlates positively with the spirit of village self-governance. Furthermore, the promulgation of the revised Organic Law of the Village Committees in November 1998 sent a very clear and strong signal to the provincial governments that the central government is committed to implement village self-governance. As a consequence, Guangdong and Hainan provinces finally started to implement village elections for the first time in 1998–99, and Yunnan province in 2000–2001.

In light of the success of village elections, the Chinese government appears now to be considering the possibility of holding elections for officials at the township or even the county level. An experiment of the direct election of a township magistrate was conducted in Buyun township, Sichuan province in December 1998. Another experiment was conducted in April 1999 in Dapong town, Guangdong province, where candidates for the township magistrate were popularly nominated. The third experiment was conducted in Zhuoli township, Linyi county, Shanxi province, where an incumbent of the top three government posts would not be allowed to seek reelection if he/she failed to receive 50 percent of the approval votes cast by township residents.

These experiments in the elections of township government officials, however varied they may be procedurally, hopefully will pave the way for more democratic township elections to be held in 2002. More significantly, the successful implementation of electoral processes at the village level and the recent adoption of some of these methods at the higher, township level indicates that the use of democratic procedures for achieving political aims is being met with increasing popular support. These encouraging signs at the grassroots level are fulfilling Peng Zhen's prophetic vision and will hopefully promote a continuing peaceful and democratic transition in China.

NOTES

1. The administrative government of the People's Republic of China (PRC) is organized into five levels, with the central government as the highest. Then, in descending order, are the provincial government, the city government, the county, and the township. Villages, which are technically subsidiaries of the township government, do not figure into the hierarchy of administrative organizations for the People's government. Instead, the 1982 Constitution of the People's Republic of China stipulates that village committees are self-governing bodies.
2. The organizational structure of the village committee is similar to the administrative system of the production brigade created during the People's Commune period. The production brigade was governed by a brigade leader and an administrative committee.
3. According to the Organic Law, all villagers, regardless of their ethnic nationality, race, sex, occupation, family status, religious belief, education, property status, or length of residence, are eligible to vote and be elected to the village committee. Individuals who have legally lost their political rights may not vote or be elected to the village committee.
4. Guangdong, Qinghai, Ningxia, and Xizang were excluded from the samples because only 27 entrants in total were from those four provinces.

REFERENCES

Bai, Yihua. 1995. *Reforms of the Chinese Basic-Level Governments* [in Chinese]. Beijing: Chinese Society Press.
Burns, John P. 1988. *Political Participation in Rural China*. Berkeley: University of California Press.
Epstein, Amy B. 1996. Village Elections in China: Experimenting with Democracy. In *China's Economic Future: Challenge to U.S. Policy—Study Papers*. Washington, D.C.: U.S. Congress, Joint Economic Committee.
Ju, Bo-Jun. 1987. *Collection of Electoral Laws of China* [in Chinese]. Taipei, Taiwan: Central Election Commission.
Kelliher, Daniel. 1997. "The Chinese Debate over Village Self-Government." *China Journal* 37:63–91.
Lawrence, Susan V. 1994. "Democracy, Chinese Style." *Australia Journal of Chinese Affairs* 32:61–68.
Li, Lianjiang, and Kevin J. O'Brien. 1999. "The Struggle over Village Elections." In *The Paradox of China's Reforms*, edited by Roderick MacFarquhar and Merle Goldman. Cambridge, Mass.: Harvard University Press.
Li, Xueju. 1994. *A Study of the Development of Town and Township Basic-Level Governments in China* [in Chinese]. Beijing: Chinese Society Press.

Manion, Melanie. 1996. "The Electoral Connection in the Chinese Countryside." *American Political Science Review* 90:736–48.
Mi, Youlu. 1997. Villager Participation in Autonomy and Its Evaluation. Working paper.
———. 1998. "A Quiet Revolution Started Here: Searching for the First Village Committee in China [in Chinese]." *Tribune of Villages and Townships* (December 1998): 6–8.
Nathan, Andrew J. 1985. *Chinese Democracy.* New York: Knopf.
O'Brien, Kevin J. 1994. "Implementing Political Reform in China's Villages." *Australian Journal of Chinese Affairs* 32: 33–62.
O'Brien, Kevin J., and Lianjian Li. 2000. "Accommodating 'Democracy' in a One-Party State: Introducing Village Elections in China." *China Quarterly* 162:465–89.
Oi, Jean C. 1996. "Economic Development, Stability and Democratic Village Self-Governance." In *China Review 1996*, edited by Maurice Brosseau, Suzanne Pepper, and Tsang Shu-ki. Hong Kong: Chinese University of Hong Kong.
Pei, Minxin. 1995. "Creeping Democratization in China." *Journal of Democracy* 6:65–79.
Peng, Zhen. 1991. "Direct Democracy at the Grassroots Level through Mass Autonomy" [in Chinese]. In *Anthology of Pengzhen*. Beijing: People's Press.
Shi, Tianjian. 1999a. "Economic Development and Elections in Rural China." *Journal of Contemporary China* 8:425–42.
———. 1999b. "Village Committee Elections in China: Institutionalist Tactics for Democracy." *World Politics* 51:385–412.
Thurston, Anne F. 1998. *Muddling toward Democracy: Political Change in Grassroots China.* Washington, D.C.: United States Institute of Peace.
Wang, Zhenyao, et al. 1993. *Study on the Election of Village Committees in Rural China.* Beijing: Chinese Society Press.
———. 1995. *Legal System of Village Committees in China* [in Chinese]. Beijing: Chinese Society.
Womack, Brantly, ed. 1982. *Electoral Reform in China.* Armonk, N.Y.: M.E. Sharpe.
Xin, Qiushui. 1998. *Villagers Autonomy and the Team Campaigning System* [in Chinese]. Working paper.
Ye, Ming-teh. 1993. *Political Participation of the Chinese People* [in Chinese]. Taipei, Taiwan: Shi-Ying.

CHAPTER 2

Continuity and Change in Taiwan's Electoral Politics

by John Fuh-sheng Hsieh

THE REPUBLIC OF CHINA (ROC) on Taiwan has long been ruled by the Kuomintang (Nationalist Party, KMT). Even after the country's transition to democracy beginning in 1986, it had won all major national elections. It is only in the presidential election of 18 March 2000 that it was defeated by the Democratic Progressive Party (DPP). Even if DPP's Chen Shui-bian becomes the new president and forms a nonpartisan government, however, the KMT as the majority party of the Legislative Yuan (parliament) has been able to dictate the policies from time to time. It remains a formidable force. Indeed, the dominance of the KMT and its prolonged competition with the DPP have been continuing features in Taiwan's electoral politics.

Of course, there are changes in Taiwanese politics as well. The fragmentation within the traditional KMT and DPP camps over the years is quite obvious. Previously, only one party was in each camp, but now there are several.

The purpose of this chapter is to scrutinize the continuity and change in Taiwan's electoral politics. But first, I investigate Taiwan's democracy, its electoral history, and the electoral systems used for various types of elections. A discussion of continuity and change in Taiwan's party configuration as revealed in electoral competition then follows. Finally, election campaigning and voting behavior are examined.

DEMOCRACY IN TAIWAN

Democracy has been defined in many different ways. Some identify the key element of democracy as free and fair elections, and others insist upon adding more features to it.[1] In the following discussion, I follow the lead of, among others, Joseph A. Schumpeter (1976) and Samuel P. Huntington (1991) in adopting a procedural definition of democracy as a system under which candidates for the most powerful positions in the government are chosen by the general public in free and fair elections. This may not be the best definition, but it conforms to common sense and is easy to operationalize.

Given such a definition, the first task in judging whether a country is a democracy is to identify the most powerful positions in the government. To do so, one needs to take a close look at its constitutional arrangement. In this regard, the ROC Constitution provides essentially for a parliamentary form of government (Hsieh 1993).

According to the original stipulations of the Constitution promulgated in 1947, the highest administrative organ in the country is the Executive Yuan (cabinet), not the president; the Executive Yuan is responsible to the Legislative Yuan, not to the president; and in promulgating laws and issuing ordinances, the president shall obtain the countersignatures of the premier and, if applicable, the ministers concerned. All these requirements seem to indicate that the constitutional form of government is essentially parliamentary and that governing power resides, to a large extent, in an Executive Yuan supported by the majority party or majority coalition of parties in the Legislative Yuan.[2]

The Constitution has been amended several times in the past few years. Now, the Legislative Yuan has an explicit vote of no confidence against the Executive Yuan, and the president and/or the Executive Yuan, after the Legislative Yuan passes the no-confidence vote, may dissolve the Legislative Yuan, thus moving the ROC even closer to the Westminster model. Even if, according to the new stipulations, the president is directly elected by the citizens of the country rather than indirectly elected by the National Assembly as in the past, and even if he can appoint the premier, the head of the Executive Yuan, without the consent of the Legislative Yuan, the president's formal powers remain limited and are essentially the same as they were previously.[3] Thus, at least formally, the governing power is still in the hands of the Executive Yuan supported by the majority party or majority coalition of parties in the Legislative Yuan.

Nevertheless, in the past several decades, the presidents, with the exception of Yen Chia-kan, have almost always exerted a great deal of power. This closely relates to their dual roles as president and leader of the KMT, the majority party in the Legislative Yuan; furthermore, some of them were military strongmen. As a consequence of such practices, future presidents may follow suit. But if the president is unable to command the majority party or the majority coalition of parties in the Legislative Yuan, constitutional crises may ensue. It will probably require some time before the constitutional practices attain the "equilibrium" defined by the Constitution.

Thus, in judging how democratic Taiwan is, one must first take a close look at the Legislative Yuan elections. Although elections for some of the representatives have been held since 1969, it is only since 1992 that all members of the Legislative Yuan have been elected by Taiwanese citizens. And the electoral process since 1992 has been, in general, free and fair. Consequently, Taiwan can be said to satisfy the procedural definition of democracy from about that time. Four years later, even the president was directly elected by the populace, further evidencing Taiwan's successful transition to democracy.

ELECTORAL HISTORY

Although truly significant elections are a new phenomenon, as mentioned above, elections have been held in Taiwan for a much longer time. In fact, since the KMT moved to the island in the late 1940s, local elections have occurred quite regularly. These include elections for village heads; township chiefs; county magistrates; city mayors; township, county, and city councils; and the provincial assembly.

At the national level, however, elections had been halted for almost two decades. According to an old interpretation rendered by the Council of Grand Justices, the body responsible for the interpretation of the Constitution, there were three national legislative bodies in the ROC: Legislative Yuan, National Assembly, and Control Yuan. But in actuality, only the Legislative Yuan can be seen as a parliament in a normal sense. The main functions of the National Assembly are to amend the Constitution and, prior to the recent constitutional reform, to elect and recall the president and vice president. And the Control Yuan's job is to supervise the conduct of civil servants, similar to parliamentary ombudsmen in Nordic countries. As stipulated in the original Constitution, the members of the Legislative Yuan and the National Assembly are elected directly by the general populace, while the members of the Control Yuan are chosen indirectly by the provincial assemblies and the councils of the provincial-level cities. Nonetheless, as a result of the recent constitutional reform, the members of the Control Yuan are now nominated by the president and confirmed by the Legislative Yuan.[4] It is no longer seen as a legislative body.

The members of these three bodies were first elected in the late 1940s in China as a whole, including Taiwan. After losing mainland China, the Nationalist government claimed that new elections for the national legislative bodies were impossible because most of the members lost their constituencies. Hence, those elected in the late 1940s continued to hold their offices and were referred to as senior members. As time went by, however, many of them passed away, and the demand for more popular participation in national politics increased. Consequently, in 1969, supplementary elections were held to fill the vacancies in the national legislative bodies. The senior members continued to serve, and those elected in 1969 were treated as if they were senior members who did not need to stand for reelection.

After 1972, new seats were created in the national legislative bodies. These additional members, unlike those elected earlier, had to be reelected in accordance with the terms stipulated in the Constitution. With the exception of 1978, when the United States decided to shift its diplomatic recognition from the ROC to the People's Republic of China (PRC) on the mainland, the additional-member elections had been held quite regularly.

In 1990, the Council of Grand Justices rendered an important interpretation, demanding the resignation of the senior legislators in 1991. This decision paved the way for the elections of the entire National Assembly and Legislative Yuan in 1991 and 1992, respectively. Afterwards, new elections were held for the National Assembly in 1996 and for the Legislative Yuan in 1995 and 1998.

As noted earlier, following the recent constitutional reform, the president is no longer elected by the National Assembly. The first popular election of the president was held in March 1996 amid military threat against Taiwan from the PRC.[5] In March 2000, another round of presidential election was held.

ELECTORAL SYSTEMS

Two types of electoral systems have been used in Taiwan. For legislative elections at various levels of government, the single nontransferable vote (SNTV) has been the norm, under which each voter casts only one vote in a district where multiple seats are at stake, and the top several candidates who receive more votes than others get elected. Such a system has rarely been used in advanced democracies except in Japan prior to the recent electoral reform.[6] In Taiwan's Legislative Yuan election of 1998, the average number of seats to be elected from the districts was 5.68.[7]

A different type of electoral system has been applied to the elections of executive offices such as president, Taiwan provincial governor, city mayor, county magistrate, township chief, and village chief. It is the single-member district (SMD) plurality system under which only one seat is available in a given district, and the candidate who obtains the most votes, not necessarily a majority of votes, wins the election. This is the electoral rule commonly found in Anglo-American countries, not only for the elections of executive offices but also for those of legislative bodies.

Since 1991, part of the National Assembly and the Legislative Yuan has been elected by proportional representation (PR). Voters in Taiwan do not have a chance to cast ballots directly for the party lists, however; instead, they still vote in the SNTV districts, and the votes for each candidate are aggregated by party with seats allocated proportionally among the parties receiving more than 5 percent of the total valid votes. Thus far, only a small portion of the seats have been elected this way. In the National Assembly election of 1996, 100 out of 334 seats (29.94 percent) were elected by PR. In the Legislative Yuan election of 1998, it was 49 out of 225 (21.78 percent). Nonetheless, in August 1999, the National Assembly passed a constitutional amendment to change the electoral rule of the National Assembly from the current mixed system to pure PR.

Generally speaking, the SMD plurality system favors two-party competition because voters, on the one hand, may turn to the lesser of the two big evils so as not to waste their votes on third-party candidates who stand little chance of winning, and candidates/parties, on the other hand, may find it advantageous to join forces against the strongest candidate or party (Riker 1982; Cox 1997). Such a proposition has been called Duverger's Law by William H. Riker (1982).

A parallel proposition dubbed Duverger's Hypothesis (Riker 1982) refers to the PR system. Under such a system, it is generally easier for small parties to gain seats because seats are allocated proportionally among the parties according to each party's share of the vote. Therefore, the incentive for voters to choose between the lesser of two evils and for candidates or parties to join forces diminishes. Consequently, a multiparty system may emerge.

Similarly, under the SNTV system, small parties may survive because they only need a small fraction of the vote in a given district for their candidates to get elected. Indeed, even an independent, the smallest type of party, may win the election by capturing a certain portion of the vote. Furthermore, it can be expected that the larger the number of seats available in a district, the better the chance a small party has of electing a candidate.[8] As a result, it is likely that a multiparty system may come into being.

Because the SNTV system has been used for the elections of the Legislative Yuan as well as other legislative bodies in Taiwan, we should expect a multiparty system to emerge. But since elections for executive offices are conducted under the SMD plurality system, it must have, to some degree, constrained the proliferation of political parties in the legislative arena (cf. Shugart and Carey 1992, chap. 10). Accordingly, although the SNTV system used in legislative elections may be conducive to the emergence of a multiparty system, the SMD plurality system adopted for the elections of executive offices may cap the number of political parties in Taiwan.

Of course, the electoral system is not the only factor affecting party configuration. The political cleavages in the country determine why certain parties emerge in the first place.

Political Parties and Party System

Among Taiwan's political parties, the Kuomintang has been a dominant force since the end of World War II. Indeed, an interesting feature of Taiwan's democratization is that, even after the end of authoritarian rule, the KMT remained in power, a rarity among the newly emerging democracies where the previous ruling parties often collapse after transitions to democracy. But the KMT survived until the presidential election of March 2000 and remains a formidable political force; in fact, it still controls the Legislative Yuan.

A second party and longtime opposition force, the Tangwai (literally, outside the party), emerged in the mid-1970s and evolved into the DPP in September 1986. The competition between the KMT and the Tangwai/DPP has been a continuing feature of party politics in Taiwan before and after democratization,

Table 2.1 Vote Shares of the Various Political Parties in the Legislative Yuan Elections, 1969–98 (in percentages)

Year	Party		
	KMT	DPP	NP
1969	76.00		
1972	73.94		
1975	79.39		
1980	73.66		
1983	73.10		
1986	69.20	22.17	
1989	60.22	28.26	
1992	53.02	31.03	
1995	46.06	33.17	12.95
1998	46.43	29.56	7.06

Source: Calculated from the Central Election Commission data. The designation of DPP candidates for the 1986 election is based upon Li 1987.

suggesting that there has been a great deal of continuity in Taiwan's party configuration despite the rapid transition to democracy.

Nonetheless, the situation is not totally frozen on the island. Indeed, some changes in Taiwan's party politics have occurred in the past several years. As a consequence of democratic transition, competition between the KMT and other political forces has become more open and less restricted. Although the KMT still wins in parliamentary elections, its vote shares have been decreasing over time (see table 2.1). Moreover, the KMT has experienced serious ruptures within the party, resulting in the formation of the New Party (NP) in August 1993. In the recent presidential election, the KMT-turned-independent James Soong captured more votes than the KMT nominee Lien Chan. Soon afterwards, Soong and his followers formed the People First Party (PFP).

Indeed, similar events took place in the DPP as well. A group of staunch Taiwan independence supporters left the DPP to form the Taiwan Independence Party (TAIP), and some DPP lawmakers also split from the DPP to set up the New Nation Association (NNA). It seems that a multiparty, rather than a two-party, system is emerging in this new democracy.

The Dominance of the KMT

As noted above, one of the most conspicuous continuing features of Taiwan's party politics in the past decade is the dominance of the KMT. Until the presidential election of March 2000, the KMT had won all national elections. An interesting question is this: What are the factors contributing to its long dominance in Taiwanese politics?

It is undeniable that the KMT's organizational strength, its huge party enterprises, its control (albeit less direct now than before) over the major TV networks, its influence on the military, and so forth may all have contributed to its dominant position in Taiwan. But to attribute the KMT's dominance solely to such "technical" factors is superficial. In fact, if these were the only factors, and if people's aversion to the party was strong, the KMT probably would have ceased to be the dominant political force in Taiwan long ago.[9]

Thus, to account for the KMT's dominant position, we need to look into something more germane to the emergence of political parties on the island, that is, political cleavages, meaning the major issues that greatly differentiate the general public politically. Hsieh and Emerson Niou (1996a, 1996b) argue that the most salient issues in Taiwan's electoral politics are often political rather than socioeconomic. Political issues such as national identity and reform versus stability are, more often than not, more important than socioeconomic issues such as social welfare and environmental protection in affecting voters' selections (cf. Lin, Chu, and Hinich 1995). Among the political issues, national identity is often regarded as most significant in distinguishing among the various political parties (Hsieh and Niou 1995; Wu 1996).

The national identity issue refers to the divergent views with regard to Taiwan's relationships with mainland China. For some, Taiwan is part of China and should be reunited with the mainland. For others, Taiwan is different from China and should be separated from China permanently. Still others hold views somewhere in between. Undoubtedly, this is a highly emotional issue.

To estimate the distribution of the Taiwanese population on such an issue, the following question has been asked in election surveys:[10]

> On the issue of unification and independence, some people advocate that Taiwan should declare independence at once regardless of Communist China's reaction; some believe that Taiwan should soon negotiate with Communist China so as to accelerate the unification process; and there are others standing in between. Suppose the view that Taiwan should declare independence at once is at one extreme, represented by a score 0, and the view that Taiwan should soon negotiate with Communist China on unification is at the other extreme, represented by a score 10, then
>
> a. What is your ideal position on this issue on a 0–10 point scale?
> b. Where will you position the KMT on this scale?
> c. How about the DPP?
> d. How about the NP?

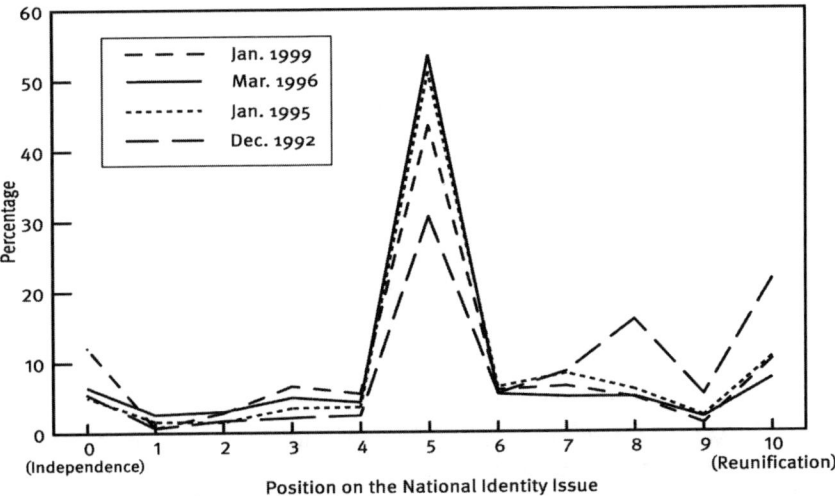

Figure 2.1 The Distribution of Voters on the National Identity Issue, 1992–99

Source: The 1992 survey was conducted by Opinion Research Taiwan. Others were done by the Election Study Center, National Chengchi University.

The results with regard to the respondents' personal positions are shown in figure 2.1.[11]

As shown in figure 2.1, except for the data obtained from the January 1999 survey, a clear trend may be seen among the general public: a slight increase in the number of people who are more or less in favor of Taiwan independence and a drastic decline in the number of people who support reunification. As a result, the vast majority of respondents may be placed at the center of the scale, the status quo—in favor of neither independence nor reunification. The latest data show a somewhat reverse trend, with public opinion becoming a bit more polarized. Many more people are still placed at the center of the scale, however, than at any other position.

Figure 2.2 summarizes voters' own positions and their perceptions of the positions taken by various political parties on this issue. Again, it is evident that the respondents have moved from a position somewhat favoring reunification to a relatively neutral one. Similarly, their perceptions of the KMT's position have also shifted to one less strongly favoring reunification. Their perceptions of the DPP's position, however, have remained the same, an unmistakable proindependence position. The NP's position, relatively favoring reunification, has not changed greatly, either.

These perceptions generally conform to common sense among the observers of Taiwanese politics except that the relative positions between the KMT and the NP in the earlier period look odd. In common parlance, the latter is often considered more proreunification than the former, but in the earlier surveys, this was not the case. The inconsistency may be explained by the fact that the NP was

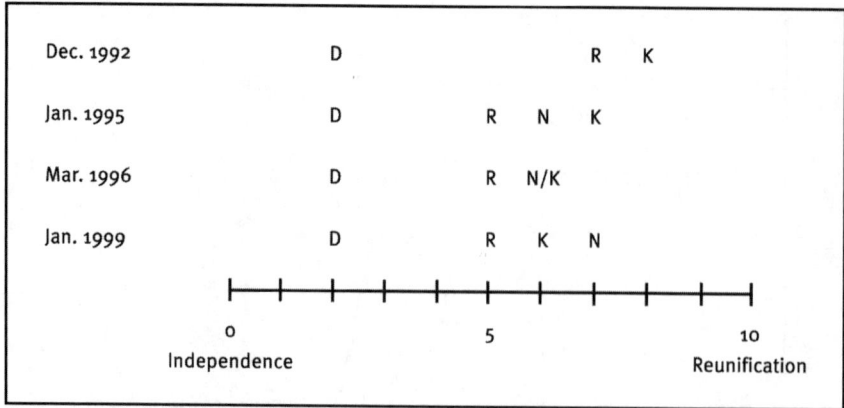

Figure 2.2 Voters' Own Positions and Their Perceptions of the Various Parties' Positions on the National Identity Issue

Source: The 1992 survey was conducted by the Opinion Research Taiwan. All others were done by the Election Study Center, National Chengchi University.

Note: R = respondents; K = Kuomintang; D = Democratic Progressive Party; N = New Party. These points all represent the median values.

then truly a new party, and thus less well known, and that the KMT might be viewed as an aggregate of individuals, including some prominent proreunification figures. And it seems that the respondents do possess better information now concerning the differences between the two parties.

Thus, in Taiwanese politics, the three parties should be aligned, from proindependence to proreunification, as follows: the DPP, the KMT, and the NP, with the DPP as a proindependence party, the KMT as a status quo party leaning somewhat toward reunification, and the NP as a proreunification party. Recently, the DPP has tried to tone down its proindependence rhetoric, thus alienating some staunch independence supporters who finally split from the party to form the TAIP. Undoubtedly, the TAIP is more proindependence than the DPP. Another DPP splinter group, the NNA, is also in favor of Taiwan independence. The newly-formed PFP's position is not clear yet, but it is likely to be somewhere between that of the KMT and that of the NP.

Given the distribution of voters' own positions and the positions taken by various political parties, it is evident that the KMT is closest to the largest segment of voters and thus is in an advantageous position vis-à-vis other political parties. This is indeed an important source of the KMT's strength.[12]

Another important factor contributing to the KMT's dominance in Taiwanese politics is the voters' attitude toward stability. Hsieh and Niou (1996a, 1996b) argue that Taiwanese voters are greatly concerned about this issue. When asked

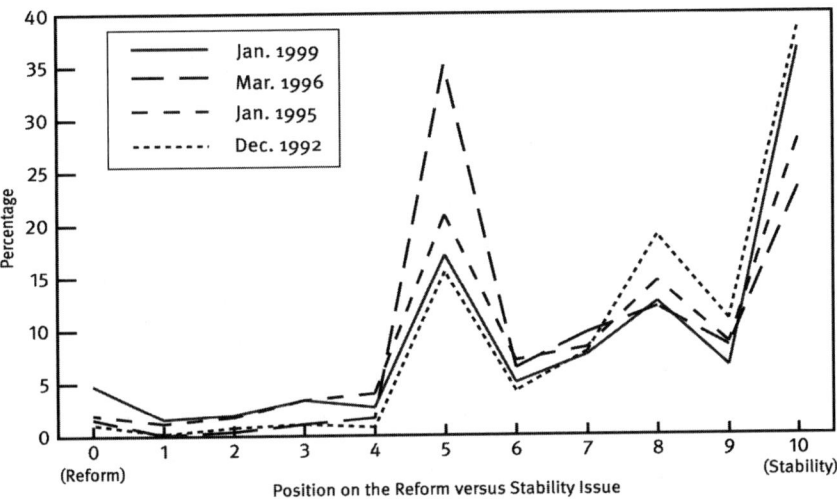

Figure 2.3 The Distribution of Voters on the Reform versus Stability Issue, 1992–99

Source: The 1992 survey was conducted by Opinion Research Taiwan. Others were done by the Election Study Center, National Chengchi University.

about the trade-off between reform and stability, a large number of respondents choose stability over reform (see figure 2.3). Figure 2.4 shows that voters' own positions on this issue have been much closer to that of the KMT than those of other political parties. This is another great advantage enjoyed by the KMT. (Voters may identify the KMT as the party of stability, to a large extent, because political and social stability has been very much maintained under KMT rule in the past several decades—even during the period of democratic transition.)

The national identity and reform-stability issues are, to a certain extent, related to the national security problem. For many Taiwanese, the threat posed by the Chinese Communists across the Taiwan Strait is a constant fear. In particular, because Communist China has reiterated its intention to use force against Taiwan if Taiwan declares independence, many voters may hesitate to support independence. Likewise, many may fear that the breakdown of political and social stability on the island would encourage Communist China to take brutal action against Taiwan. They are thus very much concerned about stability in Taiwan. Accordingly, the incumbent KMT party—supporting the status quo and stressing political and social stability—enjoys a great deal of support from those people.

Aside from these issues, the KMT's past performance in economic matters also may have been instrumental in winning votes. The economic "miracle" that Taiwan has been experiencing under KMT rule is undoubtedly a positive asset for the KMT in fighting against opposition parties in the elections. In the survey conducted by the Election Study Center of National Chengchi University in

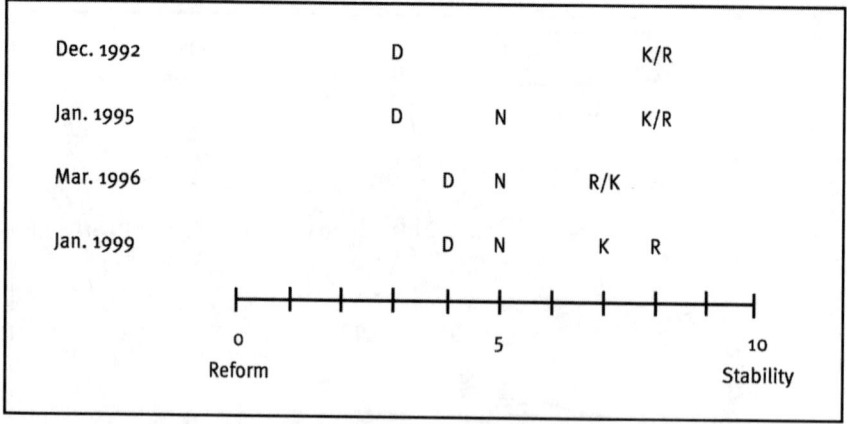

Figure 2.4 Voters' Own Positions and Their Perceptions of the Various Parties' Positions on the Reform versus Stability Issue

Source: The 1992 survey was conducted by the Opinion Research Taiwan. All others were done by the Election Study Center, National Chengchi University.

Note: R = respondents; K = Kuomintang; D = Democratic Progressive Party; N = New Party. These points all represent the median values.

January 1999, for instance, 51 percent of the respondents believed that the KMT could best handle the economy, and only 9.1 percent and 1 percent picked the DPP and the NP, respectively.

Thus, as long as it is able to hold together, the KMT will certainly be a formidable political force in Taiwan.

The DPP as the Main Power Contender

In addition to the KMT's dominance in politics, another continuing feature of Taiwan's party politics is the role played by the Tangwai/DPP as the main power contender in Taiwan. As noted earlier, some people in Taiwan favor independence; these people constitute the core support received by the Tangwai/DPP. Although the DPP leadership recently has tried to tone down the independence rhetoric, thus resulting in the exodus of some staunch independence supporters, the DPP remains a major force representing the ideal of Taiwan independence. (Indeed, the major difference between the DPP and the DPP's splinter groups may lie in the timing and strategies to achieve independence rather than the ideal of independence itself.)

Another strength of the DPP lies in its past efforts to promote democratic reform in Taiwan. Thus, for reform-minded voters, the DPP is their choice.

Over the years, the DPP has also strengthened its organization, thus enhancing its chances in the elections. And given the performance of many of its officeholders at various levels of government, the party is now able to attract many more voters who have had doubts previously about its capabilities in governing. It can be expected that the DPP will continue to play an important role in Taiwanese politics.

Changes in Taiwan's Party System

Although there are immense continuities in Taiwan's party politics, some changes have occurred as well. For example, the KMT's strength in the elections has eroded vis-à-vis other political parties. As shown in table 2.1, the KMT's vote shares in Legislative Yuan elections have dropped from more than 70 percent prior to the early 1980s to less than 50 percent lately. As for the DPP, its vote shares have increased from slightly more than 20 percent to about one-third.

One of the factors that may have contributed to the decline of the KMT's vote shares as compared to other political parties is the image of corruption associated with the KMT. The accusation of corruption committed by KMT officials and legislators will not easily go away, and will continue to be a liability for the party in future elections. Another factor is the split of the party—it is just simple arithmetic.

Nevertheless, if one combines the vote obtained by the KMT and the NP (which split from it), that is, the pan-KMT vote, and compare it to the DPP vote, one can see that the pan-KMT vote has remained relatively unchanged while the DPP's momentum has been slowed in the past decade or so. In 1989, for instance, the DPP obtained 28.26 percent of the vote, and the KMT 60.22 percent. In 1992, the DPP's vote share was increased to 31.03 percent. As for the KMT, although the official figure stood at 53.02 percent, by adding those candidates who were KMT members but were unable to gain the party's endorsement, the KMT's vote share was 60.5 percent, almost the same as in the previous election.[13] Three years later, the DPP received 33.17 percent of the vote, slightly increased from the previous election, while the combined total of the KMT and the NP vote was 59.01 percent, again similar to the earlier KMT figures. In 1998, if the votes won by the Democratic Alliance, which includes many former KMT and NP politicians, are added to the pan-KMT vote on the one hand, and the TAIP's and the NNA's vote are added to, say, the pan-DPP vote on the other, then the vote shares between the two sides were roughly the same as in the past. Thus, even though there have been changes in the relative strengths between the traditional KMT and the traditional DPP camps in the early period of the democratization process, such changes have slowed recently. In the elections in which the SMD plurality system is in use, which tends to benefit the two major parties, the vote distribution between the two camps is somewhat different. The DPP has been able to gain 40 percent or more in such elections. In the 2000 presidential election, DPP's Chen Shui-bian won by 39.3 percent of the vote, which is quite typical in this sense.

Table 2.2 shows the distribution of seats in the Legislative Yuan following the 1992, 1995, and 1998 elections. As shown in the table, Taiwan's party system as

Table 2.2 The Distribution of Seats in the Legislative Yuan

Party	1992 Election	1995 Election	1998 Election
Kuomintang	95	85	123
Democratic Progressive Party	51	54	70
Chinese Social Democratic Party	1	—	—
New Party	—	21	11
Taiwan Independence Party	—	—	1
New Nation Association	—	—	1
Democratic Alliance	—	—	4
Nonparty Alliance	—	—	3
Independents	14	4	12
Total	161	164	225
Effective Number of Parties[a]	2.23	2.54	2.51

Source: Central Election Commission.

a. Effective Number of Parties = $1/\Sigma(p_i^2)$, where p_i refers to the proportion of seats obtained by the ith party. The independents are treated as parties consisting of only one person.

exemplified by the distribution of seats in the Legislative Yuan has been moving toward a multiparty one: The effective number of parties has been increased from slightly more than 2 to about 2.50.[14]

Two major factors may be attributed to the growing fragmentation in Taiwan's party configuration. One is related to the electoral system, particularly the one used in legislative elections. As noted earlier, the SNTV system adopted for the election of the legislative bodies in Taiwan is beneficial to small parties. Thus even if the SMD plurality system may encourage two-party competition, small parties may still be able to find a niche in the legislative races and continue to survive.

The other factor accounting for the fragmentation in Taiwan's party politics is the political cleavages that give birth to political parties in the first place. In Western democracies, class and religious divisions, coupled occasionally with urban-rural, linguistic, and certain other cleavages, dominate the political scene, shaping the party structures in these countries. Such cleavages have proved to be quite resilient in many Western societies (Lipset and Rokkan 1967). Recently, new divisions have emerged based upon "new politics" issues such as environmental protection, but the old cleavages remain salient in many of the Western democracies (Dalton 1996).

The situation in Taiwan, however, is quite different. As mentioned earlier, the major cleavage that molds Taiwan's party configuration centers on the national identity issue. A careful examination of figure 2.1 reveals that Taiwanese voters' attitudes on that issue may be depicted as a trimodal type with the largest mode at the center—the status quo—and two smaller modes on two sides of the spectrum. Indeed, although the two extreme positions are occupied by a small number of people, their intense preferences may actually magnify the salience of those positions in Taiwanese politics. Given the multimodal shape of Taiwanese voters' distribution on the national identity issue, it is quite likely that there may emerge more than two political parties in Taiwan (cf. Downs 1957, chap. 8).[15]

In examining changes in Taiwan's party configuration over the past decade, it is interesting to note that whenever a major party moved to a new position, another took up its old position. For example, as the KMT moved from a more prounification stance to a less prounification one, the NP was formed. When, later on, the DPP tried to attract middle-of-the-road voters, the TAIP and the NNA split from it. In light of the distribution of Taiwanese voters' attitudes toward the national identity issue, such a result is not surprising. As a matter of fact, it is perhaps quite natural.

ELECTION CAMPAIGNING AND VOTING BEHAVIOR

Under the SNTV system, a major party may need to nominate several candidates in a district. In order to win as many seats as possible, it has to ensure that each of its candidates will receive enough votes to get elected. Two strategies are employed: first, the party must not nominate too many candidates, and second, it must try to distribute the votes evenly among its candidates. In a nine-member district, for instance, if a party figures out that, given its support, it is able to win only five seats, it will nominate no more than five candidates; otherwise, the sixth candidate may attract votes from the other five, thus reducing their chances of winning. In addition, the party should try to allocate the votes evenly among its five candidates so that no one will gain too many votes at the expense of other copartisans.

In the past, the KMT's record in allocating the votes among its candidates was superior to that of other parties in Taiwan. Given the KMT's strong organization at all levels of government, this is not surprising. The KMT had several methods for allocating votes evenly. The basic one is called a responsibility zone (RZ) system. To take the above nine-member district again as an example, the KMT would divide the whole district into five RZs, each of which, judging from its past experience, will draw an approximately equal number of votes for the party. Then, in each RZ, only one of the KMT candidates will be allowed to campaign, and all other copartisans are prohibited from entering it. In this way, the KMT was able to allocate the votes quite successfully (Liu 1991). In addition to the RZ system, the KMT also relied upon the mobilization of its functional branches representing, say, the military, civil servants, and school teachers to help equalize the votes among its candidates.

The other parties generally have been less capable of allocating votes. But gradually, they have been able to devise other ways to offset their disadvantages vis-à-vis the KMT. For instance, they try to nominate candidates with different backgrounds to attract different segments of the population. In recent elections, the DPP and the NP supporters were even asked to vote according to, for example, their birthdays: Those born in the spring were to vote for candidate A, and so on.

Because the major parties often need to nominate multiple candidates under the SNTV system, party labels and issue positions may be less important for voters choosing among candidates of one party. Consequently, elections may become highly personalized. Candidates' previous records of services in the districts, their personal ties to the local groups, and so forth may influence voters' choices greatly. Factionalism may creep in. Even such illegal practices as vote-buying and threats from gangsters may find their way into the electoral process.[16]

Does this mean, however, that partisan voting and issue voting are absent in Taiwan? Of course not. As noted above, although some changes have occurred, Taiwan's party configuration has very much stabilized. In a sense, it may be more institutionalized than that of many other new democracies in the region such as South Korea, the Philippines, and Thailand (Hsieh 1997). This reflects the long history of competition between the KMT and the Tangwai/DPP, and the relative stability of the national identity cleavage underpinning the party system. As voters choose a political party to support, the national identity issue is very much in their minds, and their partisan attachment is often quite enduring. But when it comes time to choose among several candidates of the same party, party label and issue position become less meaningful.

It has often been asserted that partisan voting is not very significant in Taiwan, accounting for, say, only about 15 percent of voters' selections (Chen and Huang 1992). This is, to a large extent, a misconception due to the particular question wording usually found in the surveys. The respondents were often asked, "What is the most important reason for you to vote for him/her?" Since there may be several candidates of the same party running in the district, the respondents may point to factors other than partisan attachment as their reason for voting for a specific candidate, but in fact, they may have already screened the candidates by partisanship and then selected one of their favorite party's candidates. In the 1992 survey mentioned earlier, a different question was asked: "Under our current electoral method, there may be several KMT candidates or several DPP candidates running in a district. Under such a circumstance, will you first decide which party to vote for, and then select one of that party's candidates?" In this survey, 44.1 percent of the respondents answered "yes," indicating that partisan voting is not unimportant in the case of Taiwan (Hsieh 1997).

The situation under the SMD plurality system is quite different. Generally, only the two largest parties, that is, the KMT and the DPP, are able to run successful campaigns. And since each party, under normal circumstances, nominates only one candidate in a district, party label may become more prominent in the race. Although it is hard to say whether issues play a significantly more important role, some evidence suggests that issue voting does exist in those elections (e.g., Hsieh, Lacy, and Niou 1996, 1998).

CONCLUSION

As a new democracy, Taiwan's electoral politics has exhibited a surprisingly high degree of continuity in the past decade or so. In particular, the competition between the (pan-)KMT and (pan-)DPP camps has largely stabilized. This correlates with the relative stability of the national identity cleavage underpinning the party configuration. Beneath the surface, however, we see changes as well, such as fragmentation within each camp, caused to a certain extent by the multimodal distribution of voters on the national identity issue. The fragmentation is also related to the particular type of electoral system used in Taiwan's legislative elections. Some discussion recently has focused on reforming the electoral system, but given the vast differences among political parties on the issue, electoral reform is not that easy. As long as the electoral system remains essentially the same, and the political cleavages do not change drastically, it is likely that the two-camp competition with fragmentation within each camp will continue in the foreseeable future.

NOTES

1. For a discussion of various definitions of democracy, see, for example, Sartori 1987.
2. It should be noted that the parliamentary form of government as stipulated in the original ROC Constitution is different from, say, the Westminster model. Notably, the members of the Legislative Yuan cannot serve in the government; the Executive Yuan cannot dissolve the Legislative Yuan; and the Legislative Yuan possesses only a very weak type of vote of no confidence against the Executive Yuan after the former overrides the latter's veto by a two-thirds majority. The ROC is not unique among the parliamentary countries, however; the parliamentarians in Norway, the Netherlands, and Luxembourg, for instance, cannot serve in the cabinet as well, and the cabinet cannot dissolve the parliament in Norway.
3. This is indeed a controversial issue in Taiwan. Many people believe that, after the recent constitutional reform, a mixed system modeled after French Fifth Republic was instituted. But this is not quite accurate because the ROC president cannot do many things that a French president can (e.g., dissolving the parliament in a more active manner, asking the parliament to reconsider a law, bypassing the parliament by appealing directly to the general public in a referendum, and presiding over the Council of Ministers).
4. According to the constitutional amendment of 1992, the members of the Control Yuan are nominated by the president and confirmed by the National Assembly. In 2000, it was further amended that the Control Yuan members be confirmed by the Legislative Yuan rather than the National Assembly.
5. For an account of the impact of the PRC's military threat on Taiwan's 1996 presidential election, see Hsieh, Lacy, and Niou 1998.
6. See chapter 5 in this volume.
7. The previous figures for Legislative Yuan elections were about four. The higher figure in 1998 was caused by the increase of the total membership of the Legislative Yuan as a result of the constitutional reform.

8. It has been shown that, under the SNTV system, the larger the number of seats there are elected from a district, the greater the number of viable candidates will be. In general, the number of viable candidates is equal to the number of seats plus one (Reed 1990; Hsieh and Niemi 1999).
9. As noted by Barbara Geddes, in Poland, Hungary, Romania, and Bulgaria, as transition to democracy began, "Communist parties . . . had tremendous advantages over other parties in regard to local organization, control of government resources and patronage, and control of the media," but soon afterwards, "support for Communist parties and their successors declined—dramatically in most countries" (Geddes 1996, 19). Obviously, the KMT is not such a party. In addition to its organizational strength, the KMT has something more to offer, which may have distinguished it from those Communist Parties.
10. These are nationwide surveys conducted by the Opinion Research Taiwan in December 1992 on behalf of Professor Emerson M.S. Niou and me, and by the Election Study Center of National Chengchi University in January 1995, March 1996, and January 1999.
11. The wordings in these surveys are not identical but do not deviate too much.
12. It should be noted that the national identity issue and ethnicity are closed intertwined in Taiwan. The Minnan Taiwanese are more inclined than other ethnic groups to support Taiwan independence, while the mainlanders are more likely to favor reunification. The Hakka Taiwanese stand somewhere in between (Hsieh 1999). But politically, it is national identity, rather than ethnicity per se, that, for the most part, determines one's attachment to a political party.
13. In the previous official records published by the Central Election Commission, all those candidates who claimed to be members of a specific party were counted as that party's candidates. But such was no longer the case in 1992. Since then, only those who obtained the party's official endorsement could be regarded as the candidates of that party. Thus, to be comparable to the earlier data, the figures in 1992 and afterwards should include those who were members of a particular party but were unable to get the endorsement of that party.
14. Effective Number of Parties is defined as $1/\Sigma(p_i^2)$, where p_i refers to the proportion of seats or votes obtained by the ith party. In Taiwan's Legislative Yuan election of 1992, for instance, the KMT and the DPP obtained 59 percent and 31.68 percent of the seats, respectively, with the Chinese Social Democratic Party and the independents each getting 0.6 percent of the seats. If independents are treated as parties consisting of only one person, then the effective number of parties as a result of that election was $[1/(0.59^2 + 0.3168^2 + 15 \times 0.006^2)] = 2.23$. This is a popular way of counting the number of parties in a political system (Taagepera and Shugart 1989; Lijphart 1994).
15. It has been argued that the number of parties is equivalent to the number of issue dimensions plus one (Taagepera and Shugart 1989). Apparently, such an argument does not take into account the particular shapes of the voters' distributions on the issues.
16. For an interesting account of the similar situation in Japan, see Ramseyer and Rosenbluth 1993.

References

Chen, Yih-yan, and Li-chiu Huang. 1992. *Electoral Behavior and Political Development* [in Chinese]. Taipei, Taiwan: Li-ming.
Cox, Gary W. 1997. *Making Votes Count: Strategic Coordination in the World's Electoral Systems*. Cambridge, U.K.: Cambridge University Press.
Dalton, Russell J. 1996. *Citizen Politics: Public Opinion and Political Parties in Advanced Industrial Democracies*, 2d ed. Chatham, N.J.: Chatham House.
Downs, Anthony. 1957. *An Economic Theory of Democracy*. New York: Harper and Row.
Geddes, Barbara. 1996. "Initiation of New Democratic Institutions in Eastern Europe and Latin America." In *Institutional Design in New Democracies*, edited by Arend Lijphart and Carlos H. Waisman. Boulder, Colo.: Westview.
Hsieh, John Fuh-sheng. 1993. "Parliamentarism vs. Presidentialism: Constitutional Choice in the Republic of China on Taiwan." *Chinese Political Science Review* 21:173–202.
———. 1997. "Electoral Politics in New Democracies in the Asia-Pacific Region." *Representation* 34:157–65.

———. 1999. "Ethnicity, National Identity, and Democratic Transition in Taiwan." Paper presented at the 28th Sino-American Conference on Contemporary China, Duke University, Durham, North Carolina, June.
Hsieh, John Fuh-sheng, Dean Lacy, and Emerson M.S. Niou. 1996. "Economic Voting in Taiwan's 1994 Elections." *American Asian Review* 14:51–70.
———. 1998. "Retrospective and Prospective Voting in a One-Party-Dominant Democracy: Taiwan's 1996 Presidential Election." *Public Choice* 97:383–99.
Hsieh, John Fuh-sheng, and Richard G. Niemi. 1999. "Can Duverger's Law Be Extended to SNTV? The Case of Taiwan's Legislative Yuan Elections." *Electoral Studies* 18:101–16.
Hsieh, John Fuh-sheng, and Emerson M.S. Niou. 1995. "What Are the Differences among the Three Parties? An Analysis of Taiwan's Party Cleavages" [in Chinese]. Paper presented at the Conference on the Post–World War II Political Development in Taiwan, Taipei, Taiwan, October.
———. 1996a. "Issue Voting in the Republic of China on Taiwan's 1992 Legislative Yuan Election." *International Political Science Review* 17:13–27.
———. 1996b. "Salient Issues in Taiwan's Electoral Politics." *Electoral Studies* 15:219–35.
Huntington, Samuel P. 1991. *The Third Wave: Democratization in the Late Twentieth Century*. Norman: University of Oklahoma Press.
Li, Hsiao-feng. 1987. *Forty Years of Taiwan's Democratic Movement* [in Chinese]. Taipei, Taiwan: Independence Evening Post.
Lijphart, Arend. 1994. *Electoral Systems and Party Systems: A Study of Twenty-Seven Democracies, 1945–1990*. Oxford, U.K.: Oxford University Press.
Lin, Tse-min, Yun-han Chu, and Melvin J. Hinich. 1995. "Conflict Displacement and Regime Transition in Taiwan: A Spatial Analysis." *World Politics* 48:453–81.
Lipset, Seymour M., and Stein Rokkan. 1967. "Cleavage Structures, Party Systems, and Voter Alignments: An Introduction." In *Party Systems and Voter Alignments: Cross-National Perspectives*, edited by Seymour M. Lipset and Stein Rikkan. New York: Free Press.
Liu, I-Chou. 1991. "A Study on the Effectiveness of the KMT's System of Responsibility Zones" [in Chinese]. Paper presented at the Conference on Party Politics and Constitutional Democracy, Taipei, Taiwan, March.
Ramseyer, J. Mark, and Frances McCall Rosenbluth. 1993. *Japan's Political Marketplace*. Cambridge, Mass.: Harvard University Press.
Reed, Steven R. 1990. "Structure and Behaviour: Extending Duverger's Law to the Japanese Case." *British Journal of Political Science* 20:335–56.
Riker, William H. 1982. "The Two-Party System and Duverger's Law: An Essay on the History of Political Science." *American Political Science Review* 76:753–66.
Sartori, Giovanni. 1987. *The Theory of Democracy Revisited*. Chatham, N.J.: Chatham House.
Schumpeter, Joseph A. 1976. *Capitalism, Socialism and Democracy*. New York: Harper and Row.
Shugart, Matthew Soberg, and John M. Carey. 1992. *Presidents and Assemblies: Constitutional Design and Electoral Dynamics*. Cambridge, U.K.: Cambridge University Press.
Taagepera, Rein, and Matthew Soberg Shugart. 1989. *Seats and Votes: The Effects and Determinants of Electoral Systems*. New Haven, Conn.: Yale University Press.
Wu, Naiteh. 1996. Liberalism, Ethnic Identity and Taiwanese Nationalism. *Taiwanese Political Science Review* 1:5–39.

CHAPTER 3

Hong Kong: A Decade of Change

by David Newman

THE 1990S BEGAN with Hong Kong's roughly 5 million residents looking back in time with solemnity and forward with apprehension. Just six months before the decade began, Chinese mainland authorities ordered the People's Liberation Army to fire its weapons against Chinese students demonstrating for democracy in Tiananmen Square. This singular event politicized millions of Hong Kong residents in an unprecedented manner. Millions marched in solidarity with the slain students; money was collected to provide support for the demonstrators; and it is rumored that even the triads, local organized crime families, assisted by transporting Chinese students wanted by the mainland authorities to safety in Hong Kong.

These 5 million looked forward to a date certain, 1 July 1997, when the British colonial power would lower the Union Jack for the last time and return sovereignty over Hong Kong to the People's Republic of China. Hundreds of thousands of Hong Kong residents believed the post-Tiananmen future in Hong Kong was bleak, and they fled to Canada, England, Australia, and New Zealand, among other places. Those who remained put their faith in the one country–two systems concept and Deng's promise of "Hong Kong people ruling Hong Kong," and by 1997, most of those remaining were optimistic about the future (DeGolyer 1997).

The events of Tiananmen Square also changed the plans of the colonial administration. Britain historically viewed Hong Kong as an easily administered and relatively docile colony populated by hard working individuals—many of whom had fled the neighboring communist regime. Tiananmen created a concern that Britain was no longer turning Hong Kong over to a reformed China but rather a revealed China. Since there was no turning back, the British chose (somewhat late, critics argued) to create a set of democratic institutions and democratically oriented politicians who were prepared to defend Hong Kong after the British departure (Lo 1997). For China, the British actions were viewed as a repudiation of previous understandings that had to be resisted.

This chapter examines the development of political parties, party identification, and party performance in competitive elections, principally the legislature, in Hong Kong leading up to the change in sovereignty and in the thirty months following the handover. In addition, due attention is focused on changes in rules governing selections and their effect on political competition over the decade. Perhaps more than anywhere else in Asia, Hong Kong has been an exemplar of how politicians can use electoral rules to achieve particular electoral outcomes. The chapter concludes with a discussion of prospects for the future of democracy in Hong Kong. First, however, one needs to understand the unique structure of Hong Kong's political institutions and electoral system.

Hong Kong's Political Structure

The political structure of Hong Kong was traditionally, and in large part remains, that of a large city. Hong Kong was a small colony in which the foreign colonial administrators, in cooperation with the local elite, which was primarily drawn from the business community and the civil service, managed political affairs in consultation with various interest groups in the territory (Miners 1991). As one would expect, the organs of government were divided into executive, legislative, and judicial. At the top of the hierarchy was the governor, appointed by the Prime Minister of the United Kingdom, who served as a very powerful chief executive. The governor was assisted by a "cabinet"; the Executive Council (referred to as "Exco"), consisting of ex officio members holding key posts, such as the Finance Secretary; and nonexecutive advisers drawn from the community. While the governor theoretically had immense political powers, most were never used. The governor's executive powers were exercised through the civil service, which was drawn from expatriates and locals and directed by the Chief Secretary.

The legislative functions of government were carried out by the Legislative Council (referred to as "Legco") while basic services such as trash collection, health care, and cultural activities were provided by two municipal councils—the Urban Council, operating in the urban areas, and the Regional Council, operating in the rural areas. To ensure that government was accountable and responsive at the local level, in 1982, Hong Kong was divided into districts with boards of elected and appointed members. The District Boards were designed to "advise the government on matters affecting the well-being of the residents and to provide a mechanism for collecting public views" (Hong Kong Government 1993). Beginning in 1994 there were 18 District Boards with 346 elected members and 27 ex officio members who were rural committee chairmen.[1]

The three branches of government were not coequal in any sense. Hong Kong, as a colony, utilized an "executive-led" model of government in which the governor held commanding authority. The colonial power, Britain prior to 1997, wanted to vest power in a single individual they could hold responsible and accountable for matters in the territory. For example, legislators could not introduce bills relating to public expenditure, the political structure, or operation of government. All bills had to be signed by the governor and he retained the power to dissolve Legco. These restrictions were collectively powerful limitations on Legco's authority.

The creation of the Hong Kong Special Administrative Region (HKSAR), following the change in sovereignty, did little to change the basic structure of governance in Hong Kong. Although the colonial governor was replaced by the chief executive, his powers, noted above, are quite similar. Moreover, the limitations on Legco were preserved. In addition, the structure of the legislature, the Municipal Councils, and the District Boards was provisionally retained.

THE POLITICAL CONTEXT

It is important to appreciate that prior to 1985, the legislature in Hong Kong was entirely unelected. Moreover, until that year, the governor served as president of Legco, and the Chief Secretary (the head of the civil service), the Finance Secretary, and attorney general all also served as ex officio members. The remainder, a maximum of 57 members, were appointed by the governor. Of the 57, the governor could appoint a maximum of 25 government officials as "official members" of Legco. Official members had to vote with the governor unless specifically released. The remaining maximum 32 "unofficial members," as they were referred to, could vote as they chose.

In 1985, the size and composition of the legislature was changed. The size was reduced to a maximum of fifty-seven members—twenty-two appointed, twenty-four elected, the governor, three ex officio members, and seven official members. The elected members, however, were not selected from broad-based popular constituencies. Instead, twelve members were selected from occupational and professional groups and twelve members elected by an Electoral College consisting of members of the local district boards and municipal councils. Specifically, one representative was elected from each of the six following functional categories: financial, social services, medical, teaching, legal, and engineering/architectural/surveying/planning; two representatives were selected from commercial, industrial, and labor interests. The use of functional constituencies was adopted from the British experience in other colonies as part of the preparation for independence. The functional constituencies were viewed as a tool for a gradual but controlled expansion of democratic participation. Somewhat hidden from view was the mechanism by which voters were certified in functional constituencies. Stated criteria generally referred to members of various bodies in a particular sector as eligible electors. If the particular bodies allowed for corporate memberships, then those corporate bodies were granted a vote. For example, the financial services functional constituency included banks as defined under the banking ordinance. So the bank as a corporate body had a vote that it could exercise through an appointed agent. Alternatively, the statute might refer explicitly to a particular corporation or entity eligible to vote.

Of the remaining twelve elected representatives, the members of the District Boards chose ten and each of the Municipal Councils chose one. Though a majority of the legislature was elected, it was not in any sense by popular, broad-based franchise. The assumption was that popular sentiment was expressed by those electors in the Electoral College, some of whom were themselves directly elected.

The 1985 changes in the Legislative Council foreshadowed the future set of issues that would dominate the political debate in the 1990s. These included the number of elected representatives and the nature of their constituencies, the breadth of popular participation, the number of functional constituencies, the use of an Electoral College and its composition, and the voting rules to be adopted for selecting candidates.

Britain, never a leader in pressing the pace of reform while the colony was under its stewardship, did not press for certainty regarding democratic processes in the protracted negotiations with China between 1982 and 1984.[2] Efforts for further reform after 1985 were put on hold awaiting the mainland's promulgation of the Basic Law. It was widely felt that whatever political reform was to occur between 1985 and 1997 should be consistent with the Basic Law that China was responsible for drafting.

The Decision of the National People's Congress on the Method for the Formation of the First Government and the First Legislative Council of the Hong Kong Special Administrative Region (the "Decision"), adopted with the Basic Law in 1990, provided that the first Legislative Council of the HKSAR would consist of sixty members with twenty directly elected by geographic constituencies, thirty selected by functional constituencies, and ten chosen by an Electoral College. It further provided that if the legislature elected in 1995 conformed to the provisions of the Decision, then it could straddle the transition and serve until the next subsequent legislative election scheduled for 1999.

In a mere twenty-seven months, Hong Kong's political landscape was dramatically altered. One cannot overstate the impact of the Tiananmen Square massacre in June 1989 on the politicization of the Hong Kong people. For many, Tiananmen crystallized political attitudes toward China, the transition to Chinese rule, and political identification in Hong Kong. Fifteen months after Tiananmen, the National People's Congress promulgated the Basic Law to govern Hong Kong after 1997. And finally, in September 1991, the first Legislative Council composed, in part, of directly elected geographical constituencies, was formed. To a large extent, in this relatively short period of time, modern politics, politicians, and political parties blossomed in Hong Kong. Between 1981 and 1991, the size of the electorate increased by more than a factor of 50 (see table 3.1). In 1991, there were three times as many elections, four times as many elected

Table 3.1 Growth in the Hong Kong Electorate

Year	Electorate (A)	Population (B)	Percentage (A/B)
1952	9,000	2,250,000	0.40
1971	37,788	3,936,630	0.96
1981	34,381	5,109,812	0.67
1991	1,916,925	5,674,114	33.78
1995	2,572,124	5,993,000	42.92
1998	2,795,371	6,617,000	42.25

Sources: Li 1995 for 1952–95 data; Wong 1998 and Hong Kong Government 1998 for 1998 data.

bodies, twenty-two times as many elected officials, and 250 times as many votes cast as in 1981 (DeGolyer 1994). Politics took center stage with political parties, politicians, and party members.

POLITICAL PARTIES AND PARTY IDENTIFICATION IN HONG KONG

The 1970s and early 1980s saw the emergence of various special interests, pressure groups, and community organizations to represent distinct interests. With the introduction of a universal franchise in 1982, these groups were poised to transform their connections into political parties at some time in the future (Louie 1991; Li and Newman 1997). As Maurice Duverger (1963) suggests, elections give rise to political parties (Louie 1991), and meaningful elections were needed to provide the final impetus for parties to form. As noted, the introduction of geographic constituency elections for Legco in 1991 made contesting for seats in Hong Kong meaningful and gave rise to the conversion of interest groups into political parties.[3]

The Joint Declaration, negotiated by the British and Chinese governments in 1984 to resolve the status of Hong Kong after 1997, gave a further, and perhaps unintended, push to the formation of political parties. The Joint Declaration promised a "high degree of autonomy" incorporating the ideal of "Hong Kong people governing Hong Kong." Moreover, the Declaration and the Basic Law envision elections with universal suffrage as the mechanism for returning the chief executive and the entire Legislature sometime after 2007. Although disagreements exist over the meaning of the word "election" and the pace of introducing electoral reforms, the goal of abolishing the appointment system is clearly stated.

The 1990 edition of an annual survey of Hong Kong affairs entitled its chapter on politics "Politicians" (Lee 1990). Political parties were not yet the focus of scholarly attention. The 1992 annual survey recognized the new reality and entitled its chapter on politics "Politicians, Political Parties and the Legislative Council" (Louie 1992).

The Parties

The Democratic Party, the most popular mass party in Hong Kong, and the Hong Kong Association for Democracy and People's Livelihood (ADPL) evolved from liberal democratic groups formed to represent Hong Kong's emerging educated middle class. Through the 1980s and into the early 1990s, these groups merged into larger political parties and these interests are now generally represented by the larger Democratic Party and the somewhat smaller, but still important, ADPL. Throughout the 1990s, more than 60 percent of survey respondents generally identified with the Democratic Party. Because of the democratic support of dissidents in China, the democrats have been isolated by the Chinese government and some leaders have been characterized by the Chinese as subversive. In 1996, Emily Lau formed the Frontier, and in 1997, Christine Loh formed the Citizens Party. Both are prodemocratic parties pursuing an expansion of democratic participation and the rule of law in Hong Kong independent of the Democratic Party.[4]

The Democratic Alliance for the Betterment of Hong Kong (DAB) is a grassroots working-class party with a history of good relations with China. This party was formed with the support of leftist trade unions and traditional local organizations. On matters relating to local politics, the traditional pro-Beijing forces and democrats often agree on social and commercial matters but diverge on relations with China.

The Liberal Party evolved from the Cooperative Resources Centre formed in 1991. The party represents commercial interests in Hong Kong. While believing in a free economic market, it opposes any further politicization of Hong Kong or expansion of the social welfare system in Hong Kong. The Liberal Party has primarily targeted seats in the functional constituencies with many of its candidates running unopposed.

The Hong Kong Progressive Alliance was formed in 1994 with the blessings of the Chinese government. This group primarily consists of pro-Beijing business interests.

United Ants was formed just after the electoral reform debate in 1994 by prodemocratic elements disturbed by the caution exercised by other democrats. The Civic Force, yet another party, was primarily concerned with local issues in one community in Hong Kong—Sha Tin. Neither party survived the decade intact.

Identifying with a party proved difficult for some candidates. Some were unaligned and ran in elections as independents. Others, perhaps for strategic reasons, decided it was to their advantage to run without a party affiliation. While some candidates running as independents were pro-Beijing and received support from the Chinese establishment in Hong Kong, others were easily identifiable as democrats but ran without the crest of one of the democratic parties.

In addition to the above political parties that actively contested geographical constituency seats, other political organizations ran candidates for the functional constituency and election committee seats at various times. These include the 123

Democratic Alliance, a pro-Taipei group formed in 1994; the Federation of Trade Unions (FTU), a working-class labor union that may have organizational links to Beijing; the Confederation of Trade Unions (CTU), a pro-Taipei labor union; and the New Hong Kong Alliance (NHKA), a probusiness group in Hong Kong led by a former Exco and Legco member.

Party Identification

Unlike in the United States, where in many states a voter must register as a member of a political party as part of the voter registration process, no such requirement exists in Hong Kong. Most of the political parties are very small in terms of actual paid membership and somewhat larger in terms of volunteers. Party membership in Hong Kong, excluding Chinese Communist Party and Kuomintang members, was estimated at 3,800 in 1991 (DeGolyer 1994). This number is perhaps inflated by the fact that some of the "parties" were more social or community organizations. In 1999, the Democratic Party reported that it had about 600 paid members; the Citizens Party reported about 50 paid members and Frontier reported 120 paid members.

A 1991 survey of the electorate found that only 11 percent of likely voters considered party affiliation an important factor in deciding for whom to vote (*South China Morning Post*, 15 September 1991). In another survey of likely voters, 50 percent indicated that they would consider a candidate's position on the prodemocracy movement in China before voting (*Hong Kong Standard*, 14 September 1991). This cleavage gave rise to the two major political camps in Hong Kong—the democratic and pro-Chinese parties. The other division, primarily within the pro-China camp, was between the business interests and the traditional leftist organizers and their supporters. This cleavage distinguishes the DAB from the Liberal Party (see Li 1997).

In a 1995 election survey asking respondents "which political party would you say is closest to your own political stance?" 36 percent said "no party represented their views," and more than 50 percent said the candidate's political affiliation was not an important consideration in their vote choice (Scott 1996). Using a slightly different methodology, Kin-shuen Louie (1996) found that 14.6 percent of the 1995 Legco voters were strong party identifiers and 9.5 percent were weak party identifiers. Moreover, comparing 1995 results with those from the 1991 Legco election, Louie found that the percentage of party identifiers (strong or weak) did not advance significantly despite the prominence of the political debate over the same period.

Strongly identifying with one political camp or another had potential costs, and political entrepreneurs, or politicians, in Hong Kong were faced with a difficult and uncertain calculation at the beginning of the 1990s. Seven and one-half years still remained until the change in sovereignty. The "old" Chinese elite had been co-opted by the colonial administration (Lee 1990). The new elite had to decide whether to align with the current colonial administration or align with the future one—China. Would seven and one-half years of future rewards sufficiently establish one as a political figure without tarnishing one's future prospects? Should one align early, or even ultimately, with China, in a post-Tiananmen period, knowing that China was almost universally scorned in Hong Kong following Tiananmen? Should one align with local Hong Kong sentiments, assuming the Joint Declaration and Basic Law statements regarding a high degree of autonomy were meaningful, but ultimately knowing that China controlled all the cards following the transition? These were difficult decisions at a difficult time, and they dominated Hong Kong politics throughout the decade.

Academic studies of voter behavior, something new in Hong Kong, identified several issues as fundamental to the electorate—democracy, the transition, and China (Sun and Wong 1996; Li 1996). While Milan Tung-wen Sun and Timothy Ka-ying Wong highlighted the importance of democracy in the 1995 election, their conclusions can be extended to the 1991 and 1998 Legco elections as well.

> Considering Hong Kong people's general worry about possible intervention by the Chinese government, it is not surprising to see "Democracy" overwhelm all other concerns in the campaign. . . . On the other hand, "Transitional Issues" was usually associated with the pro-China camp which emphasized "one country, two systems," "economic prosperity," "supporting the Basic law," etc. That the elected candidates had tended to emphasize more democratic issues than transitional issues whereas the defeated ones [had tended] to emphasize the reverse lends support to the common belief that pro-democracy candidates performed better, at least in strategic terms, than the pro-China candidates in the 1995 election. (Sun and Wong 1996, 185)

Weak party identification in Hong Kong can be explained by several factors:

1. the political parties are all relatively new;
2. the parties themselves have been subject to considerable change and consolidation over a short period of time;
3. Hong Kong's population is largely composed of immigrants from the mainland, where the cultural norm is to avoid politics; and
4. the colonial administration of the territory sought to avoid civic education and political socialization.

An additional constraint on party identification is the well-understood institutional arrangement in which political parties, under either British colonial ad-

Table 3.2 (S)election Methods of Government Officials in Hong Kong

Year	Municipal Council	District Boards	Legislative Council	Chief Executive
1991	Urban and regional council elections	District Board elections	Legislative Council elections	
1992	Patten Reforms proposed	Patten Reforms proposed	Patten Reforms proposed	
1994		District Board elections		
1995			Legislative Council elections	
1996	Provisional Municipal Councils appointed	Provisional District Boards appointed	Provisional Legislature appointed	Chief Executive selected
1997	Transfer of sovereignty	Transfer of sovereignty	Transfer of sovereignty	
1997			New election scheme introduced	
1998			Legislative Council election	
1999	Eliminated	District Board elections		

ministration or Chinese rule, are permanently relegated to a role of loyal opposition. No matter how active one may be in a party and no matter how well a party may do in an election, the party can never govern.

Legislative Elections in Hong Kong

As is evident in table 3.2, Hong Kong emerged from a long period of political hibernation to one of rapid and almost continuous electoral activity. Hong Kong averaged almost one election per year. Moreover, as table 3.3 illustrates, the election systems employed were in constant flux as the goals to be achieved through the use of elections changed. One should keep in mind that with changes in method of selection came changes in boundaries and districts. While the pace of change clearly kept the concept of elections on the front pages of newspapers and in the minds of the electorate, the possibility remained that the intensity and frequency of the debate alienated some potential voters.

The 1991 Legco Election

By 1991, Legco's size was fixed at sixty members: four ex officio members, seventeen appointed members, and thirty-nine elected members. Of the elected mem-

Table 3.3 Changes in the Composition of the Hong Kong Legislature over Time

Year	Appointed/ Ex Officio	Geographic Constituencies		Functional Constituencies		Electoral College	
		Narrow	Broad	Narrow	Broad	Narrow	Broad
Prior to 1985	61						
1985	32	12		12			
1991	17/4		18	21			
1995			20	21	9		10
1997	60						
Provisional 1998			20	30		10	
2000			24	30		6	
2004			30	30			

Note: The terms broad and narrow are used in context. While the use of an Electoral College is a restrictive device, it allowed for broad participation in 1995 as compared to previous or subsequent years.

bers, twenty-one were chosen by functional constituencies and, for the first time ever, eighteen were directly elected by nine geographical constituencies (see table 3.4, p. 60). The functional constituencies used a preferential elimination voting system, and the geographical constituencies used a plurality voting scheme. In the several functional constituencies returning two candidates, each elector possessed two votes. This system clearly conformed to the requirements outlined in the Basic Law.

Given that each geographic district was to elect two representatives, the parties needed to calculate their prospects relative to the those of other parties in determining how many candidates to run in each district. Parties with large popular support could field two candidates per district with the hope of electing both. A party with modest support would consider fielding only one candidate so that the party's supporters did not split their support across two candidates and elect neither of them. The United Democrats, an element of today's Democratic Party, fielded fourteen candidates in the nine constituencies and coordinated with Meeting Point, another element of today's Democratic Party, in three of the constituencies (see table 3.5, p. 62). There was a maximum of eight candidates in one constituency and a minimum of four in another; more than half of all candidates ran either as independents or from minor parties. Even though the election of directly elected legislators was the subject of considerable interest in Hong Kong,

Table 3.4 Hong Kong Party Representation in Legco by Constituency in 1991, 1995, Provisional, and 1998 Legislatures

Party (Date of founding)	1991 Legislature[a]	1995 Legislature	Provisional Legislature	1998 Legislature
Geographic Constituencies				
Democratic Party (1994)	15	12		9
DAB (1992)		2		5
Liberal Party (1993)		1		0
Other prodemocratic parties and independents (Frontier, 1996; Citizens Party, 1997)	1	4		5
Unaffiliated	2	1		1
Functional Constituencies				
Democratic Party (1994)	4	5		4
DAB (1992)/ Federation of Trade Unions		2/1		2
Liberal Party (1993)	8	9		9
Hong Kong Progressive Alliance (1994)				2
ADPL (1986)		1		
123 Democratic Alliance (1994)/ Confederation of Trade Unions		2		
Unaffiliated	9	10		13
Election Committee				
Democratic Party (1994)		2	0	0
Liberal Party (1993)			9	1
DAB (1992)		2	11	2
Hong Kong Progressive Alliance[b] (1994)		2	10	3
ADPL (1986)		1	4	
Unaffiliated/Minor Parties		3	26	4
Appointed				
Liberal Party (1993)	12			
Unaffiliated	5			
Ex officio	4			

a. Party classification reflects current party configurations.
b. Includes Chu Yu-lin, formerly of the Liberal Democratic Foundation and now of HKPA.

on election day, turnout fell just short of 40 percent. The democratic parties swept to victory, winning fifteen of the eighteen geographic seats. A prodemocratic independent, Emily Lau, won one seat, independent Andrew Wong won one seat, and Tai Chin-wah was elected with the support of rural groups in the New Territories. Tai later resigned after it was revealed that he forged professional qualifications. In a by-election to fill his seat, Meeting Point won a third seat in Legco. The pro-China forces had considerable support, receiving more than 44,000 votes in the Kowloon Central constituency—enough votes to win a seat in most other constituencies—but failed to win a seat either in Kowloon Central or elsewhere.

While interest in the functional constituency races was overshadowed by the geographical constituency races, there were forty candidates for the twenty-one seats; ten candidates ran unopposed. Of the 104,609 eligible voters, just less than two-thirds registered. The smallest constituency had only 36 electors and the largest 38,678. In neither the functional nor the geographic constituencies was there a concern with protecting the notion of one person, one vote whereby each voter's influence in selecting a candidate is roughly equal. The democratic parties picked up four functional constituency seats, the Liberals eight, and unaffiliated nine.

The election results clearly made the mainland Chinese authorities unhappy (Ching 1992). The democratic parties in Hong Kong commanded the loyalty of more than 60 percent of the voters, and prior to the formation of the DAB in 1992, no credible pro-Chinese political parties existed. Assuming no change in the preferences of the voters, any increase in the number of geographic constituency seats was likely to make Chinese administration of Hong Kong more difficult after 1997.

The Patten Reforms and the 1995 Legco Election

As the 1990s unfolded, change was directed toward broadening the processes for selecting Legislative Council members (see table 3.3, p. 59). The impetus for change came in part from local demands for greater democratization following the Tiananmen Square crackdown (Louie 1992). The high points of this period were the electoral reform bills introduced by Christopher Patten, the last governor of Hong Kong, and the subsequent 1995 Legislative Council elections. As the government stated, the goal was to "broaden the participation of the community in the conduct of Hong Kong's affairs; and to devise arrangements for the district board election in 1994 and the Legislative Council and municipal council election in 1995 which command the confidence and the support of the community" (Hong Kong Government 1994). This period of reform came to a crashing halt with the change in sovereignty and the appointment of the provisional legislature in which all sixty members were unelected.

Governor Patten proposed two rounds of reforms in October 1992 to govern, in part, the Legco Elections of 1995. While Patten did not explicitly favor the democrats, the reforms that he proposed and to which the Chinese objected cer-

Table 3.5 Comparison of the 1991, 1995, and 1998 Geographic Constituency Elections in Hong Kong

Party	1991 Candidates Fielded (Elected)	1991 Percentage Vote Received	1995 Candidates Fielded (Elected)	1995 Percentage Vote Received	1998 Candidates Fielded (Elected)	1998 Percentage Vote Received
Democrats						
United Democrats of Hong Kong	14 (12)	45.1	*	*		
Meeting Point	3 (2)	7.2	*	*		
Democratic Party			15 (12)	42.3	18 (9)	42.9
Assoc. Democracy and People's Livelihood	3 (1)	4.4	5 (2)	9.5	4 (0)	4.0
HK Democratic Foundation	1 (0)	1.4			1 (1)	2.6
Neighborhood and Workers Service Center	1 (0)	2.8			4 (0)	.002
123 Democratic Alliance					2 (1)	2.8
Citizens Party					4 (3)	10.0
Frontier					1 (0)	
United Ants			2 (0)	2.0		
Prodemocratic Independents	3 (1)	5.0	2 (2)	7.3		4.0
Subtotal	25 (16)	65.9	24 (16)	61.1	34 (14)	66.3
Conservatives						
Liberal Democratic Foundation	5 (0)	5.1	1 (0)	1.3		
Rural	3 (1)	5.3	2 (0)	3.0		
New Hong Kong Alliance	2 (0)	0.9				
Liberal Party			1 (1)	1.7	12 (0)	2.2
HK Progressive Alliance			2 (0)	2.8	1 (0)	3.4
Proconservative Independents	6 (0)	8.2	2 (0)	1.9		
Subtotal	16 (1)	19.5	8 (1)	10.7	13 (0)	5.6

HONG KONG: A DECADE OF CHANGE

Leftists						
Federation of Trade Unions	1 (0)	3.3				
Hong Kong Citizen Forum	1 (0)	2.2				
Kwon Tong Man Chung Association	1 (0)	1.6				
Democratic Alliance for the Betterment of HK			7 (2)	15.7	20 (5)	25.2
Pro-Beijing Independents			2 (0)	2.2	8 (0)	.01
Subtotal	3 (0)	7.1	9 (2)	17.9	28 (5)	25.2
Rightists						
Trade Union Council	1 (0)	0.2				
Others	9 (1)	7.2	9 (1)	10.3	6 (1)	2.9
Total	54 (18)	99.9	50 (20)	100.0	81 (20)	100.0

Note: * indicates party merged.

tainly increased the likelihood that democrats would dominate Hong Kong's legislature. Patten's 1992 Policy Address explicitly argued that expanding democratic participation in Hong Kong was one way to protect Hong Kong's way of life (Patten 1992, 101).

While the Basic Law envisioned twenty members of Legco being elected from geographic constituencies, the Electoral Provisions (Miscellaneous Amendments) (N. 2) Bill 1993 lowered the voting age to eighteen, introduced a "single-seat, single-vote" electoral system for all three levels of government—district boards, municipal councils, and legislative council. The second round of reforms, the Legislative Council (Electoral Provisions) (Amendment) Bill created nine new functional constituencies, which effectively granted almost all voters a second vote and eliminated corporate voting in the functional constituencies. Finally, the legislation provided for the indirect election of the remaining ten Legco members by employing the directly elected district board members as the election committee. The net effect of the two rounds of reforms was to expand the franchise to include more than 2.5 million people. While the proposals were technically in conformity with the requirements of the Basic Law, the mainland authorities held that they violated understandings between the British and the Chinese on the pace of democracy (see Ching 1993; Dimbleby 1997). When Patten persisted, mainland officials decreed that the legislature elected in 1995 could not sit beyond 30 June 1997.

The 1995 Election Results

As a result of the Patten reforms, the British and others could claim that the 1995 Legco elections were the first designed to have all sixty seats elected—though not all by popular franchise. Moreover, the candidates seeking a seat knew that although they were running for a four-year term, they would only be allowed to serve until 1 July 1997 because the Chinese authorities had announced that the sitting legislature would be dissolved on that day.

Fifty candidates competed for the twenty single-member, popularly elected geographical constituency seats. The democrats received about 7 percent fewer votes in 1995 compared to 1991, but the switch to single-seat constituencies allowed them to capture sixteen of the twenty geographic constituency seats. The pro-China forces won two seats, the Liberal Party won one, and an independent, Andrew Wong, won the last. The decline in votes for the democrats was not surprising given the diminishing influence of Tiananmen on Hong Kong politics and the general confidence in the future change in sovereignty.

The big overall winner was the pro-China DAB, which captured almost 16 percent of the vote in their first electoral outing. The DAB could claim success despite the fact that four of the seven DAB candidates lost, including party leader Tsang Yok-sing. The DAB more than doubled the previous 1991 vote tally of all pro-China groups.

In the functional constituencies, nine of the twenty-one "old" seats were uncontested. In districts with the twelve contested seats, 42,885 votes were cast, compared to 393,521 votes cast in the nine new broad-based constituencies introduced by the Patten reforms. While these reforms broadened the electorate, they did not enshrine the notion of one person, one vote where each vote had potentially equal weight in selecting a candidate. One vote in one of the old contested functional constituencies was still worth 12 times as much as one vote cast in a new functional constituency.

Of the thirty functional constituency seats, the Democratic Party won five seats, the Liberal Party won nine seats, independents won ten seats, the CTU and DAB each won two seats, and the ADPL and FTU each won one seat (see table 3.4, p. 60).

Even though the Liberal Party emerged with ten seats, the fact that only one candidate, party leader Allen Lee, was able to win in a geographic constituency highlighted the party's lack of broad-based popular support.

The Election Committee, which consisted of 283 partisan and independent district board members, returned ten legislators from a list of eighteen candidates. Of the ten, seven were advisers to the mainland on Hong Kong affairs, two were members of the Democratic Party, and one was a member of the 123 Democratic Alliance.

Overall, the election results were again seen as a rebuff to the mainland. The strong showing of the democrats was seen as evidence of local concern with posttransition politics. The democrats polled better than any pundits had predicted before the election. The pro-China forces fared best in the Election Committee, a small forum where pressure could most easily be exerted; this was surprising because the mainland had had the most objections to this constituency under the Patten reforms. For the Chinese authorities, it was clear that any posthandover electoral system using either single-member or two-member constituencies rewarded the democrats.

SELECTING THE CHIEF EXECUTIVE AND PROVISIONAL LEGISLATURE

A Decision of the National People's Congress on the Method for the Formation of the First Government and the First Legislative Council of the Hong Kong Special Administrative Region (the "Decision") governed the selection of the first HKSAR chief executive, Tung Chee-hwa, and the formation of the first legislature—the 1998 legislature, because the Decision did not anticipate the Provisional Legislature.

The Decision, adopted by the National People's Congress, China's legislature, on 4 April 1990, provided that in preparation for the (s)election of the chief executive, the Standing Committee of the National People's Congress choose 150 members to serve on what was called the Preparatory Committee—94 members from Hong Kong and 56 members from the Mainland. The Preparatory Committee, as its name suggests, prepared for the posthandover administration of the

HKSAR; it was to (s)elect a 400-member Selection Committee to choose the first chief executive. For the first time in Hong Kong's history, it was claimed, Hong Kong's chief executive would be elected rather than appointed.

Individuals could apply to serve on the Selection Committee, and more than 5,000 Hong Kong residents did so. From the pool of applicants, the Preparatory Committee chose 100 from each of four sectors—business, politics, the professions, and grassroots organizations. In round one of a two-part selection process, an aspirant for the post of chief executive needed to secure the support of fifty members of the Selection Committee in order to become a candidate. In round two, using a two-stage runoff system, the first candidate to achieve a majority, 201 votes, would be selected as chief executive for a five-year term.

On 15 November 1996, three aspirants secured the requisite 50 votes. Tung Chee-hwa, a former executive whose shipping company was bailed out by mainland interests in the 1980s, received 206 votes. Yang Ti-liang, the former Chief Justice, received 82 votes, and Peter Woo, a prominent local businessman, received 54 votes. A fourth aspirant with strong ties to the mainland, Simon Li, received only 43 votes and failed to move on to the second round.

The final selection of the chief executive was held on 11 December 1996. With Tung's strong showing a month earlier, it was a foregone conclusion that he would be selected the first chief executive. In the end, he secured more than 80 percent of the votes.

Subsequent chief executives of the HKSAR were to be selected according to Article 45 of the Basic Law and Annex 1. Annex 1 provided for the creation of an 800-member selection committee drawn equally from the industrial, commercial, and financial sectors; the professions; labor, grassroots, religious, and other sectors; and former political figures, Hong Kong deputies to the NPC, and Hong Kong members of the National Committee of the Chinese People's Political Consultative Council. This committee was to nominate a candidate to the Central People's Government to serve as chief executive in 2002 and 2007. While it was a stated goal of the Basic Law that the chief executive will ultimately be chosen by universal suffrage, the first several chief executives were to be chosen through a very contorted process designed to constrain the set of candidates who can vie for office.

The Provisional Legislature was selected by the same 400-member "selection committee" constituted for the selection of the chief executive. One needed ten supporters from the Selection Committee to be nominated, and each of the 400 electors cast 60 votes—one for each member of the provisional legislature. It was not referred to as the first legislature since it was not selected according to the Decision.

For many, the Provisional Legislature had a tenuous legal basis (Rabushka 1997; Lau 1996) because the Basic Law did not stipulate the use of the Selection

Committee for this purpose. Even members of the pro-China camp had problems with its legality. One member of the National People's Congress and the Selection Committee, Dorothy Liu Yiu-chu, stated that "it was a violation of the Basic Law for both the legislature and executive bodies to be selected by the Selection Committee." She further went on to say that "[t]he establishment of the provisional legislature was without legal basis and would embarrass China" (*South China Morning Post*, 22 December 1996). Instead, it was an expedient tool once the British and the Chinese reached an impasse over the methods used to choose the 1995 Legco, and the committee met on 21 December 1996 in Shenzhen, China, to make its selections.

There were 134 candidates for the 60 positions. Of these, 91 were members of the Selection Committee and 34 were sitting members of the 1995 Legislative Council. Few real surprises arose in the Provisional Legislative selection. As a general conclusion, since the democrats boycotted the election, there was room in the Provisional Legislature both for those who lost in 1995 and for those who won in 1995 and were willing to continue serving. Ten candidates defeated in the 1995 Legco election, including the head and deputy head of the DAB, were selected in 1996. All but one sitting member of the Legislative Council who sought a seat was selected. Chan Choi-hei, a former member of the Democratic Party who served as a District Board member, who defected before the selection, was rewarded with a seat. Tam Yiu-chong, Vice Chairman of the DAB, received the most votes—345. Fifty-one of the sixty members selected served on the Selection Committee. "If one had to summarize the criteria sought by the Selection Committee, it was a legislative and political background with many of the candidates having current and former experience in either Legco or Executive Council, and service in an advisory capacity to the Beijing government" (Li and Newman 1997).

Although there were allegations of vote switching and mainland interference in the selection process, to the extent it occurred, it was largely hidden. Just before the voting began, Qian Qichen, China's Vice Premier and Chairman of the Preparatory Committee, advised selectors to "give support to those with practical experience in legislative work" and "make the provisional legislature as widely representative as possible" (*South China Morning Post*, 22 December 1996). Two nights before the voting, Chan Wing-kee, a member of the National People's Congress, announced that he would cast a vote for each of the thirty-four incumbent members of the Legislature standing for selection *(South China Morning Post*, 20 December 1996).

The First HKSAR Legislature

On 29 September 1997, the Provisional Legislature enacted guidelines for the election of the First Legislative Council of the HKSAR on 24 May 1998. The law provided that the First Legislature comprise the following:

- Twenty members directly elected, according to proportional representation, from five districts, each returning between three and five members;
- Thirty members chosen by functional constituencies, including nine new ones to replace the nine broad ones created by the Patten reforms;
- Ten members selected by an 800-member Election Committee composed of handpicked representatives from four sectors: (1) industry, commerce, and finance; (2) the professions; (3) labor, social services, and religion; and (4) politics. Each sector is further divided into subsectors representing thirty-eight sets of interests in Hong Kong, including the twenty-eight functional constituencies. (S)election of the 800 electors was by election or consensus or as a matter of right granted to members of the National People's Congress, the Chinese People's Political Consultative Conference, and members of the Provisional Legislative Council.

Some have speculated that because the Provisional Legislature was in part composed of appointed members who were either personally defeated in previous elections or affiliated with political parties that performed poorly under previous election schemes, they were motivated, at least in part, to design a system that would improve their chances of winning future elections (Newman and Rabushka 1998). Five individuals ran in 1995 and lost, served in the Provisional Legislature, and then ran for a seat in 1998. All five won.

The 1998 Election Results

The intended, but unstated, effects of the changes in the electoral system were the following: (1) to reduce the influence of the democrats; (2) to reduce the influence of all political parties so that no one party could claim to represent a majority of the populace and challenge the appointed chief executive; and (3) to ensure that a conservative, pro-China, probusiness majority be preserved in the Legislative Council. The election scheme adopted for the first posthandover Legislative Council elections achieved all three goals.

The election results can be summarized by the headlines found in two newspapers the following day—"Record Turnout Poised to Give Democrats Sweeping Victory" and "Pro-China Parties Likely to Dominate Legislature." The democrats collectively received 56 percent of the popular vote but garnered only 30 percent of the seats (eighteen seats). The democrats won fourteen of the twenty geographic constituency seats and four of the thirty functional constituencies, including two of the four largest functional constituencies.

Election Committee Voting

Electors to the Election Committee were selected from narrowly constituted interests within the commercial sector; the professions; social, cultural, and religious groups; and politicians. These "interest groups" were each given a number of votes on the Election Committee and allowed to select their "subsector" representatives. Some groups such as the Hong Kong Chinese Enterprise Association had uncontested "elections" to choose its eleven electors. Of the 800 seats, 137 (17 percent) were reserved for members of the Provisional Legislature, Delegates to the National People's Congress, and members of the Chinese People's Political Consultative Conference.

Even though roughly 140,000 people registered to vote in these subsector elections, only 23.4 percent of them bothered to show up and cast a vote. This was the lowest functional constituency turnout in the past four elections. The turnout in the Election Committee subsector elections is contrasted to the functional constituency elections since, in large part, the electors are the same in both. Even Professor Lau Siu-kai, a spokesman for and member of the Preliminary Working Group, Beijing's advance team in Hong Kong, had to concede that "the middle class was resistant to the Election Committee system which goes against their democratic ideals."

The 800-member Election Committee represented a major change from its predecessor. The committee was heavily composed of pro-China, probusiness members from similar backgrounds. Moreover, the election rules for the Election Committee were changed to bloc voting whereby each elector *must* cast ten votes and the winners are those with the most votes. The adoption of the first-past-the-post system in the Election Committee shows that the Hong Kong authorities are not philosophically opposed to this system. Instead, using different electoral systems in various settings enhanced the chance of pro-China voices being elected. The argument that Legco should reflect a broad set of opinions through proportional voting was selectively applied to impair the democratic voices.

The democrats had little expectation of retaining their two seats from the at-large constituencies in the 800-member Election Committee, which was dominated by pro-China figures, including the sixty Hong Kong members of the National People's Congress and the Chinese People's Political Consultative Conference. The switch from the single transferable vote to the pro-China bloc vote by members of the new Election Committee crippled the chances of democrats winning any of these seats. Their popular appeal had no attraction to 800 pro-China (antidemocratic) electioneers. So-called independents captured four seats, the HKPA three seats, the DAB two seats, and the LP one seat.

Corporate Voting in the 1998 Election

The use of corporate voting in the 1998 election was one of the most significant rule changes to be implemented in posttransition Hong Kong. The adoption of corporate voting by the unelected Provisional Legislature ensured that the interests of the corporate/business elite, aligned with mainland China, would effectively hold a veto over any potential legislation. Members of the various democratic parties had little or no chance in the refashioned nine functional constituencies because of both the switch to corporate voting and the change to some constituencies' functional identities.

The following data illustrate the undemocratic character of the corporate vote system: One Hong Kong billionaire, Lee Shau-kee, had a controlling interest in twenty companies in the real estate constituency. This gave him votes equal to five percent of that constituency. Li Ka-shing, another billionaire, had even more votes in that constituency. Many of the functional constituencies had only a few hundred voters, with the smallest having fewer than 100 voters. An investigation reported in the *South China Morning Post* of 23 February 1998 disclosed that the Real Estate Functional Constituency contained 410 corporate "voters" but that a number of tycoons possessed additional votes for themselves by owning shelf companies—generally companies without any real assets, registered in a tax haven, each of which received a vote. Robert Ng's Sino Group had nineteen companies registered, of which eighteen nominated representatives for the election; of these, five were US$1 companies registered in the Cayman Islands and one a US$2 company registered in Panama. Ng's 18 votes were equivalent, in representative voting power, of 6,100 voters in a geographic constituency that contained more than 200,000 voters. In total, the real estate functional constituency in 1998 had 340 corporate votes and only 70 individual voters.

The Sino Group was not the only property conglomerate to possess the right to cast multiple votes; the Hang Lung Group held ten votes, and Sun Hung Kai and Henderson Land each held thirteen. These four companies combined possessed 14 percent of the eligible votes. Such perversities of the election system were not limited to so-called domestic companies. British insurance companies held almost 14 percent of the votes in the insurance functional constituency, an electoral equivalent to 19,300 people in a geographic constituency. Foreign firms, in total, possessed more than one-half of the votes in the insurance functional constituency. Even foreign governments that control foreign-flagged airlines operating in Hong Kong were eligible to vote through designated representatives who were permanent residents of Hong Kong. Foreign airlines constituted 5 percent of the total vote in the tourism functional constituency.

While the potential electorate perceived that the process was undemocratic, the extent was not highlighted. These same functional constituencies were often used to select members of the Election Committee. For example, the 152 voters in the agriculture and fisheries constituency elected 40 members of the committee, whereas the 11,503 voters in the education constituency elected 20 members. One of the basic elements of a democratic election is "one person, one vote." A vote in the agriculture and fisheries constituency was worth more than 150 votes in the education constituency. Moreover, it was possible that a majority of the 800 seats could derive their authority and legitimacy from as few as 1,230 votes cast in the subsector elections.

A frequent argument in favor of the functional constituencies is that the companies casting votes contribute significantly to the economic welfare of the HKSAR. In the 1998 election, however, no effort was made to restrict voting rights to just those making a positive contribution. Firms in bankruptcy could cast a vote so long as they had designated an "authorized representative" to act on behalf of the company. Even the government admitted it had no estimate of the number of firms that have voting rights, since these rights are often conveyed by membership in private trade associations. The corporate vote system fits the description of "pocket" or "rotten" boroughs in eighteenth-century Britain that were eliminated with electoral reforms in the mid-nineteenth century. The only other political jurisdiction in the world that maintains corporate voting is the upper house of the Slovenian Parliament.

The Theme of Changing the Rules

Perhaps the central theme of Hong Kong politics in the 1990s was the almost continuous debate concerning the appropriate (s)election rules to be used for choosing Legislative Council members. The candidates, parties, aspirants, and mainland authorities were all conscious of the fact that particular rules advantaged some and disadvantaged others. During the decade, no two elections were conducted under the same set of rules. These changes, first under the British colonial administration and later enacted by the appointed provisional legislature, were designed initially to open up the electoral process and later to constrain it. The changes in the electoral rules focused on the number of directly elected seats in the legislature, the selection mechanism (first-past-the-post versus proportional representation), the number of representatives from each geographic constituency, the number and composition of the functional constituencies, the composition of the "electoral committee," the voting age, and appointed seats. These changes were so significant that the orderly transition anticipated by the Joint Declaration entered into between the British and the Chinese broke down.

Even as the decade came to a close, change persisted. In his 1998 Policy Address to the Legislative Council, Chief Executive Tung Chee-hwa called for the abolition of the Municipal Councils. The government's arguments focused on cost savings and efficiencies particularly in light of several food scares following the handover (Constitutional Affairs Bureau 1999). While the government noted the role played by the councils in political participation and elite recruitment, these concerns were dismissed. A bill eliminating the councils was placed on the agenda in April 1999 to take effect when the unelected Provisional Councils' terms ended on 31 December 1999.

Further change was also slated for 2000 and 2004. As noted, the number of Legco seats selected by the Electoral College would decrease to six in 2000, and the Electoral College would cease to function after the 2000 election. Moreover, each of the five geographic districts would be altered either in boundaries or in the number of candidates selected as the number of geographic seats increased in both 2000 and 2004.

Conclusion: The Pace of Democracy

In his 1992 maiden Policy Address, Governor Patten argued:

> So the pace of democratization in Hong Kong is—we all know—necessarily constrained. But it is constrained, not stopped dead in its tracks. . . . The Governments of the United Kingdom and China have agreed in the Joint Declaration that democracy should be carried forward with a Legislature constituted by elections. The Basic Law provides for a steady increase in the number of those directed elected to the Legislature. It does not visualize stagnation. (Patten 1992, 105–6)

Patten's view was buttressed by others even after the breakdown of the through train, the plan envisioned by the Basic Law whereby the legislature elected in 1995 would straddle the 1997 transition and serve until elections in 1999, and the imposition of the Provisional Legislature. Wong asserts that the 1998 Legco elections "put Hong Kong back onto course of gradual democratization" (1998, 147).

The evidence and structure now in place in Hong Kong, however, suggest a very different analysis. If one defines further democratization in the Hong Kong legislative context as an increase in the number of popularly elected legislative seats along with the broadening of the constituencies empowered to elect legislators, then democracy is now fully constrained. With the exception of the changes already provided for in 2004, the process has come about as far as it can and the end is in sight.

The pace of democracy in Hong Kong is constrained, in part, by the terms of the Basic Law, and in part, by the concerns of mainland Chinese authorities and local politicians who are served by the current political structure. According to the Basic Law, future changes in the electoral system will require separate majorities of *both* the geographic and the functional constituency members in Legco. It is difficult to envision the functional constituency members agreeing to vote themselves out of office when little evidence suggests that they could successfully compete in open elections requiring broad-based public support. Hence, for the foreseeable future, any expansion in the number of directly elected seats in Legco is unlikely despite the demands of democrats to the contrary.

Although the Basic Law provides that the chief executive will be (s)elected by an 800-member Selection Committee in 2002, this is hardly a radical expansion of democracy. Article 45 provides that "[t]he ultimate aim is the selection of the chief executive by universal suffrage upon nomination by a broadly representative nominating committee in accordance with democratic procedures," the process of amending the rules for selecting the chief executive in the years beyond 2007 are quite difficult. Any modification requires "the endorsement of two-thirds of the Legislative Council, the consent of the chief executive, and the approval of the Standing Committee of the NPC" (Committee on the Promotion of Civic Education 1997).

The democratic camp will press as early as possible for selection of the chief executive by universal suffrage, but so long as it commands the allegiance of a majority of the Hong Kong populace, the mainland is likely to resist any mechanism that may result in the selection of a objectionable candidate.[5] The political divide will occur over the composition of the nominating committee and the rules for making a selection. The mainland, in response to democratic pressure, is likely to propose a popular-vote confirmation of a candidate selected from a very closed structured nomination process. Such proposals are likely to put the democratic camp in the uncomfortable position of vetoing what will be held up as a reform measure on the path to further democracy. Direct election of the chief executive through a broad, open, competitive, and free process is just not in the cards in the foreseeable future.

Notes

1. While analyses of District Board and Municipal Council elections are beyond the scope of this chapter, the proposal to eliminate the Municipal Councils is briefly addressed.
2. Extensive literature covers the negotiations between the British and the Chinese relating to "who said what" (Roberti 1994; Cottrell 1993).
3. The date each party was founded is presented in table 3.4 (p. 60).
4. Following convention, "democratic" refers to individuals and groups broadly favoring an expansion of democratic institutions in Hong Kong; "Democratic" refers to the Democratic Party.
5. Support for the democrats cannot be assumed. Potentially realigning issues have already appeared on the political agenda. For instance, the democrats have supported the Court of Final Appeal's decision with respect to the right of abode of mainland children born of Hong Kong parents because of its rule of law implications. If Hong Kong were swamped with mainland children, however, middle class support for the democrats could be severely undercut.

References

Bueno de Mesquita, Bruce, David Newman, and Alvin Rabushka. 1997. *Red Flag over Hong Kong*. Chatham, N.J.: Chatham House.
Ching, Frank. 1992. "The Implementation of the Sino-British Joint Declaration." In *The Other Hong Kong Report 1992*, edited by Joseph Y.S. Cheng and Paul C.K. Kwong. Hong Kong: Chinese University Press, 79–94.
———. 1993. "Politics, Politicians, and Political Parties." In *The Other Hong Kong Report 1993*, edited by Po-king Choi and Lok-sang Ho. Hong Kong: Chinese University Press, 23–37.
Committee on the Promotion of Civic Education. 1997. *The Basic Law of the Hong Kong Special Administrative Region of the People's Republic of China*. Hong Kong: Hong Kong Government Printing Department.
Constitutional Affairs Bureau. 1999. Hong Kong Government.
Cottrell, Robert. 1993. *The End of Hong Kong: The Secret Diplomacy of Imperial Retreat*. London: John Murray.
DeGolyer, Michael E. 1994. "Politics, Politicians, and Political Parties." In *The Other Hong Kong Report 1994*, edited by Donald H. McMillen and Si-wai Man. Hong Kong: Chinese University Press, 75–101.

———. 1997. "Political Culture and Public Opinion." In *The Other Hong Kong Report 1997*, edited by Joseph Y.S. Cheng. Hong Kong: Chinese University Press, 169–206.
Dimbleby, Jonathan. 1997. *The Last Governor*. London: Warner Books.
Duverger, Maurice. 1963. *Political Parties: Their Organization and Activity in the Modern State*. Translated by B. North and R. North. New York: Wiley Science Edition.
Election Affairs Commission. 1998. *Report on the 1998 Legislative Council Elections*. Hong Kong Government. 24 August.
Hong Kong Government. 1993. *Hong Kong 1993—A Review of 1992*, edited by Hugh Witt. Hong Kong: Hong Kong Government Information Services.
———. 1994. *Hong Kong 1994—A Review of 1993*, edited by Renu Daryanani. Hong Kong: Hong Kong Government Information Services.
———. 1998. *Hong Kong—A New Era*, edited by Bob Howlett. Hong Kong: Hong Kong Government Information Services.
Lau, Emily. 1996. "Peking Forms Illegal Legislature for Hong Kong." http://www.emilylaw.org.hk/dec2396e.html.
Lee, Ming-kwan. 1990. "Politicians." In *The Other Hong Kong Report 1990*, edited by Richard Y.C. Wong and Joseph Y.S. Cheng. Hong Kong: Chinese University Press, 113–30.
Li, Pang-kwong. 1995. "Elections, Politicians, and Electoral Politics." In *The Other Hong Kong Report 1995*, edited by Stephen Y.L. Cheung and Stephen M.H. Sze. Hong Kong: Chinese University Press, 51–65.
———. 1996. "1995 Legislative Council Direct Election: A Political Cleavage Approach." In *The 1995 Legislative Council Elections in Hong Kong*, edited by Hsin-chi Kuan, Siu-kai Lau, Kin-sheun Louie, and Timothy Ka-ying Wong. Hong Kong: Hong Kong Institute of Asia-Pacific Studies, Chinese University Press, 245–73.
———. 1997. "Executive and Legislature: Institutional Design, Electoral Dynamics and the Management of Conflicts in the Hong Kong Transition." In *Political Order and Power Transition in Hong Kong*, edited by Pang-kwong Li. Hong Kong: Chinese University Press, 53–78.
Li, Pang-kwong, and David Newman. 1997. "Give and Take: Electoral Politics in Transitional Hong Kong." *Asian Perspective* 21, no. 1: 213–32.
Lo, Shiu-hing. 1996. "Political Parties in a Democratizing Polity: The Role of the 'Pro-China' Democratic Alliance for the Betterment of Hong Kong." *Asian Journal of Political Science* 4, no. 1: 98–129.
——— 1997. *The Politics of Democratization in Hong Kong*. London: Macmillan Press.
Louie, Kin-shuen. 1991. "Election and Politics." In *The Other Hong Kong Report 1991*, edited by Yun-wing Sung and Ming-kwan Lee. Hong Kong: Chinese University Press, 51–65.
———. 1992. "Politicians, Political Parties and the Legislative Council." In *The Other Hong Kong Report 1992*, edited by Joseph Y.S. Cheng and Paul C.K. Kwong. Hong Kong: Chinese University Press, 79–94.
———. 1996. "Party Identification in Hong Kong Elections: A Further Inquiry." In *The 1995 Legislative Council Elections in Hong Kong*, edited by Hsin-chi Kuan, Siu-kai Lau, Kin-sheun Louie, and Timothy Ka-ying Wong. Hong Kong: Hong Kong Institute of Asia-Pacific Studies, Chinese University Press, 137–64.
Miners, Norman. 1991. *The Government and Politics of Hong Kong*. 5th ed. Hong Kong: Oxford University Press.
Newman, David, and Alvin Rabushka. 1998. "Hong Kong under Chinese Rule: The First Year." *Hoover Institution Essays in Public Policy* 90:1–33.
Patten, Christopher. 1992. *Our Next Five Years: The Agenda for Hong Kong*. Hong Kong: Government Printer.
Rabushka, Alvin. 1997. "Freedom's Fall in Hong Kong." *Hoover Institution Essays in Public Policy* 79.
Roberti, Mark. 1994. *The Fall of Hong Kong: China's Triumph and Britain's Betrayal*. New York: John Wiley and Sons.
Scott, Ian. 1996. "Party Politics and Elections in Transitional Hong Kong." *Asian Journal of Political Science* 4, no. 1: 130–52.

Sun, Milan Tung-wen, and Timothy Ka-ying Wong. 1996. "Priming and Election: An Analysis of the 1995 Legislative Council Election." In *The 1995 Legislative Council Elections in Hong Kong*, edited by Hsin-chi Kuan, Siu-kai Lau, Kin-sheun Louie, and Timothy Ka-ying Wong. Hong Kong: Hong Kong Institute of Asia-Pacific Studies, Chinese University Press, 165–200.

Wong, Ka-ying Timothy. 1998. "The First Legislative Council Election of the Hong Kong Special Administrative Region: Meaning and Impact." *Issues & Studies* 34, no. 9: 124–49.

Yeung, Chris K.H. 1997. "Political Parties." In *The Other Hong Kong Report 1997*, edited by Joseph Y.S. Cheng. Hong Kong: Chinese University Press, 49–70.

CHAPTER 4

Macau's Political Evolution and Prospects

by Lo Shiu Hing

MACAU'S ELECTORAL SYSTEM has evolved since 1972, when the Legislative Assembly was formally established in accordance with the political tradition in Portugal's overseas colonies. In 1972, the Macau Legislative Assembly was composed of fourteen members, of which five were directly elected by the Portuguese residents, eight indirectly elected, and one appointed by the Portuguese governor. The prerequisite for members of the Legislative Assembly in 1972 was Portuguese citizenship. This requirement excluded many local Chinese from being legislators, although some members of the Chinese community held Portuguese passports.

In 1974, a military coup in Portugal toppled the authoritarian government in Lisbon. The Portuguese revolution affected electoral politics in Macau. Some Portuguese and Macanese—racially mixed Macau residents with Portuguese-Chinese or Portuguese-Malayan ancestry—formed the Centre Democratico de Macau (CDM), which put up candidates in the election for a Macau representative to sit in Portugal's Constituent Assembly. The CDM also criticized the Macau government for corruption. Some progovernment local Macanese formed the Association for the Defence of the Interests of Macau (ADIM) to oppose the CDM. In 1975, the ADIM candidate won election to Lisbon's Constituent Assembly (Lo 1995, 60–61). In 1980, the Macanese-dominated ADIM took four of the six directly elected seats in Macau's Legislative Assembly. Hence, the Portuguese revolution provided a catalyst for the local Macanese to participate in the direct election held for the Macau Legislative Assembly.

The Portuguese revolution shaped Macau's electoral system in another aspect. In 1976, the Organic Statute of Macau was ratified by the Portuguese Parliament, stating that the local legislature would make laws, scrutinize public expenditure, and amend the Organic Statute—Macau's colonial constitution (Yee 1999, 29–30). According to the Organic Statute, the Legislative Assembly would be composed of seventeen members, of which six were directly elected, six indirectly

Table 4.1 The Composition of Macau's Legislative Assembly, 1976–2009

Year	Directly Elected	Indirectly Elected	Appointed	Total
1976–80	6	6	5	17
1980–84	6	6	5	17
1984–88	6	6	5	17
1988–92	8	8	7	23
1992–96	8	8	7	23
1996–2001	8	8	7	23
2001–2005	10	10	7	27
2005–2009	12	10	7	29

elected by interest groups, and five appointed by the governor (see table 4.1). Yet from 1976 to 1983, the franchise in the Legislative Assembly was limited. The electoral law stated that to be eligible to vote, Chinese residents must be Macau residents for five years. In contrast, the Portuguese and Macanese were exempt from this strict requirement.

In 1984, the Portuguese administration in Macau introduced a new electoral law that gave equal voting rights to all Macau residents regardless of their length of residence. Governor Vasco de Almedia e Costa decided to introduce such a law because his policy of centralizing the administration of the Leal Senado (the Municipal Council with jurisdiction on the Macau Peninsula; the Camera Municipal das Ihas has jurisdiction on Taipa and Coloane Islands) was opposed by the Macanese legislators. Infuriated by their attempts to amend his administrative decrees without his approval, Governor Costa was determined to change the law to allow more room for the Chinese residents to participate in local elections. This way, he hoped to curb the political influence of the Macanese legislators. During the 1976–84 Legislative Assembly elections, economic or business groups could choose three indirectly elected legislators. Costa's reform, however, allowed the Chinese-dominated economic interest groups to select five indirectly elected legislators. As a result of these changes, Chinese participation in the Legislative Assembly was politically institutionalized.

In 1990, the Portuguese Parliament approved revisions to the Organic Statute in order to prepare the Macau Special Administrative Region (MSAR) to have "a high degree of autonomy" after 19 December 1999. The Sino-Portuguese Joint Declaration of 1987 stipulated that Macau's administrative right would be returned to the People's Republic of China (PRC) and that the Portuguese administration would come to an end. The change in the Organic Statute of 1990 could be interpreted as a result of the Sino-Portuguese agreement, which would prepare the Macau people to govern the MSAR. According to the revised Organic Statute, the old seventeen-member legislature would be enlarged to twenty-three members, of which eight would be directly elected by citizens, eight indirectly elected by interest groups, and seven appointed by the governor.

As shown in table 4.1, the Basic Law of the MSAR—the constitution of Macau under Chinese rule—stipulates that the number of directly elected seats would increase slightly to ten in 2001–2005 and to twelve in 2005–2009. Obviously, the drafters of the law were aware that the public would likely demand a gradual increase in the number of directly elected seats in the MSAR. To preempt such a demand, the drafters of the Macau Basic Law adopted a gradualist approach to democratization. It remains unclear, however, whether this gradualist approach will really reflect the wishes of the Macau society, composition of which has changed in the past decade as recent mainland immigrants have been more educated than those who arrived during the 1960s and 1970s. Needless to say, any review of the composition of the Macau Legislative Assembly will require the approval of the central government in Beijing and the support of the PRC officials responsible for the MSAR affairs. Most importantly, from the perspective of the PRC officials, any increase in the number of directly elected seats in Macau Legislative Assembly will have to take into consideration its effect on the Hong Kong Special Administrative Region (HKSAR), where the prodemocracy movement has traditionally been much stronger than its counterpart in Macau and where the liberal-minded democrats have a track record of grasping the majority of directly elected seats in the Legislative Council (Lo and Yu 1999). Given the relatively weak prodemocracy movement in Macau, it is unlikely that it can push the MSAR government and Beijing to accelerate democratization of the Legislative Assembly, at least in the short run.

It must be noted that neither the Portuguese administrators nor the Basic Law drafters liked to introduce radical changes to the composition of appointed seats, which usually number about one-third of the members of the Legislative Assembly. Traditionally, the Portuguese governors used appointed seats to co-opt Portuguese and Macanese and to balance the ethnic composition of the legislature. This strategy is unlikely to be drastically changed by the MSAR government, which would probably appoint fewer Portuguese and Macanese legislators than the Portuguese governors. Appointed seats, however, provide useful means by which the MSAR chief executive may balance the political as well as ethnic composition of the legislature. For example, if the Macanese fail to be directly elected by citizens to the legislature, the MSAR chief executive may appoint some Macanese in order to protect their interests. In contrast, in the event that the liberal-minded democrats were successful in MSAR's Legislative Assembly direct election, the chief executive would appoint more pro-Beijing legislators. The maintenance of appointed seats can be viewed as a safety device for balancing the political and ethnic composition of the MSAR's Legislative Assembly. In fact, the first MSAR chief executive, Edmund Ho Hau-wah, appointed four Chinese and three Portuguese as well as some Macanese legislators. Of the four Chinese legislators, one is Stanley Au Chong Kit, a candidate who competed with Ho in the first election for the MSAR chief executive in May 1999. Ho won the election by getting 81.9 percent of the votes (163 votes) in a Select Committee's election for that office. Au obtained 34 votes or 17.1 percent of the ballot *(South China Morning Post*, 16 May 1999). Anyway, appointment became a means by which the chief executive conferred upon his defeated opponent a political position in the Legislative Assembly. This practice could become a constitutional convention—unwritten rules of the political game—in the event that the defeated candidates running for chief executive were also appointed to the legislature.

Elections are also held for the MSAR's Executive Council and the two Municipal Councils (the Leal Senado and the Camera Municipal das Ihas). The Executive Council, formerly named the Consultative Council in Macau under Portuguese rule, remains the top policymaking body in Macau. The Executive Council is composed of seven to eleven people, and the chief executive can invite concerned people to sit in the council's meetings (http://safpsql.informac.gov.mo/gcs/e-index41c2.htm). In Macau under the final years of the Portuguese rule, the Consultative Council was composed of ten members, of which five were appointed by the governor and the rest were elected by (1) an electoral college consisting of employers, (2) an electoral college consisting of labor unions, (3) an electoral college consisting of cultural and educational interest groups, (4) members of the Leal Senado, and (4) members of the Camera Municipal das Ihas.Indirect elections held for the Consultative Council, however, were by no means competitive. In theory, elections were held for the Consultative Council. In practice, candidates running in the indirect elections for positions on this council were often automatically elected without opponents. It appeared that the Macau governors appointed representatives of the interest groups concerned to the Consultative Council, rather than interest groups making compromise among themselves and selecting their deputies.

The first MSAR Executive Council is composed of ten persons; five of them are government officials: (1) Florinada da Rosa Silva Chan, the Secretary for Administration and Justice; (2) Francis Tam Pak Un, the Secretary for Economy and Finance; (3) Fernando Chui Sai On, the Secretary for Social Affairs and Culture; (4) Ao Man Long, the Secretary for Transports and Public Works; and (5) Cheong Kuoc Va, the Secretary for Security. For the other five members of the Executive Council, three are also members of the Legislative Assembly: Victor Ng Wing Lok, Tong Chi Kin ,and Leong Heng Teng. It looks as if the Chief Executive, Edmund Ho, is determined to make the Executive Council an elite think tank with some experienced legislators and senior civil servants rather than following the indirectly elected model of the Consultative Council under Portuguese rule. Perhaps Ho is keen to adopt the Hong Kong model of the Executive Council, which is composed of members entirely appointed by the HKSAR chief executive.

Although elections are to be held for MSAR's Municipal Councils, both the Basic Law and the MSAR Government stress that the councils are not "organs of political power" (http://www.macau.gov.mo/macauinfo/e-politicreg.html). In Macau under Portuguese rule, the Municipal Councils were reconstructed by a new electoral law in July 1988. At that time, the Leal Senado had fifteen members, of which three were appointed by the Governor, six were indirectly elected, and six were directly elected. The Camera Municipal das Ihas, which had no elected members before July 1988, has had since then eleven members, of which three were appointed, four indirectly elected, and four directly elected.

Nevertheless, the powers of the two Municipal Councils were limited. Most members of the Municipal Councils were dominated by progovernment forces. Although a minority of pro-Beijing members were sometimes critical of the Portuguese administration, they did not constitute an effective check on the power of the executive branch, which remained politically preponderant because of the majority of progovernment councillors. Moreover, the Leal Senado was usually controlled by an executive committee composed of a chairperson, a vice chairperson, two other councillors, and a full-time member who was often a senior civil servant appointed by the governor to the council. The crux of the problem was that the Leal Senado tended to co-opt progovernment councillors into the executive committee, making the Leal Senado almost like an appendage of the government rather than a loyal opposition.

Given that prodemocracy politicians in the MSAR are relatively outnumbered and isolated, calls for democratization of the Municipal Councils remain very weak. The MSAR government, however, could consider democratizing the composition of the Municipal Councils as a first step toward long-term democratic reforms (*South China Morning Post*, 19 December 1999). Having said that, the MSAR government may interpret the Basic Law in a relatively narrow way, saying that democratic reforms cannot proceed beyond the requirement that Municipal Councils are not to become "organs of political power." In the event that the Basic Law's provision on Municipal Councils is interpreted rigidly, it could probably be an obstacle to reforming Macau's electoral system at the municipal level in the long run.

CHANGING PATTERNS OF PARTICIPATION IN DIRECT ELECTIONS FOR THE LEGISLATIVE ASSEMBLY

Compared with elections for the Municipal Councils and the Executive Council (formerly Consultative Council), those for the Macau Legislative Assembly have traditionally attracted more citizen participation and attention from the mass media. In the 1980 Legislative Assembly direct election, for example, only 2,600 registered voters cast their ballots, mainly because of the very narrow franchise restricted to the Portuguese residents. In 1984, after Governor Costa's electoral reform, 28,970 citizens went to the polls—an outcome of the widened franchise

Table 4.2 Voter Turnout in Macau's Legislative Assembly Direct Elections, 1976–96

Year	Registered Voters	Voter Turnout	Percentage
1976	3,647	2,846	78.03
1980	4,195	2,600	61.98
1984	51,454	28,970	56.03
1988	67,604	20,094	29.65
1991[a]	97,648	18,202	18.68
1992	48,137	28,520	59.25
1996	116,441	75,093	64.49

Sources: Lo 1995, 99; Yee 1999, 30; and Yee 1997, 956.

a. The 1991 election was a by-election.

(see table 4.2). In 1984, an intellectual and liberal-minded political group called the Flower of Friendship and Development of Macau participated in the direct election and obtained 3,500 votes. Its leader and candidate, Alexandre Ho Si Him, was elected. Its success marked the emergence of the Macau Chinese intellectuals in direct elections for the Legislative Assembly. Moreover, the number of Chinese interest groups registered in the indirect elections for the legislature increased from 84 in 1980 to 141 in 1984.

The 1984 direct election was politically significant in Macau because there was for the first time an electoral alliance between the pro-Beijing Chinese and Macanese community leaders. The late Macanese leader Carlos d'Assumpcao formed the Electoral Union to participate in the election. He was fully supported by the Chinese community leader Ma Man Kei. As a result, the Electoral Union won four directly elected seats in the Legislative Assembly. The Chinese community leaders cooperated with the Macanese counterpart again in the 1988 Legislative Assembly direct election, but they were viewed as being "defeated" by the rise of the liberal-minded group led by Alexandre Ho, Leong Kam Chuen, and Wong Cheong Nam (*Far Eastern Economic Review* 1990). Ho's group shocked the pro-Beijing force by capturing three of the six directly elected seats in the Legislative Assembly.

In the 1992 Legislative Assembly election, however, the liberals suffered a setback: both Wong and Leong failed to be reelected. The 1992 direct election was characterized by some significant changes to the *d'Hondt rule* or the list system. According to the old (pre-1992) d'Hondt rule, each political group that participated in direct elections for the legislature needed to nominate a list of three to six candidates in consecutive order. It stipulated that the first candidate of each group obtained the total votes that group received; the second candidate acquired half; the third received one-third; the fourth one-quarter; and so forth. Under the list system, a political group could win a number of seats directly proportional to the votes it obtained in direct elections. For example, a group that obtained one-third of all the votes would capture one-third of the directly elected seats. Under this electoral system, the candidate who was ranked higher would have a better chance of being elected.

Prior to the 1992 Legislative Assembly direct election, d'Assumpcao proposed changes to the d'Hondt rule. He tried to curb the political power of the liberal-minded intellectuals, which would prevent them from capturing more directly elected seats and provide more room for the Macanese groups to those seats. Under his proposed model, the first candidate would still get full votes and the second candidate half, but the third candidate would obtain one-quarter, the fourth one-eighth, the fifth one-sixteenth. This rule, if adopted, would mean that candidates ranked third in any political group would almost have no chance of being directly elected. The pro-Beijing legislators supported d'Assumpcao's revised rule, for it would not affect the pro-Beijing groups in direct elections.

When the rule was revised, the liberal-minded intellectuals tried gaining more directly elected seats by splitting themselves into three groups: the Amity Association, led by Alexandre Ho and Leong Kam Chuen; the Association in Promotion of Democracy and Livelihood, led by Wong Cheong Nam; and the New Democratic Macau, led by Ng Kuok Cheong. As a result, Ng and Ho managed to get elected, but Wong and Leong were defeated (see table 4.3).

The direct elections for the Legislative Assembly in 1992 were unique in several aspects. First and foremost, the pro-Beijing political groups effectively mobilized their supporters to vote for the candidates of the Union for the Promotion of Progress and the Development Union. Their strategy was successful as they transported voters to the polling stations on the election day, provided fringe benefits to workers affiliated with pro-Beijing trade unions, and utilized the pro-Beijing mouthpiece *Macau Daily News* to give favorable coverage of the activities of their candidates. Second, the independent Chinese businesspeople who formed the Three Unions failed to challenge such mainstream pro-Beijing political groups as the Union for the Promotion of Progress and the Development Union. Although the Three Unions were dissatisfied with governmental bureaucratism and the failure of the pro-Beijing Federation of Trade Unions to fight for the working-class interest, their mobilizational strategy was no match for the pro-Beijing groups. Third, the outnumbered Macau liberals were fortunate to get two candidates elected to the legislature. Yet given the relatively poor performance of Alexandre Ho, his ability to retain his seat in the future became a problem fully exposed in the 1992 direct election. In fact, Ho was later defeated in the 1996 Legislative Assembly direct election. Fourth, the Macanese groups, especially the Electoral Union, performed unsatisfactorily. Although the Labour Solidarity won a directly elected seat, the traditionally powerful Electoral Union failed to get any

Table 4.3 Results of Macau's 1992 Legislative Assembly Direct Elections

Party/Group	Background	Votes Received	Percentage of Valid Votes	Candidates Elected
Union for the Promotion of Progress	Pro-Beijing	6,956	25.25	Leong Heng Teng, Kuo Hoi In
Development Union	Pro-Beijing	6,543	23.75	Tong Chi Kin, Chui Sai On
New Democratic Macau	Liberal	3,412	12.39	Ng Kuok Cheong
Independent Union for Future Macau	Independent, split from pro-Beijing forces	2,201	7.99	Susanna Chou
Labour Solidarity	Independent, Macanese	2,037	7.39	Alberto Noronha
Amity Association	Prodemocracy, liberal group led by Alexandre Ho	1,965	7.13	Alexandre Ho
Three Unions	Independent, Chinese business group	1,788	6.49	None
Association in Promotion of Democracy and Livelihood	Liberal, led by Wong Cheong Nam	1,696	6.16	None
Electoral Union	Pro-China and Macanese	948	3.44	None

Sources: Compiled from *Macau Official Bulletin*, No. 39, 30 September 1992, and *Macau Daily News*, 21 September 1992, 6.

candidate elected. Hence, the 1992 direct election signaled the downfall of d'Assumpcao's old political group—the Electoral Union—which failed to get the genuine and wholehearted support from pro-Beijing forces. Obviously, the focus of the pro-Beijing forces was to provide manpower and resources to ensure the electoral victory of the Union for the Promotion of Progress and the Development Union.

Finally, the Macau electoral law failed to prevent and reduce vote-buying activities in the 1992 direct election. Since the electoral law did not specify the maximum amount of campaign expenditure, it tended to be biased in favor of the affluent political groups, which offered free lunch, dinner, and souvenirs to supporters in the 1992 direct elections. Liberal candidate Wong Cheong Nam publicly complained that some political groups had bought votes for 50 to 500 patacas (Lo 1995, 97). Given the lack of political will on the part of the Portuguese administration to fight corruption in both nonelection time and the election campaign period, however, vote-buying became a common practice without any penalty in the 1992 direct elections for the Legislative Assembly.

VOTE-BUYING IN THE 1996 LEGISLATIVE ASSEMBLY ELECTIONS

Vote-buying became more serious and widespread during the 1996 Legislative Assembly elections than ever before. Twelve political groups participated in the direct elections that year—an indication that the number of directly elected seats was insufficient to accommodate the increasing public demand for more channels of political participation (see table 4.4).

The 1996 direct elections had a number of prominent features that were distinct from those of the 1992 elections. First and foremost, the number of independent and Chinese businesspeople participating in the direct elections held for the Legislative Assembly increased from one in 1992 to six in 1996. Perhaps most importantly, of the six independent Chinese business groups, two had casino interests and one was directly elected. Days before the handover of Macau at midnight on 19 December 1999, Chow Kam Fai told some Hong Kong reporters that he would like to see more competition introduced in Macau's casino industry. With the benefit of hindsight, his participation in the 1996 Legislative Assembly election seemed to confirm speculations that some businesspeople would like to protect their casino interest through electoral politics. On the election day, many casino employees were mobilized to cast their ballots. Although another political group—the Alliance for Entertainment Associations—was defeated in elections, businesspeople with casino background openly participated in the Legislative Assembly direct elections for the first time in Macau's political history. This change also reflected the insufficient channel for them to participate in the Legislative Assembly through indirect elections, which were traditionally dominated and controlled by the mainstream pro-Beijing groups. Their open political participation also raised the question of whether the business sector in Macau had become politically fragmented, and whether the Macau government should address this issue by co-opting them into the policymaking process. For example, the Macau Land Developers Association openly supported the Union for the Construction of Macau—an indication that some emergent land developers wanted to participate in elections formally (*Macau Daily News*, 20 September 1996). Instead of waiting for the Macau government to appoint land developers into the Legislative Assembly, these two groups

Table 4.4 Results of Macau's 1996 Legislative Assembly Direct Elections

Party/Group	Background	Votes	Candidates Elected
Association for the Promotion of Macau's Economy and Livelihood	Independent, Chinese business group	12,090	Chan Kai Kit, Liu Yuk Lun
Union for the Promotion of Progress	Pro-Beijing	11,045	Leong Heng Teng, Kou Hoi In
Development Union	Pro-Beijing	10,528	Tong Chi-kin
Union for the Construction of Macau	Pro-Beijing, Chinese business group	7,516	Fong Chi Keong
Alliance for a Prosperous Macau	Independent, Chinese business group with casino interest	7,439	Chow Kam Fai
New Democratic Macau	Prodemocracy, liberal	6,332	Ng Kuok Cheong
Association for Fujian Residents in Macau	Independent, Chinese business group	4,671	None
Alliance for Entertainment Associations	Independent, Chinese business group with casino interest	3,107	None
Alliance for Economic Construction	Independent, Chinese business group	5,085	None
Association in Promotion of Democracy and Livelihood	Prodemocracy, liberal group led by Wong Cheong Nam	960	None
Amity Association	Prodemocracy, liberal group led by Alexandre Ho	1,690	None
Root in Macau	Independent, Macanese	2,100	None

Sources: Macau Daily News, 23 September 1996, 1, 6; 24 September 1996, 1.

Note: Chan Kai Kit disappeared from Macau in 1999 after he was investigated by the Hong Kong Independent Commission against Corruption. His position became vacant until the Preparatory Committee that arranged Macau's transition affairs elected Iong Weng Ian to replace him straddling 19 December 1999.

organized themselves to challenge the mainstream pro-Beijing groups. Arguably, their electoral participation signaled a crisis of governance in the Portuguese administration, which was more concerned about cooperation from the pro-Beijing forces than about co-opting the emergent Chinese middle and business classes into the existing political framework.

Second, the 1996 Legislative Assembly direct elections signaled the decline of the mainstream pro-Beijing groups. Apart from Tong Chi Kin, who won a seat, the Development Union failed to elect any candidates. The pro-Beijing forces were unhappy about vote-buying activities, which directly and indirectly contributed to the Development Union's failure to obtain two seats. They openly complained about vote-buying, which to Tong Chi Kin was "a big humiliation to the society" and according to Leong Heng Teng "distorted the system of democratic elections" (*Macau Daily News*, 25 September 1996 and 24 September 1996, respectively). Strategically speaking, the pro-Beijing forces were overconfident in the 1996 Legislative Assembly direct elections, failing to register sufficient supporters to vote and, more importantly, neglecting to hold activities and social functions that could mobilize supporters effectively. In the 1992 Legislative Assembly elections, the pro-Beijing forces held dinners and social events celebrating the national day of the PRC and appealing to voters to support their candidates on the election day. Yet in the 1996 Legislative Assembly direct elections, such social functions were held after, not before, the elections on 22 September 1996. Arguably, this was a strategic error made by the pro-Beijing forces, who underestimated the extent of vote-buying and mobilizational ability of the newly emergent, independent Chinese business groups. A careful analysis of the election result showed that although the pro-Beijing groups gained some new supporters in most of the seven districts compared with the 1992 Legislative Assembly elections, the Union for the Promotion of Progress lost some voters in both Taipa Island and Coloane Island in 1996 (*Macau Daily News*, 24 September 1996; 23 September 1992).

In contrast, probusiness groups such as the Association for the Promotion of Macau's Economy and Livelihood and the Alliance for a Prosperous Macau, as well as the Union for the Construction of Macau, made tremendous progress in mobilizing new supporters, especially in the Fatima District, where many workers and middle-lower-class people resided. These business groups had already conducted voter registration drives among their employees and supporters from 1993 through 1996 (Yee 1997). This strategy of pre-election registration is extremely important in Macau because the voters are relatively vulnerable to mobilization by their employers. Some workers, for example, admitted that they received 100 patacas by a political group for registering to vote in 1996 (*Macau Daily News*, 26 September 1996). They were also worried that private data, such as their names, home addresses, and voters' identification numbers were known by strangers and triad members, who might threaten their personal safety (*Macau

Daily News, 26 September 1996). Since the independent Chinese business groups imitated the old mobilizational strategy of the pro-Beijing groups, and since the latter failed to fully mobilize their supporters and new electorate in the 1996 direct elections, it was not surprising that the big winner in the 1996 direct elections was the emergent Chinese business groups.

Third, the performance of the liberals was a disappointment to Macau's prodemocracy movement. The New Democratic Macau received 6,332 votes; the Amity Association 1,690 votes; and the Association in Promotion of Democracy and Livelihood 960 votes. Altogether they managed merely 8,982 votes—a small increase over the total of 7,073 obtained in the 1992 Legislative Assembly direct elections. This small increase, however, could not compete with the large amount of support given to the newly emergent business groups and the pro-Beijing forces. In terms of political platform, the three prodemocracy groups appeared to be weak, perhaps with the exception of the New Democratic Macau. The three groups failed to pool their resources in projecting a clear, prodemocracy, opposition image to the young voters of Macau. It was difficult for them to achieve mutual cooperation, however, partly because of the d'Hondt rule, which encouraged their political fragmentation, and partly due to their personality differences—a phenomenon parallel to the Hong Kong democrats (see Lo 1999b). The Macau liberals also failed to establish their power base in some districts in Macau, targeting the middle classes and intellectuals. Not surprisingly, only Ng Kuok Cheong managed to be reelected to the Legislative Assembly. Indeed, under the circumstances of widespread vote-buying, the underfinanced democrats became the victims of the last, unfair direct election in Macau under Portuguese rule.

Fourth, the Macau government was totally incompetent to handle complaints about vote-buying. Trying to portray an image of the last fair, successful election in Macau under Portuguese rule, the government authorities simply had neither the intention nor the incentive to look into vote-buying cases seriously. After all, as long as the election law did not specify the maximum amount of campaign expenditure, it was difficult to reprimand, not to mention prosecute, candidates who spent money to buy gifts for voters.[1] Hoping that the last direct election would symbolize a prelude to a "glorious" withdrawal of Portugal from Macau, some Portuguese administrators thought that vote-buying cases, even if they existed, should not affect the election result. Compounding the difficulties of investigating vote-buying cases was the weakness of the anticorruption commission, which failed to have sufficient legal power, manpower, and resources to look into vote-buying cases in elections. Boy scouts were mobilized to help election officers in various polling stations instead of relying on the assistance of the staff members of the underdeveloped and powerless anticorruption agency. Although police were sent to maintain law and order on election day, no police officer was allowed within 100 meters of the polling station in accordance with the election law. A minority of Macau residents complained to police officers about vote-buying cases (*Macau Daily News,* 25 September 1996), but ironically the police force itself was also affected by internal corruption. Therefore it was impossible for the public to expect the police to be effective in pursuing any vote-buying cases in elections.

Fifth, although the Macau government reiterated the secretive nature of voting, many Macau residents were reluctant to report cases of vote-buying to the authorities. For one thing, the Chinese residents in Macau understood the importance of maintaining harmonious relationships with their patrons or employers. A patron-client network was gradually established and firmly entrenched in the direct elections (Lo 1999a). Voters and supporters were given gifts, money, and fringe benefits by their patrons. In return, the voters were expected to cast ballots for the patrons on the election day. This patron-client network became extremely important in the 1996 Legislative Assembly direct elections. In Chinese tradition, once a person receives any help or gift from another, he or she is morally obliged to return the favor as a gesture of goodwill, polite support, and reciprocal exchange. It was this patron-client relationship that explained why very few local residents dared to report vote-buying cases to the authorities after the 1996 direct elections. In Chinese saying, a phenomenon of "sentimental votes" often occurred in Legislative Assembly direct elections. Once a voter developed a degree of emotional or sentimental relationship with his or her patron, he or she must return something beneficial to the patron.

Interestingly, a minority of voters were so materialistic and pragmatic that they tried to develop relationship with several patrons simultaneously. One voter received favors from eight political groups (*Macau Daily News,* 24 September 1996). He attended the lunches and social functions of these groups and pretended to vote for their candidates. Voter identification cards cost 1,000 to 1,500 patacas (*Macau Daily News,* 24 September 1996), so winning a voter is a considerable expense for a political group. Another voter refused to go to the polls until he could get on a bus where his free lunch tickets were validated by the campaign workers of a political group (*Macau Daily News,* 24 September 1996). Another political group reportedly mobilized workers of several factories in the Northern District, distributing free lunch tickets to them and exchanging each of their votes for 500 patacas (*Macau Daily News,* 24 September 1996). Ngan Yin Ling, the defeated candidate of the Association for Fujian Residents in Macau, was so angry with the election result that he publicly implied that some Legislative Assemblymen were directly elected because of their extensive vote-buying activities (*Macau Daily News,* 25 September 1996 [Ngan said: "Legislators themselves should abide by the law"]). After the election, some workers publicly complained about the government's incompetence in tackling vote-buying and suggested that a special inquiry commission be set up to investigate complaints (*Macau Daily News,* 26 September 1996). It was reported that some workers were intimidated by their workplace superiors to support a particular political group, and that they had no choice but to yield to the pressure (*Macau Daily News*, 26 September 1996).

Last but not least, triads, the gangster organizations engaging in criminal activities, were rumored to be involved in the election campaign. Although no concrete evidence proved that some candidates had suspicious or triad backgrounds, some campaign supporters and workers were triad members. Some triad members guarded the entrance of restaurants, which were closed to the public on the election day and which were specially reserved for some candidates and their supporters. Some workers also complained that people like triad members threatened voters, especially the elderly people, to vote for particular political groups (*Macau Daily News*, 26 September 1996). Arguably, some triads tacitly or openly participated in the 1996 Legislative Assembly direct elections. The latter half of the 1990s in Macau was not only characterized by triad wars but also marked triads' active participation in elections (Lo 1999c). Their political participation definitely tarnished the image of having a "fair" election held for the last legislature under the Portuguese administration.

Conclusion and Comparative Implications

Macau's electoral system has evolved gradually since the Portuguese revolution in 1974. While changes in the composition of the Legislative Assembly were introduced in 1984 and again in 1990, the d'Hondt rule remained unchanged until 1992 when the Macanese community leaders attempted to curb the rise of prodemocracy Chinese political groups. The franchise in Macau's direct elections was narrow until 1984 when Governor Costa decided to widen it to allow more Chinese to participate in local elections. Overall, electoral reform in Macau under Portuguese rule could be seen as an aftermath of several different factors at various historical moments. It was partly a result of political changes in Portugal in 1974, partly an outcome of the Sino-Portuguese Joint Declaration in 1987, and partly a product of political struggle against the Macanese by Governor Costa in 1984 and later against the prodemocracy Chinese groups by d'Assumpcao in 1992.

From a comparative perspective, Macau's electoral system was significant for the HKSAR, which eventually adopted an electoral method similar to Macau's list system in the 1998 Legislative Council direct election (Lo and Yu 1999). What is more, the widespread vote-buying activities in Macau can now be seen in local District Council elections in the HKSAR in 1999. Vote-buying in the HKSAR took the form of (1) organizing tours for voters in nonelection time and during the campaign period, (2) distributing gifts to voters regularly before the official campaign period, and (3) mobilizing supporters to register in elections and to vote on the election day (very similar to Macau in this aspect).[2] Indeed, anticorruption agencies and election laws in the HKSAR appear to be more developed than their counterparts in the MSAR. Nevertheless, the campaign expenditures in the Hong Kong Special Administrative Region can often exceed the official limit without penalty or effective checks by the Election Commission.[3] If this analysis is accurate, the HKSAR elections may be gradually "Macau-ized" without much attention from political observers.

This does not mean that the MSAR is bound to be characterized by unfair elections and incompetent electoral administration. If the MSAR government is determined to increase the power of the anticorruption agency, if the election law's loopholes can be plugged, and if the public is extensively educated about the evils of vote-buying and the need to report complaints to a competent Election Commission, the prospects of having clean and fair elections for the Legislative Assembly are not necessarily so gloomy. Indeed, all reforms depend on the political will of the MSAR government, which should learn from the mistakes made by the electoral administration in Macau under Portuguese rule. The Election Commission in both the 1992 and 1996 Legislative Assembly direct elections failed to publicize the election law to the public. It also failed to project an image of a competent body with the determination to investigate and combat vote-buying activities. In the event that the MSAR government does not reform the electoral administration, the direct elections for the MSAR Legislative Assembly would probably exhibit legacies of the Portuguese colonial era. The model of direct elections for Macau's Legislative Assembly under Portuguese rule is by no means a worthy experience for any neighboring cities, especially the HKSAR, to emulate.

In the final analysis, Macau voters appeared to be politically vulnerable to mobilization and short-term material benefits. Unlike the HKSAR voters, who at least in the meantime tend to be more independent-minded,[4] Macau voters appeared to be more easily attracted by gifts and money offered by candidates and political groups in the 1992 and 1996 Legislative Assembly elections. If the materialistic orientation of voters in the MSAR persists—a phenomenon that is quite likely—vote-buying will probably continue in the MSAR Legislative Assembly elections. Perhaps it is merely a matter of the degree of vote-buying activities in the MSAR.

Any tendency toward materialism on the part of the HKSAR voters, however, would lead to the phenomenon of being "Macau-ized." The question of vote-buying in Macau is far more complicated than conventional wisdom assumes. It is often taken for granted by some Macau observers that vote-buying reflects the political "immaturity" of Macau voters.[5] Objectively speaking, vote-buying activities might indicate a degree of political "immaturity" of Macau voters in the sense that they might not vote "rationally" for candidates with substance and platform, and that they might be easily politically intimidated. Nevertheless, vote-buying may also point to a deeper sociopolitical phenomenon: the gradual expansion of patron-client networks as suggested in this chapter. If vote-buying is proliferating in the HKSAR but in slightly different forms, such as organizing tours and regular services for the elderly as mentioned above, then patron-client networks are gradually intermingling with local electoral politics in both Macau and Hong Kong. If this observation is accurate, it can be anticipated that Macau's extensive vote-buying and patron-client relationship will shape the electoral politics of the HKSAR. In short, the political convergence between the HKSAR and MSAR has certainly one element in common: the electoral system of the HKSAR has not only imitated Macau's list system, but the Macau version of patron-client relationship between voters and candidates is also penetrating the HKSAR. The Macau electoral system should receive more serious treatment and in-depth study because it its impact has already touched its neighbor, the HKSAR.

NOTES

1. The election law only stated that thirty days after the election, candidates should report their campaign expenditure to the District Election Commission. Then the commission would check the campaign expenditure within thirty days and would finally publish it in a Chinese and Portuguese newspaper. See *Booklet on the Elections Held for the Legislative Assembly and the Consultative Council* 1998.
2. Results are from the author's extensive interviews with thirty-five candidates in the District Council elections in October and November 1999.
3. In personal interviews with the author during the November 1999 District Council elections, at least two candidates said that the election in the HKSAR was actually unfair, and that campaign expenditure could easily exceed the official limit.
4. In a personal interview with the author, one candidate in the 1999 HKSAR District Council election complained to the author that his defeat was attributable to the "immaturity" of voters who attached more importance to the material gains offered by candidates, such as tours, visits, and other elderly services.
5. Herbert Yee, for example, remarks that "a majority of the Macau citizens do not possess a mature or democratic political culture." See Yee 1997, 958. I also implied a similar point in Lo 1995, 274. But a more in-depth analysis shows that, as I contend earlier in this chapter, patron-client relationships exist and proliferate in Macau.

REFERENCES

Booklet on the Elections Held for the Legislative Assembly and the Consultative Council [in Chinese and Portuguese]. 1998. Macau: Secretary of Public Administration and Civil Service, 253.
Far Eastern Economic Review. 1990. *Asia Yearbook*. Hong Kong: Far Eastern Economic Review.
Lo, Shiu Hing. 1995. *Political Development in Macau*. Hong Kong: Chinese University Press.
———. 1999a. "Macau's Political System." In *Macau 2000*, edited by Jean A. Berlie. Hong Kong: Oxford University Press.
———. 1999b. "The Democratic Party in the Hong Kong Special Administrative Region." *Round Table* 352:635–58.
———. 1999c. "Gambling and Organized Crime: Towards the End of the Stanley Ho Connection?" *China Perspectives* 26:56–65.
Lo, Shiu Hing, and Yu Wing Yat. 1999. *Election and Democracy in Hong Kong: The 1998 Legislative Council Election*, no. 4. Occasional paper/reprint series, School of Law, University of Maryland.
Yee, Herbert. 1997. "Money Politics and Political Mobilization in Macau." *Asian Survey* 37:944–60.
———. 1999. "Prospects of Democratization: An Open-ended Game?" *China Perspectives* 26:29–30.

CHAPTER 5

Changing How the Japanese Vote: The Promise and Pitfalls of the 1994 Electoral Reform

by Michael F. Thies

IN EARLY 1994, the Japanese Diet (parliament) passed two electoral reform bills after months of wrangling. Political reform of various sorts had been under discussion since the early 1950s, with very little to show for it. But when the Liberal Democratic Party's (LDP's) thirty-eight-year stranglehold on power ended with a party split in June 1993, a new governing coalition staked its life on the promise of actual reform. Finally, after several false starts, the promise was fulfilled. The first reform act abandoned the single-nontransferable-vote (SNTV) electoral system that had been in use as far back as 1925 and replaced it with a mixed system of single-member districts and proportional representation. The second act tightened up campaign finance regulation and introduced a system of public financing of elections.

The electoral reform punctuated a dramatic break from nearly four decades of single-party government. Why were these bills passed, and what have been their effects on Japanese politics? In order to answer these questions, one must first understand the workings of the old system and its implications for political competition. The coalition that jettisoned SNTV was a heterogeneous collection of politicians, with different complaints about the old system and different (often incompatible) expectations for the new one. The second task of this essay is to examine the effects of the 1994 electoral change thus far, and to speculate as to its long-term ramifications. Along the way, the changes in the party system, internal party organization, campaign strategies, and voting behavior are explored. The essay concludes with an assessment of the state of electoral democracy in Japan.

Electoral Rules and the Legislature

Japan's postwar constitution, imposed by the American-led occupation authority in 1946, established the basic institutions of Japanese democracy. Citizens were granted a panoply of rights and responsibilities. Women were given the vote for the first time. The cabinet was made responsible to the Diet, which was assigned supreme legislative authority.

The Diet remained bicameral, but the prewar House of Peers was replaced by the elected House of Councillors. Councillors serve fixed, six-year terms, with half elected every three years.[1] Members of the more powerful House of Representatives (HR, the Lower House) are elected to four-year terms. As under most parliamentary systems, however, the prime minister may dissolve the Lower House and call for elections at any time, so terms usually end earlier than scheduled. With twenty-one Lower House elections in the fifty-five years since the end of World War II, the average House has lasted just over thirty-one months.

From 1946 through 1955, elections produced shifting coalitions of parties, party splits and mergers, formations and collapses. Signs of stability appeared in 1955, with the formation of the Japan Socialist Party (JSP) and, a month later, the LDP. Thereafter, every Lower House election until 1993 produced an LDP majority and single-party control over government. Some have commented that this lack of partisan turnover in government has stunted the development of democracy in Japan (Johnson 1987), while others simply attribute the LDP's perpetual dominance to the foibles of a disorganized opposition, the boon of a strong economy, savvy electioneering, and, for the most part, good government (Ramseyer and Rosenbluth 1993).

Certainly, voters were free to vote against the LDP, and they were offered a variety of partisan alternatives. And while the LDP consistently managed to eke out majorities, by the mid 1970s these were not guaranteed.[2] At the level of individual electoral districts, candidates clearly behaved as if outcomes were in doubt. The combined opposition's main problem was that with Japanese citizens getting richer every year, they were relegated to bemoaning the social costs of such growth, leading the fight against such blights as corruption, pollution, overcrowding, and business domination of the economy. They were unable to unify on an alternative policy mix, however, and the LDP was quick to pounce on any opposition issue that seemed to be resonating with voters (e.g., pollution control).

Nevertheless, the lack of partisan turnover, along with the constant stream of corruption scandals involving the LDP, came to be seen by many as sufficient reasons to change the electoral system. Of course, prescriptions varied. Some wanted to knock the LDP off its pedestal by causing it to break up, thus introducing a period of coalition governments, in which more political parties would have a chance to achieve governmental power. Others hoped instead for a reconsolidation of the party system around two large programmatic parties, each of which enjoyed a good chance of winning a legislative majority, governing alone, and implementing its party program—the classic Westminster ideal of responsible party government (Lijphart 1984). Still others hoped that if the LDP could simply be forced to compete on a level playing field (i.e., with less recourse to money politics and the pork barrel), then the current electoral system might otherwise be retained.

The Old System: The Single Nontransferable Vote with Multimember Districts

From 1947 through 1993, Lower House elections were based on the electoral formula of SNTV. Each voter cast a single vote for an individual candidate rather than a party or party list, and this vote could not be transferred to the voter's second-choice candidate if her favorite candidate received more votes or fewer votes than required to win a seat. The number of electoral districts and seats in the Lower House has increased over time. In the last election held under the SNTV rules in 1993, 511 Lower House members were elected from 129 electoral districts, which ranged in size from two to six seats. Thus, the top two-to-six vote-getters (depending on the number seats available in a district) each received a seat (see table 5.1).

Passage of Electoral Reform

During the LDP's long incumbency, calls for electoral and campaign-finance reform waxed and waned among the opposition parties as well as within the LDP. But many within the LDP were wary of changing a system that had served them so well for so long. Individual party members had no way of knowing how a new system might affect their chances for reelection. Finally, in June 1993, a vote of no-confidence against the cabinet of Prime Minister Kiichi Miyazawa succeeded when a group of LDP legislators defected and voted against the government. This defection, led by Ichiro Ozawa and Tsutomu Hata, split the LDP, and the ensuing election saw the emergence of several new political parties. Electoral reform was the main issue prompting the LDP split (Cox and Rosenbluth 1995; Reed and Thies 2001).

The LDP won only 223 seats out of 511 in the 1993 general election, which allowed it to remain by far the largest party in the Diet but spelled the end of its long reign as majority party. The LDP tried to convince two of the new parties to join it in a coalition government, but all had run on political reform platforms, and a postelection alliance with the LDP would have appeared hypocritical to their supporters. The result was an unwieldy, seven-party coalition that excluded only the LDP and the Japan Communist Party (JCP). The coalition came together under the leadership of Morihiro Hosokawa, the leader of the small, centrist Japan New Party.

The one point of agreement within the coalition was to enact an electoral reform that would end LDP dominance and the political corruption many attributed to the SNTV system. But while all seven parties shared a desire to change the electoral system *from* SNTV, there was a marked lack of agreement over what

Table 5.1 Japan's Lower House Electoral Rules: Before and After Reform

	The Old Rules	The New Rules	
		Single-Member Districts	Regional PR Districts
Time Period	1947–94	1994–present	1994–present
Electoral System	SNTV	SMD	Closed-list PR
Number of Districts	129[a]	300	11
Number of Seats	511[a]	300	180 (was 200 in 1996)
Average Seats per District	4.0	1	16.4 (was 18.2 in 1996)
Intraparty Competition	Always	None	For good list slots but not in election campaigns

a. The numbers of districts and seats changed several times during the SNTV period. These numbers are correct for the last time SNTV was used, in 1993.

to change it *to*. The Socialists and the Buddhist-backed *Komeito* (Clean Government Party, CGP) favored a more proportional system. The new parties preferred a system that relied more heavily on single-member districts. In the end, the coalition split over this issue—after a compromise plan passed the Lower House, several Socialists voted against it in the Upper House, causing the plan to fail—so the Hosokawa government was forced to turn back to the LDP for the support necessary to pass the reform. Given the chance to participate again, the LDP obtained concessions that made the new system much more majoritarian than the Hosokawa government had originally intended.[3]

The new electoral rules originally set the size of the House of Representatives at 500 seats. Of these, 300 were chosen by (relatively) equal-sized single-member districts (SMDs) and 200 by proportional representation (PR) in eleven regional districts. (The number of PR seats was reduced to 180 in January 2000, bringing the total number of Lower House seats down to 480 beginning with the 2000 election). Each voter may cast two votes: one for a candidate in the SMD, and one for a party in the PR region. This new system is similar to the one used in Germany, where a candidate may run in a district *and* appear on the corresponding party list in the larger region. But it differs from the German system in that the district seats and the list seats are allocated separately.[4]

Another important feature of the Japanese electoral system is its restrictive rules for campaigning. Candidates are not allowed to advertise on television or the radio, with the exception of two five-minute spots on the government-controlled public broadcasting system. They are restricted to a limited number of newspaper ads and handbills, and door-to-door canvassing is prohibited (Hrebenar 1992). The official campaign period begins with the call for Lower House elections and lasts for only twelve days. The law, moreover, officially limited how much money candidates could spend on their campaigns. Though some of these rules were easily evaded—especially the limits on political activities and campaign spending—the rules that were easily enforced played a role in sustaining LDP hegemony.[5]

The 1994 reforms maintained most of these restrictions (and shortened the official campaign period even further, to ten days) but tightened up the flow of money to candidates (Christensen 1998). Public funding through central party organizations was introduced, and the flow of private money was constricted. Corporate contributions to the fund-raising organizations of individual candidates were limited, and each candidate was restricted to only two such organizations.[6] Corporate donations were to be phased out completely within five years, with all future giving to be funneled solely through party channels. The remaining loophole, however, is that such donations may be given to local party organizations, and in single-member districts, a donation to the local party office is tantamount to a direct donation to an individual politician.

Once electoral reform was achieved, the Hosokawa-led seven-party coalition fell apart when the Socialists and the New Party Harbinger dropped out. Two months later, these two parties joined forces with the LDP in the so-called "coalition of strange bedfellows." After all, the LDP and Socialists had been bitter rivals since 1955. To entice the Socialists into the partnership, the LDP allowed Socialist leader Tomiichi Murayama to become prime minister. It was the first time since 1947 that a Socialist had held the top post.

IMPLICATIONS FOR THE PARTY SYSTEM

Prior to the 1993 LDP split and the 1994 reforms, five main parties held seats in the House of Representatives. Figure 5.1 shows the dynamics of the party system beginning in 1955. The center-right LDP, of course, controlled a majority of seats (having won 275 of 511 seats in the 1990 election). The Japan Socialist Party was the largest opposition group, winning 136 seats in 1990. This was the JSP's best showing in an HR election since 1963, making its rapid decline after 1994 all the more interesting. The other three parties in the system were the *Komeito* (45 seats), the Democratic Socialists (DSP, 14 seats), and the Communists (16 seats). All three won fewer seats than usual in 1990, given the Socialists' strong showing that year. The *Komeito's* decline was minor relative to its average seat share over the two preceding decades, but the DSP fell to 14 seats, an all-time low, and the JCP fell to its lowest total in twenty years.

The postsplit LDP actually managed to gain one extra seat in the 1993 election, as did the DSP and the Communists. *Komeito* gained six seats. The JSP was the biggest loser. Voters interested in opposing the LDP now had new vehicles, namely the parties led by LDP defectors. These parties were attractive both to traditional opposition voters and to traditional LDP voters who wished to support reform (many of whom could do so while continuing to vote for the same incumbents as before). Not surprisingly, the new parties were the clear winners in the election (see table 5.2, p. 98).

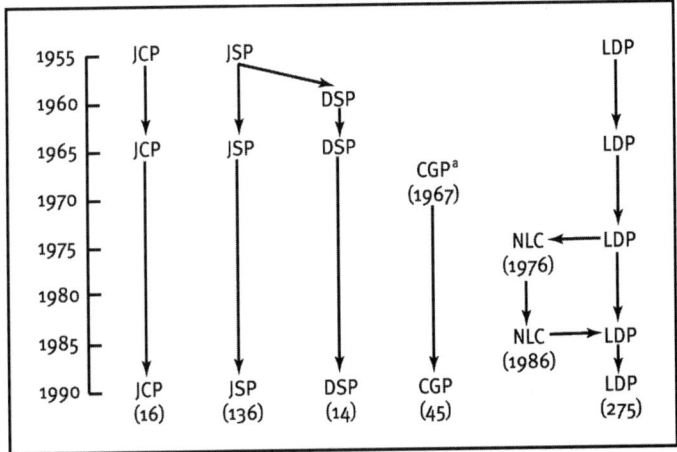

Figure 5.1 Japan's Party System, 1955–90

Political Parties
CGP = Clean Government Party (*Komeito*)
DSP = Democratic Socialist Party
JCP = Japan Communist Party
JSP = Japan Socialist Party (renamed SDPJ)
LDP = Liberal Democratic Party
NLC = New Liberal Club

a. The CGP supported candidates in the Upper House as early as 1956, but it did not endorse Lower House candidates until 1967.

The Postreform Party System

In general, single-member districts tend to produce two-party competition, while proportional representation allows the survival of several parties (Duverger 1954; Riker 1982). The new Japanese electoral system contains both of these elements. What has been the effect on the party system so far?

Some movement toward party system consolidation has occurred in Japan, with the LDP as one of the main parties. But the formation of a second major party has proceeded in fits and starts, and it likely will never manage to encompass all non-LDP supporters. In December 1994, various LDP splinter groups, the DSP, and the *Komeito* merged to form the New Frontier Party (NFP). Right away, the NFP became the largest opposition force, with 156 seats. Then, in its first electoral test—the 1995 Upper House election—the NFP solidified its position, even outpolling the LDP in the PR tier of the election, 31 percent to 27 percent. It remained the second largest party in the 1996 Lower House election, but by that time, it had already begun to splinter as a result of internal conflicts over ideology and tactics.

Table 5.2 Party Strength in Japan's House of Representatives, 1990 and 1993

	Seats Won	
	1990 HR Election	1993 HR Election
Liberal Democratic Party	275	223
Japan Socialist Party	136	70
Democratic Socialist Party	14	15
Clean Government Party	45	51
Japan Communist Party	16	15
Renewal Party	—	55
Japan New Party	—	35
New Party Harbinger	—	13
Other Minor Parties	5	4
Independents	21	30
Total	512	511

The NFP disbanded in late December 1997 (see figure 5.2); several members rejoined the LDP. The former *Komeito* reemerged almost intact as the "New *Komeito*." Some loyalists of erstwhile NFP leader Ozawa formed the Liberal Party. Then, in early 1998, the rest of the NFP refugees joined the Democratic Party of Japan (DPJ).[7] The final change in the party system to date was the May 2000 split of the Ozawa's Liberal Party (LP). When differences over policy objectives caused the LP to leave the governing coalition, half its membership split off to form the Conservative Party and rejoin the government, while the other half, led by Ozawa, retained the old party name and moved into opposition.

Thus far, only the 1996 and 2000 elections have been contested under the new electoral rules, so it is too early to assume that the party system has settled down. Nonetheless, it is worthwhile to take stock of what has happened over the last several years. The main similarities between the 2000 and 1992 party systems are that the LDP is still on top at near-majority strength (and it did climb above majority status for a period before the 2000 election) while the JCP and *Komeito* look relatively unchanged. The most important differences in the party system are that the Democratic Socialists have disappeared, the JSP has been relegated to minor-party status, and the Democrats, who have united much of the former JSP labor-support base with the largest group of LDP defectors, have emerged as the main big-party competitor of the LDP. At this writing, the Democrats hold only 128 Lower House seats, compared to the LDP's 233 (see table 5.3, p. 100). They were the only party, however, to have any success in the single-member districts (tallying 80 seats to the LDP's 177 in 2000), and they ran almost even with the LDP in the PR tier (winning 48 seats, to the LDP's 56). Thus, the primary effects of the electoral reform on the party system have been to hamper the LDP's pursuit of single-party

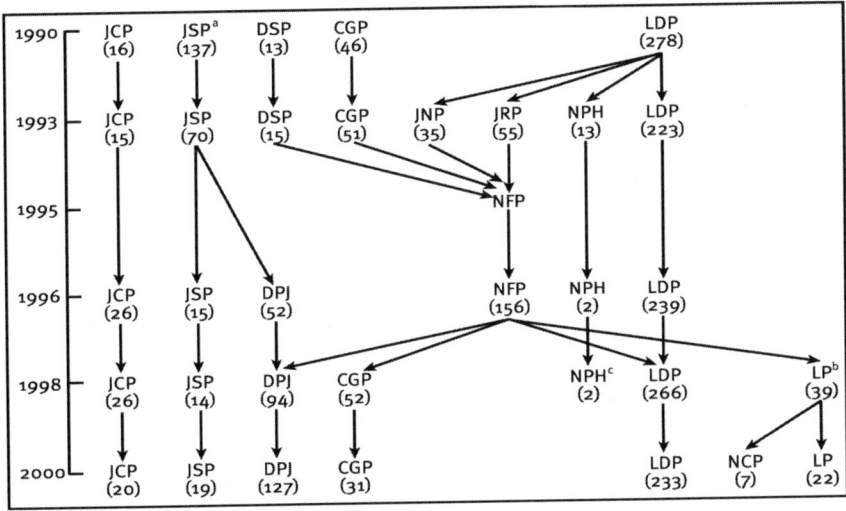

Figure 5.2 Japan's Party System, 1990–2000

Political Parties
CGP = Clean Government Party (*Komeito*)
DPJ = Democratic Party of Japan
DSP = Democratic Socialist Party
JCP = Japan Communist Party
JNP = Japan New Party
JRP = Japan Renewal Party

JSP = Japan Socialist Party[a]
LDP = Liberal Democratic Party
NCP = Conservative Party
NFP = New Frontier Party
NPH = New Party Harbinger

Note: Numbers in parentheses are the number of Lower House seats that each party held at five points in time: before the 1993 LDP split, after the 1993 and 1996 elections, as of 31 December 1998, and after the 2000 election.
a. The JSP changed its name to Social Democratic Party of Japan in the early 1990s, but I retain the old name here and in the text, for purposes of clarity.
b. After the Liberal Party (LP) was expelled from the governing coalition in May 2000, it split in half, with the new Conservative Party rejoining the government and the rump-LP moving into opposition.
c. Of the two remaining NPH incumbents, one rejoined the LDP, and the other ran as an independent in 2000.

majorities and, not coincidentally, to move the locus of the opposition rightward along the ideological spectrum. The Democratic Party looks considerably more "centrist" and moderate than the JSP did when it led the opposition.

The main reason that a stable, two-party system is not likely to emerge in Japan is the existence of the proportional representation tier of seats (200 seats in 1996, since reduced to 180). In the largest of the eleven PR districts, thirty legislators are selected, which means a party can win a seat there with just over 3 percent of the PR vote. The PR component of the new system therefore offers incentives

Table 5.3 Party Strength in Japan's House of Representatives, 1996 and 2000

	Seats Won, October 1996 HR Election	June 2000 HR Election Before	After[a]
Liberal Democratic Party	239	271	233 (177)
New Frontier Party	156	—	—
Liberal Party	—	18	22 (4)
New Conservative Party	—	18	7 (7)
New Komeito	—	42	31 (7)
Democratic Party	52	95	127 (80)
Japan Socialist Party	15	14	19 (4)
Japan Communist Party	26	26	20 (0)
Others/Independents	12	15	21 (21)
Total	500	499	480

a. Total seats (SMD seats).

for small parties to eschew coalition with one another in favor of continuing to compete independently. This is especially true for the Communists and *Komeito*. Both parties maintain small, but extremely loyal, support bases, so both can expect to continue to win Lower House representation via the proportional representation seats. In the 2000 election, the Liberals and Socialists also won most of their seats (eighteen of twenty-two and fifteen of nineteen, respectively) through the generous PR tier.

Next, although returnees from the disintegrating NFP allowed the LDP to regain its Lower House majority by September 1997, it fell eight seats short of the mark in 2000. This outcome was due in part to the LDP's decision to step aside in twenty-five SMDs and instead support candidates from its current coalition partners (the NCP and *Komeito*). Had the LDP insisted on running its own candidates in most or all of those districts, it might very well have retained its Lower House majority. So why didn't it do so?

The reason is that the LDP has not been able to recapture control of the House of Councillors (HC, the Upper House), and it needs the support of its coalition partners to push through legislation (see table 5.4). It remains the largest party in the Upper House, but the 1998 election further reduced its strength there. The LDP's inability to deal with persistent economic stagnation and financial turmoil contributed to the 1998 defeat, and it remains unclear when Japan's current economic distress will be overcome. The outcome for the opposition parties in the 1998 Upper House election was just as important as the LDP's poor showing. The Democrats strengthened their position as the primary opposition group, while the JSP continued its slide toward oblivion.

Table 5.4 Party Strength in Japan's House of Councillors

	Held Over from 1995 Election	Seats Won, 1998 Election[a]			Current Strength (July 2000)
		Districts	National Lists	Total	
Liberal Democratic Party	58	33	14	47	105
Democratic Party of Japan	20	21	12	33	58
New *Komeito*	13	4	7	11	24
Japan Communist Party	8	7	8	15	23
Japan Socialist Party	8	1	4	5	13
Liberal Party	6	1	5	6	5
New Conservative Party	—	—	—	—	7
Minor Parties/Independents	13	9	0	9	16
Total	126	76	50	126	251[b]

a. Figures account for 13 candidates who won as independents but joined parties immediately after the election. Of those 13, the LDP added 3, the DPJ 6, CGP 2, and minor parties 2 (*Yomiuri Shimbun*, 4 August 1998).
b. One seat is currently vacant.

EXPECTATIONS FOR THE FUTURE

The two elections held under this new electoral system have already produced a pattern that is likely to continue, barring any further tinkering with the rules. Two national parties will dominate the single-member districts, while a handful of small parties will survive only by virtue of the PR portion of the electoral system. Specific parties might dissolve or merge, and new small parties might appear, but the system should continue to produce two large parties and a few small ones.[8]

The Democratic Party should remain the primary challenger to LDP politicians in most single-member districts. But how well the Democrats fare will depend in large part on how small parties and their voters behave. In the 2000 election, the LDP won only 31 percent of PR seats, but it took advantage of a fractured opposition to garner 59 percent of the SMD seats. By contrast, the Democrats won 26.7 percent in each tier (80 of 300 SMDs and 48 of 180 PR seats), not because they lost a lot of SMDs to other opposition parties, but because the LDP benefited when the other opposition parties insisted on running their own candidates in competition with one another, splitting the "anti-LDP" vote in the process.

For two reasons, the prospects for united opposition candidacies are bleak. First, the JCP can be expected to continue to field a candidate in every single-member district. They will be competitive only rarely (all 300 of their SMD candidates lost in 2000), but the Communists have always treated elections as opportunities to "educate the public" as much as to win seats in the Diet. Dissuading hopeless JCP candidates from running and "wasting" precious anti-LDP votes will be a difficult proposition for the Democrats. Second, all parties have an incentive to field SMD candidates because doing so can help their PR-tier prospects. If a party can put a local face in each district to supplement its list for the larger region (not to mention use that candidate's organization to campaign), it will have an easier time mobilizing voters for the PR vote, even if it loses in every SMD (Cox and Schoppa 1998).

IMPLICATIONS FOR CAMPAIGN STRATEGIES

The SNTV electoral rule created a variety of incentives and consequences to which parties and candidates had to respond. A party had to win at least 256 seats, or an average of about two seats per district (256 seats/129 districts), to secure a majority in the legislature. Therefore, a party had to nominate an average of at least two candidates per district—possibly more, since not every candidate could be expected to win. Because copartisan candidates shared a common party label and platform, the SNTV system forced them to compete with one another on the basis of appeals to personal support groups. The intraparty competition engendered by SNTV created an incentive to favor organized groups that could provide a steady supply of votes and/or money for same-party candidates to compete against one another. This made elections expensive and led to considerable corruption.

The LDP solved this vote-division problem by encouraging its candidates' efforts to create decentralized campaign organizations. Individual LDP candidates targeted groups in their districts, through either geographic or professional relationships, and specialized in distributing political favors to those groups. They then used the money raised from the groups they assisted to build up loyal personal support bases. The party aided its candidates' efforts by doling out pork-barrel projects for which candidates could claim credit and by enforcing a policy-specialization scheme. The party saw to it that its candidates within a given district specialized in different areas of policymaking. This way, they could differentiate themselves from one another by pointing to exclusive influence over "their" policy turf (McCubbins and Rosenbluth 1995). Each would thereby have a natural group of supporters within the district that was protected from competing claims by copartisan rivals.

The LDP's response to the need to divide the vote also had consequences for political competition. This system produced huge entry barriers for challengers, especially non-LDP challengers. Control of the budget was critical for the personalistic and distributive strategy to work, and those parties who did not have control (i.e., everyone but the LDP) could not credibly offer the kinds of payoffs necessary to attract votes. Voting for the opposition, even when the opposition espoused policies closer to voters' own preferences, might never pay off. Of course, the LDP's reliance on personalistic (as opposed to programmatic) campaigns periodically led to corruption scandals or to "hot" issues that the opposition could exploit to excite the public. But these gains were transitory, as voters inevitably would return to the LDP and the tangible benefits that party offered in exchange for their support.

The severe restrictions on electioneering activities also advantaged the LDP at the expense of opposition parties, and not only because the LDP always had the most incumbents. Note that these rules make it very difficult for candidates to appeal to large groups of voters at once. Television and radio would be the easiest ways to issue broad-based policy appeals, but they were prohibited, and even since the electoral reform, they continue to be restricted. This was fine for LDP candidates who were too preoccupied with intraparty competition to be concerned with broad-based, partisan appeals. But opposition parties, especially those that ran only one candidate per district, would have benefited enormously from the ability to present their platforms to a mass audience via television and radio. The easiest restrictions to circumvent—because they are the most difficult to enforce—were the spending limits and the canvassing ban. And these were the areas in which the LDP maintained distinct advantages (Cox and Thies 1998).

Arguably, all of this incumbent protection means that the LDP was simply lucky to have been the first majority party under SNTV. Had the Socialists started out on top back in the 1950s, they might have been able to use the budget and the proincumbent electioneering rules to maintain a majority just as the LDP has done (Reed and Bolland 1999). It might also be argued, however, that the niche strategies pursued by LDP candidates were available only to a business-oriented conservative party, because producer groups were easier to organize (and better able to provide campaign finance) than the groups that progressive parties might have targeted (e.g., labor, environmentalists, or women).

The 1994 reforms were expected to affect campaign strategies in two main ways. First, in the SMDs, with no party nominating more than one candidate per district, personalistic appeals are no longer necessary. Now, even LDP candidates can campaign on the party platform. Similarly, in the PR tier, the competition will be explicitly party versus party, so voters have no choice but to focus on party platforms. Of course, candidates in the SMDs might still prefer to maintain their personal vote machines as insurance against a downturn in party fortunes. Putting all one's eggs in the partisan basket is efficient, but it is risky as well.

The second expected change in campaign tactics was the elimination of niche strategies in favor of more broad-based appeals. Since candidates now will have to aim to win a majority (or at least a large plurality) of votes, they might be induced to forgo pandering to a collection of small groups within the district, in favor of campaigning for the support of the median voter. The eventual elimination of corporate contributions should reinforce this shift. This, in turn, could reduce the bias toward producer groups and focus more attention on consumer-type interests. Whereas a focus on producer status served to divide voters according to their employment status and category, the one common denominator among all voters is their status as consumers. Accordingly, they share such interests as lower prices, better selection in the marketplace, lower taxes, and greater social welfare, and candidates might choose to appeal on the basis of those shared interests.

So much for theory. Unfortunately, the 1996 election did not provide much support for the above hypotheses. Candidates whose traditional bases of support were geographically concentrated in new SMDs generally went after the higher vote share needed there not by switching to programmatic appeals to the median voter, but by stoking the fires of their money machines even higher. Where possible, they would exchange support with a same-party candidate in an adjoining district if each candidate's old support groups extended to the other's district. Several LDP incumbents whose personal support groups spilled across the new district lines and candidates who had to contend with other incumbents for SMD nominations switched parties when they realized they would not receive the LDP's endorsement in the SMD of their choice. To some extent, then, parties came to represent short-term strategic interests of ship-jumping members rather than underlying policy differences. It is not surprising, then, that the party system that existed before the election fragmented soon after the election.

Still, there are three good reasons to believe that the 1996 election is not indicative of future trends. First, with so many candidates left over from the old electoral system (both incumbents and returnees), it would have been unreasonable to expect all these old dogs to learn new campaign tricks immediately. It is more reasonable to expect the "new equilibrium" to be reached gradually, as much by replacement of old candidates with younger ones as by the retraining of the holdovers. Just because campaign strategies did not change in the first election under the new rules does not mean they will never change.

Second, the electoral reform's ban on business donations to candidates, designed to reduce the influence of money in elections, did not take force until 2000, so "old tricks" were still permitted in the 1996 election. It is too early to tell whether the now complete ban on corporate contributions to individuals had any effect on the 2000 election, although the loophole that allows donations to local party branches may frustrate reformers. Not surprisingly, the Democrats have been calling for that loophole to be closed, and further changes in campaign finance laws would not be surprising.

Third, the prediction of programmatic parties presupposes that politicians and voters alike can clearly identify those parties. As discussed, the 1996 election occurred in the midst of tremendous flux in the party system. The 2000 election again took place amid a different party system than existed in 1996. The NFP no longer exists. *Komeito* did not run as an independent entity in 1996, but did so in 2000. The Democrats formed only one month before the 1996 election, which made it impossible to run a coordinated campaign even if they had wanted to do so. And JSP defections to the newly formed Democrats left the JSP as a small shell of the party that contested the 1993 election. Therefore, only the LDP and

JCP were relatively intact going into the 1996 election, and in 2000, only these two parties resembled parties that competed in 1996.

Several factors suggest that the party system is beginning to produce the sorts of ideological cleavages that will allow for more programmatic campaigns. To some extent, the Liberals and Democrats have begun staking out policy positions designed to differentiate themselves from the LDP. The Liberals have positioned themselves as the party of economic deregulation, a policy over which the LDP opinion remains divided. Second, the Liberals have taken on a hawkish posture in military matters, favoring an amendment to the Constitution to allow an increased international role for the Japanese Self-Defense Forces, along with a decreased dependence upon the United States for national defense. Though some LDP members share this view, popular opinion continues to prefer the status quo on military matters, so the LDP is unlikely to advocate such dramatic changes. Similarly, the Democrats are developing a position to the left of the LDP. With the near demise of the JSP, they have been able to secure the support of the umbrella labor union organization *Rengo*. This should offer a solid base of support to build upon in urban areas, although it remains unclear how the Democrats will appeal to voters in agricultural regions.

Further, the new campaign regulations allow parties to conduct media campaigns that, though limited, are expected to increase in importance in the future (Christensen 1998). In other words, once the party system stabilizes somewhat, parties should begin to use the new tactics to promote their platforms and candidates.

Implications for Internal Party Organization

With the introduction of single-member districts and party lists, the expectation was that central party leaderships would be strengthened at the expense of individual candidates. Now, each party must choose the one candidate per district with the best chance of outpolling all other candidates (as opposed to just finding one who could win one of several available seats, as under SNTV) and must devise a rank-ordering of party candidates on each regional list. Similarly, the introduction of public funding of campaigns and the restriction of contributions to individual politicians should again increase the discretion and control of party leaders.

LDP Factions

SNTV profoundly affected the internal organization of large parties. For parties that ran more than one candidate in many electoral districts (i.e., the LDP, and sometimes the JSP), the resulting intraparty competition gave succor to intraparty factions. Copartisan candidates could not compete with one another over policy, because doing so would confuse voters as to what the party represented. Hence, they resorted to personalistic appeals, each carving out a niche of supporters within the district.

Factions helped candidates to maintain their personal support machines. They were organized as parallel, seniority-based hierarchies within the party, in which members supported their factional leader (or his choice) for the party presidency in exchange for campaign finance, help in securing the official LDP endorsement, and access to party and government posts. If intraparty competition under SNTV provided succor for LDP factions, then the elimination of intraparty competition under the new electoral rules should cause factions to change, if they persist at all. Early research shows that factions have already begun to change in at least three ways.[9]

First, factional discipline broke down in the LDP's party presidency-selection process in both 1995 and 1998. In the former case, Ryutaro Hashimoto convinced many younger members from all existing factions to ignore the dictates of their factional leaders and to support him over Yohei Kono, who had followed the traditional practice of brokering deals with other factional chiefs. Such an open rebellion against factional leaders was unprecedented, but it succeeded, propelling Hashimoto to victory. Then, in 1998, after Hashimoto resigned his post to take responsibility for the LDP's Upper House electoral debacle, the contest for succession again revealed cracks in the old faction-based modus operandi. The Obuchi faction nominated their leader, Keizo Obuchi, for the job, only to have factionmate Seiroku Kajiyama announce that he would run as well. Obuchi ended up winning (a third candidate, Junichiro Koizumi, split the anti-Obuchi vote with Kajiyama), but not because his faction was united behind him, and not because other faction leaders succeeded in throwing their factions' united support to him.

Second, in the 1996 Lower House election, candidates without factional backing performed better than ever before, and almost all newcomer LDP candidates eschewed factional affiliation during the campaign. Since they did not face competition from factionally backed copartisans, these newcomers apparently did not feel the need to sign up with factions themselves. Interestingly, most of the LDP candidates who won seats without factional ties proceeded to join factions soon after the election. The elimination of intraparty competition in elections has altered the role of factions (a sole LDP candidate can now campaign largely on the basis of his partisan platform), but LDP members must still compete for party and government posts, and for these, factional support continues to be important. Nonetheless, the electoral bond connecting faction leaders and members has weakened.

Third, the post-1994 period has witnessed a series of shifts in the factional structure. The defection that led to the LDP split was led by the Hata group, which was itself a splinter group of the party's largest faction. Since that time, several other factions have divided, and a few of the smaller groups have coalesced to form new factions. The party split cost the LDP many of its most prominent members, so it is natural that remaining members would jockey to fill the void at the top. But this factional shifting is beginning to reveal an ideological divide within the party as well. In the past, LDP factions were notorious for their lack of ideological baggage. Because the candidates who competed against each other in each SNTV electoral district generally came from different factions, all factions had roughly the same geographical composition. Because these intraparty battles were fought with personal support networks and truckloads of money—and not on the basis of policy differences—individual factions never became known for distinct policy programs. Finally, since LDP newcomers were "obliged" to choose a faction not already represented in their districts, they were more likely to use a process of elimination, not a search for the best ideological fit. To be sure, some policy battles were waged within the party, but they did not tend to be fought along factional lines (Ramseyer and Rosenbluth 1993).

Now, however, the two main ideological streams that can be identified within the LDP are beginning to coincide with factional affiliations.[10] Since factions will no longer do battle at the electoral level (with only one LDP candidate running in each SMD), there is nothing to constrain policy-based factional affiliations. In sum, factions might persist within the LDP despite the demise of SNTV, but they will be very different organizations than before: they will have less relevance for elections at the district level and perhaps less pertinence for leadership battles, but they will have continued importance for post allocation and increased significance for policymaking.

The Pretenders to the Throne: The New Frontier Party and the Democrats

Prior to the electoral reform, the only party anywhere near as large or as heterogeneous as the LDP was the Japan Socialist Party. The JSP contained factions too, dating back as far as the party's founding by the 1955 merger of the Left and Right Socialist Parties. In contrast with LDP factions, JSP factions were always ideologically based. This cleavage reflected, to a great extent, the divide between public-sector and private-sector unions that provided the JSP with candidates, votes, and financing but did not see eye-to-eye on policy matters. Of course, as a permanent opposition party, the JSP did not have access to the pork-barrel spending or huge campaign war chests with which the LDP smoothed over factional disputes, so there was no unifying force to keep dissatisfied groups from simply leaving the party. The splits in the JSP that produced the Democratic Socialist Party in 1960 and the Social Democratic League in 1977 testify to this point.

Other prereform parties were much smaller and much more homogeneous. The Communists and *Komeito* were (and are) distinctive for their rigid party hierarchies. Though the two parties are the most bitter of rivals (Hrebenar 1992), they resemble each other in their ability to organize their members all the way down to the neighborhood level. Because these parties never endorsed more than one candidate in any electoral district under SNTV, intraparty competition did not cause them any problems. Similarly, the Democratic Socialist Party, though not nearly as hierarchical as the JCP or *Komeito*, was relatively free of factional strife.

The introduction of the new electoral system was expected to have two main effects on party organization outside the LDP. First, the need to win a plurality of votes to capture seats in the single-member districts provides an incentive for small parties either to merge into larger parties, or at least to coordinate their endorsements. Second, the needs to produce party lists for large districts and to dole out publicly provided campaign funds were expected to strengthen the hands of party leaders.

Thus far, these two incentives have been irreconcilable. The rise and fall of the New Frontier Party is a case in point. In retrospect, one might view the failure of this attempt to build a large-party rival to the LDP as a result of the party's high level of heterogeneity bumping up against the efforts of its leader, Ichiro Ozawa, to centralize decision making. The NFP was formed by a merger of the *Komeito*, the DSP, and the two largest LDP splinter parties. These formerly independent parties behaved somewhat like ideological factions within the larger umbrella party. While they were united in their efforts to bring down the LDP and to jettison SNTV, they had little else in common.

The NFP's troubles in the 1996 election revealed the fundamental incompatibility of the arrangement. The NFP had a very difficult time uniting behind candidates for the SMDs, with each "faction" demanding that its own members be allowed to continue their district associations. Given the *Komeito*'s pariah status[11] among many supporters of the NFP's other constituent parties, the NFP was obliged to "hide" many of its Komei members on the party lists. But to keep the Komei group happy, those candidates were given relatively high positions on the lists, which upset other party members who had hoped to win via the lists. It also meant that the NFP was the only party that did not place its SMD candidates on its list in the PR tier. Whereas SMD candidates from the LDP and the Democrats could hope to be saved by the lists should they fall short in their districts, the NFP's district candidates were forced to play a much higher-stakes game.

The major beneficiary of the NFP's collapse was the fledgling Democratic Party of Japan. The DPJ was formed on 17 September, just before the October 1996 election, when former comrades Ozawa and Tsutomu Hata (who led the rebellion within the LDP in 1993) had a falling out. Hata joined forces with three other prominent LDP defectors and Ozawa opponents, Yukio and Kunio Hatoyama and Naoto Kan. Formed so close to the start of the 1996 electoral campaign, the DPJ was not able to find candidates for every district, but it still did pretty well in the election, winning fifty-two seats to become the second largest opposition party after the NFP.

When the DPJ accepted the NFP refugees into its fold in 1998, it ascended to the highest position among the opposition parties. So far, it is nowhere near as heterogeneous a group as was the NFP, since Ozawa's Liberals and the New *Komeito* have remained on the outside. But if the Democrats really do expect to challenge the LDP for preeminence in the Lower House, they will have to either unite the opposition or await another LDP split. Either way, they would likely become *more* heterogeneous and *more* internally factionalized along ideological lines. A safer option, in terms of internal party harmony, might be for the DPJ to concentrate on depriving the LDP of its majority, and then work to form a multiparty coalition around itself. Then, the hardest question to answer would be whether to include the Communists in such a coalition.

Finally, there is little reason to expect the new electoral rules to cause changes in the internal organization of the other holdover parties from the old regime, the JCP and *Komeito*. Both were already highly centralized, and the new rules will only reinforce this tendency. After the *Komeito*'s ill-fated attempt to become part of a large, majority-seeking umbrella party, it is back on its own and, to all indications, back to business as usual in terms of internal operations. In October 1999, the *Komeito* joined the LDP and Liberal Party in a coalition government (its seats are needed to give the government an Upper House majority). This time, however, the *Komeito* will not merge with its partners, but will remain an independent party.

Implications for Voting Behavior: Turnout, Party Identification, Vote Swings, Interest Groups

Voter turnout in the 1996 HR election dropped to 59.6 percent, an all-time low for the Lower House, and nearly 8 points below the previous nadir of 67.3 percent in 1993. Though many commentators expressed dismay over this decline, it is unclear whether it represents a dangerous new political alienation or is simply a sign that Japanese democracy has matured, now that Japanese voters seem as apathetic and complacent about politics as do their counterparts in other liberal democracies.

Starting as early as the first election after the reintroduction of SNTV in 1947, turnout has experienced a slight but statistically significant decline. If one looks only at the three decades since 1969, however, and excludes the especially poor turnout of 1996, the trend is not statistically significant. So most of the drop can be attributed to the first postwar decades and the 1996 election. Further, the decline has not been monotonic. Instead, turnout rates have varied considerably up and down over time. Why then was there such a significant drop off in 1996?

Figure 5.3 (p. 110) shows national turnout rates for both Diet chambers during the postwar period. Note first that the low turnout of 1993 is not far off the other periodic lows in the this era. It is possible that turnout hit bottom in 1996 as a result of voter uncertainty over the new electoral rules and the chaotic party system. In postelection interviews, many voters did express confusion over the new rules. Moreover, the districting scheme left many Japanese voters without the option to vote for the same candidate as in the previous election because that candidate had been moved to a neighboring district. Finally, voters faced an array of new parties whose platforms were difficult to distinguish from one another,

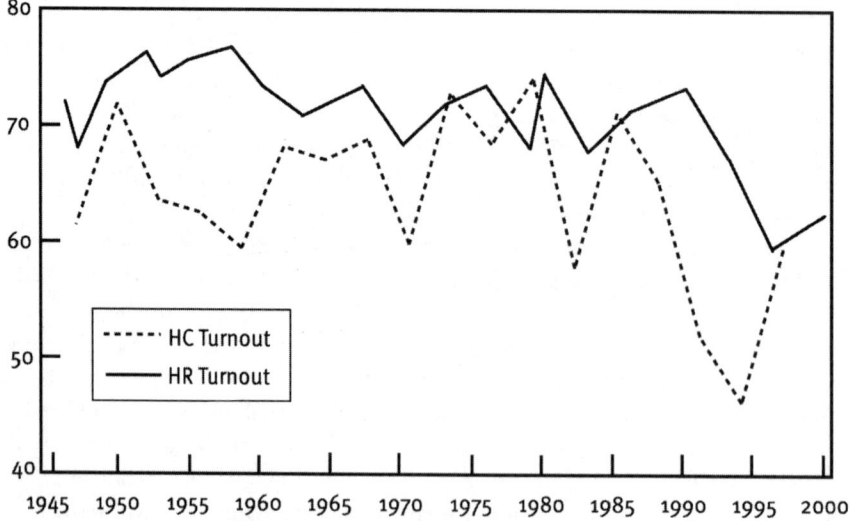

Figure 5.3 Change in Japanese Voter Turnout, 1946–2000

which probably resulted in increased abstention. As the party system settles down and as the electoral rules are better understood, voters may respond by returning to the polls. In fact, turnout did increase to 62.5 percent in the 2000 Lower House election, despite poor weather over most of the country.

The recent history of turnout in House of Councillors elections supports this hypothesis. After turnout dropped to an all-time low of 44.5 percent in the 1995 Upper House poll, it rebounded to 58.8 percent in 1998. In the case of the Upper House in 1995, voters did not have to decipher a new electoral system, but they did have to wade through the chaotic party system that resulted from the Lower House reform. Not surprisingly, in their second crack at that new party system, more voters turned out. It is also important to note that volatility in HC turnout rates is not at all new. Upper House elections have seen regular and dramatic downturns in voter turnout every twelve years, when nationwide local elections immediately precede them, and 1995 was indeed such a year.

At the district level, turnout is affected by the same variables, and in the same ways, as in other industrial democracies. These variables include age, education, urban or rural residence, and closeness of an election. Districts with more educated and more elderly voters have higher turnout (Richardson 1973; Matsubara and Kabashima 1984). Ronald Hrebenar (1992, 16) found that voter turnout in rural and semirural areas exceeded turnout in big cities by an average of 16.5 percent from the late 1970s into the 1980s. This variation is best explained by differences in social cohesion. Voters in rural areas are members of stable communities with numerous organizational ties based on such factors as occupation and home ownership. They are also more likely than urban voters to work in the electoral district in which they reside. In turn, high levels of group membership and participation facilitate voter mobilization at election time. The closeness of an election also plays a role. Close elections drive political elites, such as party and factional leaders, to increase their efforts at mobilizing their likely supporters. Campaign mobilization efforts, in turn, are more effective in districts with higher social cohesion (Cox, Rosenbluth, and Thies 1998).

For many voters, in particular LDP supporters who had multiple candidates from whom to choose, personal characteristics of candidates play as important a role as partisan connection under SNTV. Even strong partisans who favored LDP policies still had to select one LDP candidate among several, so partisan affiliation was an insufficient decision rule. As noted above, the LDP's electoral strategy tied voters to specific LDP Diet members based upon the specific policy expertise and pork a given LDP member could offer particular constituents. This exchange of vote support for government goodies produced a stable bond between representative and voter.

OTHER ELECTIONS IN JAPAN

The Lower House of the National Diet is certainly the most important political institution in Japan, and the 1994 reform that changed how its membership is chosen is clearly the watershed political event of the past decade. But there is more to Japanese electoral democracy than the Lower House. The Upper House of the Diet has long been dismissed as a rubber stamp, but this is largely because the LDP controlled both chambers for so long. Since the LDP lost its Upper House majority in 1989, that chamber's importance has become more apparent. Constitutionally, it ranks somewhere between the U.S. Senate and the German *Bundesrat* among second chambers in terms of legislative authority.

Japanese voters also elect legislative assemblies and governors at the prefectural level, and town councils and mayors at the municipal level. Since Japan is a nonfederal country, these local governmental units enjoy only that authority delegated by the central government, but collectively, they spend upwards of two-thirds of all public monies and administer most of the day-to-day operations of government. Moreover, local and prefectural political offices are often the stepping stones to the Diet, and local politicians maintain close patron-client relationships with Diet members.

Upper House

The 252 members of the House of Councillors are selected under different electoral rules than those used for the Lower House. They serve fixed six-year terms, with half elected every three years. Of the 126 seats available in each triennial election, 50 are chosen from party lists by proportional representation from the country at large,[12] and 76 are elected from forty-seven SNTV districts (the districts are the country's forty-seven prefectures). Each voter has two votes: one for a party in the national PR district, and one for an individual candidate in the prefectural SNTV district.

The major difference between the Upper House electoral system and the (old) Lower House rules is that the Upper House system does not generate very much intraparty competition. In the national PR district, voters cast their ballots for a party, so there is no need for individual party candidates to differentiate themselves from one another. Of the prefectural districts, more than half (twenty-six) are single-seat constituencies, in which there is no reason for a party to nominate more than one candidate. Even in the fifteen two-seat districts, it is uncommon for a party to nominate more than one candidate. So the possibility of intraparty competition and the need to divide the vote, as in the Lower House, is limited to just the six districts that send three or four members to the Diet. Thus, with a few exceptions, the Upper House electoral system closely resembles the *new* Lower House system (Cox, Rosenbluth, and Thies 2000).[13]

The Upper House rules favor issue-based rather than money-based campaigning because competition is among parties rather than candidates, and in much larger districts. This has made the LDP more vulnerable to the mood of the electorate over unpopular policies or scandals than it has been in the Lower House. That is, "personal votes" insulated LDP candidates from general voter dissatisfaction with the party in Lower House elections because *their* voters were still likely to support *them*, due to the personal ties. From the late 1960s through 1990, when the five-party system was most firmly established, vote share volatility (measured as the share of total vote that shifts between parties in a pair of elections) averaged 15 percent, and seat share volatility averaged 22 percent for the SNTV component of the House of Councillors. In contrast, only 6 percent of votes and 8 percent of seats shifted from one party to another in Lower House elections.[14]

In 1989, electoral volatility was high enough to cost the LDP its Upper House majority, apparently as a result of voter anger over a recently enacted sales tax, as well as numerous scandals. Again, in the 1998 HC election, the LDP experienced a humiliating loss because voters blamed the party for the country's recent economic crisis. With the elimination of intraparty competition under the new Lower House electoral system, the sensitivity of votes and seats to changes in public opinion that has plagued the LDP in the Upper House should become increasingly common in the Lower House as well. In the 2000 election, the LDP and its coalition partners (*Komeito* and the NCP) collectively lost sixty seats, while the main opposition party, the Democrats, gained thirty-six seats (and that despite the twenty-seat cut in the overall number of Lower House seats).

Local Elections

The LDP's post-1955 dominance of national politics has not been replicated at the local level. Particularly in large metropolitan areas, parties long relegated to opposition status in the Diet have managed to acquire at least some power on several occasions. For this reason, the LDP uses local election outcomes as a barometer of public opinion on specific issues. The best known example of this phenomenon occurred in the 1960s, when the success of progressive candidates running on antipollution platforms convinced the LDP to change its policies at the national level to defuse the issue, lest its Diet majority be threatened as well.

Each of Japan's 47 prefectures elects a governor and an assembly. Municipalities elect mayors and town councils. Members of prefectural assemblies are chosen in SNTV elections in which districts elect between one and six candidates to fixed four-year terms. Electoral competition often parallels Diet competition with personal support groups forming the basis of vote seeking at the local level.

The link between local and national elections has manifested itself in an interesting periodic effect on voter turnout. With nationwide local elections on a four-year cycle and Upper House elections on a three-year cycle, the two coincide every twelve years. Local elections occur in spring, whereas Upper House elections occur in early summer. So every twelve years, local elections precede Upper House elections by only a few months. It has been demonstrated that in these years, voter turnout for Upper House elections declines heavily relative to years when local and Upper House elections do not coincide. The explanation for these turnout declines is that local politicians help their Upper House patrons or friends to campaign, at least in part to remind their own voters that another local election is around the corner. But in years in which local elections immediately precede Upper House elections, local politicians have less incentive to be helpful (having just finished their own election, they need not stand again for four years) and fewer resources with which to help, having just depleted them locally. Since voter turnout is largely a function of mobilization, lower mobilization effort translates to lower turnout (Ishikawa 1994).

Assessment—Electoral Democracy in Japan, circa 2000

The SNTV electoral rule used in Japanese Lower House elections through 1993 generated or sustained personalistic campaigns, the factionalization of Japan's ruling party, and the fragmentation of the opposition. Though the rules also may have produced incentives for corruption in the sphere of campaign finance, this was not enough to undermine the postwar institutionalization of democracy. Analogously, the LDP's dependence on powerful interest groups led it to provide pork-barrel projects and profit-padding regulation that were economically inefficient at times, but this was not enough to undermine Japan's thirty years of "miraculous" economic growth.

It is probably no coincidence that the LDP's fall from power occurred in the middle of Japan's longest postwar recession. The LDP reaped the electoral benefits of three decades of tremendous economic growth, and it received the blame when that growth stopped. Moreover, when the economy is weak, voters seem less willing to forgive corruption, and the late 1980s and early 1990s produced new records for corruption at the highest levels. Accordingly, the LDP has performed poorly in consecutive Upper House polls in 1989, 1992, 1995, and 1998. In the Lower House as well, the LDP lost its majority via a party split and its first electoral defeat.

Whatever the SNTV system's culpability for the prolonged rule of the LDP, for corruption, or for personalistic electoral politics, the coalition that ousted the LDP in 1993 saw fit to replace it. The new electoral system provides different political incentives for Japanese politicians, and political behavior has begun to change.

Only six years and two elections have passed since the demise of the SNTV system. In this short period, it is not surprising that most of the visible political changes are to be found in the party system and the internal organization of parties. Eventually, these changes should affect policy as well. The main expectation for policy is that politicians will now have to appeal to larger segments of their districts than was necessary under SNTV, and that they will do so with a greater emphasis on policy-based appeals than was possible given the intraparty competition common to the former system.

Some evidence already exists as the ongoing economic downturn and financial crisis has focused political attention on the regulatory regime covering financial services. Current regulatory changes are ending the inefficient cartels that dominated financial services and are promoting competition: a favorable trend both for firms seeking such services and for ordinary consumers. This is just the result one would expect given the new context of electoral competition. Of course policies will change only after powerful vested interests either see the wisdom of change themselves, or are rendered less powerful in the eyes of policymakers.

The shift to a new style of political competition has been bumpy. The opposition has so far failed to consolidate or coordinate sufficiently to really challenge the LDP for Diet supremacy. This confusion has encouraged many LDP members to hang on to their tried-and-true tactics of nurturing personal-vote machines, courting business supporters at the expense of the general public, and generally resisting policy change. But as traditional electoral strategies become increasingly untenable, the old way of politics should gradually dissolve.

It is not surprising to find that more than a few politicians, both LDP and opposition, are calling for a return to SNTV. The New *Komeito*, in particular, sees its effective relegation to the PR tier as less desirable than its "old" status as the number three party in three-to-five-seat SNTV districts. While it seems unlikely that the electoral reform will be undone, further tinkering with the details of the new rules is not impossible. One example was the January 2000 decision to reduce the PR tier from 200 seats to 180. This small modification should do little to dissuade small parties from going it alone in the PR tier, but it does reduce the total number of seats needed for a Lower House majority from 251 to 241, which might help the LDP most of all.[15]

As Japan's decade-long recession continues, voters are likely to lose patience with any further attention that politicians pay to institutional fiddling, partisan alliances, and the other sordid details of elite politics. In the long run, the new electoral rules ought to produce more centralized, programmatic political parties, whose pursuit of majority support in SMDs and of maximum *partisan* support in the PR tier should redound to the benefit of the average voter. In the short-to-medium term, however, the result of electoral system change has been party system instability, shifting coalitions, and a general inattention to policy matters by politicians scrambling for new footholds. Japanese party politics will likely never be as stable as it was from 1955 to 1993; indeed, many of the reformers saw too much stability (i.e., LDP hegemony) under the old rules. But in the next election or two, the party system should sort itself out and settle down, voters should begin to figure out how the new system works and for what each party stands, and this intermediate period of flux should give way to that "long run."

NOTES

1. The details of the Upper House electoral system are discussed later in the chapter.
2. In fact, in the 1976 and 1979 Lower House elections, the number of official LDP candidates that won seats fell short of a majority. The LDP was able to reclaim its majority each time, however, when a handful of conservative independents joined the party after the election.
3. See Christensen 1994 for a recounting of the various reform proposals during the 1990s. For a longer-term perspective, see the discussion of reform efforts dating back to 1954 in Reed and Thies 2001.
4. That is, each party wins a proportional share of the PR-list seats *plus* as many SMD seats as it wins outright. In Germany, by contrast, each party wins a proportion of the total number of legislative seats equal to its vote share in the PR tier. Any SMD seats won count against that total. Thus, the new Japanese system is not as proportional as the German one, and it favors big parties that have a realistic chance of garnering SMD seats.
5. Certain restrictions were easily monitored and therefore difficult to evade. These include the limitation on newspaper advertisements and handbills, as well as the prohibition of all but government-sponsored television and radio ads. Of course, each of these campaign rules limited the ability of challengers to increase name recognition, which gave incumbents a clear advantage over newcomers. Since the LDP's persistent majority gave it the lion's share of incumbents, it reaped most of the benefits of these restrictions. See Cox and Thies 1998 for an extended discussion.
6. This closed an infamous loophole of the 1975 reform, which limited the amount of money each funding organization could amass but did not limit the number of organizations that each candidate could create.
7. The DPJ had been formed by NFP and JSP defectors just before the 1996 election, supplanting the JSP as the number three party and frustrating the NFP's hopes for unified opposition candidacies in many single-member districts.
8. As long as the LDP needs coalition partners to control majorities in both houses, it will have to coordinate its own electoral ambitions with those of its partners, so a few SMDs will go to these otherwise overmatched parties.
9. The following material on factions is discussed more thoroughly in Cox, Rosenbluth, and Thies 1999.
10. One recent manifestation of this cleavage took place over the question of whether or not to form a coalition with Ozawa's Liberal Party. While Prime Minister (and LDP President) Obuchi pushed the arrangement, party presidential hopeful Koichi Kato denounced it, arguing instead for a return to a coalition with the Socialists and the small New Party

Harbinger. Ozawa's calls for constitutional revisions that would allow Japan to play a larger role in international peacekeeping were of particular concern to the Kato group. Most LDP members lined up behind one of the two leaders, and the grouping more or less followed (new) factional affiliations.

11. The *Komeito* was formed by the lay Buddhist organization Soka Gakkai. Although formal ties between Soka and the party have been severed, the party still draws almost all of its electoral and financial support from fiercely loyal Soka adherents. Soka, and by extension, *Komeito*, are viewed with suspicion by many nonadherents, which makes other parties wary of appearing to be too close to *Komeito*.

12. Prior to the 1983 election, the fifty national-tier seats were elected by SNTV as well. Because the top fifty vote-getters nationwide would win seats, the best candidates during that time were celebrities (newscasters, actors, former athletes) and interest-group representatives. The shift to closed-list PR in 1983 was brought about by parties who wanted greater control.

13. In addition to the half-dozen multiseat districts in the Upper House, and the fact that there are 47 large districts there, compared with 300 small ones in the Lower House, there are two other differences: (1) the PR tier for the Upper House uses one national district, compared to eleven PR districts for the Lower House; and (2) candidates may not run in both tiers simultaneously in the Upper House. The first of these differences is probably important only insofar as the larger (fifty-seat) PR district allows even tinier parties to win representation. The second difference probably matters somewhat more for internal party organization, campaign strategies, and voter calculations.

14. Of course, elections for the two chambers rarely occur simultaneously, and the specific timing of elections could affect these results. In particular, the fact that Lower House election timing is chosen by the ruling party, whereas Upper House elections are on a fixed schedule, might help to explain low Lower House volatility. Simultaneous Upper and Lower House elections have occurred twice, however, in 1980 and 1986. Looking at these elections only, the results in the text hold up: vote swings between parties in the Upper House averaged 17 percent, compared with only 4 percent in the Lower House (for seat swings, the figures were 21 percent and 9 percent, respectively).

15. One LDP coalition partner at the time, the Liberal Party, originally demanded a 50-seat reduction, to 150, but when *Komeito* agreed to join the coalition in October 1999, they would only acquiesce to the more modest 20-seat cut (*Japan Times*, 4 October 1999).

REFERENCES

Christensen, Raymond V. 1994. "Electoral Reform in Japan: How It Was Enacted and Changes It May Bring." *Asian Survey* 34:589–605.

———. 1998. "Putting New Wine into Old Bottles: The Effect of Electoral Reforms on Campaign Practices in Japan." Paper presented at the annual meeting of the Association of Asian Studies, Washington, D.C., 26 March.

Cox, Gary, and Frances McCall Rosenbluth. 1995. "Anatomy of a Split: The Liberal Democrats of Japan." *Electoral Studies* 14:355–76.

Cox, Gary, Frances McCall Rosenbluth, and Michael F. Thies. 1998. "Mobilization, Social Networks and Turnout: Evidence from Japan." *World Politics* 50:447–74.

———. 1999. "Electoral Reform and the Fate of Factions: The Case of Japan's Liberal Democratic Party." *British Journal of Political Science* 29:33–56.

———. 2000. "Electoral Rules, Career Ambitions and Party Structure: Comparing Factions in Japan's Upper and Lower Houses." *American Journal of Political Science* 44:115–22.

Cox, Gary, and Michael F. Thies. 1998. "The Cost of Intra-party Competition: The Single, Nontransferable Vote and Money Politics in Japan." *Comparative Political Studies* 31:267–91.

Cox, Karen, and Leonard J. Schoppa. 1998. "The Consequences of 'Sticky Voting' in Mixed-Member Electoral Systems." Paper presented at the annual meeting of the American Political Science Association, Boston, September.

Duverger, Maurice. 1954. *Political Parties*. New York: Wiley.

Hrebenar, Ronald J. 1992. *The Japanese Party System.* 2d ed. Boulder, Colo.: Westview Press.
Ishikawa, Masumi. 1994. *A History of Postwar Politics* [in Japanese]. Tokyo: Iwanami Shinsho.
Johnson, Chalmers. 1987. "Political Institutions and Economic Performance: the Government-Business Relationship in Japan, South Korea, and Taiwan." In *The Political Economy of the New Asian Industrialism,* edited by Frederic C. Deyo. Ithaca, N.Y.: Cornell University Press.
Lijphart, Arend. 1984. *Democracies: Patterns of Majoritarian and Consensus Government in Twenty-One Countries.* New Haven, Conn.: Yale University Press.
Matsubara, Nozumu, and Ikuo Kabashima. 1984. "The Logic of an Overwhelming Tanaka Faction Victory amidst an LDP Defeat" [in Japanese]. *Chuo koron* 99:74–85.
McCubbins, Mathew D., and Frances M. Rosenbluth. 1995. "Party Provision for Personal Politics: Dividing the Vote in Japan." In *Structure and Policy in Japan and the United States,* edited by Peter F. Cowhey and Mathew D. McCubbins. New York: Cambridge University Press.
Ramseyer, J. Mark, and Frances McCall Rosenbluth. 1993. *Japan's Political Marketplace.* Cambridge, Mass.: Harvard University Press.
Reed, Steven R., and John Bolland. 1999. "The Fragmentation Effect of SNTV in Japan." In *Elections in Japan, Korea, and Taiwan Under the Single Non-Transferable Vote: The Comparative Study of An Embedded Institution,* edited by Bernard Grofman, Sung-Chull Lee, Edwin Winckler, and Brian Woodall. Ann Arbor: University of Michigan Press.
Reed, Steven R., and Michael F. Thies. 2001. "The Causes of Electoral Reform in Japan." In *Mixed-Member Electoral Systems: The Best of Both Worlds?* edited by Matthew Soberg Shugart and Martin P. Wattenberg. New York: Oxford University Press.
Richardson, Bradley. 1973. "Urbanization and Political Participation: The Case of Japan." *American Political Science Review* 67:433–52.
Riker, William H. 1982. "The Two-Party System and Duverger's Law: An Essay on the History of Political Science." *American Political Science Review* 76:753–66.

CHAPTER 6

Elections in Democratizing Korea

by Chan Wook Park

THIS CHAPTER EXAMINES, for the most part, Korea's presidential and national legislative elections that have taken place since the country's democratic transition in the late 1980s. Specifically, to set the context for the analysis, the chapter begins with a brief overview of political developments in the Republic of Korea and describes the country's party politics in the democratic era. Then it analyzes key aspects of Korean elections, including the electoral system, campaign issues and practices, and citizens' voting behavior. Finally, it assesses the significance of Korean elections as a democratic procedure.

POLITICAL DEVELOPMENTS AND ELECTIONS: AN OVERVIEW

From the inception of the First Republic in 1948 through the current Sixth Republic, South Korea has undergone a series of political upheavals. Despite its founding ideology of liberal democracy, the First Republic soon degenerated into authoritarianism where President Syngman Rhee wielded arbitrary power. The Rhee government's flagrant rigging of the 1960 presidential election triggered the student uprisings that led to the fall of the First Republic. During the Second Republic, Koreans briefly experienced democratic politics and a parliamentary system of government, but the Second Republic was toppled in May 1961 by the military under General Park Chung Hee's command. After ruling the country for two and a half years as the junta's leader, Park was elected president of the Third Republic. In October 1972, President Park fortified his dictatorial rule by proclaiming martial law, and he instituted the Fourth Republic two months later. After seven years, Park's assassination precipitated another round of military intervention led by General Chun Doo Hwan. Chun rose to the presidency of the Fifth Republic. In June 1987, President Chun faced massive prodemocracy demonstrations, and he conceded to citizens' demand for democratization. This concession, dubbed the June 29 Declaration, was formally announced by Roh Tae Woo, then President Chun's handpicked would-be successor. The declaration marked the beginning of Korea's transition to democracy. Shortly afterwards, political leaders and their parties negotiated a new democratic constitutional framework heralding the Sixth Republic.

In each republic, with the exception of the short-lived Second Republic, a presidential system of government was adopted. In the beginning of the First Republic, Syngman Rhee was elected president by the National Assembly. Later, the constitution was revised for direct popular election of the president. President Rhee won his second term by popular vote in 1952. In 1954, his supporters in the National Assembly revised the constitution and removed the two-term limit on the presidency. For the third time, Rhee ascended to the presidency following the 1956 election. The Third Republic constitution also provided for direct election of the president. Park Chung Hee consecutively won the 1963 and 1967 presidential elections. In 1969, President Park's party pushed a constitutional revision again lifting the two-term restriction on the presidency. Park was narrowly elected to a third term in 1971. During the Fourth and Fifth Republics, the president was indirectly elected through the National Conference for Reunification or an electoral college.

The Sixth Republic constitution has restored the method of electing the president by direct popular vote. In the three-way presidential election held on 16 December 1987, the ruling party's Roh Tae Woo squeezed out an electoral victory with about 37 percent of the votes cast. Roh won a plurality largely because two prominent civilian leaders, Kim Young Sam and Kim Dae Jung, split the opposition vote. This election was historic because the Korean voters directly elected the president for the first time in sixteen years (Lee 1990, 45–69, 71–92). In early 1990, Kim Young Sam joined with President Roh to form the Democratic Liberal Party (DLP). Kim became the party's presidential nominee, and he won the December 1992 presidential election by securing 42 percent of the vote over the 34 percent received by Kim Dae Jung of the Democratic Party (DP). Kim Young Sam was sworn in as the first civilian president since the military intervention in 1961 (Lee 1995; Park 1993b). Five years afterwards, in December 1997, Kim Dae Jung of the National Congress for New Politics (NCNP) was elected in his fourth presidential bid. Kim narrowly defeated Lee Hoi Chang of the Grand National Party (GNP) by 40.3 percent to 38.7 percent of the vote. Kim's victory accomplished the first peaceful transfer of presidential power to the opposition (Park 1998/99; Steinberg 1998).

Sixteen general elections have been held for the National Assembly. The election for the first Constituent Assembly, with a two-year term, took place in May 1948. Subsequent elections for choosing legislative members for a four-year term were held in May 1950, May 1954, and May 1958. The Fifth Assembly election, held in July 1960, served as the founding election for the Second Republic. Legislative elections for the Third Republic were held in November 1963, June 1967, and May 1971. The Ninth and Tenth Assembly elections, both of the Fourth

Republic, were held in February 1973 and December 1978, respectively. Also, two elections took place during the Fifth Republic: for the Eleventh Assembly in March 1981 and for the Twelfth Assembly in February 1985. Since the dawn of the Sixth Republic, Korea has held four more national legislative elections. This chapter, which focuses on electoral politics since Korea's democratic transition, analyzes these four most recent Assembly elections in detail.

In the Thirteenth Assembly election held on 26 April 1988, the president's party failed to gain a majority for the first time in Korea's legislative politics, with the National Assembly split among four parties. While President Roh's Democratic Justice Party (DJP) held the largest bloc of seats, its legislative strength fell 25 seats short of an overall majority (Park 1988b; Kim 1989). As shown in table 6.1 (p. 122), the DJP captured 87 district seats with 34 percent of the vote. After receiving an additional 38 at-large seats, according to the electoral rules described later, the ruling party's total seats constituted approximately 42 percent of 299 seats. Kim Dae Jung's Party for Peace and Democracy (PPD) emerged as the largest opposition party with about 23 percent of the seats. It surpassed Kim Young Sam's Reunification Democratic Party (RDP) in terms of seats, even though the former party's vote share (19.3 percent) was 4.5 percent lower than the latter's. Kim Jong Pil's New Democratic Republican Party (NDRP) drew 15.6 percent of the vote and won a respectable number of seats, 35 in total.

In the Fourteenth Assembly election held on 24 March 1992, the ruling DLP again was unable to obtain a majority of legislative seats (Lee 1994; Park 1993a; Kang 1998). It came up one seat short of 150 seats needed for a majority (see table 6.2, p. 123). The main opposition DP took almost one-third of all legislative seats by garnering 29.2 percent of the vote. Within only two months of its inauguration, the Unification National Party (UNP) won 17.4 percent of the vote and 31 seats, sufficient to form a bargaining body within the National Assembly. In brief, the ruling party's ability to act alone was severely weakened, and the stage was set for a three-party competition.

The results of the Fifteenth Assembly election reflected a typical pattern (see table 6.3, p. 124). President Kim Young Sam's New Korea Party (NKP) won 34.8 percent of the vote and a much greater share of seats (46.5 percent), still short of a legislative majority (Leuthold 1997). Kim Dae Jung's NCNP obtained 26.4 percent of total legislative seats with 25.5 percent of the vote. The party failed to attain its own pre-election goal, one-third of the seats. While Kim Jong Pil's United Liberal Democrats (ULD) demonstrated its strength by winning 50 seats, the DP obtained only 15 seats. The latter party failed to secure a foothold in the National Assembly.

In the Sixteenth Assembly election that took place on 13 April 2000, the opposition GNP finished first by receiving 48.7 percent of the total seats with 39.0 percent of the vote. President Kim Dae Jung's Millennium Democratic Party (MDP) won 35.9 percent of the vote, which yielded 42.1 percent of the seats. No other third party crossed the 20-seat threshold required for forming a party group within the National Assembly (see table 6.4, p. 125). This election produced an incomplete two-party system in which neither of the two major parties singly commanded a legislative majority.

Elections for local chiefs and councillors were held prior to 1961. Some local autonomy was restored in 1989 with local council elections beginning in 1991 and election of local chiefs beginning in 1995. These progressive developments notwithstanding, local autonomy and decentralization are at a rudimentary stage. As such, this chapter focuses on national elections for the president and the National Assembly.

Political Parties in the Electoral Arena of the Democratic Era

Korean political parties are personality dominated and rally around particular bosses to maintain their vigor. The fate of a party, including a split or the formation of a new party, hinges on the decision of its boss. Members of the National Assembly have changed party affiliation according to their relationship with focal leaders or political convenience. Being identified with its top leader, an existing party's crucial base for mobilizing electoral support is the region in which the leader is a native son or with which he has a special connection. Bossism and regionalism are two catchwords succinctly describing Korean party politics.

Frequent regime changes have made political parties fluid. Political parties, represented in the national legislature, are all centrist or conservative. Instead of ideologies or policy programs, personalities loom large in Korean party politics. In the authoritarian era, the party system was most often characterized by a dominant party system with a tendency toward bipolar competition. The issue of authoritarianism versus democracy gained salience in dividing the ruling and opposing parties, with the ruling party continuing to have the upper hand. In this democratic era, this issue has lost its vigor, but no other major ideological or policy issue has crystallized yet. As a result, the party system is much less stable in this democratic era than previously.

In the 1987 presidential and Thirteenth Assembly elections, four major parties competed: the DJP, RDP, PPD, and NDRP. Kim Young Sam and Kim Dae Jung had jointly led the RDP at the closing stage of the Fifth Republic until the two Kims failed to agree on a single presidential candidate and the latter Kim formed the PPD in late October 1987. Kim Jong Pil, a former prime minister under President Park, rehabilitated the old ruling party, the Democratic Republican Party, which had ruled from 1963 through 1979. Roh Tae Woo of the DJP won the election in 1987.

The contour of party politics underwent a sudden reshaping when President Roh, Kim Young Sam, and Kim Jong Pil made a surprise announcement on 22 January 1990 to merge their three parties into the DLP. This ruling party, a motley

Table 6.1 Korea's National Assembly Election Results, 1988

Party	Percentage of Vote (A)	District Seats (B)	At-Large Seats (C)	Total (B+C)	Percentage of Districts (D)	Total Percentage (E)	District Advantage Ratio (D/A)	Overall Advantage Ratio (E/A)
DJP	34.0	87	38	125	38.8	41.8	1.14	1.23
PPD	19.3	54	16	70	24.1	23.4	1.25	1.21
RDP	23.8	46	13	59	20.5	19.7	0.86	0.83
NDRP	15.6	27	8	35	12.1	11.7	0.78	0.75
Nine Minor Parties	2.5	1	0	1	0.5	0.3		
Independents	4.8	9	0	9	4.0	3.0		
Total	100.0	224	75	299	100.0	99.9		

Source: Election statistics were compiled by the Central Election Management Committee and calculated by the author.

Note: DJP = Democratic Justice Party; PPD = Party for Peace and Democracy; RDP = Reunification Democratic Party; NDRP = New Democratic Republican Party.

Table 6.2 Korea's National Assembly Election Results, 1992

Party	Percentage of Vote (A)	District Seats (B)	At-Large Seats (C)	Total (B+C)	Percentage of Districts (D)	Total Percentage (E)	District Advantage Ratio (D/A)	Overall Advantage Ratio (E/A)
DLP	38.5	116	33	149	48.9	49.8	1.27	1.29
DP	29.2	75	22	97	31.6	32.4	1.08	1.11
UNP	17.4	24	7	31	10.1	10.4	0.58	0.59
NPP	1.8	1	0	1	0.4	0.3	0.22	0.17
Two Minor Parties	1.6	0	0	0	0	0		
Independents	11.5	21	0	21	8.9	7.0		
Total	100.0	237	62	299	99.9	99.9		

Source: Election statistics were compiled by the Central Election Management Committee and calculated by the author.

Note: DLP = Democratic Liberal Party; DP = Democratic Party; UNP = Unification National Party; NPP = New Politics Party.

Table 6.3 Korea's National Assembly Election Results, 1996

Party	Percentage of Vote (A)	District Seats (B)	At-Large Seats (C)	Total (B+C)	Percentage of Districts (D)	Total Percentage (E)	District Advantage Ratio (D/A)	Overall Advantage Ratio (E/A)
NKP	34.8	121	18	139	47.8	46.5	1.37	1.34
NCNP	25.5	66	13	79	26.1	26.4	1.02	1.04
ULD	16.3	41	9	50	16.2	16.7	0.99	1.02
DP	11.3	9	6	15	3.6	5.0	0.32	0.44
Independents	12.0	16	0	16	6.3	5.4		
Total	99.9	253	46	299	100.0	100.0		

Source: Election statistics were compiled by the Central Election Management Committee and calculated by the author.

Note: NKP = New Korean Party; ULD = United Liberal Democrats; NCNP = National Congress for New Politics.

Table 6.4 Korea's National Assembly Election Results, 2000

Party	Percentage of Vote (A)	District Seats (B)	At-Large Seats (C)	Total (B+C)	Percentage of Districts (D)	Total Percentage (E)	District Advantage Ratio (D/A)	Overall Advantage Ratio (E/A)
GNP	39.0	112	21	133	49.3	48.7	1.26	1.25
MDP	35.9	96	19	115	42.3	42.1	1.18	1.17
ULD	9.8	12	5	17	5.3	6.2	0.54	0.63
DPP	3.7	1	1	2	0.4	0.7	0.11	0.19
Four Minor Parties	2.3	1	0	1	0.4	0.4		
Independents	9.4	5	0	5	2.2	1.8		
Total	100.1	227	46	273	99.9	99.9		

Source: Election statistics were compiled by the Central Election Management Committee and calculated by the author.

Note: GNP = Grand National Party; MDP = Millennium Democratic Party; ULD = United Liberal Democrats; DDP = Democratic People's Party.

giant, commanded more than a two-thirds majority in the National Assembly. On the opposition side were two parties: Kim Dae Jung's PPD and the minor DP organized by a small faction of Kim Young Sam's former followers. These two opposition parties merged under the banner of the DP in the fall of 1991. Every member of the Thirteenth Assembly changed his or her party affiliation due to the merger of three parties into a new ruling party and the formation of a unified opposition, and in the wake of nomination for the Fourteenth Assembly election.

In the Fourteenth Assembly election held in March 1992, a three-party system emerged—the DLP, DP, and UNP. The UNP was organized by Chung Ju Yung, the founder of the Hyundai business conglomerate. As mentioned earlier, Kim Young Sam won the December 1993 presidential election. Due to his electoral defeat, Kim Dae Jung withdrew from politics as well as from the top leadership of the DP. Chung Ju Yung and his UNP were politically buried after this presidential election. Legislative members formerly affiliated with the UNP were eventually absorbed by other major parties or became independents. During 1994, a bipolar configuration emerged within the National Assembly—the DLP versus the DP.

During the Fourteenth Assembly, numerous legislative members changed party affiliation yet again. In January 1995, Kim Jong Pil and his followers bolted from the DLP when he was put under heavy pressure to resign from the leadership position. Kim Jong Pil subsequently founded the ULD. Kim Dae Jung, even while allegedly retired from politics, kept a firm grip on the DP, and he greatly influenced the party's strategies for local elections held in June 1995. Kim Dae Jung was highly encouraged by the DP's impressive showing in these local elections. In the summer of 1995, Kim Dae Jung suddenly decided to come back to the political stage and organized the NCNP, drawing his loyal followers away from the DP. In the latter half of the Fourteenth Assembly, the partisan configuration in the legislature could be characterized as a four-party system, including the DLP, NCNP, ULD, and DP. The ruling DLP changed its name to the NKP in late 1995, about four months prior to the general election of the Fifteenth Assembly.

The Fifteenth Assembly election changed a four-party competition format into a three-party one. Of those four parties—the DLP, NCNP, ULD, and DP— the DP obtained only fifteen seats, five short of the requisite for forming its own party group in the legislature. This outcome was a precursor to its ultimate demise about one and a half years later.

In the December 1997 presidential election, three major candidates competed. The ruling NKP nominated Lee Hoi Chang. In the run-up to the election, Lee's popularity dropped because his two sons allegedly dodged military conscription. This induced Rhee In Je, the runner-up in the NKP contest for the party's nomination, to break away from the NKP and declare his candidacy under the banner of the New Party by the People in mid-September. By mid-November, Lee managed to revamp his party by merging the NKP with the minor DP into the GNP (Park 1998/99, 160–64). The main opposition, the NCNP, unsurprisingly nominated Kim Dae Jung as its presidential candidate. This Kim succeeded in persuading Kim Jong Pil of the ULD to withdraw in favor of an electoral coalition, "the DJP alliance," for Kim Dae Jung's triumph.

Kim Dae Jung was elected president in the second year of the Fifteenth Assembly. At that time, President Kim's NCNP could not command a legislative majority, even when combined with its junior coalition partner, the ULD. Over time the ruling coalition has gradually recruited legislative members from the opposition. For instance, the New Party by the People was drawn into the NCNP in the fall of 1998. By co-opting members, the ruling coalition finally managed to achieve a majority in the Fifteenth Assembly. In an effort to boost the ruling party's legislative strength less than three months before the Sixteenth Assembly election, President Kim Dae Jung reinvented the NCNP by recruiting prominent civic activists and other high-visibility individuals and introducing the MDP. A few weeks before the election, Kim Jong Pil's ULD officially severed its coalition ties with the ruling MDP in hopes of remaining a significant political force after the election. Under the leadership of Lee Hoi Chang, the opposition GNP denied several big-name politicians its nomination for the upcoming election. In a dramatic turn against Lee, these politicians seceded from the GNP to form the Democratic People's Party (DPP) in early March 2000.

Rules of the Electoral Game

Thus far in the direct popular election of the country's president, the plurality system has always been employed. Although alternative systems such as the majority-runoff system have been suggested by reform-minded academics, such proposals do not gain popular support. Moreover, most of the debate on the electoral system has centered on the election of the National Assembly.

The electoral system used for the Eleventh and Twelfth Assembly elections during the Fifth Republic was a one-vote mixed system in which a nominal component of proportional representation (PR) is combined with a single nontransferable vote (SNTV) in two-member districts. Two-thirds of 276 seats were elected from 92 two-member districts. The remaining one-third were filled by means of nationwide at-large party lists under a PR system. The PR component was nominal for several reasons. First, a voter did not cast a separate vote for choosing a party's slate of candidates but rather a single ballot to elect the district representative. This vote was counted again as the vote for the chosen candidate's party list. Second, the PR formula was not substantively proportional to provide smaller parties with a reasonable chance of representation in the National Assembly. Two-thirds of 92 at-large seats were allocated to the party winning the greatest number of district seats. The rest were allotted proportionally among the other parties according to the number of district seats each obtained.

The electoral system described above is a typical example of the electoral manipulation that enabled the ruling party to secure a stable legislative majority.

The two-member SNTV component helped elect many candidates of the ruling party as second highest vote-getters in urban districts, traditionally the bulwark of the opposition (Kim and Koh 1980, 72–80). By ensuring the largest bloc of district seats this way, the ruling party additionally garnered two-thirds of the at-large seats. In the Twelfth Assembly election, the ruling DJP won 46 percent of district seats but secured a 54 percent majority in the legislature (Koh 1985). Thus the opposition parties had good reason to criticize this electoral system as it was biased in favor of the ruling party.

In early 1988, parties engaged in a series of negotiations for the Thirteenth Assembly election scheduled for April of that year. Since the presidential election was held a few months earlier, the parties at the time had reasonably accurate information about the distribution of their electoral support. The parties presented different proposals addressing the number of seats per district in an attempt to maximize their seats in the new legislature. The DJP initially offered a one-to-three-member district plan. Under this proposal, two or more legislative members would be elected in each urban district, typically the citadel of the opposition, while one member would be elected in each rural district, the ruling party's stronghold. The RDP, the largest opposition party before the election, was highly divided over the most favorable electoral system. While its leader, Kim Young Sam, was known to be the long-time advocate of the single-member district system, the results of the previous presidential election indicated that this system would not help the party maintain its status as the largest opposition party. The party was likely to receive electoral support that was fairly widespread but intense only in a relatively small number of districts. The party's legislative members from rural districts supported a plan of two-to-three members per district, a slight modification of the existing system. This plan was initially pushed by the RDP. The PPD, the chief rival of the RDP within the opposition, also aimed to become the largest bloc of opposition seats. Kim Dae Jung pressed for single-member districts. Under this winner-take-all arrangement, Kim Dae Jung's party would likely perform better than Kim Young Sam's because of the former's more concentrated regional support. The NDRP, which had meager support in regions other than South Ch'ungch'ong, considered changes to the existing system as fatal. The party favored a two-to-four-member district system, another slight modification of the status quo. This marginal party was largely left out of the negotiation process.

The two largest parties, the DJP and RDP, saw common ground between themselves and reached a tentative agreement on a one-to-three-member district system on 19 February 1988. On 23 February, Kim Young Sam met Kim Dae Jung in an attempt to unify their parties under strong public pressure for such action. Following this, Kim Young Sam announced that his party would not pursue the agreed-upon multimember district system but rather the single-member system demanded by Kim Dae Jung as a condition for the merger. In response, the DJP proposed its own version of single-member district system on 28 February, which was enacted unilaterally by the party on 9 March. The DJP changed its preference concerning the electoral system for several reasons. First, the DJP was optimistic about gaining votes in the upcoming Assembly election due to the spillover effect of Roh Tae Woo's victory in the presidential election. Second, it saw that the opposition's merger talks were not immediately bearing fruit; the ruling party expected the opposition candidates to split their electoral support again in the Thirteenth Assembly election. Third, the merger talks between the two opposition parties finally broke off on 22 March. It was believed that Kim Dae Jung lost interest in the merger as soon as a single-member district system was adopted (see Brady and Mo 1992; Park 1988b, 61–62).

Under the new electoral rules, the size of the National Assembly was expanded to 299 seats from the Thirteenth through Fifteenth Assemblies. The electoral system remained a one-vote mixed system. For the Thirteenth Assembly, 224 seats were elected from single-member plurality districts. An additional 75 at-large seats were elected by means of nationwide party lists under a PR system. If the party with the largest number of district seats did not obtain an absolute majority of district seats, it was ensured 38 of 75 at-large seats. The remaining seats were allocated to the other parties that won 5 district seats or more, in proportion to each party's share of district seats. If the largest party won a majority of district seats, the at-large seats were supposed to be allocated, in proportion to each party's share of the district seats, to all the parties obtaining 5 district seats or more. The seat allocation rules involved the application of the largest remainder method based on simple or Hare quota. Importantly, the PR formula guaranteed that the party with the largest share of district seats would receive at least half of the nationwide at-large seats. This kind of system was not proportional in a substantive sense.

Tables 6.1, 6.2, 6.3, and 6.4 (pp. 122–25) show the extent to which a given party has benefited or suffered from the single-member district component or the mixed system as a whole (the advantage ratios). A ratio greater than one shows how much the party's share of seats exceeded its share of the popular vote. Conversely, a ratio smaller than one shows to what extent the party's seat share fell short of its vote share. In the Thirteenth Assembly election, the ruling DJP received 14 percent more district seats and overall 23 percent more seats than it deserved, relative to its vote share. As mentioned above, the PPD succeeded in emerging as the largest opposition party after this general election. Its district advantage ratio (1.25) indicated that the party, enjoying enormously concentrated support in the Honam region as described later, made the most of the single-member district system. It turned out that the party's leader, Kim Dae Jung, was correct in insisting on the adoption of the single-member district system during the interparty negotiations. Indeed, throughout the history of the National Assembly elections, the Thirteenth Assembly election had been the only election held wholly or partly under the single-member district system in which an opposition party was favored more than the ruling party (Kim and Koh 1980, 77–79; Park 1996). In contrast, the RDP was affected unfavorably by the rule changes. It received the second largest number of popular votes, but it was thrown into third place in the number of seats. This party, along with the NDRP, was shortchanged by the electoral system.

A comparison of the district advantage and overall advantage ratios in table 6.1 (p. 122) suggests that at-large seats allocated under a PR system served poorly as a corrective for the disproportionality, that is, the vote-seat share differences, generated by the plurality component. The DJP's advantage ratio was amplified by the existence of the PR component, whereas the RDP and NDRP suffered a bit from it. In the case of the PPD, the favorable bias of the plurality system was reduced to a small extent. In effect, this Korean version of one-vote mixed system was much closer to the plurality system than to the PR system.

Prior to the Fourteenth Assembly election, some adjustments were made to the electoral system. The number of nationwide at-large seats was reduced from 75 to 62, and that of district seats was increased from 224 to 237. The formula for allocating at-large seats also changed. The guarantee of half the at-large seats for the largest party was abolished. Under the new formula, any party that failed to win a district seat but received 3 percent or more of the popular vote nationally was entitled to one at-large seat. After accommodating the parties that failed to win a district seat, the remaining at-large seats were allocated among the parties with 5 district seats or more, in proportion to each party's share of district seats.

The results of the Fourteenth Assembly election (see table 6.2, p. 123) show that the higher the percentage of the vote a party received, the greater advantage ratio it enjoyed. Both the ruling DLP and the main opposition DP collected more seats than they deserved in terms of their vote shares. Under the plurality component, the UNP and the New Politics Party were discriminated against. This distortion was not rectified by the PR component.

The electoral system for the Fifteenth Assembly was also changed somewhat from the previous one. Of 299 seats, 253 were elected from single-member districts, while the remaining 46 were filled by means of nationwide party lists under a proportional system. In this one-vote mixed system, the plurality component has become more dominant. The nationwide at-large seats are divided as follows: one seat is first allocated to the party that has won no district seat but received 3 to 5 percent of the vote. The remaining seats are assigned in proportion to each party's nationwide vote share among the parties with at least 5 district seats, or at least 5 percent of the vote. Each party's vote share at the national level has replaced each party's number of district seats in allocating at-large seats. The data in table 6.3 (p. 124) suggest that the rule changes did not alter the pattern of seat allocation among parties; larger parties gained a disproportionately greater share of legislative seats. The splinter DP, which had no regional bastion of support, suffered the most: it realized only 5 percent of the total seats with a bit more than 11 percent of the vote. The PR component did not much compensate this party for the unfavorable distribution of district seats under the plurality component.

The Sixteenth Assembly had 273 seats—26 seats fewer than the Fifteenth Assembly—of which 227 were elected from single-member districts and 46 by PR. Other aspects of the electoral system remained largely unchanged. Table 6.4 (p. 125) shows that the pattern of seat allocation among parties is not dissimilar to that in the previous three elections for the National Assembly.

Table 6.5 (p. 132) presents four measures of the deviation of party seats and votes. These measures are Rae index, Loosemore-Hanby or Gini index, Gallagher's least-squares index, and largest-deviation index (Lijphart 1994, 58–77). The greater the value of each measure, the more disproportional the results. Overall, the one-vote mixed system used for the Thirteenth Assembly generated much more disproportional results than did that used for any of the three subsequent general elections.

To bring the Korean electoral outcomes into comparative perspective, relevant measures are provided for the United Kingdom, Japan, and (West) Germany in table 6.5. The United Kingdom is well known for using the single-member plurality or first-past-the-post system, which produces highly disproportional results. Before its electoral reform in 1994, the Japanese House of Representatives was elected by an SNTV system in medium-sized (three-to-five-member) districts. In a strict sense, this system is not a PR system, but it is often described as semiproportional based on its reasonably proportional conversion of votes into seats. Germany elects the lower house by employing its own version of two-vote mixed system in which one half of the total seats are elected from single-member districts and another half are through a PR system. In the German system, a voter has two votes, one for choosing a candidate in the district and another for choosing a party list. Each party's share of the total seats is proportional to its share of the party vote. Looking at the values of all four measures, one can conclude that the one-vote mixed system used in democratizing Korea is similar to the United Kingdom's plurality system in its effect on disproportionality.

Table 6.5 also displays some measures for assessing the effect of the electoral system on the party system. For Korea, the effective number of elective parties averages 4.0, and that of legislative parties, 3.0. A glance at the relevant measures for three other countries reveals that disproportionality tends to reduce the effective number of parties. The Korean case is an exception in this regard. Despite the great deviation between parties' vote and seat shares in the general elections for the National Assembly, the fractionalization of Korea's party system is greater than that in the United Kingdom or Japan. The Korean party system is as fractionalized as the German system. Why is this so in Korea? As examined later, regional cleavage is a salient factor in the party and electoral politics of democra-

Table 6.5 Indices of Disproportionality and Party System Characteristics

	Korean Thirteenth Assembly Election	Korean Fourteenth Assembly Election	Korean Fifteenth Assembly Election	Korean Sixteenth Assembly Election	Mean Thirteenth–Sixteenth Korean Elections	United Kingdom[a]	Japan[b]	Germany[c]
Rae index	6.5	4.9	5.0	4.7	5.3	5.5	1.9	1.0
Loosemore-Hanby/ Gini Index	16.2	12.3	9.9	12.2	12.7	12.9	10.7	3.3
Gallagher's Least-squares Index	14.5	9.8	9.6	8.8	10.7	10.6	5.8	2.2
Largest-deviation Index	19.2	11.3	12.0	9.7	13.1	11.6	6.6	2.1
Effective Number of Elective Parties	4.3	3.8	4.4	3.4	4.0	2.7	3.5	3.2
Effective Number of Legislative Parties	3.5	2.7	3.3	2.4	3.0	2.1	2.9	3.0
Frequency of Legislative Majorities					0.0	0.92	0.65	0
Frequency of Manufactured Majorities					0.0	0.92	0.47	0

Sources: Lijphart 1994, 160–62, for the United Kingdom, Japan, and Germany data. The measures for Korea were calculated by the author.

Note: Only parties with 0.5 percent of vote or seat share were included in computation. For definition of each measure, see Lijphart 1994, 58–77.
a. Thirteen general elections were held from 1945 through 1987.
b. Seventeen general elections were held from 1947 through 1980.
c. Eight general elections were held from 1957 through 1983.

tizing Korea. A multipolar pattern of regional cleavage inhibits the plurality-dominated electoral system from developing a two-party system. A single party legislative majority was not generated in any of the past three general elections. No majority party was artificially generated out of parties that did not win a vote majority. In this regard, the Korean case is similar to the German case. Its strong effect on disproportionality notwithstanding, the Korean electoral system's effect for suppressing party fractionalization is quite limited.

The current electoral system for the National Assembly can be criticized both for its high degree of disproportionality and for its failure to shape a legislative majority or a genuine two-party system. Given that the single-member plurality component helps major parties reap disproportionately bountiful benefits of sweeping legislative seats in their regional strongholds, many reform-minded intellectuals, civic activists, and politicians argue for reducing or changing the single-member plurality system. Some alternatives often suggested include the German two-vote mixed system, Japan's newly introduced two-vote parallel system, or other peculiar types of two-vote mixed system (for example, a parallel combination of SNTV in medium-sized districts with PR). At this time, it is not certain what future changes will be made to the electoral system for the National Assembly.

Campaign Issues and Practices

Campaign issues raised during the December 1987 presidential election centered on the legitimacy of the authoritarian Fifth Republic and also political stability in the nascent democratic era. Kim Young Sam tried to attract voters under a single overarching theme, "the termination of military rule." Kim Dae Jung also challenged the legitimacy of the past regime, but his campaign theme was complex. Kim Dae Jung portrayed himself as the people's choice and made a broad range of campaign promises, including national reconciliation, economic growth with justice, political neutrality of the military, promotion of national reunification, human rights, and an investigation of the military's brutal crackdown on Kwangju citizens. Countering the offensive taken by these two major opposition candidates, Roh Tae Woo of the ruling party emphasized that social disorder, confusion, and instability would be inevitable if the opposition seized power. He attempted to defend the Fifth Republic by reminding voters of good economic conditions during that period. Roh's campaign themes encompassed inauguration of the era of the common man, and the military's neutrality in politics. The opposition's capacity to deliver a sincere message to the voters was limited because of its division and a neck-and-neck competition between the two Kims. In contrast, Roh's emphasis on stability and leadership made voters feel secure (Lee 1990, 72–73, 91).

Campaign issues in the Thirteenth Assembly election held four months later also did not focus on substantive policy problems but on the nature of the political regime and leadership. To be more specific, the ruling party faced opposition charges of widespread election rigging, which opposition politicians believed had taken place in the previous presidential election and could possibly take place in the upcoming Assembly election. Also, opposition parties aggressively alleged that the former President Chun and his relatives were involved in corruption on a massive scale. Late in March 1988, President Chun's younger brother, "little Chun," was arrested on charges of bribery taking, influence peddling, and embezzling. Opposition parties asserted that the government had uncovered only "a tip of the iceberg" of the Chun family wrongdoing (Park 1988b, 63–64).

In the Fourteenth Assembly election and the subsequent presidential election, both held in 1992, the basic nature of the political regime and the incumbent leadership were no longer the dominant issues. Other matters, such as democratic change versus status quo maintenance or checks and balances versus political stability, remained significant. A new kind of issue concerning policy performance and future policy direction emerged to some degree. The UNP and its leader Chung Ju Yung made the sluggish economy a major issue. Using newspaper advertisements, the party set off policy debates on prices, interest rates, housing problems, small- and medium-sized enterprises, and the like. Policy slogans such as "apartments at half price," "twice the amount of currency in issue," and "ten billion dollar trade surplus within a year of taking power" attracted voters' interest, though most slogans seemed unattainable (Park 1993a, 12).

In the December 1992 presidential election, Kim Young Sam made great efforts to distance himself from President Roh and the policy failures of the Roh government. Interestingly enough, President Roh's withdrawal from the DLP three months before the election seemed to help this campaign strategy. Kim campaigned on the themes of "creating a New Korea" and "reform amid stability." He claimed that the country suffered from the "Korean disease" as indicated by rampant corruption, withering work ethics, and weakening authority. He promised to restructure the nation's politics, economy, and social life. The changes proposed by Kim were not radical but moderate. By reform he meant a predictable change to the system from within the establishment.

In this presidential election, two leading themes of Kim Dae Jung's campaign were "interparty shift of power" and "grand national reconciliation." The first one was a virtually fixed-in campaign theme for the main opposition. The second theme was intended to stretch Kim Dae Jung's support base beyond his stronghold, the Honam region.

Chung Ju Yung's presidential campaigning, as his party's in the March general election for the National Assembly, focused mainly on the problems of the flagging economy. He tried to project an image of himself as an "economist-president," capable of fixing all the economic ills by his magic touch. He promised to triple the per capita income level to US$20,000 in five years, bring down the inflation rate from 10 percent at that time to 3 percent, and turn the US$10 billion trade deficit into a US$30 billion surplus within a couple of years. As the time went on, however, Chung's appeal to voters weakened and his promises were increasingly viewed as unrealistic. All three major candidates tried to get the message across that they would give the highest priority to galvanizing the economy once elected. It was made difficult for Chung's party alone to capitalize on voters' economic concern (Park 1993b, 433–36).

In the Fifteenth Assembly election of 1996, the ruling NKP stressed stability and reform in its campaign. The NCNP and ULD advocated further checks on the power of the Kim Young Sam government. The latter opposition party also argued for a constitutional amendment to establish a parliamentary system. The DP called for an end to the era of the "Three Kims"—Kim Young Sam, Kim Dae Jung, and Kim Jong Pil—and for a generational change in leadership. Compared to the Fourteenth Assembly election, these campaign issues reflected neither the language of ordinary voters' feelings nor people's concerns. All parties put an emphasis on their own version of reform, which was an empty catch-phrase insufficient to attract the attention of most voters. Since the economy was not bad, the handling of the economy did not become a significant issue. Given the absence of dominant national issues, many candidates instead emphasized development projects at the electoral district level.

In the December 1997 presidential election, the issue of economic crisis became solely dominant because the crisis culminated at the height of the campaign. The International Monetary Fund (IMF) bailout program signed about two weeks before the election day triggered public anger over the grave mismanagement of the national economy. Of three major candidates, only Kim Dae Jung could completely distance himself from the Kim Young Sam government. Kim Dae Jung and his party were remarkably successful in persuading voters that a shift to the opposition would be the best solution to the crisis as well as the best approach to finding fault with their opponents (Park 1998/99, 169–70).

In the Sixteenth Assembly election held in April 2000, the ruling and opposing parties again debated political stability versus checks and balances. The ruling MDP stressed that its inability to secure a legislative majority would have a negative impact on the economy, the stock market, labor issues, and inter-Korean relations. In contrast, the GNP defined the election as an interim assessment of the Kim Dae Jung administration and asked voters to pass judgment on its abuse of power and policy failures, such as increased national debt, a widening gap between haves and have-nots, and favoritism toward the Honam region in personnel policy. Overall, however, the haggling over candidates' quality overshadowed policy debate. This was mainly due to conspicuous civic activism for ostracizing corrupt and incompetent established politicians from the political arena, and also to the publicized records about candidates' military service, criminal punishment, and tax payment. In particular, the Citizens' Alliance for the 2000 General Elections, an umbrella organization of more than 400 civic groups, blacklisted a total of 113 politicians considered unqualified based on their past involvement in corrupt practices and other egregiously illegal activities. The giant civic group made strenuous efforts to put pressure on the political parties not to nominate these politicians and further to persuade voters from supporting them.

The preceding description suggests that outside extraordinary times Korean elections lack any major debate on substantive policy. Salient campaign issues concern the basic nature of political regime and leadership or overarching abstract objectives of the nation. This is basically due to the characteristics of existing political parties. Parties dominated by personalities do not seek an identity based on ideological or policy orientations. With frequent name changes, the parties have not invested in developing a distinct policy image.

As elections show a lack of policy contest, personalized negative campaigning substitutes. In the December 1987 presidential election, the ruling party distributed "copies of a 14-page booklet that described Kim Young Sam as incapable, ignorant, and unqualified." It portrayed "Kim Dae Jung as excelling in fraud, betrayal, agitation, and radicalism; and Kim Jong Pil as a puppet of the dictatorial regime of the *Yushin* era under Park Chung Hee" (Lee 1990, 72). In the December 1992 presidential election, Kim Young Sam of the ruling party did not have much knowledge about policy issues. His campaign team compensated for this vulnerability by advising him to criticize Kim Dae Jung for forging links with the National Alliance for Democracy and Unification, an allegedly left-wing political group, and for being soft on North Korea. By invoking "red scare" tactics, Kim Young Sam put Kim Dae Jung on the defensive. Faced by Chung Ju Yung's aggressive criticism intended to siphon off progovernment voters, Kim Young Sam responded by blaming Chung for his attempt to "purchase" the presidency with huge sums of money. Voters were constantly reminded of the negative imagery of *chaebol*, a family-owned conglomerate, identified with Chung (Park 1993b, 434–36). The presidential election of 1997 was also characterized by a variety of personalized negative campaigning. Recently, the Internet was abused for negative campaigning. About a month or so before the Sixteenth Assembly election, a ULD nominee for a Seoul district was caught vilifying his opponents in cyberspace. He had accused the ruling MDP candidate in his district of being a communist sympathizer, and he portrayed his GNP rival as a candidate who sold himself for money and power.

Since Korean political parties do not exist independently from the top leader or presidential candidate, there is not much meaning in distinguishing party-centered from candidate-centered campaigning in a presidential election. Presidential campaigning is basically candidate centered. A set of campaign themes is developed not based on the party's policy orientation but according to the candidate's political style and image. The party, labeled as the "official" or "formal" organization, is basically a personalized instrument in the contest for political power. In the election season, the presidential candidate additionally organizes and runs informal vote-gathering machines, such as groups of young people, professionals, or other kinds of followers. Likewise, the district party is essentially a political machine organized on the basis of patron-client ties and for the achievement of a particular politician's electoral success. All the campaign activities done by the district party in the National Assembly elections are indeed candidate centered. Together with the district party, every legislative member elected from the district maintains informal groups serving political purposes, such as various friendship societies and hiking or other recreational groups (Park 1988a, 1051–55). The campaign initiative taken by the central headquarters of the party may be said to be party centered. Yet such party-centered campaigning has an impact only in the region where the top leader enjoys strong support. In brief, in parts of Korea where parties are not institutionalized, election campaigning is largely candidate centered.

A typical method of campaigning in Korean elections, especially presidential ones, used to be the massive outdoor rally. The election law revised just before the December 1997 presidential election, however, has prohibited candidates from holding such campaign rallies. Before this most recent presidential election, political parties competed by gathering as many people as they could at rally sites. Parties mobilized crowds to rallies by every means possible, including illegal and corrupt practices. In general, the ruling party had advantages over the opposition in organizational strength, financial resources, and information for mobilizing voters to the rallies. A close observer of the 1987 presidential election described the massive outdoor rally held by the ruling party on 12 December at the Youido Plaza, Seoul, as follows:

> [The party] mobilized civil servants and company workers dependent on the government. Government offices and state-run companies, normally open on Saturdays, were closed. State-run company employees were reportedly paid [US]$6 to [US]$7 to attend the rally. Bank employees were given about [US]$30 for their dinner after the rally. It was like a holiday for office workers.... Nearly 6,000 buses and 30,000 policemen were mobilized—some of them disguised as civilians. (Lee 1990, 80)

Another typical method of campaigning in Korea used to be door-to-door canvassing. Campaign workers, often paid, made individual contacts with voters. This method could serve as a route for buying votes with gifts or cash. The 1994 comprehensive election law banned door-to-door canvassing.

The 1987 presidential election and the 1988 Thirteenth Assembly election were not clean or fair; campaign violence tainted these elections. For instance, when Kim Dae Jung campaigned in Pusan, Kim Young Sam's bastion of support, hundreds of angry youths badly damaged the hotel where Kim Dae Jung stayed. Kim Young Sam's rally in Kwangju was ruined when Kim Dae Jung supporters burnt campaign placards and brochures, and hurled stones, rocks, eggs, and apples at Kim Young Sam. Young protesters in Kwangju threw a barrage of rocks and tear gas grenades at Roh Tae Woo when he made a speech (Lee 1990, 75–78). Moreover, violence frequently occurred among party workers on all sides, including hostage taking and assaults. Also, allegations of corrupt campaigning practices were rampant in the 1987 presidential election (see Lee 1990, 74). In the Thirteenth Assembly election as well, it was reported that some candidates and their campaigners made attempts to buy votes with gifts, food, spa trips, and cash. On the election eve, opposition party workers discovered that a ruling party candidate had tried to mail more than 3,000 envelopes each containing about US$28 in cash (Park 1988b, 64).

Both the Fourteenth Assembly and presidential elections in 1992 were cleaner and smoother than the two previous elections. Undeniably, there were still complaints of election rigging and corrupt practices. Several months after the Assembly election, a county chief's clandestine campaigning for the ruling party candidate in an election district was revealed. Also, it was discovered that in a military barrack soldiers were pressured to cast their ballots for ruling party candidates. In the presidential election, money and gifts were distributed particularly by Chung Ju Yung's UNP and Kim Young Sam's DLP (Lee 1995, 35). Despite these reports, the Fourteenth Assembly election and the presidential election showed, by and large, signs of gradual progress in electoral fairness.

Importantly, at the urging of President Kim Young Sam, the National Assembly in 1994 passed a comprehensive electoral reform law designed to produce freer, cleaner, and less costly elections. On the one hand, while this law has brought more freedom for electoral campaigning than the previous law and increased public spending for candidates' campaigns, it has imposed numerous new restrictions. For example, the law prohibited candidates or campaign workers from going door to door, because this method of campaigning was used in the past to hand money directly to voters. The law lowered the ceilings on candidates' campaign spending and strengthened regulations against corrupt campaign practices. It required that all parties and candidates use only the funds withdrawn from their bank accounts for campaigning, and that they submit their account books to the Central Election Management Committee. The law also stipulated more severe penalties for violations.

The Fifteenth Assembly election, held in April 1996, was largely fair. The election was still costly, however, with many candidates reportedly exceeding the campaign spending limits. Elections were expensive because there were few volunteer campaign workers or activists. Many supporters expected to be paid for their assistance, and others expected at least to be fed. Some voters also came to expect pay for their votes. Vote-buying schemes did not disappear immediately with the new law (Leuthold 1997, 17–20).

The election law was further revised prior to the December 1997 presidential election, which brought about major changes in campaign styles. Candidates were barred from holding massive outdoor rallies. Instead, the law induced candidates to engage in campaigning through the mass media, especially television. Television debates were to be sponsored by the state. Each candidate could air a limited number of paid campaign commercials. Due to these new provisions, television actually played a prominent role in 1997. The candidates at various times were questioned on the air by knowledgeable interrogators who were not reluctant to press candidates with difficult questions. The television debates, introduced for the first time in the presidential election, included only the three major candidates. In three rounds of debates, the candidates engaged in personal attacks against one another rather than discussing substantive policy issues. Despite these shortcomings, television debates still contributed to reducing costly and illegal campaign practices. Candidates were given the opportunity to appeal directly to millions of voters, and voters became informed about candidates. No evidence suggests, however, that one particular candidate excelled in debate performance and gained the most favorable electoral support (Park 1998/99, 164–65; Steinberg 1998, 60).

Of the three presidential elections held during the past decade, the December 1997 election was the least costly. In this election, illegal campaign practices accountable for high election costs dwindled drastically. Parties spent much less money on mobilizing voters' support than before. No egregious reports were made concerning the massive provision of services, favors, and goodies to voters. Parties poured the bulk of their campaign money into advertising through the mass media within the legal framework. The Sixteenth Assembly election, held in April 2000, did not make a sharp break with the perennial undesirable campaign practices. Parties and candidates encouraged regional rivalries, exchanged tirades, and slandered one another. Also, candidates' heavy reliance on paid campaign workers and vote-gathering machines made the election expensive.

Voters' Electoral Behavior

The average turnout for the four presidential elections in the current democratic era is 83.9 percent. Throughout the recent three Assembly elections, turnout averaged 67.2 percent. Since a presidential election is a wholly national event for choosing the country's most powerful leader, it tends to attract more eligible voters to polling places than does an Assembly election. The 1987 presidential election and the Thirteenth Assembly election recorded the highest turnout, 89.2 and 75.8 percent, respectively. But turnout has declined in subsequent elections, for both the president and the National Assembly. In particular, the Sixteenth Assembly election reported the lowest-ever turnout among the Assembly elections—57.2 percent.

The analysis of election results, either presidential or legislative, aggregated by the administrative unit or electoral district, consistently shows that voter turnout is inversely associated with the rate of urbanization (see Kim and Koh 1980).

This prevailing phenomenon is called *tocho ch'ongo* (low in cities, high in villages). The Fifteenth Assembly election is a good example: The turnout rate in metropolitan districts was 61.2 percent. The comparable figure rose to 64.4 percent in urban districts, to 69.7 percent in semirural districts, and finally to 71.3 percent in rural districts (Park 1996, 7–8).

Also, previous analyses of the individual-level sample survey data have invariably shown that in addition to a voter's residence, age is a significant factor influencing participation (Mo, Brady, and Ro 1991). Up to the age of sixty, age is positively correlated with the likelihood of voting. For instance, in the Fifteenth Assembly election, 44.0 percent of those in their twenties voted, and 62.8 percent of those in their thirties voted. Of those in their forties, 75.3 percent turned out, and 81.3 percent of those in their fifties did so. Voters sixty years of age or older still participated at a high rate, 74.4 percent, but as one would expect at a rate lower than those slightly younger (Park 1996, 10). Socioeconomic variables such as education, income, and occupation reveal no consistent pattern of association with voting participation in Korea.

Why is the turnout rate higher among rural voters than among urban voters? One explanation, formulated by several studies on Korean elections, is that the higher turnout among rural residents results from mobilized voting. Rural people are vulnerable, to a greater extent than are urban people, to pressures for mobilization by individual politicians or government officials. A sizable portion of rural voters do not participate based on independent judgments and motivations but are pressed to conform to the wishes of the heads of their families, villages, clans, or government officials in their districts (Kim and Koh 1980, 66; Kim 1980; Mo, Brady, and Ro 1991). The "decline-of-community" thesis is another explanation, complementary to the theory of mobilized voting, concerning the effect of urbanization on voter turnout in Korea. As the size of the community increases, the capacity of the community to enforce conformity to a prevailing norm tends to decline rapidly. This means that there exist ineffective community social networks for mobilizing voters in urban areas (Kim and Choe 1988). These two theses developed in the authoritarian era still hold significantly true in democratic Korea.

The low turnout rate among young people is probably a universal phenomenon in democracies all over the world. Given their unsettled socioeconomic status, their stakes in elections are not high. Also, their high geographical mobility may make it hard for them to vote in elections. In Korea, younger people have shown more antipathy and cynicism about the existing politics and politicians. Due to their strong sense of alienation from the electoral process, a large portion of eligible voters in their twenties and thirties abstain from casting ballots.

As noted, regional voting is a salient pattern of the Korean electorate's behavior in the democratic era. In presidential elections, a voter supports the candidate who hails from the same region as the one where the voter was born or with which the voter strongly identifies. In the National Assembly elections, voters often support the candidate of the party whose leader is a favorite son of their region.

Regional voting was particularly conspicuous in the 1987 presidential election. Roh Tae Woo dominated in the northern part of the Yongnam region: in his home city of Taegu (with 69.8 percent of the votes in this city) and in North Kyongsang (with 64.9 percent of the votes in this province). Kim Young Sam's strength was centered in the southern part of the Yongnam region: in Pusan (with 54.6 percent of the votes in this city) and in South Kyongsang (with 49.9 percent of the votes in this province). Kim Jong Pil enlisted the strongest support in his native South Ch'ungch'ong (with 44.1 percent of the votes in this province). These three leaders, however, are not on a par with Kim Dae Jung in terms of fervent support in the home region. This Kim received an overwhelming majority of the votes in his native Honam region, including the city of Kwangju (93.3 percent) and North and South Cholla (80.8 percent and 86.2 percent, respectively) (Park 1988b, 68–69; Lee 1990, 81–85). In the 1992 election, Kim Young Sam received 72.6 percent in Pusan and 71.5 percent in South Kyongsang, while Kim Dae Jung obtained 95.1 percent in Kwangju, 88.0 percent in North Cholla, and 91.1 percent in South Cholla (Lee 1995, 51–53). In the 1997 presidential election, Kim Dae Jung was the only major candidate who retained a strong regional support base. Needless to say, he received overwhelming support in the Honam region: 97.3 percent in Kwangju, 92.3 percent in North Cholla, and 94.6 percent in South Cholla (Park 1998/99, 171–74).

Notably, the Honam residents have been especially well known for rallying around their favorite son, Kim Dae Jung. The residents have felt discriminated against under the governments of Park Chung Hee, Chun Doo Hwan, Roh Tae Woo, and Kim Young Sam, all from the Yongnam region. In particular, Kwangju citizens have the experience of being brutally crushed when they resisted General Chun's military takeover in 1980.

Not only the aggregate data but also the individual survey data indicate the prevailing pattern of regional voting. In the survey, the respondents are asked about their native region. The identification of the voter's native region is useful especially in the case of Seoul and Kyonggi residents, because a good majority of them originally came from somewhere else. It goes without saying that the candidate's or the party leader's native region is the most important cue for voters' choices. For example, an analysis of the survey results collected immediately after the 1997 presidential election has shown that about nine out of ten voters from the Honam region nationwide voted for Kim Dae Jung (Park 1998/99, 173).

In the National Assembly election, most candidates for district seats are closely tied to their electoral districts by birth or other connections. In this case, regional voting refers to the regional base of the candidate's party or that of the party's top leader. In the general election for the Thirteenth Assembly, Roh's DJP did not fail to win all the seats in his home city of Taegu, and the party secured 81 percent of the district seats in Noth Kyongsang. The PPD most vividly demonstrated regional strength by capturing thirty-seven of the thirty-eight district seats in the Honam region. Regional voting helped the RDP to sweep Kim Young Sam's home city of Pusan. Finally, owing to "JP (Kim Jong Pil) whirl," the NDRP obtained 94 percent of district seats allocated to South Ch'ungch'ong (Park 1988b, 69). Similarly, in the Fourteenth Assembly election, the regional factor served as the dominant cue for voters' choices (Park 1993a, 8–10; Lee 1994, 767; Kang 1998, 99–103). The DLP of Roh Tae Woo, Kim Young Sam, and Kim Jong Pil won at least 50 percent of the district seats in the Yongnam region and South Ch'ungch'ong. Kim Dae Jung's DP secured all but two district seats in the Honam region. This pattern of electoral support continued to exist in the Fifteenth Assembly election. The NKP of President Kim Young Sam, the NCNP of Kim Dae Jung, and the ULD of Kim Jong Pil all garnered an overwhelming share of the district seats in their own regional strongholds.

Candidate image voting, which in Korea refers to the pattern of voters' candidate choices based on the affection or imagery of trustworthiness, attributed by them to a candidate, is also significant. In Korea's personalistic political culture, the candidate-voter linkage is consolidated considerably by *jong* (human feelings). In the campaign, a successful candidate does not neglect to convey warm personal tones to his potential supporters.

Kim Dae Jung's campaigning strategy illustrates the importance of candidate image. Despite his impressive assets as a charismatic leader, Kim acquired a reputation for being radical, left leaning, unreliable, and even dangerous. This was largely due to the propaganda efforts made by the past authoritarian governments. Given that Korean voters are favorably disposed toward a leader with a moderate and warm image, Kim's perceived reputation was detrimental to his electoral fortunes in his 1971 and 1987 presidential bids. In the 1992 presidential campaign, Kim and his party resorted to the so-called "New DJ Plan," to bury his old image as a radical politician. The plan advised Kim to smile and use humor frequently. This strategy was aimed at gaining support especially among conservative middle-class voters (Lee 1995, 54–5). The strategy, however, was not effective enough for him to win the election. Kim still maintained an alliance with progressive dissident groups, while appealing to moderate middle-class voters. It was difficult for Kim to tread this fine line throughout the campaign period. More importantly, this Kim trailed behind the ruling party's Kim Young Sam in voters' positive perceptions about candidate attractiveness and reliability. The emotional aspect of candidate image was indeed a crucial factor for Kim Young Sam's victory (Park 1993b, 435, 447–49, 453). In the 1997 presidential election, Kim Dae Jung's continuing strategy for moderating his old image worked to his electoral success. In particular, the electoral coalition with Kim Jong Pil helped Kim Dae Jung expand electoral support in the Ch'ungch'ong region and among conservative middle-class voters as well (Park 1998/99, 167–69).

Partisan voting in Korea is not exactly the same as that found in Western democracies. As depicted earlier, Korean political parties are ever shifting because of frequent splits and mergers. The notion of party identification, a relatively long-term psychological attachment to a specific political party, has no direct applicability. Also, political parties are determined by personalities, not by ideological or policy lines. Thus, a voter's party preference solicited by a survey question is in fact his or her preference toward the party's focal leader. Still, one cannot say that the party factor does not play an important role in voters' choices. Most Korean voters have *yoyasonghyang*, a sociopsychological tendency that a voter is disposed to maintain a progovernment or proopposition stance. This partisan disposition is not necessarily tied to a specific party or prominent political leader. In the context where the presidential power was never transferred to the opposition before 1997, the partisan tendency persisted over a relatively long span of time.

An analysis of voters' candidate choices in the 1992 presidential election showed that progovernment or proopposition predilection significantly served as an anchorage for voting decision among the Korean electorate (Park 1993b, 449, 452). Also, in the 1997 presidential election, the voter's partisan disposition was relevant to his or her calculus of voting choice. On the one hand, the voter who had a stronger partisanship in favor of the government was more likely to vote for Lee Hoi Chang. On the other hand, the voter who leaned more toward the opposition was more supportive of Kim Dae Jung (Park 1998/99, 176–77). It is not clear, however, whether this partisan tendency will remain a significant factor now that the national leadership has been taken over by the opposition.

It is conventional wisdom that issue voting is not remarkable among the Korean voters. Until the Fourteenth Assembly election, the issues meant for the most part regime or leadership characteristics: typically, democratization versus status quo maintenance. The lack of issue variety was definitely a reason for the overall neglect of issues, particularly substantive policy issues, in the previous studies on Korean elections. As the nature of the times changes, however, the significance of the election as a forum for the voters to express their support for or opposition to the regime itself has abated. In the Fourteenth Assembly election, the UNP could ride a strong wave by making the economy a major issue. Many voters concerned about the gloomy prospects for the national economy responded to and chose the party (Park 1993b; Kang 1998). This suggested that an election could have a meaning as a referendum on the government's policy performance.

Evidence for both retrospective and prospective economic voting could be found in the 1997 election, which was held in the wake of economic crisis and the International Monetary Fund bailout. In a postelection survey conducted by the Institute for Korean Election Studies, a majority of the respondents mentioned Lee Hoi Chang's GNP as the party most responsible for messing up the economy. About six out of ten voters who responded in this way supported Kim Dae Jung at the polling booth. Moreover, well over half of the respondents said that Kim

Dae Jung was most competent for resolving the nation's economic crisis. Around 70 percent of those who said so registered their support for Kim (Park 1997/98, 176–78). The effect of these retrospective and prospective economic variables on the vote remained intact even after controlling the region factor in a multivariate context of analysis (Lee 1998).

Concluding Remarks: An Assessment

An overview of Korean elections in the past decade or so suggests that Korean democracy has made significant progress. In the past authoritarian regime, the indirect election of the president legitimized the arbitrary rule by a strong leader. The general elections for the National Assembly also provided the chief executive with an effective means for buttressing his dictatorial rule most of the time. With the democratic transition, however, the election of the president by the popular vote has been reintroduced. Three consecutive presidential elections, every five years since 1987, have now legitimated the method of allocating ultimate political power in Korea. In the 1997 presidential election, Korea opened a new chapter in democratic development by achieving the transfer of executive power between competing political parties. Moreover, the National Assembly elections in this democratic era no longer guarantee a legislative majority for the president's party. The electoral outcome can produce a healthy condition to counterbalance presidential power. As shown by the results of the Fourteenth Assembly election and the 1997 presidential election, voters are now using elections for passing judgment on the policy performance by the incumbent government and leadership. Voters are unafraid to express their wishes regarding prospective political leadership by electoral choice. In brief, Korean elections now serve as a significant arena for political competition, and also as a meaningful avenue for mass participation.

Elections have become increasingly clean and fair. Campaign violence and corrupt campaign practices, including vote-buying attempts, which were widespread at the beginning of the democratic era, have now disappeared or diminished over the decade. In this regard, the comprehensive election law of 1994 was significant. The latest presidential election of 1997 indeed proved fair and just. With television debates introduced, this election witnessed a sea change in campaigning style. Labor-intensive campaigning, such as door-to-door canvassing and the mobilization of voters to mass rallies, are being replaced by candidates' communication with voters through the mass media, especially television. The new style of campaigning is capital-intensive, but to a large extent it is funded by public monies. On the part of candidates and parties, they spend less on illegal practices.

Despite these appreciable developments, Korean elections as a democratic procedure still leave much to be desired. The urban-rural cleavage or the cleavage of democracy versus authoritarianism has weakened in the democratic era. Instead, a high level of regional cleavage, strongly manifested in the 1987 presidential election, has persisted on the electoral landscape. Although the opposition took over the national leadership in the 1997 presidential election, this has not fundamentally changed electoral politics dominated by regional cleavage.

The overwhelming cleavage of regionalism stifles policy-based electoral competition while encouraging appeal to emotion and sentiment. Given the fact that political parties differ little in ideologies or key policy directions, the variety of election issues and the range of voters' choices are limited.

The electoral system for the National Assembly has yet to provide fairness of political representation. Due to its discrepancies between vote and seat shares, the system discriminates against newly emerging and alternative political forces with fresh ideas. Furthermore, this system has failed to shape a legislative majority party or a stable system with a low degree of fractionalization.

The lack of policy contest in elections has led to personalized negative campaigns. Elections are characterized by a variety of undesirable practices, such as personal attack, mudslinging, groundless accusation, black propaganda, the arousing of regional antipathy, and the like. Despite the reduction in illegal campaign spending, a concern about high-cost and clandestine voter mobilization remains.

These drawbacks and shortcomings of Korean elections indicate the need for further change. Reform toward a cleaner and fairer election remains a buzzword in Korean politics. The consolidation of Korean democracy hinges much on further steady progress in electoral reform.

REFERENCES

Brady, David, and Jongryn Mo. 1992. "Electoral Systems and Institutional Choice: A Case Study of the 1988 Korean Elections." *Comparative Political Studies* 24:405–29.
Kang, Won-Tak. 1998. "The Rise of a Third Party in South Korea: The Unification National Party in the 1992 National Assembly Election." *Electoral Studies* 17:95–110.
Kim, Chong Lim. 1980. "Political Participation and Mobilized Voting." In *Political Participation in Korea: Democracy, Mobilization, and Stability*, edited by C.L. Kim. Santa Barbara, Calif.: ABC-Clio Books.
Kim, Hong Nack. 1989. "The 1988 Parliamentary Elections in South Korea." *Asian Survey* 29:481–95.
Kim, Hong Nack, and Sunki Choe. 1988. "Urbanization and Changing Voting Patterns in South Korean Parliamentary Elections." In *Political Change in South Korea*, edited by Ilpyong J. Kim and Young Whan Kihl. New York: Paragon House.
Kim, Jae-On, and B.C. Koh. 1980. "The Dynamics of Electoral Politics." In *Political Participation in Korea*, edited by C.L. Kim. Santa Barbara, Calif.: ABC-Clio Books.
Koh, B.C. 1985. "The 1985 Parliamentary Election in South Korea." *Asian Survey* 25:883–97.
Lee, Hyun-woo. 1998. "Economic Voting in Korea" [in Korean]. In *Korean Elections* II, edited by Nam Young Lee. Seoul, Korea: Purungil.
Lee, Kap-Yun. 1994. "Democratization, Party Failure, and the Emergence of the Unification National Party." *Korea and World Affairs* 18:749–71.
Lee, Man-woo. 1990. *The Odyssey of Korean Democracy: Korean Politics, 1987–1990*. New York: Praeger.
———. 1995. "South Korea's Politics of Succession and the December 1992 Presidential Elections." In *Politics and Policy in the New Korean State: From Roh Tae-woo to Kim Young-sam*, edited by James Cotton. New York: St. Martin's Press.
Leuthold, David A. 1997. "Further Steps toward Democracy: The 1996 National Assembly Elections." *Korea Observer* 28:1–24.

Lijphart, Arend. 1994. *Electoral Systems and Party Systems: A Study of Twenty-seven Democracies, 1945–1990.* New York: Oxford University Press.

Mo, Jongryn, David Brady, and Jaehun Ro. 1991. "Urbanization and Voter Turnout in Korea: An Update." *Political Behavior* 13:21–31.

Park, Chan Wook. 1988a. "Legislators and Their Constituents in South Korea: The Patterns of District Representation." *Asian Survey* 28:1049–65.

———. 1988b. "The 1988 National Assembly Election in South Korea: The Ruling Party's Loss of Legislative Majority." *Journal of Northeast Asian Studies* 7:59–76.

———. 1993a. "The Fourteenth National Assembly Election in Korea: A Test for the Ruling Democratic Liberal Party." *Korea Journal* 33:5–16.

———. 1993b. "Korean Voters' Candidate Choice in the 1992 Presidential Election: A Survey Data Analysis." *Korea and World Affairs* 17:432–58.

———. 1996. "An Aggregate Data Analysis of the Fifteenth National Assembly Election" [in Korean]. *Korea and International Politics* 12:1–26.

———. 1998/99. "The Korean Presidential Election in December 1997: Kim Dae-jung's Victory as a Momentum for Democratic Consolidation." *Han'gukchongch'iyon'gu* [*Journal of Korean Political Studies*] 8/9:159–82.

Steinberg, David I. 1998. "Korea: Triumph Amid Turmoil." *Journal of Democracy* 9:76–90.

CHAPTER 7

Elections as Complicated and Important Events in the Philippines

by Steven Rood

ELECTIONS IN THE PHILIPPINES are festive occasions. During the campaign, politicians sing and dance, bring singers and dancers to rallies and meetings, bandy slogans, and create colorful gimmicks. Leaflets are scattered about, posters pasted onto any vertical surface, strings of bunting put up one day by one candidate only to be replaced the next day by those of a rival candidate. Election day itself is a holiday, turnout is high, and residents often gather at the polling station in the evening to watch the precinct workers (public school teachers deputized to the task) perform the long process of manually tallying all the handwritten names on the ballots.

Elections are not, however, to be taken lightly. Outcomes are uncertain, and power is transferred by means of these exercises. The most striking example of this occurred in 1986, when Ferdinand Marcos (in power since 1965) sought to legitimize his continued tenure in office by means of a snap election—and set in motion events that led to his ouster by means of the People Power revolution in front of the military camps along Epifanio Delos Santos Avenue (EDSA). Elections since that time have been less traumatic but no less important for determining the course of governance.

The Philippines is ethnically and geographically very complex. Of the 7,107 islands in the Philippines, hundreds are occupied by dozens of different ethnic groups. The nation is composed of 78 provinces, which contain 1,608 municipalities and cities, which in turn encompass some 42,000 barangays (villages). Each of these units of government has an elected executive (governor, mayor, or barangay captain) and a legislative council (provincial council, city council, or barangay council), creating literally hundreds of thousands of local elective offices to be voted upon by 34 million voters.

The national government also has executive and legislative branches—but there are two houses of Congress. Each province[1] has one or more congressional

Table 7.1 Sequence of Philippine Elections from 1992 to 1998

Year	Officials Elected
1992	President Fidel Ramos, Vice President Joseph Estrada, 24 senators (half for six years, half for three), 200 representatives, governors and councils for more than 70 provinces, mayors and councils for more than 1,500 cities and municipalities
1993	Youth Council elections at the Barangay Level (for those fifteen to twenty-one years old)
1994	Barangay officials (captains and councils) in more than 42,000 barangays
1995	12 senators (replacing those with three-year terms—now for six-year terms), 200 representatives, and local officials for provinces, cities, and municipalities
1996	Barangay Youth Council elections again (after a three-year term)
1997	Barangay officials elected again (after a three-year term)
1998	President Joseph Estrada, Vice President Gloria Macapagal-Arroyo, 12 senators, 221 representatives (some by a new nationwide proportional representation under a party list system), and all the governors and Provincial Council members, and mayors and City and Municipal Council members

districts from which a single representative is elected for a three-year term to the lower house (the House of Representatives), while 24 senators are elected at large (that is, nationwide)—with half being elected every three years to six-year terms. The president and vice president are elected nationwide for six-year terms.

Thus, an obvious characteristic of these important fiestas is that there are many of them. We can consider 1992 as the first "normal" election in recent times. Corazon Aquino was stepping down after her constitutionally allowed one term as president, and the officials elected in 1992 were to serve the normal length of office (three or six years, depending on the position) rather than the extended periods that had been allowed in interests of stability during the period after the 1986 revolution. Table 7.1 summarizes the complex rhythm of election exercises.

Elections for the major national and local offices involve roughly 100,000 candidates, while those for youth council and barangay elections involve almost one million candidates.

To be fair, this frenetic pace has somewhat diminished because the youth councillors and barangay officials have had their terms extended to five years; a more relaxed pace of only four elections over a six-year period instead of annual elections has been adopted.

This is truly a welter of elections for different levels of government, with electorates ranging from nationwide (34 million voters for president, vice president, and senators) through the 200 congressional districts with voters ranging from the tens to hundreds of thousands, to the municipalities and cities, down to the barangays with electorates ranging from several hundred to several thousand.

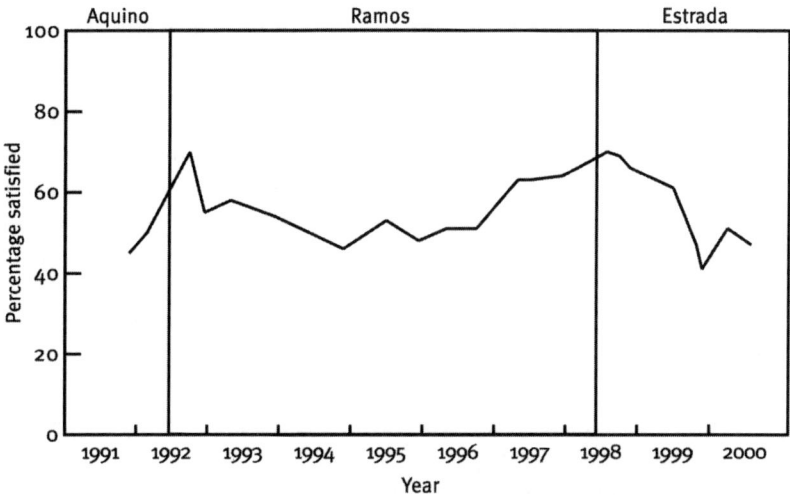

Figure 7.1 Filipinos' Satisfaction wih the Way Democracy Works, 1991–2000

Source: SWS, various years.

Not too surprisingly, it is hard to generalize about "elections." To take a particular example, the barangay youth council elections are sometimes rehearsals for adult politics, often by scions of political families. In other instances, they have nothing to do with adult politics but are limited to concerned youth from the neighborhood—all of whom know one another.

One generalization that is easy to make is that Filipinos believe elections are important. For instance, survey data from a nationwide sample of adults demonstrate that citizens think elections help make government responsive. Asked just before the May 1995 elections to react to the statement "Elections are a good way of making the government pay attention to what the people think," 72 percent agreed and only 9 percent disagreed (Social Weather Stations [SWS], March 1995 survey).[2]

Another generalization that invites a concentration on national elections is that the national elections are the ones that are connected to people's sense of democracy. Since 1991, Social Weather Stations, an independent academic research group, has been asking whether people are satisfied with the way democracy works in the Philippines. Figure 7.1 shows the pattern of responses over time.

The figure shows that the holding of synchronized national and local (provincial, city, and municipal) elections in 1992 and 1998 was associated with a peak in satisfaction with democracy. A smaller peak was also evident in 1995, but since the presidency was not at stake, citizens were less impressed with the functioning of democracy. The chief executive occupies center stage in political thinking.

This citizen focus on the presidential election is one reason why this chapter uses the presidency as the focus for much of its analysis. (Another is the presidential dominance of local political affiliations, as discussed later in this chapter.)

Election day is a nonworking holiday, which accounts in part for the high turnout (86 percent in the 1998 elections, according to the Commission on Elections) despite the fact that voting is not compulsory. The day's media coverage begins even before the polls open. The coverage can be excruciatingly dull, however, as nothing really happens for some days afterwards. The prolonged counting of ballots is the culprit. At the precinct level, the handwritten ballots are counted and tallied, and the tallies are forwarded to the municipal or city hall—typically by the morning of the day following the election. Repeated steps in the process of accumulating totals by hand—barangay totals in the municipality, municipal totals in the province—can take an exceedingly long time, particularly when poor transportation over some distances is involved.

In 1998, the Commission on Election proclaimed the official results of the presidential election on 27 May, sixteen days after election day. The twelve winning senators were indeed proclaimed on 29 May, long before the July opening of Congress. This eighteen-day pace was a considerable improvement on earlier elections, when there was doubt whether the tallying would allow all elected senators to take their seats at the beginning of the congressional session. Repeated calls for changes in electoral procedures to shorten the process—including those for computerization of elections—have been unavailing. As the twentieth century gives way to the new millennium, the Philippines remains mired in low-technology handwritten electoral processes.

Electoral History

Beginning in 1907, less than a decade after the conquest of the Philippines by the United States, regular elections for an Assembly were introduced. During the colonial period, the franchise was restricted, but by the commonwealth period (1935–46), the franchise was extended to all literate adults—male and female.

After full independence in 1946, even the literacy requirement was dropped, but many local officials (mayors and governors) were still appointive. The number of elections kept increasing, with the institution of elective local governments and, finally, barangay elections throughout the country. In short, the current vast number of elections has been in place for more than thirty years (albeit in a distorted fashion during the 1972–86 period of authoritarian rule by Ferdinand Marcos).

Election results were typically controversial—with accusations of the use of "guns, goons, and gold," refusals to concede defeat, and long legal wrangles before the Commission on Elections and the courts. Still, elections were the mechanisms for determining the alternation of officials in power.

That this alternation was frequent is witnessed by the fact that Ferdinand Marcos—elected in 1965 and reelected in 1969—was the first Philippine president to win reelection. During his second term, there was a growing consensus that the political system needed fixing, so a constitutional convention was elected and convened. Before its work was finished, Marcos declared martial law in September 1972.

The period between September 1972 and Marcos's ouster in February 1986 can be seen, in retrospect, as an aberration. Elections were not the means of determining who would wield ultimate power. If "Hypocrisy is the homage vice plays to virtue," however, elections were Marcos's homage to democracy. Several "elections" were held in that time period, as all agreed that the only real route to legitimation in the Philippines was through voting. While the ultimate outcome of these elections was never in doubt, at the local level, factions within the ruling party, or purely local groupings, had some chance to reach the margins of power. When asked to comment on the surprisingly strong showing of opposition candidates in parliamentary elections in 1984, Marcos replied that his lieutenants had taken too seriously his orders for a fair election.

In February 1986 Marcos submitted himself to a special "snap" presidential election in the hope of convincing the world that he still retained popular support. As might be imagined given the authoritarian nature of the regime, Marcos dominated the media and manipulated the rules. The surprising strength of the opposition, united behind Corazon C. Aquino (widow of Marcos's assassinated rival, Benigno "Ninoy" Aquino), forced the ruling party to resort to overt fraud—much of it finally televised in the tumultuous days of the election. Computer operators walked out of the election count in full view of the cameras, rather than enter fraudulent data. The actual results remain controversial, given the level of manipulation. In fact, various academic analyses tried to deconstruct the fraudulent count to arrive at an honest tally, and the verdict was that Aquino won with approximately 52 to 53 percent of the vote (Rood 1988).

Marcos, of course, did not concede, but he was ousted only weeks later by the People Power EDSA revolution, fueled in large part by outrage over election fraud. After a short interregnum, elections were held for Congress (May 1987) and local posts (January 1988)—to be followed by the current rhythm of elections as presented in table 7.1 (p. 148).

Electoral System

The electoral system has several unusual features. As noted above, there is a large number of elected officials. First, there are local government officials. Each of more than 42,000 barangays has a barangay captain and councillors; each of more than 1,600 cities and municipalities has a mayor and councillors, each of 78 provinces has a governor and councillors.

Then there is the national legislature, with more than 200 members of the House of Representatives elected in single-member plurality districts (each province is a district, or is divided into several districts if population warrants). The

Senate has 24 members, elected at large for six-year terms by the entire nation, with 12 senators elected every three years. In the Senate elections, the top 12 candidates win, with the top-ranking candidate getting some 50 to 60 percent of the total vote, while the twelfth candidate generally receives roughly 25 percent.

The president and vice president are elected every six years (e.g., 1992, 1998, 2004). But they can come from different parties—and, in fact, that is the typical situation. In both 1992 and 1998, the winning vice president was from a different party than the winning president—but in both instances the president gave substantive responsibility to the vice president (a special anticrime task force for then–Vice President Estrada, and the Department of Social Work and Development for Vice President Macapagal-Arroyo).

Another unusual feature is that the voter is required to write in the name of the candidate he or she selects for each post. This means that the voter must generally write more than twenty-four names to vote for all the myriad of offices up for election in a presidential year. Depending on the source, this practice is "virtually unknown elsewhere in the world" (Montilla 1999, 135), or the Philippines is "one of two countries in the world that require voters to write the name[s] of the candidates on the ballot"(NAMFREL 1999, 5). Truly, this is a unique feature of Philippine elections. Since 1951, votes for parties have not been allowed (with the recent exception of party list elections to the House of Representatives, discussed below), so a premium is placed on name recognition and recall.

The exception noted above with regard to writing the name of parties on ballots has to do with the 20 percent of seats in the House of Representatives reserved by the 1987 Constitution for party list representatives. The avowed purpose of this new provision is to encourage more policy-oriented elections, rather than the personality-focused mechanisms for most offices. This provision went into full effect only in 1998, when it was intended that 50 seats (20 percent of 250) be allocated by the party list vote.

Each voter thus had one more vote: for a party. Turnout for this part of the ballot—that is, the proportion of voters who bothered to fill in this blank—was only 30 percent. And the law was badly drafted (each party was to get one seat for every 2 percent of the party-list vote, with no provisions for redistributing the votes of parties who did not make the cutoff) so that only 21 representatives were actually seated. Even this limited success has injected a little more ideology into governmental processes. Party list representatives, who are more concerned with issues than are regular representatives elected by district, are often quoted in the press. Further, a party list representative from a women's party, *Abanse Pinay*, is chair of the House committee dealing with family law.

The entire election process is supervised by an independent constitutional commission, the Commission on Elections (COMELEC). The COMELEC had fallen into disrepute during the Marcos years, for the obvious reason that they were not able to ensure free and fair elections. During the Aquino administration

(1986 to 1992), the COMELEC began to regain its credibility and was ranked with the Senate and Supreme Court in public esteem. COMELEC was then tainted by a scandal during the 1995 election known as "*Dagdag-Bawas*" (add-subtract), where it was widely believed—by 64 percent of respondents in the June 1996 SWS survey—that some candidates for the Senate benefited from votes added while others were disadvantaged by votes subtracted. After the scandal faded (the alleged chief victim was, in fact, elected to the Senate in the 1998 elections), the COMELEC once again regained its credibility.

The administrative capacity of the COMELEC, however, is often in doubt. As noted, voting is still conducted by paper ballots and counting is still done by hand. Computerization of elections has been touted since the early 1990s, and even pilot-tested in one region of the country, but the funds and capacity for this shift are nowhere in sight. In fact, despite the computerization in the pilot region, 1998 ballots from that region were once again counted by hand (NAMFREL 1999).

Party System

Any discussion of the party system in the Philippines is reminiscent of a political cartoon: A protester is carrying a sign, "Down with the system"—to which a bewildered bystander responds incredulously, "This is a system?" The chaos among parties is visible each election on the printed sample ballots candidates distribute and many voters take into the polling booth to help with name recall while writing on the ballot. These sample ballots contain virtually all permutations of candidates, because individual candidates would like to link their names with others that are perceived to be popular—even if those other candidates are from other parties.

Before the imposition of martial law in 1972, two main parties existed, the Liberals and the Nacionalistas. Control of government shifted between these two virtually identical groupings. More to the point, politicians switched readily from one side to the other. Ferdinand Marcos, unable to obtain the Liberal Party nomination for president in 1965 (because incumbent President Macapagal, a Liberal, was seeking reelection), switched to the Nacionalista Party and won the election. At lower levels of government, the hierarchy switching ("turncoatism") was also prevalent, usually to whichever party had just won the presidency. For instance, Benigno "Ninoy" Aquino, while governor of Tarlac, switched (along with the mayors of municipalities in the province) from the Nacionalistas (the party under which he had joined politics) to the Liberals in response to the victory of Diosdado Macapagal in 1961. When Ferdinand Marcos won in 1965, Aquino declined to switch back to the Nacionalista Party—but most of the mayors of Tarlac did switch (Joaquin 1983, chap. 7).

While remnants of the Liberal and Nacionalista Parties survived the fourteen years of martial law, they have not come close to winning national elections

Table 7.2 Low Public Trust in Philippine Political Parties

Institution	Percentage Reporting "Much Trust"
Courts	27
Congress	26
Commission on Elections	24
Government Offices	23
Political Parties	12

Source: SWS, September 1996 survey.

since 1986. For the most part, political parties in the Philippines are shifting kaleidoscopes of office seekers, with many name changes, coalition building and breaking, and legalistic maneuvering. While important for politicians as markers of who are (at least temporarily) on the same team, they are of virtually no use in either organizing governmental action or influencing votes.

Voter responses to this dismal reality are quite realistic. Asked in a September 1996 survey to characterize their trust in various political institutions, respondents ranked political parties low in terms of having "much trust" (see table 7.2). Not surprisingly, given this low level of trust, few citizens feel close to parties. Only 15 percent identify with any party (Laylo and Dayag-Laylo 1999).

At the elite level, even the politicians who so readily adopt party labels don't really take them seriously. As noted by Errol Leones and Miel Moraleda, "Party structures, as elaborate as they seem, do not have permanent local headquarters and local full time staff" (1998, 310). Similarly, Carl Lande summarizes these entities as "groupings that call themselves parties, but . . . have little organizational or doctrinal cohesion" (1996, 139).

The upshot is that elections might be fought by politicians wearing party labels, but party affiliation has no effect on citizens' votes, nor on the organization of government. In the past two presidential elections, most winning congressional candidates were in fact from parties other than those headed by the winning presidential candidate. Once they realized who had won the election, the politicians promptly switched parties.

"When Ramos won and became president [in 1992], from the original ragtag 39 LAKAS [Ramos's party] members, the party roster swelled to 120" (Leones and Moraleda 1998, 314). The same thing happened in 1998, as shown in table 7.3—candidates grouped under the banner of former Speaker Jose de Venecia won a majority of the seats in the House of Representatives. By the time Congress opened its session, however, the grouping associated with Joseph Estrada, the victorious presidential candidate, had a comfortable majority.

Table 7.3 Shifting Party Affiliations after the 1998 Elections in the House of Representatives of the Philippines

Two Main Party Groupings	May 1998 Election Results	July 1998 Congress Organized
LAKAS-NUCD-UMDP etc. (Former Speaker Jose de Venecia)	110	39
LAMMP (President Joseph Estrada)	56	142

Source: Philippine House of Representatives.

It is worth noting in this regard that President Estrada's "party" had, eighteen months after the May 1998 elections, already changed its name again (the acronym is now LAMP). Yet in classic disdain for party structure, there is no party organization whatsoever—no constitution, no by-laws, no registration with the COMELEC. This is a classic illustration of the irrelevance of parties to the personalistic game that is Philippine electoral politics.

CAMPAIGN STRATEGIES

Given the weaknesses just described in the party system, there seems to be a strong disconnectedness between political reality and politician activity. Politicians typically begin by wondering who will win "the party's nomination." Disappointed candidates are then tempted to "change parties," but with a contemporary difference. In pre–martial law politics (that is, before 1972), in the effective two party trade-off between the Liberals and the Nacionalistas, the method was "party switching." So Marcos, failing to obtain the Liberal Party nomination in 1965 in the face of incumbent President Macapagal, switched to the Nacionalista Party to run his victorious campaign.

Nowadays, the disappointed candidate is likely merely to create a new party. Thus, we have a bewildering variety of party names, and five or six serious candidates on the ballot—all with their own party affiliations. In 1998, aside from the two groupings shown in table 7.3, there were such innovations as REPORMA and PROMDI, parties whose names or acronyms attempted to encapsulate the image of their presidential candidate. It does not matter that the party in question, at this point any party with a chance to win the election, has been in existence less than six years, and often less than six months. They are treated in political discussions as if they were real entities that would have profound consequences, but these are, in fact, temporary coalitions to win elections.

This bizarre behavior on the part of politicians rests on an outmoded theory of voter behavior known as the patron-client model of politics. This theory is discussed in greater detail below, but for now it is important to know that many politicians are convinced that local leaders can deliver votes, and the channel to those local leaders is through party affiliation. Thus, efforts are made to make temporary alliances for the duration of the election campaign, alliances marked by the use of a common name for candidates' "parties," on the theory that these alliances build up votes.

Sooner or later brute reality should set in, as people contemplate the 1992 and 1998 elections. In both these elections, a losing candidate (former Speakers of the House of Representatives Ramon Mitra in 1992 and Jose de Venecia in 1998) shared party affiliation with the majority of winning congressional (that is, local district) candidates but lost the election (to Fidel Ramos and Joseph Estrada, respectively). And as shown in table 7.3, not only did these winning candidates not contribute to a winning coalition, but shortly after the election they flocked to join the presidential winner's political grouping.

The individualism of electoral politics is reflected in all the campaign paraphernalia that abounds in election season. Political advertising in broadcast or print media is not allowed during the campaign, although it is indulged in during the months running up to the formal campaign season—unfortunately for the cost-effectiveness of the advertising, it occurs before voters are paying much attention. As a result, posters gradually cover every vertical space in an urban area and are also very prevalent in rural areas. Leaflets run the gamut of biographies of candidates, statements of platforms, or just lists of names in the form of the ballot—in order to aid the memory of voters tasked with writing so many names.

News coverage of elections is, in fact, extensive—which to some extent makes up for the lack of campaign advertisements. Television news is centralized in Manila, but radio stations proliferate throughout the archipelago. Thus, a national campaign must balance news events that are covered by the national media with those in provincial localities far from the capital.

Because national elections are, in the end, media campaigns, there is an obvious incentive to maximize media coverage. Not surprisingly, a parallel system springs up as the functional equivalent of campaign advertising—purchased news coverage. It has recently emerged that a common form of corruption in the media is accepting money from candidates in order to provide guaranteed coverage in the newsroom. This has become institutionalized, going beyond bribing individual reporters to file stories. For instance, in 1998, a radio station with nationwide coverage offered four campaign packages for presidential candidates to ensure adequate news coverage. Thus, under-the-table money for advertising in the guise of news coverage once again flows to the media (Florentino-Hofileña 1998).

Voters' Electoral Behavior

The traditional explanation of voters' behavior is what is known as "patron-client" relations. In a society with marked inequality and few formal mechanisms for social security, informal mechanisms take the form of clients' dependence on patrons. This dependence is characterized as relatively long-term, and it involves some degree of affective relations (rather than a mere exchange of dependence for social support). In this model, one of the favors a client can do for a patron is to vote for the patron, or the candidate endorsed by the patron. Local patrons accessed resources to service their clients from higher-ups, and so the determining factor in political alliances was particular benefits to be gained, in return for mobilizing voters (Kerkvliet and Mojares 1991). This hierarchical chain of officials dependent on whoever won power at the national level led to the phenomenon of switching parties after every election, so common that there was cynical reference to "commuting."

In fact, traditional politics along these lines was already breaking down in the late 1960s. As noted, Ferdinand Marcos was in 1969 the first president to win re-election—by realizing that he could bypass local patronage pyramids and use government resources to link directly with communities. He mobilized government funds to work with the lowest-level political leaders, such as barangay captains, whether or not the mayors and governors were aligned with him (Kerkvliet 1996).

Beyond this innovative style of governance (using the national government's bureaucracy rather than local politicians to distribute patronage), economic development both reduced the dependence of typical citizens and increased the size of the middle class—that is, the pool of potential patrons. It is not unusual to find four to six serious candidates for mayor, governor, or Congress, just as the 1992 and 1998 elections saw numerous candidates for president.

This increased competition has reduced the certainty of election results at local levels and has shifted the balance of power to voters. Now, as Jaime Cardinal Sin, Archbishop of Manila, has advised, voters feel free to accept money from candidates but still make up their own minds as to their votes.

Thus, it has become more useful to analyze voting behavior in the same way as might be done in an advanced country. The characteristics of the voters can be analyzed for clues as to which candidate they prefer. Generally, the most relevant characteristic is ethnolinguistic group. The Philippines has eight languages spoken as mother tongue by more than one million people, as well as seventy other significant languages. Thus, in 1998, Senator Roco polled the most votes for president in the Bicol-speaking region—because he is from that region.

Another possible characteristic is religion. The Philippines is 85 percent Roman Catholic, but this has surprisingly little effect on voting. Despite its prominence in media political discourse, voters do not take their policy cues from the Catholic hierarchy. The most prominent example of this is the average citizen's support for artificial methods of birth control despite the steady opposition of the Church (Mangahas 1991). Similarly, the Church campaigns against the death penalty, but executions are widely seen as necessary by the public. Religion's impotence as a factor can be seen in the 1992 results, when Fidel Ramos won despite the fact that he is Protestant, and in the 1998 results, when Joseph Estrada won despite the

Catholic hierarchy's adamant opposition due to his allegedly immoral lifestyle (he is alleged to have several families in a country where divorce is not legal).

In the past, discussions of the shift from patron-client to more individualistic voting touched only lightly on class. Two reasons, however, can be advanced for emphasizing class analysis. The first reason is that a growing middle class has generated a demand for reform candidates. In 1992, this was tapped by Miriam Santiago, running almost solely on an anticorruption platform. In 1998, the reform vote was divided among three other candidates who were favored by elements of the middle class (even though Santiago was once again running—see below).

The second reason for the recognition of class relates directly to the 1998 election. President Estrada ran a campaign that tapped into class sentiments: "Estrada for the Poor" rhymes in Filipino ("Erap para sa Mahirap") and genuinely rang a bell among those to whom it was addressed. Not only did Estrada have a long movie career behind him—where he played the champion of the underdog—but he also had stylistic elements that endeared him to the poor. His ability to dress like and eat like the poor, while appearing natural, as well as his (deliberately) fractured English—all set him off as not a member of the middle class.

As a result, the poor voted for Estrada and the middle and upper classes voted against him. But this should not be taken as social determinism, for in fact the image of the candidate mediates between the voters' social characteristics and their votes. In a path-breaking analysis, Pedro Laylo and Carijane Dayag-Laylo (1999) show that when candidate image is taken into account, social characteristics fade into statistical insignificance as influences on presidential voting.

A practical example of this theory is Miriam Santiago. In 1992, as noted, she captured the imagination of the middle class as a "reform candidate." In 1998, she was once again in the race, but no longer was she supported as "reform." The change occurred because from 1995 to 1998 she had been in the Senate and had gained a reputation as a constant attacker of the Ramos administration. In short, she dissipated her unusual appeal and appeared more as a normal partisan "fiscalizer." (Prosecutors in the Philippines are termed "Fiscals," so attacking one's opponent on moral or legal grounds is called "fiscalizing.") This is somewhat unfair to Santiago, as there is no way she ever would have switched to join forces with Ramos, but the grain of truth can be seen in her close association with the Estrada administration (her husband has become an undersecretary).

Another example of the power of candidate image is drawn from the 1998 race results by region. As noted, Senator Roco topped the presidential race in his home region of Bicol. Former governor of Cebu Emilio Osmeña also won the presidential race in the central Philippines regions dominated by Cebuano speaking people. In contrast, regional differences hardly existed in the vice presidential race, where Gloria Macapagal-Arroyo won across the nation—even though another Osmeña (Sergio) was running. The difference lay in the image being projected, with Emilio Osmeña ostentatiously running as a regional candidate (his party was called

"PROMDI"—a Filipino-English term for somebody from outside of Manila—roughly equivalent to "hick"). Thus, his image drove a regional differentiation of presidential vote that was missing from the vote for vice president.

So candidate image does the trick. Given the ban on advertising during the campaign, candidate image has to be earned in the years before the election. Movie stars and sportsmen are joined by media personalities—newscasters or presenters in feature programs. Not surprisingly, this means that candidates express their interest well in advance of the actual campaign, to begin to position themselves in the public mind.

Interesting in this context is the recent development of polling technology in the Philippines. Standardized, rapid, repeated nationwide polls of voters only became available during the 1992 election campaign, and they were used more extensively in 1998. Politicians have had some trouble adjusting to the growing importance of these polls—even though their utility is obvious.

It is striking that in both 1992 and 1998, the frontrunner in the polls more than a year ahead of time eventually won the election. In fact, neither Ramos nor Estrada ever trailed. Perhaps it is a coincidence that for both of these elections, the most serious rival was the Speaker of the House of Representatives—Ramon Mitra and Jose de Venecia, respectively. Both of these men had access to the sort of party building beloved of the politicians, they won the endorsement of most local politicians, their local politicians won election—and Mitra and de Venecia duly lost. (And the local politicians promptly defected to parties of the winning candidates, as indicated in table 7.3, p. 155).

In their belief in the machinery, these candidates and their supporters disdained the polls. Political pundit Nelson Navarro declared during the 1998 campaign that "no politicians come out number one in a poll they did not pay for." Immediately after the election, Speaker de Venecia denied the relevance of exit polls showing Estrada in the lead by stating that Estrada had paid for the survey—only to be reminded by the newscaster that the ABS-CBN television network had funded the Social Weather Stations' work (Mangahas 1998).

In short, the behavior of the electorate is becoming more individualistic and predictable on the basis of polling data—as witnessed by the success of Social Weather Stations in predicting election outcomes. In the future, politicians who understand and use polls will have a comparative advantage (as will those with a realistic view of the impact of parties).

Assessment

Elections are clearly important for understanding Philippine politics. The average citizen believes in them as the hallmark of democracy. And they genuinely determine political outcomes, selecting the rationalist technocrat Ramos in 1992 and the emotive populist Estrada in 1998. What are we to make of elections in the Philippines?

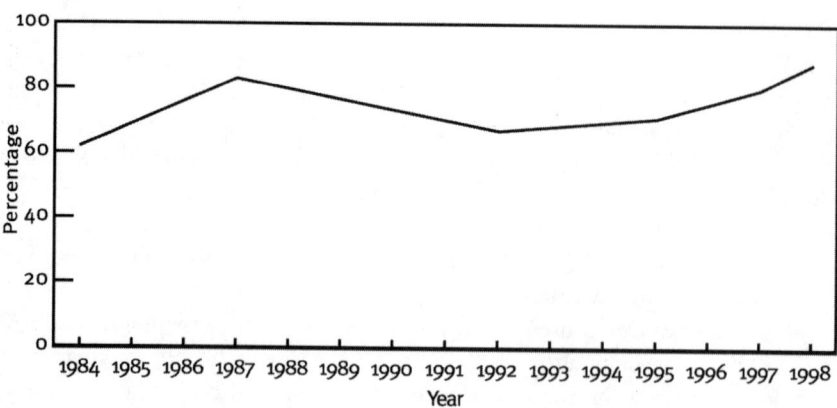

Figure 7.2 Filipinos' Belief in Free and Fair Elections at the Precinct Level, 1984–98

Source: SWS, various years.

Note: Test statement for each election: "The (date) elections were clean and free in our precinct."

May 1984	Batasan	May 1995	Congressional, senatorial, local
May 1987	Congressional	June 1997	Barangay
May 1992	Synchronized national	May 1998	Synchronized national

The first question to be answered is whether elections are free and fair. Clearly citizens believe they are—at least at the precinct level, as shown in figure 7.2. It should be emphasized that this judgment is empirically based—since the handwritten ballots are counted by hand by teachers in the local school house, many community residents stay until the counting is completed at the precinct level. This can take quite a long time (up to twenty-four hours), but some citizens are typically there at all times—if even for curiosity's sake.

But citizens are not naive. They realize that cheating can go on at higher levels, where precinct totals are agglomerated into municipal totals, then into provincial totals, and so on up the national chain. As noted, citizens were particularly suspicious of the 1995 senatorial election results. And they had, in advance, doubts about the 1998 election. A year before the election, 57 percent felt, "Probably there would be cheating, not necessarily at the precinct level, therefore the coming 1998 elections will not accurately reflect how people will feel" (SWS, June 1997 survey).

Despite early doubts about the event, however, the 1998 election passed off quite well. While citing the challenges and difficulties accompanying the process, the National Citizens' Movement for Free Elections (NAMFREL) concluded in its "Report on the Philippine General Elections—11 May 1998": "The 1998 election was clean and credible. No major incidents of massive cheating or election related violence. This led to a peaceful transition of power distinguished by the lack of election protests from the losing candidates especially for the presidential and vice presidential positions. More important, a peaceful transition of power was made possible since the results of the elections were readily accepted by the people" (NAMFREL 1999, 33).

In short, elections in the Philippines are generally free and fair—although there are lapses. Some of the best guarantees against these lapses are the activities of the election watchdog groups—NAMFREL and the Parish-Pastoral Council for Responsible Voting (PPCRV). These groups can be deputized by the COMELEC to help maintain the quality of elections—and they have been able to do so thus far.

The activities of NAMFREL in 1986 were sufficiently widespread that covert cheating became much more difficult. This forced Marcos into more blatant cheating, which in turn led to his losing legitimacy. Incidentally, one of the limitations of NAMFREL's activities reinforces the centrality of elections. Early in the Aquino administration, NAMFREL took on the task of monitoring funds spent in localities under a special economic recovery initiative. While this effort certainly enhanced the efficiency of spending, NAMFREL was unable to sustain this more general "citizen watchdog" role and has reverted to its original core competence, election monitoring. In this role, the citizenry is sufficiently motivated, due to the perceived importance of elections, to make NAMFREL a world-famous resource for other countries trying to manage elections. NAMFREL was involved in the Cambodian elections in 1998 and in the Indonesian elections in 1999.

Given the picture of elections presented above, there are three points to consider where change may be in the air. First, as noted, elections are becoming media events, and candidates burnish their image in order to win. Currently, electoral advertising is prohibited, but this ban creates an unstable situation. Given the overriding importance of image and name recall, this regulation flies directly in the face of the self-interests of all candidates (and, for that matter, the media that loses advertising revenues). In this situation, corruption is the unsurprising result. In the relatively short term, advertising will likely once again be allowed, bringing more clearly to the fore the role of media. This will add to the transparency of election coverage, erasing doubts about the honesty of the media, but it will undoubtedly increase the role of money as restraints on election expenditures are loosened.

The analysis in this chapter has focused largely on elections for president, wherein elections truly have controlled the shifting of power. In the presidential system of government, the top office is clearly the central locus of political authority, causing others to gravitate to it, as seen in table 7.3. Political power, however, is beginning to shift to the local governments—provinces, cities, municipalities, and even barangays—given the new Local Government Code. These elections show considerable variation—from traditional patron-client interaction to modern media hype. As of now there are no systematic data to analyze

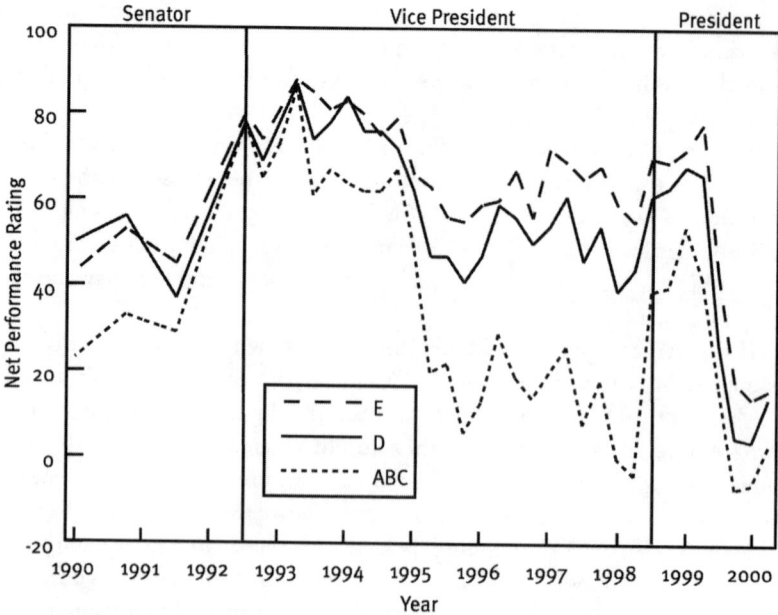

Figure 7.3 Filipinos' Net Performance Ratings of President Joseph E. Estrada by Socioeconomic Class, 1990–2000

Source: SWS, various years.

Notes: Net performance ratings = percentage satisfied minus percentage dissatisfied. ABC = upper and middle classes; D = the bulk of the Philippine population; E = the poorest class.

voter behavior at these lower levels, but the technology of polling is spreading (Divine Word College in Tagbilaran has, for its province, instituted a Bohol poll based on SWS-style technology).

The importance of these local elections is rising, as the locus of governmental action shifts away from Manila. We may in the medium term gain a much better understanding of local-level electoral dynamics and the variations in those dynamics. Preliminary indications are that local officials are becoming more likely to have a professional background (doctors, entrepreneurs, etc.) that is more varied than the predominance of lawyers that has been so usual. In addition, they seem to be oriented more towards "good governance," particularly as variations in the quality of local governance has more effect now on local economic and social development (Rood 1998).

The third point has to do with a current strain on the system due to middle-class disaffection with President Estrada. This should not be characterized, as it so often is, as just a reaction to his personal style. In fact, as shown in figure 7.3, the class differentiation towards Joseph Estrada developed only in 1995, some eight years after he became a national political figure. The event associated with middle-class disaffection was his support for the action of his subordinates in the Presidential Anti-Crime Commission, when they killed all the members of the *Kuratong Baleleng* gang after capturing them. (Accounts vary as to whether this was due to a shoot-out, or a deliberate execution.) The middle class began disapproving of Joseph Estrada at that point, and it has ever since.

The systemic strain is that, having to suffer a president of whom they don't approve, the middle class may begin to drift away from its ardent support of elections as the hallmark of democracy. Nobody disputes that Estrada is the duly elected president in the Philippines, but there are many who feel he ought not be president. Thus, there is a dissonance between belief in elections and rejection of the result of those elections—that elections are the hallmark of democracy, but that the current president is seen as unfit for office.

Disaffection of this stratum of society is possibly a problem. If the middle class, which has provided the backbone of electoral monitoring through the NAMFREL, and which supplies the plethora of candidates that broke the hold of traditional patronage-oriented politicians, loses faith in elections, there may be long-term consequences for the Philippines. Modernization of the electoral system could be delayed, and reform of government deficiencies pushed back. Elections do determine who rules in the Philippines, so support for better elections can produce better governance.

NOTES

1. The political and electoral relation between provinces and cities is complicated by the fact that some highly urbanized cities (e.g., Baguio City) are independent of the provinces within which they are geographically located (Benguet), and also form an independent congressional district. This detail is ignored in this chapter.
2. Throughout this chapter, considerable use is made of data produced by Social Weather Stations (SWS). Each citation to data provides the date of the survey. All SWS data are maintained in an archive at the office of SWS and are available for use by scholars and the general public.

    SWS is an independent, nonprofit, academic research institution specializing in opinion surveys based on probability samples. Founded in 1985, SWS conducts at least four nationwide surveys each year, with more frequent surveys during national elections. Comparison of SWS results with election returns shows a very close correlation, bolstering the credibility of their other findings. SWS is funded by a variety of clients—Philippine government agencies, official donors such as the U.S. Agency for International Development (USAID) and the World Bank, private donors such as the Ford Foundation and The Asia Foundation, and even political candidates. The diversity of funding helps SWS to maintain its independence, and its practice of making its survey results public allows general judgment as to its accuracy. SWS makes election data files public after each election so that scholars and others can analyze the data themselves. The interpretations of SWS data offered in this chapter are those of the author, and not the responsibility of Social Weather Stations or any of the other institutions mentioned herein.

References

Florentino-Holfileña, Chay. 1998. *News for Sale: The Corruption of the Philippine Media.* Manila: Philippine Center for Investigative Journalism and Center for Media Freedom and Responsibility.

Joaquin, Nick. 1983. *The Aquinos of Tarlac.* Manila: Cacho Hermanos.

Kerkvliet, Benedict J. 1996. "Contested Meanings of Elections in the Philippines." In *The Politics of Elections in Southeast Asia,* edited by R.H. Taylor. Washington: Woodrow Wilson Center Press.

Kerkvliet, Benedict J., and Resil B. Mojares. 1991. "Themes in the Transition from Marcos to Aquino: An Introduction." In *From Marcos to Aquino: Local Perspectives on Political Transition in the Philippines,* edited by Benedict J. Kerkvliet and Resil B. Mojares. Quezon City: Ateneo de Manila University Press.

Lande, Carl H. 1996. *Post-Marcos Politics.* Singapore: Institute of Southeast Asian Studies.

Laylo, Pedro, Jr., and Carijane Dayag-Laylo. 1999. "Candidate Images and Vote Intentions in the 1998 Philippine Presidential Elections." Paper presented at the annual meeting of the American Association for Public Opinion Research, St. Petersburg, Florida, May.

Leones, Errol B., and Miel Moraleda. 1998. "Philippines." In *Political Party Systems and Democratic Development in East and Southeast Asia. Volume I: Southeast Asia,* edited by Wolfgang Sachsenroder and Ulrike E. Frings. Brookfield, Vt.: Ashgate.

Mangahas, Mahar. 1991. "Who's Afraid of the Catholic Church?" *Social Weather Bulletins* 91-4.

———. 1998. "SWS Surveys on the 1998 Elections." *Social Weather Bulletins* 98-7/18.

Montilla, Gabriella R. 1999. "Parties and Accountability in the Philippines." *Journal of Democracy* 10:126–40.

National Citizens' Movement for Free Elections (NAMFREL). 1999. *Report on the Philippine General Elections—11 May 1998.* Manila: Report submitted to the Commission on Election.

Rood, Steven. 1988. "Baguio Citizen Response to the February 1986 Snap Election and Revolution." *Pilipinas* no. 10.

———. 1998. "Decentralization, Democracy, and Development." In *The Philippines: New Directions in Domestic Policy and Foreign Relations,* edited by David B. Timberman. New York: Asia Society.

CHAPTER 8

Cambodia: A Shaky Start for Democracy

by Jeffrey C. Gallup

ELECTIONS OF A SORT have been known in Cambodia for centuries. The Cambodian Royal Chronicles frequently refer to the kings of Cambodia being elected by the notables of the country. In the modern era, however, elections have rarely been free and fair, or even competitive. Instead, elections have been used to bolster the legitimacy of ruling regimes and sometimes have provided convenient occasions to suppress the regimes' enemies (Heder 1998).

The two national elections that took place in the 1990s marked a departure from that historical norm. The elections for a Constituent Assembly, in 1993, and the National Assembly, in 1998, were real competitions. But they were not the natural expression of an existing Cambodian democracy. Instead, they were pushed by the international community primarily as a means of resolving Cambodia's factional conflicts. Indeed, these elections did help restore peace, at least temporarily.

As engines of democratization, they were somewhat less successful. None of the major Cambodian political parties had strong, demonstrated credentials. The polls were marred by serious flaws, including intimidation and violence. In both cases, the losers vehemently (and on dubious grounds) rejected the results as fraudulent but, under foreign pressure, eventually joined fragile coalition governments with the winners. The real victor to date has been the party with the least claim to democratic standing, the ex-communist Cambodian People's Party (CPP), which never really relinquished power despite its loss in the 1993 elections. With its win in the 1998 polls, the CPP has emerged stronger than ever.

On the positive side, the constitutional electoral process has survived despite great stress; elections have been conducted with reasonable technical proficiency and honesty; and most important, the Cambodian people have shown great enthusiasm for democracy by their overwhelming participation in the polls, the rapid growth of nongovernmental organizations, and other indications of a burgeoning civil society.

While they are precarious, the political achievements of the 1990s should not be discounted, especially when contrasted with Cambodia's extraordinarily bloody and tragic recent history that is briefly summarized here (see Chandler 1996). The early years after Cambodia's independence from France in 1953, under the leadership of then-Prince Norodom Sihanouk, are widely viewed by Cambodians as an interlude of peace, prosperity, and relatively benevolent authoritarianism. By the late 1960s, however, Cambodia became embroiled in the Vietnam War, as Vietnamese communist forces used Cambodia as a staging ground and were attacked by American bombers. Powerless to keep the foreigners out, Prince Sihanouk was overthrown by his own prime minister, Lon Nol, in 1970. Lon Nol's government engaged in an inept and disastrous attempt to rid Cambodia of the communist Vietnamese forces. Beleaguered by the Vietnamese and the growing indigenous communist movement, the Khmer Rouge, Lon Nol's Khmer Republic fell to the Khmer Rouge on 17 April 1975. Then began a four-year reign of terror almost unparalleled in history. Determined to transform Cambodia into an autarkic peasant society, the Khmer Rouge drove the urban population into the countryside and made them farm the land under conditions of extreme privation and iron discipline. Khmer Rouge cadre killed countless people for the slightest infraction. An estimated one million or more Cambodians died of famine, illness, or execution during Khmer Rouge rule, out of a total population of about 6 million. After a series of border clashes, the Vietnamese invaded Cambodia in December 1978, overthrowing the Khmer Rouge within a few weeks and installing an orthodox communist state under Vietnamese occupation, the People's Republic of Kampuchea (PRK).

The PRK, ruled by what has become today's Cambodian People's Party, was soon under attack by a resistance movement with three important factions: the Khmer Rouge, the royalist National United Front for an Independent, Neutral, Peaceful and Cooperative Cambodia (FUNCINPEC), and the republican Khmer People's National Liberation Front (KPNLF). Vietnamese forces withdrew from Cambodia in 1989, and the government, still run by the CPP, was renamed the State of Cambodia. Fitful international attempts to end the ongoing conflict finally bore fruit in 1991 with the signing in Paris of the Agreement on a Comprehensive Political Settlement of the Cambodia Conflict. This agreement laid the groundwork for the political transformation of Cambodia through free and fair elections, which were an integral provision of the text.

Conduct of the 1993 Elections

The 1993 national elections in Cambodia were the culmination of an enormous United Nations operation. Under the Paris accords, the United Nations formed the United Nations Transitional Authority in Cambodia (UNTAC), which was supposed to assert effective control over the administration of the country under the formal authority of the Supreme National Council (SNC), composed of representatives of the four Cambodian factions and Prince Norodom Sihanouk. Although the United Nations (UN) deployed some 22,000 personnel, about half military, and spent about US$2 billion on UNTAC operations, it was never able to exert effective control over the government administration, which remained in the hands of the State of Cambodia (SOC) and the ruling party, the CPP. In addition, the United Nations was able to establish neither the "neutral political environment" nor the cantonment and disarmament of the factions as intended by the accords (Doyle 1995).

The pre-election period was marked by significant political violence and intimidation. The worst violence was committed by the Khmer Rouge, which had pulled out of the election process and repeatedly attacked ethnic Vietnamese civilians, SOC government personnel, and UNTAC employees. The Vietnamese were targeted in accordance with the Khmer Rouge line that Vietnam, and Vietnamese in general, were aiming to annex Cambodia with the help of the CPP regime, a Vietnamese puppet. The Khmer Rouge threatened with death anyone who dared to vote in the elections. The other major offenders were the State of Cambodia and the CPP. As in communist states, the CPP and the government were so deeply intertwined as to be almost indistinguishable. In all, some 200 persons were killed in approximately two months before the elections for apparently political reasons, most by the Khmer Rouge, others by persons affiliated with the government or CPP (Findlay 1995).

Other serious election flaws were apparent. Intimidation by the CPP was widespread (Heder and Ledgerwood 1996; Frieson 1996). State-run television and radio were skewed toward the CPP. Giving gifts to voters was also common and was practiced more by the CPP than by other parties.

Despite failures in other areas, the United Nations was able to run the elections according to international technical standards, and it recruited international election officials with substantial reputations and experience (Sorpong Peou 1997). The election law adopted by UNTAC foresaw the establishment of a Constituent Assembly of 120 members by a system of party list proportional representation by district. The purpose of the Constituent Assembly, once elected, was to draft and adopt a new constitution and convert itself into a National Assembly.

The districts consisted of nineteen provinces and two municipalities (these were the capital, Phnom Penh, and Sihanoukville, Cambodia's main port). The number of seats allocated to each province or municipality was proportional to its population with the caveat that each was entitled to a minimum of one seat in the Constituent Assembly regardless of its size. The voters each cast a single vote for the party of their choice, and seats were allocated using proportional representation with the "largest remainder" formula.

The UNTAC election law and electoral procedures established a long list of modern technical safeguards to ensure that the election met international standards for free and fair polls. Twenty parties were duly registered to compete. At voter registration, voters were issued photo identification cards and the registration lists were computerized. Despite Khmer Rouge violence and threats, some

Table 8.1 Results of the 1993 Cambodian Elections

Party	Number of Seats Won (Percentage of Seats Won)	Percentage of Valid Votes Received
FUNCINPEC	58 (48.33)	45.47
Cambodian People's Party	51 (42.50)	38.23
Buddhist Liberal Democratic Party	10 (8.33)	3.81
Molinaka Party	1 (0.83)	1.37
Other Parties	0 (0.00)	11.12

Source: Mayall 1996, 55.

4.7 million Cambodians, more than 90 percent of the estimated voting age population, registered. Voting itself took place in enclosed voting booths, and voters' fingers were marked with ink visible under ultraviolet light to prevent double voting. Ballot boxes had locks and seals and were transported to provincial centers for counting. Party observers were allowed to monitor the voting and counting process. UN troops were deployed widely to assure security to the process, and all aspects were supervised by UN personnel with the assistance of many thousands of Cambodian staff.

Despite fears of major Khmer Rouge military attacks, the voting was largely peaceful and orderly. The turnout was extraordinary: 89.56 percent of registered voters cast their ballots in an atmosphere both serious and enthusiastic.

The results gave a plurality to FUNCINPEC (see table 8.1). Its combined total with the Buddhist Liberal Democratic Party (BLDP), which grew out of the KPNLF, produced an opposition majority, 68 seats, in the Constituent Assembly. The results apparently came as a shock to the CPP, which immediately rejected them as fraudulent.

Assessment of the 1993 Election and Afterwards

The UN Secretary-General's Special Representative for Cambodia, Yasushi Akashi, the UN official in charge of the whole Cambodian operation, declared the elections "free and fair" even before counting was complete (United Nations 1995). UN investigations found the CPP complaints to be groundless. This was, of course, a self-assessment by an interested party—the very organization that conducted the elections. But this opinion was shared by independent observers as well, and it was generally accepted by the international community. The elections were widely considered the crowning success of the UNTAC mission.

It may seem surprising that elections marred by violence and intimidation, unequal media access, and vote-buying, among other flaws, could be termed free and fair. Election experts, however, felt able to conclude that these factors had not significantly distorted the vote: the vast majority of voters had resisted Khmer Rouge intimidation and had shown their commitment to the process simply by coming out to vote. Similarly, 61.77 percent of the voters resisted CPP blandishments or threats and cast their ballots for the opposition or other non-CPP parties. In short, the opposition won; therefore the effects of intimidation, violence, and vote-buying by the CPP could be discounted.

Still, a certain risk is inherent in judging the fairness of an election by who wins. Accusations of favoritism are likely. Moreover, a "free and fair" verdict may seem to wipe the slate clean of misconduct that ought to be condemned and corrected.

The gravest crisis came after the 1993 election. Still claiming fraud, senior CPP officials declared that the eastern part of the country, beyond the Mekong River, had "seceded" from Cambodia. Although this ploy collapsed, it was a demonstration of crude power by the CPP. The CPP made it clear that it would not tolerate being left out of any government, and an interim coalition was formed with co–prime ministers—the FUNCINPEC's chief, Prince Norodom Ranariddh, son of Norodom Sihanouk, who became king under the new system, and Hun Sen, the SOC prime minister.

In sum, the 1993 elections demonstrated that it is possible to organize technically correct elections in a hostile environment, but not so easy to control all the external factors, such as intimidation, that bear upon the election process. The effect of these factors may be minimized where the voting public has confidence in the process. Whatever the election results are, however, they do not necessarily change the underlying power relationships in a country such as Cambodia where democratic traditions and the rule of law are weak. Nonetheless, in Cambodia, elections opened up a democratic space that had not existed previously.

Formation and Functioning of the New Government

The permanent government established under the new constitution was a coalition similar to the interim regime. Prince Norodom Ranariddh became first prime minister; Hun Sen became second prime minister. Decisions were to be made by mutual agreement. Other senior positions were divided between the coalition partners. The apparent power-sharing between FUNCINPEC and the CPP, however, was less than met the eye. The CPP maintained effective control over the vast majority of the security forces and local administration below the provincial level. Indeed, even where a FUNCINPEC official was a minister or provincial governor, the civil servants below were dominated by CPP members. This sometimes led to a sort of "parallel government" run by the CPP and devoted to promoting CPP aims—and obstructing those of FUNCINPEC.

In its early years, the new government took some halting steps toward the consolidation of democracy. A nascent multiparty system existed. The National Assembly functioned, although largely in obedience to instructions from the ruling parties rather than as an independent body. Popular concerns received little response, and life at the local level was minimally affected. A lively, if often irresponsible, free press was present, but outspoken journalists who criticized the government were on occasion harassed and in several cases killed.

In contrast, civil society began to blossom, with the formation of several hundred nongovernmental organizations (NGOs), ranging from ethnic associations to development groups to human rights and democracy advocates. The human rights and democracy advocates were instrumental in launching public debate on national issues and were able to influence government policy (Brown and Timberman 1998). Still, the CPP view of state power as essentially coercive and top-down had not changed. FUNCINPEC showed that it too had an authoritarian streak—but in a more traditional, royalist vein.

By 1997, the CPP managed to buy off or otherwise bring into its fold sufficient members of other parties in the National Assembly to deprive Prince Ranariddh of a working majority. The FUNCINPEC response was to prevent the National Assembly from meeting by denying it a quorum. What cooperation there had been within the government largely stopped.

The Ouster of Prince Ranariddh

In the first half of 1997, tensions between the CPP and FUNCINPEC rose to a fever pitch. Hun Sen acted on 5–6 July 1997. He accused Prince Ranariddh of collusion with the Khmer Rouge remnants still at war with the government. In two days of fighting in Phnom Penh, Hun Sen's military forces attacked, and Ranariddh and many senior FUNCINPEC and other opposition leaders fled into exile. It is unclear whether Hun Sen genuinely believed he faced real danger—the nascent ties between the moribund Khmer Rouge and FUNCINPEC were no real threat—or merely thought it timely to dispose of a growing political challenge from Ranariddh. In any event, the result was to rid the country of Hun Sen's only serious rival and to allow Hun Sen to rule alone.

Military officials affiliated with FUNCINPEC were hunted down in a campaign that lasted approximately six months, resulting in about 100 summary executions (Special Representative of the United Nations Secretary-General for Human Rights in Cambodia 1997; 1998a). After Ranariddh's overthrow, small FUNCINPEC resistance forces formed on the border with Thailand and sporadically clashed with the military controlled by Hun Sen.

The international community reacted sharply to Ranariddh's ouster. It was more worried about the damage done to Cambodia's fragile peace than about the collapse of democracy. The Association of Southeast Asian Nations (ASEAN) indefinitely postponed Cambodian entry in that organization. Various international donors, most prominently the United States, suspended or cut back financial assistance to the Cambodian government. And the United Nations General Assembly, at U.S. insistence, refused to seat the Cambodian delegation. As approximately 50 percent of Cambodia's budget came from foreign aid, cuts in assistance were a serious matter, and judging from Hun Sen's testy remarks, international rebuke stung.

THE 1998 ELECTIONS

In the midst of the upheaval following the ouster of Prince Ranariddh, Hun Sen announced that the National Assembly elections would take place in 1998 as foreseen by the Constitution. The conditions for free and fair elections hardly seemed propitious. Virtually all of the chief opposition leaders had left the country out of concern for their safety. Their offices had been closed or taken over by splinter factions cooperating with Hun Sen. Although the opposition press continued to function, actual opposition party activity was reduced essentially to zero.

Yet the prospect of elections provided a hook for the international community to bring Cambodia back to peace and, some hoped, democracy as well. From the beginning, members of the international community realized that it would be a struggle to get the Cambodian government to hold genuinely competitive elections, and thereby put at risk what Hun Sen had so recently gained by military means.

The international community, unlike in 1993, could not decree how the elections were run this time; it could only provide or withhold funding, urge, suggest, and threaten. The election itself would be a Cambodian operation.

The Electoral System of 1998

Oddly, given its disdain for the UN-run elections of 1993, the Cambodian government under Hun Sen adopted the 1993 election system almost wholesale. Some thought had been given by both FUNCINPEC and the CPP to changing the system to a majoritarian, first-past-the-post system, but both reverted to the UNTAC method of proportional representation by districts. The number of National Assembly seats was raised to 122, to include one seat each for two new municipalities, Kep and Pailin.

The major change in the electoral system, and the major achievement of the new election law of December 1997, was the creation of an independent National Election Committee (NEC) to run the polls. This step was strongly urged by the international community and by local nongovernmental organizations. The eleven members of the NEC were to come from specified groups, including a chair and vice chair from among distinguished professionals, one member from each political party in the National Assembly, two representatives of the Ministry of Interior, two citizens' representatives, and a representative of the nongovernmental organizations. This structure was accepted by all major parties, on the understanding that the electoral body would be impartial, administratively and financially independent of the government, and genuinely responsible for organizing the elections. Political balance between the government and opposition parties was not an explicit requirement, but it was clearly a consideration in the choice of members.

Unfortunately, the CPP was unwilling to live with political balance or a truly nonpartisan NEC. It manipulated the selection process for the NEC to install "opposition" party representatives and others who were in fact sympathetic to the CPP. Thus the CPP obtained an effective majority on the NEC. Still, the NEC did not actually become a puppet of the CPP, as some alleged. Although it included a few CPP stalwarts, a majority were civic-minded citizens trying to do their job properly. A decisive handicap for the NEC was that the opposition parties perceived it as biased from the start and so lacked confidence in it. In addition, like other theoretically independent Cambodian institutions, the NEC was susceptible to intimidation by the CPP's overwhelming power.

The NEC, lacking any prior election expertise, was charged with organizing a massive election effort less than six months after its inauguration, a task the United Nations had accomplished in eighteen months with an expert team. Given the many obstacles, the NEC did its technical job surprisingly well, probably as well as the UN had.

The Constitution of 1993 imposed certain broader election parameters. The National Assembly was to be chosen for a five-year term. The winning party (the one with the most seats in the Assembly) was entitled to form a new government. A two-thirds vote of the National Assembly, however, was required to approve any government. The requirement for a two-thirds vote made a coalition government a virtual necessity unless one party received an overwhelming majority. This provision was intended to allay the fear of exclusion from the government, a CPP concern in 1993. It was important because exclusion, in the Cambodian historical context, was not seen as temporary and limited in scope. Instead, exclusion could mean becoming a powerless opposition that the governing party would feel free to persecute. Hence the two-thirds majority provision for a new government might seem appropriate for a highly polarized, mutually suspicious political environment such as that in Cambodia, where trust in the political system and meaningful constraints on the use of governmental power did not yet exist. By these lights, pluralism would be protected and the authoritarian tendencies of any one party moderated. Yet there were also unintended negative consequences. Being forced together did not make FUNCINPEC and the CPP into cooperative partners after the 1993 polls. The coalition government was always fraught with tension; it eventually became paralyzed by the hostility between the coalition parties. In addition, the two-headed government of 1993 never established a clear policy direction. Arguably a one-party government could have done so.

A little-noticed technical change in the electoral law altered the method of allocating leftover votes from the "largest remainder" method of UNTAC to the so-called "highest average" method. The NEC fumbled this change by writing the Jefferson/d'Hondt highest average method into its initial regulations incorrectly. It later rectified its error without alerting the political parties. Jefferson/d'Hondt, though a standard rule, favors larger parties. After the election, the opposition parties discovered the change and realized that the first (mistaken) version was also a legitimate, if obscure, seat allocation system (called Balinski/Young) and, most important, would give them more seats (Balinski and Young 1975; Schier 1998). They insisted that Balinski/Young be applied.

The Role of the International Community

The international community had a profound and generally positive effect on the conduct of the 1998 elections. Its major contribution was to provide expertise, funding, pressure, and observers. For a number of donors, the resumption of assistance after the ouster of Prince Ranariddh was contingent on successful elections. What was success? Some countries were pushing elections mainly as a means of once more restoring peace among the Cambodian factions. For others, such as the United States, and even more so, international nongovernmental organizations, the election was about democracy. They wanted to hold the elections to the exacting standard of "free and fair." A few—the French government is most commonly cited— were perceived as promoting elections mainly to legitimize the de facto rule of Hun Sen, considered by them as the least-bad political leader.

Political pressure from the international community did succeed in making the elections competitive in one fundamental way: it persuaded the recalcitrant Cambodian government to permit the return of Hun Sen's main rival, Prince Ranariddh, to compete in the polls. The international community also made a decisive difference on smaller issues, but it was less effective in dealing with more amorphous factors, such as violence, intimidation, and equitable access to the media. In part, this was because the international community did not agree on one assessment of these problems, in part because of practical limitations in solving them.

The financial assistance and expertise provided by international donors probably did more to improve the quality of the election process than direct political pressure. The bulk of the official NEC election budget, more than US$20 million of US$27 million, was provided by the international community with about $5 million provided by the Cambodian government. The European Union underwrote nearly the full cost of the voter registration and funded voter education, training on election reporting for the media, and a European observer contingent. Japan provided the ballot boxes, voting materials, vehicles, and equipment, including a countrywide radio communications system. Additional millions were spent by the international community on other election-related items, notably international and domestic election observers and voter education.

In general, the funding was provided on condition that the NEC meet high standards for election procedures and technical safeguards. Foreign donors successfully promoted tamper-proof voter identification cards, secure ballot boxes, counterfeit-resistant ballots, and indelible ink to mark voters' fingers. Foreign experts were also largely responsible for drafting the election procedures and creating a computerized voter registration system using UNTAC election equipment.

International observers were eagerly sought by the opposition and NGO groups. Although termed "too few" by opposition parties after the polls, in reality the observers were unusually numerous for so small a country, totaling about 800. They were solicited to deter violence and fraud, and their presence was undoubtedly helpful in this regard. This achievement was obscured by subsequent, and mostly unfair, charges of bias, dishonesty, and ineptitude leveled at the observers (International Republican Institute 1999, National Democratic Institute for International Affairs 1999).

Political Parties

The basic political formations—CPP and opposition—were the same in 1998 as in 1993. Between 1993 and 1998, the opposition had undergone several splits. The small BLDP had devolved into two factions, and a host of parties broke off from FUNCINPEC. The most important was led by Sam Rainsy, who had been the FUNCINPEC finance minister until 1994, when he was dismissed for criticizing his own government. He was subsequently expelled from FUNCINPEC and the National Assembly in 1995 for his continuing verbal attacks. He formed the Khmer Nation Party, later renamed the Sam Rainsy Party in order to distinguish itself from another splinter group. Many of the other numerous splits in the opposition parties were encouraged, if not instigated, by the CPP, which was ever eager to weaken its opponents.

The CPP remained intact, indeed monolithic, throughout this period. Internal divisions between Hun Sen and National Assembly President Chea Sim or between Hun Sen and Deputy Prime Minister Sar Kheng were rumored, but if they existed, they never came into the open.

Besides the three main parties, thirty-six additional parties succeeded in presenting candidates in the 1998 elections, compared to a total of twenty parties in the 1993 elections. Most of these thirty-six parties revolved around a particular personality with some money and ambition and a circle of friends and associates, but they had almost no national base or recognition.

Each major party had specific campaign themes, but specific policy prescriptions were few. FUNCINPEC, in 1998 as in 1993, stressed its royalist character and ties to the king. Many Cambodians continued to associate the rule of then-Prince Sihanouk in the 1950s and 1960s with peace and prosperity. Moreover, many Cambodians revere the monarchy and their king as a matter of tradition. Indeed, in the Cambodian context, the king has a cosmological significance: through his presence and performance of royal duties and ceremonies, he brings divine blessings upon his country. FUNCINPEC also presented itself as the alternative to an oppressive CPP regime. The party appealed as well to a less virtuous sentiment: anti-Vietnamese nationalism. While officially phrased as opposition to illegal Vietnamese immigration and unjust borders with Vietnam, FUNCINPEC effectively played to the visceral and sometimes ugly anti-

Vietnamese feelings that many Cambodians harbor. In the FUNCINPEC view, the CPP and Hun Sen were the puppets of the hated Vietnamese.

The Sam Rainsy Party and its supporters ran a campaign that, if anything, was even more virulently anti-Vietnamese than FUNCINPEC's. But the party distinguished itself from FUNCINPEC in other ways. The Sam Rainsy Party was more clearly the party of change and reform. Sam Rainsy freely condemned both FUNCINPEC and the CPP for corruption and human rights violations and won points for his no-holds-barred style.

As in 1993, a principal CPP slogan in 1998 was that the CPP had saved Cambodia from the Khmer Rouge and would prevent its return; implicit was that FUNCINPEC (and Sam Rainsy) were tainted by their historical ties with the Khmer Rouge as forces cooperating to resist the PRK and SOC. In 1998, the CPP also took credit for the collapse of the Khmer Rouge through the massive defections Hun Sen had negotiated using controversial amnesties for Khmer Rouge leaders. The CPP touted its development activities. In the name of Hun Sen, hundreds of schools had been built since 1993. Moreover, the CPP appealed to voters as the party that was legitimate simply by virtue of its incumbency: in Cambodian tradition, those who hold power have the right to continue to hold power.

Political Parties and Class

Class has some relevance in the Cambodian political context. Many CPP leaders and members have peasant origins. The CPP party platform, although it has abandoned Marxism-Leninism, makes a great deal of being "with the people," that is, the rural majority. Of course, the CPP was also the party of civil servants and the security forces. In contrast, by all appearances, educated people of middle- and upper-class origins, including royalty, were proportionately more likely to be found in the leadership ranks of FUNCINPEC and the Sam Rainsy Party.

But social origins do not necessarily predict policy. As in the communist societies of the former Soviet Union and Eastern Europe, Cambodia's CPP developed a "new class" or *nomenklatura* of highly privileged senior party members whose principal interest seemed to be pursuing their own fortunes.

Personalities played a role as well in the 1998 elections. The leading figures of each party—Hun Sen, Sam Rainsy, and Prince Ranariddh—affected voter preferences. On the positive side, Ranariddh was royal, a good patron; Hun Sen was strong and energetic; Sam Rainsy a fearless advocate of reform. These figures also had "high negatives" in campaign parlance: Ranariddh was disliked for perceived weak leadership; Hun Sen was hated for his ruthlessness; Rainsy seemed too "Western" and confrontational to some. Most candidates for the National Assembly were scarcely known to the voters of the districts they wanted to represent, however, and the final list of candidates was approved only a few days before the election.

The Election Campaign

The standard election factors cited above are insufficient to explain how the Cambodian election process unfolded. Violence, intimidation, gift-giving, the dominance of the state by the CPP, and the polarization of Cambodian society were equally if not more important. Foreign involvement weighed heavily as well. These factors are addressed below.

Violence and intimidation against opposition political parties and voters were a serious issue in 1998 as they had been in 1993. As in 1993, the opposition parties in 1998 had only a short period to build, or in this case, rebuild, their party structures. The violence during and following the July 1997 ouster of Prince Ranariddh had a chilling effect on campaigning. Opposition parties initially encountered obstruction from local government authorities as they attempted to reorganize. Gradually, however, the political climate became freer. The opposition parties were able to establish offices and hold numerous major rallies without significant harassment during the formal campaign season. Although they conducted grassroots campaigning as well, this was more limited and cautious.

The opposition parties were already reporting murders of their political activists in early 1998. The UN Center for Human Rights, Cambodia Office (UNCHR), was at one time investigating forty-nine possibly election-related killings that took place between May 1998 and the July 1998 elections (Special Representative of the United Nations Secretary-General for Human Rights in Cambodia 1998b). The UNCHR ultimately placed only three of those murders firmly in the category of election-related killings by persons linked to the CPP or government. Thirteen deaths, of election officials and government workers, were attributed to the Khmer Rouge. The other cases were ambiguous, unresolved, or not election-related.

Therefore it appears that directly election-related deaths in the immediate run-up to the election were significantly less numerous in 1998 than in 1993. Still, the impression persisted that election-related violence was severe in 1998, due in no small degree to the intense coverage of human rights by the UN Center for Human Rights, political parties, observers, and national and international human rights groups.

Intimidation in 1998 was a significant factor in the election, although probably less so than in 1993. In general, the CPP's campaign techniques in 1998 followed closely those of 1993 and were, in part, inherently intimidating. The CPP seemed to see its campaign effort as organizing and controlling the voters rather than appealing to them as independent actors. Unlike the opposition parties, the CPP had a pervasive apparatus, down to the subvillage level, to carry out its campaign. The party's methodology was to sign up as many party members as possible, and then to try to ensure they did not stray from the CPP when they voted. The party used gifts, exhortations, and monitoring of party members' behavior to this end. This methodology reflected a basic underlying CPP concept: that the power of the state (and its ruling party) is fundamentally coercive, and that the voters should be made to do what is desired of them. A combination of pressures made it difficult for people to resist joining the CPP. Those signing up members were often local party or government officials (or both) with significant power over the people in their area. They could make trouble for voters who balked at signing up and pledging their votes.

Campaigning at times also involved direct or indirect threats. Attempts were made by CPP officials, as in 1993, to persuade people that their votes would not be secret. A further CPP campaign tactic was the widespread practice, nearer the elections, of holding mock elections in which voters were shown how to mark the ballot for the CPP. In some cases, where people failed to mark the CPP spot on the ballot, they were told to repeat their attempt until they got it right.

On balance, gross intimidation was less severe in 1998 than in 1993. The Khmer Rouge were too weak by 1998 to dissuade voters from going to the polls. CPP practices in 1998 were similar to those in 1993, but the CPP recognized that violence would damage its image internationally and so cautioned against brutal tactics. The inherently intimidating character of omnipresent CPP power at the local level nonetheless remained fundamentally unchanged.

In 1998, gift-giving by the CPP to voters and party activists was rampant, probably more so than in 1993, since the party's coffers had swelled in the interim. Gifts were given in order to cement the loyalty of party workers and voters well before the elections. Gifts produced a sense of obligation on the part of recipients, consistent with Cambodia's tradition of patron-client relationships. Later, vote-buying reportedly occurred shortly before election day. These tactics aroused less ire than CPP intimidation, likely because all parties who could give gifts did so to some degree. The bestowal of presents was a customary form of patronage on the part of Cambodian political leaders.

Much more than in 1993, several Cambodian NGOs played an instrumental role in the 1998 election as watchdogs and as voter education specialists. Three major domestic election coalitions emerged: the Committee for Free and Fair Elections (COMFREL), with about 11,000 election observers; the Coalition for Free and Fair Elections (COFFEL), with almost 7,000; and the Neutral Independent Committee for Free Elections in Cambodia (NICFEC), with close to 3,000 observers. Nonpartisan Cambodian human rights and democracy groups formed the core of these coalitions. These groups received their major funding from foreign donors. The U.S.-funded Asia Foundation, for example, provided 65 percent of the total funding for domestic observers. Observer groups, interestingly, also threatened the election. A potential overflow of local observers was averted when several possibly pro-CPP observer groups were banned by the NEC at the urging of the international community.

The established election observer groups provided a major share of the nonpartisan voter education for Cambodia's electorate. While the NEC issued posters and organized television and radio shows, the nongovernmental organizations did as much or more, flooding the country with written materials and hundreds of broadcasts of television and radio spots. They also conducted voter education seminars in which more than one million of Cambodia's 5.4 million voters participated. The NGOs were a major election success story.

As in 1993, the opposition parties labored under various handicaps, while the CPP enjoyed the benefits of incumbency and control of state resources. Government officials and property were used to support CPP activities. For instance, while all thirty-nine political parties enjoyed formal media access—five minutes daily on national radio and television during the thirty-day campaign period—broadcast news strongly favored the ruling CPP. This problem initially arose in the 1993 elections, but then UNTAC had its own radio station to ensure equitable treatment.

Despite the imbalance of media coverage, most voters, even in rural areas, seemed to be familiar with the major parties. Thus, while the CPP clearly saw media dominance as important and maintained it despite international pressure, it is unclear whether this tactic deprived the electorate of crucial information or secured many extra votes for the CPP.

Election Day and Election Results

Polling day, 26 July 1998, and the day for counting the ballots, 27 July, were almost universally peaceful, as they were in 1993. The tallying was done the following day in order to avoid counting at night—and possible attacks or intimidation. The turnout was massive—some 93.7 percent of registered voters, according to the NEC, exceeding even that of 1993—and the atmosphere was upbeat. The polling was carried out at some 11,697 stations, and counting was conducted at 1,617 commune-level sites. The voting and counting were carried out under the eyes of some 800 international observers, 21,000 Cambodian domestic observers, and thousands of party agents, primarily from the CPP, FUNCINPEC, and Sam Rainsy Parties.

In 1998, the CPP received a plurality of the popular vote and an absolute majority in the National Assembly, and it did so by garnering only 3 percent more of the votes than it did in 1993: 41.42 percent versus 38.23 percent in 1993 (see table 8.2). FUNCINPEC's percentage, meanwhile, dropped precipitously from 1993 to 1998, from 45.47 percent to only 31.71 percent, a decline of almost 14 percent. The percentage of votes for minor parties remained about the same: 11.12 percent in 1993, 12.60 percent in 1998. But the Sam Rainsy Party made a strong showing for a new party, taking 14 percent of the vote.

Clearly, FUNCINPEC's loss was Sam Rainsy's gain. The Sam Rainsy Party split the opposition vote, which as a whole remained remarkably stable between 1993 and 1998. FUNCINPEC alone received 45.47 percent of the vote in 1993; FUNCINPEC plus the Sam Rainsy Party received 45.98 percent of all valid votes in

Table 8.2 Results of the 1998 Cambodian Elections

Party	Number of Seats Won (Percentage of Seats Won)	Percentage of Valid Votes Received
Cambodian People's Party	64 (52.46)	41.42
FUNCINPEC	43 (35.35)	31.71
Sam Rainsy Party	15 (12.30)	14.27

Source: http://www.cia.gov/cia/publications/factbook/geos/cb.html.

1998. Still, the constitutional requirement for a two-thirds vote of confidence in the National Assembly for a new government meant that the CPP could not rule alone, but would have to take on at least FUNCINPEC as a coalition partner.

The voting showed some interesting regional patterns. In Phnom Penh, for example, the vote was split almost evenly between FUNCINPEC, the CPP, and the Sam Rainsy Party. The latter did well there because of its appeal to the urban and educated classes. Furthermore, Sam Rainsy was very well known in the capital as a resident and local political actor. The CPP, however, performed relatively poorly in the capital. There are several possible reasons for this outcome. Phnom Penh bore the brunt of the fighting and looting that accompanied the ouster of Prince Ranariddh by Hun Sen's forces in July 1997 and suffered more from the economic decline that followed. Moreover, CPP presence and organization were not as pervasive or intimidating in the city as in much of the countryside.

The CPP did well in poor rural provinces such as Prey Veng and Svay Rieng, but less well in provinces with a more prosperous, urban, commercial, and educated character such as Battambang, Kompong Cham, and Kandal.

One surprise was the first-place showing of Sam Rainsy in the municipality of Pailin, the former Khmer Rouge stronghold still populated largely by Khmer Rouge defectors. Several reasons have been advanced. Sam Rainsy's explanation was that the CPP did not yet have a omnipresent grassroots structure there; accordingly, people felt freer to vote as they wished despite former Khmer Rouge leaders' support for the CPP (*Khemara Jati* 1998). Other reasons may include the fact that Sam Rainsy took a quite conciliatory approach toward the Khmer Rouge, arguing against trials of their leaders. A less charitable explanation is that the Sam Rainsy Party won because its strong anti-Vietnamese rhetoric echoed, in milder form, the Khmer Rouge's longstanding hostility toward the Vietnamese.

After the Elections

The main players, exhausted by the elections, failed to prepare for the inevitable postelection crisis, a time that called for exceptional skill and sensitivity to ensure the peaceful transition to a new government.

The losers in 1998—the opposition parties—asserted, as did the CPP in 1993, that the results had been engineered by fraud. They declared they would refuse to let the parliament meet and to let the new government be formed until their 800 or so complaints were satisfactorily resolved. The NEC conducted a few inquiries and then summarily dismissed the vast majority of the oppositions' complaints. This was its gravest error, one of the few times the NEC bowed to CPP pressure. The election appeals body, the Constitutional Council, dominated by CPP supporters, rejected all appeals.

Tensions rose further when the opposition launched large demonstrations, which at first focused on its election complaints. The opposition wanted recounts in about half the nation's communes; new elections in selected areas; a public accounting for all ballots, used and unused; and a reversion to the Balinski/Young method of seat allocation, which would give the opposition four more seats and deny the CPP a majority in the National Assembly. Soon the demonstrators, perhaps emboldened by a sense of growing "people power" as in the Philippines in 1986, started calling for Hun Sen's resignation and appealed to anti-Vietnamese sentiment. Several Vietnamese were attacked, and four were killed.

The demonstrations were initially tolerated, then forcibly suppressed by government forces, only to spring up elsewhere in Phnom Penh. Students and monks were beaten, and nearly a score of bodies were found mysteriously floating in rivers and lakes. Armed counterdemonstrators were brought in by the CPP. With the death toll mounting, and a massacre possibly looming, King Norodom Sihanouk appealed for an end to the killing and to the demonstrations and asked the opposition to let the parliament meet. His call was heeded, and the tension dissipated. It was still another two months before the CPP and FUNCINPEC managed to agree to form a coalition government. FUNCINPEC received a somewhat better deal than had originally been intimated by CPP sources—more ministries and Prince Ranariddh as president of the National Assembly—but in return FUNCINPEC dropped all its election complaints. The Sam Rainsy Party was not invited to join the coalition government, and it took up its role of official opposition with some relish. The election results had finally been accepted, as in 1993, but only after a longer and even more contentious interval of struggle.

The issue of whether the 1998 election was free and fair revolves around three questions. Was there, as the opposition parties alleged, massive fraud that distorted the results? Did the pre-election flaws in the areas of vote-buying, intimidation, and violence affect the results? Or were the flaws so enormous, both pre- and postelection, that the election must be condemned even if the results faithfully reflected what the voters freely intended? The first question is the easiest to answer. Almost all international and Cambodian observer groups, who collectively watched virtually all polling and counting, agreed that these were correctly done (Sorpong Peou 1998; Brown and Zasloff 1998). The parallel vote counts done by domestic observer groups strongly suggested that no manipulation of the results took place after the original count. The voter registration process was more problematic. Underage voters and Vietnamese ineligible to vote may have been registered to benefit the CPP, but this does not seem to have been a huge factor.

The international observers subsequently were roundly condemned by the opposition parties, some media, and even one another for alleged inadequate observation techniques and a too-rosy view of the Cambodian election process. In reality, almost all were diligent, followed accepted observation practices, and came to the same balanced—and net positive—judgments at election time (Some groups, notably the International Republican Institute and National Democratic Institute for International Affairs, downgraded their judgments later, in view of postelection violence and the ineffective complaint resolution process). While the largest and most criticized international observer group, the Joint International Observer Group, used the term "free and fair" in its main postelection statement, this was not a blanket endorsement of the election process as a whole, although it was interpreted as such. The clash between the different perspectives of different groups—legalist, diplomatic, and partisan, among others—spurred much of the controversy over the observers.

In 1998, the opposition parties' cries of fraud were motivated in part by simple astonishment at their loss. They needed a satisfying explanation consistent with their belief in their own popularity. They also assumed that the scattered cases of fraud they saw exemplified a widespread trend. Lacking confidence in the Cambodian-run election process, they concluded that any misdeed was possible. As in 1993, there was also an element of calculation in the rejection of the results: to concede would be to acknowledge weakness, to surrender; to resist vigorously was to assert that the opposition still had power that had to be reckoned with in any subsequent negotiations.

Did pre-election flaws distort the results? Most observer groups agreed that these defects were serious in the 1998 elections, but they were not prepared to say that they had distorted the results. Some writers have asserted that illicit pre-election actions may well have influenced enough voters—only a few percent might be required—to hand victory to the CPP (Sanderson and Maley 1998). The difficulty here is assessing the actual effects on voter behavior. What little information exists on voter attitudes in Cambodia in 1998 suggests that the vast majority were resistant to intimidation and, perhaps to a lesser degree, to vote-buying (Center for Advanced Study 1998). Some 58.28 percent of voters cast their votes for parties other than the CPP. Indeed, only 53.44 percent of the 3.8 million members the CPP claimed to have signed up before the election actually voted for the CPP, assuming all the 2,030,802 votes for the CPP were by party members. Most voters queried by journalists and observers insisted that they knew their vote was secret and that they had voted freely. This does not necessarily discredit the Sanderson and Maley argument, however, because the small percentage of voters who were scared or bribed into voting for the CPP might conceivably have given the CPP its margin of victory over FUNCINPEC.

The argument could be taken even further, and one could postulate that the CPP is a "hollow" party, like the communist parties of Eastern Europe at the end of the 1980s that collapsed when their authority had eroded and the Soviet Union no longer kept them in power. Perhaps most CPP support does come from voter self-preservation and expediency. If the CPP's omnipresence and coercive powers evaporated, this hypothesis states, so might most of its votes. This is only a hypothesis, however.

Another approach would be to judge the polls as not free and not fair regardless of the outcome because the process was unduly flawed, compared to fully democratic elections. On this basis, one could justifiably withhold a "free and fair" label, although the same would be required of the 1993 polls. This is precisely what the largest Cambodian observer group, COMFREL, did in terming the 1998 elections only "reasonably credible."

In sum, it cannot be demonstrated that the 1998 elections were won by fraud, or that pre-election misdeeds distorted the results. The flaws were sufficient, however, that it would be inappropriate to give the polls a ringing endorsement. Otherwise, misconduct might be seen as acceptable.

Conclusion: The Political Context

Cambodia has had two competitive elections in the 1990s, both reasonably well conducted in a technical sense. What is lacking is the necessary political context—a stable democratic system in which regular, free and fair elections are a routine element. Elections—and democracy—have in essence come to Cambodia from outside. The first election was imposed as part of the initial peace settlement. Much of the motivation for free and fair elections in 1998 came from the international community as a way of bringing peace to the contending factions once again. In this respect, elections have served a useful purpose, given the horrors of Cambodia's recent history. But they have not emerged organically from Cambodian political soil and are weakly implanted. Further, although elections have opened the door to democracy, most of the steps toward consolidation of democracy have yet to be taken (Manikas and Bjornlund 1998).

Each of Cambodia's elections in the 1990s has proved to be a crisis point. These elections became crises precisely because they were genuine competitions for power in a political environment where the peaceful transfer of power has been largely unknown and unthinkable. There are several reasons why this is so.

The first is the lack of a democratic political culture, particularly among key segments of Cambodia's political leadership. Historically, Cambodian political culture has been mostly authoritarian. In recent decades, it has ranged from the autocratic, under then-Prince Sihanouk, in the 1950s and 1960s, to the murderous totalitarianism of the Khmer Rouge years. While the Cambodian people showed themselves to be enthusiastic participants in the electoral process in both 1993 and 1998, their political leadership has typically been more interested in gaining or retaining power and privilege than in promoting democracy.

Moreover, Cambodian leaders have become accustomed to seeking power through armed struggle against an enemy. Accordingly, power tends to have an all-or-nothing character for them; it is seen as a zero-sum game in which their gain is their enemy's loss, and vice versa (Brown and Timberman 1998). Cambodia's opposition and CPP factions do not accept the other as legitimate, do not want to allow the other to rule, and do not want to share power or compromise. They each believe they are the only legitimate ruler.

This long-standing factional conflict has never really been resolved. Cambodian society remains deeply polarized between the CPP and the opposition. Each has a paranoid suspicion of the other. Their conflict has been projected from the battlefield onto the election process. The opposing sides perceive the stakes as extremely high—literally life or death, with no guarantee of a second chance or even a second election. The game is fought for complete victory—or total defeat. And like a real war, it is fought with all the weapons at hand. The polarization of society has also meant that it is enormously difficult to create a neutral election administration. Even if one were found and agreed upon, it would be suspected of partisanship and its credibility would be undermined. The contentiousness of the 1998 election process and the rejection of the results were predictable.

Genuine respect for the rule of law, and for the election system in particular, would be a restraining factor on electoral conduct. In Cambodia's history, however, power has rarely been constrained by law. Instead, law has been an instrument to be used arbitrarily by the holders of power to suit their own ends. So far, the election system has yet to engender the respect that will enable it to operate in an impartial manner, free of political pressure.

A final factor, not to be discounted, is the entrenched character of CPP power, which neither two elections nor an interval of apparent FUNCINPEC rule have dislodged. The CPP's pervasive and coercive apparatus down to the grassroots level and its control of the security forces endure. Leading CPP members are resistant to the loss of power and privilege that might result from electoral defeat. Given its dominant position, the CPP, if it chooses, has the ability to keep itself in power by manipulating the election process or obstructing an unfavorable electoral verdict. That it restrained itself to the degree it did in 1998 was due to foreign oversight as well as the CPP belief that it could win without gross misbehavior and thus gain greater legitimacy.

This combination of factors has turned both Cambodian elections in the 1990s into a battlefield—mostly metaphorically but to a degree literally as well. The all-or-nothing view of power, the lack of constraints on political behavior, the image of the other as enemy all have made Cambodia's elections turbulent cliff-hangers.

Some important positive elements also may be found in the Cambodian electoral process. The election law and system, for example, are fundamentally sound. The creation of an independent election committee to run the elections, despite the bias in the appointment of its members in 1998, is a major achievement. In 1998, Cambodian election authorities demonstrated, for the first time ever, that they could conduct elections to a high technical standard (Sorpong Peou 1999).

Worth special mention is the extraordinary role played by local nongovernmental organizations in the 1998 elections. These civic groups joined together to conduct a major share of all voter education activities. They also mounted a comprehensive, countrywide election-monitoring effort that severely limited the opportunities for undetected fraud or violence. Their vigilance should have a profound positive effect on future polls.

The demonstrated seriousness and enthusiasm of the Cambodian population for elections must be counted as an encouraging part of the picture, even though extensive civic participation is not yet customary. The civic activism shown by students and Buddhist monks in the demonstrations after the elections, while it ended in tragedy, also suggests a growing political awareness among key sectors. As a broader stratum of Cambodian society becomes involved in civic life, it may become more difficult for the political leadership to ignore their hopes for democracy.

A crucial positive factor in both 1993 and 1998 was the international community. Without its direct control over the election process in 1993, and its strong influence in 1998, meaningful, competitive polls likely would not have taken place on either occasion. The risk is that in the future the international community's interest in Cambodia will wane and foreign pressures will not have the countervailing effect they had in 1998.

Hopefully the opposing factions are starting to learn that it is sensible to live together in peace rather than try to eliminate the other. The fact that they ultimately decided in 1993 and in 1998 to join a coalition government and work within the legal framework rather than take up arms again is a modest positive sign.

Considering these conflicting factors, it is highly uncertain whether elections in Cambodia will soon settle down to become a peaceful, democratic, and accepted means of transferring authority, instead of part of a broader ongoing struggle for power. A strong international hand has helped keep the peace and has forced the sides to work together so far. Even with an active international community role, elections seem likely to continue to be flashpoints, unless and until the opposing sides begin to tolerate one another as legitimate officeholders. Domestic and foreign actors need to be much better prepared with strategies to defuse the inevitable postelection crises. If international pressure disappears, and if democratic commitment does not grow among the leadership, even greater consolidation of power by the CPP seems likely, in which case elections could, as often in the past, become a ritual to confirm the legitimacy of those who rule.

A more optimistic scenario seems possible. It foresees continuing international commitment and the gradual but steady development of civil society, political awareness, and democratic institutions. Elections would still be tumultuous at first, but progressively less so as Cambodia's leaders—perhaps it will require a new generation—begin grudgingly to accept one another and to see democracy as more practical and safer than the alternatives. This scenario will be more difficult to achieve, but it would mean a more stable, peaceful, and democratic future.

REFERENCES

Balinski, M.L., and H.P. Young. 1975. "The Quota Method of Apportionment." *American Mathematical Monthly* 82:701–30.

Brown, Frederick Z., and David G. Timberman, eds. 1998. *Cambodia and the International Community: The Quest for Peace, Development, and Democracy*. Singapore: Institute of Southeast Asian Studies.

Brown, MacAlister, and Joseph J. Zasloff. 1998. *Cambodia Confounds the Peacemakers 1979–1998*. Ithaca, N.Y.: Cornell University Press.

Center for Advanced Study (Phnom Penh). 1998. *Final Report: Baseline Survey of Voter Knowledge and Awareness*. Occasional Paper Series No. 3. Phnom Penh, Cambodia: Center for Advanced Study.

Chandler, David P. 1996. *A History of Cambodia*. Boulder, Colo.: Westview Press.

Doyle, Michael W. 1995. *UN Peacekeeping in Cambodia: UNTAC's Civil Mandate*. Boulder, Colo.: Lynne Rienner.

Findlay, Trevor. 1995. *Cambodia: The Legacy and Lessons of UNTAC*. SIPRI Research Report No. 9. Oxford, U.K.: Oxford University Press.

Frieson, Kate G. 1996. "The Cambodian Elections of 1993: A Case of Power to the People?" In *The Politics of Elections in Southeast Asia*, edited by R.H. Taylor. Washington: Woodrow Wilson Center Press.

Heder, Steven. 1998. "Democracy: A Historical Perspective." *Phnom Penh Post*, 30 January–12 February, p. 10.

Heder, Steven, and Judy Ledgerwood, eds. 1996. *Propaganda, Politics and Violence in Cambodia: Democratic Transition under United Nations Peace-keeping*. Armonk, New York: M.E. Sharpe.

Khemara Jati. 1998. http://www.cambodia.org/news:camnews.v001.n743.11.

International Republican Institute. 1999. *Kingdom of Cambodia Parliamentary Elections July 26, 1998. Observation Report*. Washington, D.C.: International Republican Institute.

Manikas, Peter M., and Eric Bjornlund. 1998. "Cambodia's 1998 Elections: The Failure of Democratic Consolidation." *New England Journal of Public Policy* 14:145–60.

Mayall, James, ed. 1996. *The New Interventionism, 1991–1994: UN Experience in Cambodia, Former Yugoslavia, and Somalia*. New York: Cambridge University Press.

National Democratic Institute for International Affairs. 1999. *The July 26, 1998 Cambodian National Assembly Elections*. Washington, D.C.: National Democratic Institute for International Affairs.

Sanderson, John M., and Michael Maley. 1998. "Elections and Liberal Democracy in Cambodia." *Australian Journal of International Affairs* 52:241–53.

Schier, Peter. 1998. "How the Seat Allocation Formulas Make All the Difference." *Phnom Penh Post*, 21 August–3 September, p. 6.

Sorpong Peou. 1997. *Conflict Neutralization in the Cambodian War: From Battlefield to Ballot Box*. Kuala Lumpur, Malaysia: Oxford University Press.

———. 1998. "The Cambodian Elections of 1998 and Beyond: Democracy in the Making?" *Contemporary Southeast Asia* 20:279–97.

———. 1999. "Cambodia in 1998: From Despair to Hope?" *Asian Survey* 39:20–26.

Special Representative of the United Nations Secretary-General for Human Rights in Cambodia. 1997. *Memorandum to the Royal Government of Cambodia, 22 August 1997.*
———. 1998a. *Memorandum to the Royal Government of Cambodia, 13 May 1998.*
———. 1998b. *Monitoring of Election-Related Intimidation and Violence. Post-Election Period. Report 26 July 1998–18 August 1998.*
United Nations. 1995. *The United Nations and Cambodia, 1991–1995.* New York: United Nations, Department of Public Information.

CHAPTER 9

Political Reform and the New Thai Electoral System: Old Habits Die Hard?

by Surin Maisrikrod

SINCE THE 1932 COUP that toppled the absolute monarchy, there has been significant democratic development in Thailand despite seventeen more military coups or attempted coups. Over these sixty-eight years, the country has experimented with a number of constitutional forms and electoral systems in between military takeovers and political crises. Thailand has had sixteen constitutions, including the current one promulgated in 1997, and nineteen general elections, including four during the 1990s. The last general elections were held in 1996.

The 1997 Constitution established yet another electoral system, which was tested for the first time with the election of the Senate on 4 March 2000. Following the election, which was the first ever for the Senate, some seats were nullified due to fraud and new elections were held. It is hoped that the next election, that of the House of Representatives, which will occur shortly, will see the new system improved and will work more effectively to "clean up" Thai politics.

Skeptics have expressed concern that the new electoral system can only do so much for Thailand's political and democratic development. Criticism is often directed at the behaviors and values of Thai politicians and voters and the need for them to develop a deeper respect for democracy and not succumb too easily to the old practice of patronage and money politics. The optimists, however, hold that Thai democracy has, with trials and errors, already made a lot of headway. They note that several attempts to stage military coups failed during the 1980s, and a military takeover of the government in 1992, following the 1991 coup, was met with strong opposition; the 1992 military regime fell after only weeks in power. The recent Senate election, which saw an overwhelming turnout, was effectively able to screen out a significant number of corrupt, unscrupulous politicians and supports the optimism for future democratic development in Thailand.

This chapter discusses the political implications of elections in the 1980s and 1990s, the historical context that gave rise to the new electoral system, the characteristics of the new system, the relationship between the electoral reform and the main political actors—principally the political parties, the civil society, and the military—and, lastly, the Senate elections that tested the effectiveness of the new electoral system.

THE THAI POLITICAL REFORM MOVEMENT

The new Thai electoral system must be seen in the context of the political reform movement that crystallized following the military coup of 1991 and the military suppression of prodemocracy demonstrators in May 1992. Although the absolute monarchy was toppled in 1932 and a western-style parliamentary system introduced, Thailand was best described as a "bureaucratic polity" (Riggs 1966) wherein the military and civilian bureaucracy dominated Thai political life. Parliamentary politics was interrupted by military takeover time and again. With the onset of the Cold War, and United States' efforts to obtain the Thai military's support for the American policy of containment, the military's hold of politics was strengthened and to some extent legitimated. The military virtually had complete control of politics during the 1950s and 1960s.

The United States' support of Thailand was extensive and included military, economic, and educational assistance. Capitalist development was adopted by the Thai state. In line with this development strategy, manpower development "American style" was adopted in a big way. Hundreds of Thai students were sent to the United States each year to pursue higher education. In addition to learning modern management, these students were also exposed to what was for them a new idea—the value of democracy. Although these students were sent to the United States by an authoritarian regime, many returned opposed to the principles of the Thai military. In the university environment, where state intervention was minimal, these foreign-educated returnees propagated antiauthoritarian doctrines.

The 1973 student uprising, a manifestation of this process, marked a dramatic turning point in the history of Thai politics. The democratic era that followed was, however, short-lived as it created many powerful losers, who conspired and fought back to regain their positions of authority. Making use of the perceived threat from communist Indochina and the rising threat of the then-Communist Party of Thailand, the rightists who controlled the state were able to neutralize the liberal-leaning forces and isolate the student/intellectual leftists. The students, intellectuals, and leftists were eventually crashed in the October 1976 coup, in the name of communist suppression. Another military coup followed in 1977, and Thai politics were once again brought back into the military fold.

From 1980 to 1988, under the leadership of Prime Minister and army chief General Prem Tinsulanonda, the parliament was allowed to operate in a limited manner; Prem was not elected, but he ran a coalition government with support from political parties in Parliament. Prem as the leader of the military also retained his power to appoint members of the military and technocrats to key ministries and prime ministerial advisory positions, bypassing political parties that gave parliamentary support to him. The manner in which such power was shared was known as Thai "semidemocracy"(Chai-Anan 1990). The semidemocratic period nevertheless helped nurture democratic forces, and when the military wanted to continue with its man, Prem, as a nonelected prime minister, the democratic forces strongly opposed it. A petition was sent to the king to block a reappointment of General Prem to a new term and demonstrations were planned. The public wanted an elected parliamentarian to be a prime minister. Prem gave in and Chatichai Choonhavan, leader of Chart Thai Party, took over the prime ministership. In 1988, Chatichai became the first elected prime minister in more than a decade. This transition to civilian rule marked the beginning of a new era of Thai democracy. The public euphoria was reigning, and the elected politicians—regardless of the means they had been elected—enjoyed arguably unprecedented legitimacy. Chatichai's prime ministership was widely seen as a democratic breakthrough.

The public euphoria towards democracy in the second half of the 1980s was enhanced by Thailand's phenomenal economic growth. Business opportunities were abundant with local millionaires blossoming. Industrial as well as government-owned infrastructure projects were booming. It seemed that at that moment, Thailand had reached a momentous juncture in history, when democracy and economic growth converged. Unfortunately, this convergence had a negative side effect. More infrastructure projects and business opportunities also meant more corruption. Kickbacks involving "capitalist" politicians giving concessions to friends and receiving direct monetary benefits were rampant. Politicians, bureaucrats, and businesspeople alike took advantage of the out-of-date and weak laws governing business practices compounded by the absence of accepted norms of political behavior. Although Chatichai was popular with his economic and foreign policies, his ministerial cabinet was sarcastically called a "buffet cabinet," a take-what-you-like group of government ministers.

Along with the growth in capitalist development, the middle class expanded, which in turn led to an expansion of the civil society. In less than three years of Chatichai administration, it was obvious to the strengthening civil society, and those who had some sense about the principles of government, that elected officials did not necessarily bring about good government. The legitimacy of Chatichai government nose-dived, and the military, with tacit support from the prodemocracy forces, staged a coup in 1991 to "clean up" the political mess. Thai politics were in great dilemma; a military coup was staged to remove a democratically elected government in order to bring about a good government. (Of course, this is one of the reasons the military gave to justify its takeover; there were other reasons, including the military's and bureaucrats' fear of politicians encroaching on the former's turf.)

The problems associated with the Chatichai government exposed Thais to the many flaws in their democracy. As noted, the gradual retrenchment of the "bureaucratic polity" and the expansion of money-dominated politics had brought about an undesirable result—corruption. At the same time, the term "parliamentary dictatorship" was crafted to describe the situation where a coalition government formulated policy or acted blindly on the basis of its parliamentary majority, without regard to public opinion. The privilege of parliamentary majority was greatly abused. This dilemma set in motion a political reform movement, the main agenda of which was to get rid of corruption and abuses of power by the capitalists cum politicians, to increase government accountability and transparency, and to empower the civil society to have effective and meaningful participation in the political process. A hunger strike in 1995 by a social critic and a former politician, Chalard Vorachat, received wide public support and triggered a constitutional reform effort that culminated in the formation of the Constitutional Drafting Assembly (CDA) in 1996. Incumbent politicians, whose credibility had plummeted because of their alleged corrupt behavior, were deliberately excluded from the drafting process for fear that they might hijack the charter. Instead, the Assembly was composed of ninety-nine members, including one member each from the seventy-six provinces, eight experts in public law, eight experts in political science or public administration, and seven individuals with political or public or constitutional drafting experience. These ninety-nine men and women (but mostly men) could be broadly categorized as from the civil society.

The only role reserved for the sitting members of Parliament was to vote on the pool of nominees for the ninety-nine seats in the CDA and either to approve or to reject the draft constitution as a whole; they were not allowed to make amendments to the draft. In the event that the House of Representatives rejected the draft, a popular referendum would be called. These measures were installed by the CDA's predecessor, the Committee for Democratic Development, to guard against a possible tampering of the draft constitution by politicians who were believed to have already done much to damage the Thai democracy. To be consistent with this desire for a civil society, the CDA, through its subcommittee, the Constitution Drafting Committee (CDC), ensured that the drafting process involved as many people as possible representing various sections of civil society and professional groups from various parts of the country. Public hearings were held; the people also participated by answering questionnaires and by giving ideas through suggestion boxes. Also 300 organizations, including business, industry, agriculture, mass media, various professional groups, educational institutions, political parties, democracy groups, environmental groups, and other nongovernmental organizations, participated at one stage or another in the drafting process (CDA 1997, 170). The drafters of the constitution—dubbed the "people's constitution"—went through this process to ensure that the highest law of the land would not serve any particular group.

Understandably, some quarters, especially incumbent politicians, were not happy with the draft because they feared they would lose under the new system. Initially, they voiced their opposition to the draft charter, but the economic collapse in July 1997—which was said to have been caused, to a very large extent, by politicians' corruption and "cronyism"—brought back memories of the Chatichai era, and this served to heighten the civil society's determination to do whatever it could to force the politicians to approve the constitution. The new constitution was passed in October 1997.

Electoral Experience during the 1980s and 1990s

Thai democracy saw several significant political outcomes of elections over the past two decades. Without dwelling on the details of each election, a number of generalizations can be drawn from the experience.

First, the period has seen the emergence of "money politics," which has resulted in a number of electoral manifestations, including high-cost campaigning, candidate-buying, canvasser recruitment, vote-buying, and abusing of power by government officials (Surin and McCargo 1997, 135–40). Since the 1980s, marketing, advertising, and public relations techniques have been used widely to gain electoral support. These techniques have commonly included distributing color candidate photographs, displaying posters depicting candidates in official uniforms and decorations, printing brief policy statements and slogans, handing out cassette tapes containing speeches by party leaders, and giving out calendars with photographs of candidates. Candidates have also taken advantage of television campaign advertising, which was legalized for the first time in 1995.

Candidate-buying is a situation where former members of Parliament and other prospective candidates with good electoral prospects are offered financial incentives to join or switch political parties. A "transfer fee" in the region of 10–20 million baht might be offered. To ensure victory, a candidate must be able to recruit canvassers, particularly "influential" persons including village headmen, teachers, government officials, and local priests. Money was the prime mover in such recruitment drives. Prices for votes vary, ranging from 100–200 baht per household to 1,000 baht per vote depending on the level of competition. A successful candidate standing in a typical northeastern constituency in July 1995 would probably spend 20–25 million baht, with up to one-quarter of this financing vote-buying (Surin and McCargo 1997, 139). Worse still, government officials who oversaw the administration of elections often abused their power and cooperated with corrupt politicians to rig elections. Reports of candidates buying up polling station officials have not been uncommon.

Second, the past twenty years has seen a trend toward a more stable multiparty system, if not a variation of the two-party system. Given a chaotic situation in 1975 when as many as fifty political parties contested elections, the declining number of parties is viewed as a positive development reflecting Thailand's political maturing. While in recent years as many as eleven parties have vied for parliamentary seats, it is increasingly clear that only four or five parties are now key players. For now and the foreseeable future, the main parties are Democrat, Chart Thai (Thai Nation), New Aspiration, Chart Pattana (National Development), and the newly formed Thai Rak Thai (Thais Love Thais).

It is not possible to categorize the major parties along ideological or even policy lines. In fact, as noted, members of Parliament switch camps without jeopardizing their electoral prospects. On the contrary, switching parties correlates with a perceived gain, politically or financially.

Third, elections in the past decade have indicated a "regionalization" of support for political parties (Surin 1992, 45–46). This trend was repeated in the 1996 election; the New Aspiration Party (NAP) dominated the Northeast, the country's largest region, while the Democrat prevailed in the South. Chart Thai maintained its stronghold in the central part of the country, while the North, the second largest region, was shared by the Democrat, New Aspiration, and Chart Pattana equally. The Northeast, with about 34 percent of the 400 parliamentary seats, has been the fiercest battleground for major political parties. (The central region has about 27 percent of the members of Parliament [MPs], while the North has 16 percent and the South 12 percent). The Democrat, the underdog in the Northeast, has been trying relentlessly to gain more ground there. The NAP has been advantaged by its leader, Chavalit Yongchaiyudh, having served as a key military officer in the region during the government's anticommunist campaign in the 1970s. Chavalit can rely on his extensive network of support built up over the years from influential people in the Northeast.

Fourth, the 1990s elections have produced a politics of division between the middle classes and the rural people. As in politics in general, the middle class has had a very intriguing role in Thailand's electoral politics. The middle class, particularly the Bangkok-based one, has been crucial to the democratic development in general as it spearheaded significant political change during the 1990s (Anek 1993). In terms of electoral politics, as a core of the civil society it helped expose various flaws of the electoral process and practices. The middle class has been frustrated by electoral results that it claims are largely produced by the rural voters. That is, the rural people elect politicians largely on the basis of a patronage system formed through networks of influential people. These politicians do not care about policy issues or administrative performance; instead, their main concern was to make use of their positions to gain financially in preparation for the next election. This sort of political behavior, on the part of both the electorate and the politicians, encouraged corruption and abuses of power and eroded the legitimacy of democratic development. Yet it is these very people who then administered the country. The well-educated middle class measured politicians on the basis of policy issues and administrative performance and often found them wanting. This produced an ongoing—albeit subtle—tension between these two groups within the society. In other words, there was a situation in which a rurally elected government could not meet an expectation of the Bangkok-based middle classes (Anek 1996).

Fifth, during the 1990s, with the growth of the middle class, the civil society—a coalition of nongovernmental organizations, the intelligentsia, and members of the media—expanded tremendously. The civil society demanded more political participation on a continuing, more institutionalized basis. While traditionally reactive, the civil society engineered the formation of an election watchdog, PollWatch, in the March 1992 election. As mentioned, the civil society was crucial to the political reform movement between 1996 and 1997. It has now played a key role in administering elections, a role previously monopolized by the officials of the Ministry of Interior. The involvement of the civil society has helped discourage electoral cheats and other dishonest activities.

Sixth, since the 1980s, the Thai electorate has exhibited a relentless desire for a political alternative to "old style politics" characterized by incompetence, corruption, and money politics. In 1986, Chamlong Srimuang, a devout Buddhist and a former army general who projected himself as a half-layman, half-monk, was elected governor of Bangkok. Chamlong lived an austere life and practiced Buddhist celibacy. He used an old warehouse as his residence and donated a part of his salary to charity. Corruption was totally out of the question. Chamlong tried to prove that contrary to popular belief, politics could be virtuous. The "Chamlong Fever" in the second half of the 1980s was evidence of the public's hunger for alternative politics. Unfortunately, Chamlong's style of politics did not survive long: his decision in the 1990s to join a coalition government with tainted "old style" politicians disillusioned the public, eroding his support. Thais continued to search for a new kind of politics and a new kind of leadership.

This desire on the part of the Thai public, particularly the middle class, probably explains the rise of what could be called the "Anand phenomenon," referring to Anand Panyarachun, twice prime minister. Anand, seen as competent, transparent, visionary, and, more importantly, prodemocratic, immensely affected political reform in Thailand. Ironically, however, he obtained his prime ministership not through parliamentary election, but through a military appointment. In staging a coup in February 1991, the military claimed that it wanted to clean up the corrupt government of Prime Minister Chatichai Choonhavan. Interestingly, the coup received tacit support from the civil society. As part of its claim to create a good government, the military appointed Anand.

The very appointment of Anand by the military was also ironic because the latter dismissed him from his post as undersecretary of the foreign ministry on the charge of being a leftist after the military coup of 1976. But Anand had a proven record of competency and was well known in both Asia and the United States, having served as Thai ambassador to the United Nations and Washington for about a decade. His appointment by the military junta following the coup of

1991 won praise from the public and he did not disappoint them. He ran the government effectively and promoted the ideas of transparency, honesty, accountability, and popular participation in government. Indeed, he set a model for good government. In addition, despite being appointed by the military, he did not kowtow to the establishment. On the contrary, he did much to lay the foundation for the civil society's participation in the political process. PollWatch, a precursor of the Election Commission, was established under the Anand administration. Moreover, he curtailed the power of the state in a variety of ways, including allowing public access to government information. Within a period of about a year as prime minister, Anand won the hearts and minds of conservatives and progressive alike, with his administrative efficiency and promotion of political and bureaucratic reforms. In May 1992, following the military suppression of demonstrators, Anand Panyarachun once more rescued the nation for democracy when he again agreed to serve as interim prime minister until elections were held in September. In fact, the way he has been perceived and treated gave rise to the term "Anand phenomenon." He symbolizes the "new politics" of Thailand and typifies the values that the Thai civil society—largely the urban middle class— wants to cultivate for the country. His middle-class followers identify a number of Anand's characteristics, calling for desirable values for Thai society: the possession of a broad social vision, frankness, an instrumental orientation, decisiveness, the capacity for compromise, a team spirit, leadership, transparency, and a sense of practical strategy (Prasarn et al. 1999).

Anand is used as a reference point in Thai politics to distinguish good government from bad. In the context of the legislature, this means that the parliamentary system must be operated with accountability, honesty, transparency, and popular participation—generally known as "good government." More importantly, it means that Thais should not enlist the support of the military to get rid of government—even a corrupt one. Instead, a constitutional process in general and electoral requirement in particular should be able to prevent corrupt government, or to get rid of it, if it occurs. In short, to most Thais, a constitutional process should be able to produce a prime minister like Anand Panyarachun.

By and large, these characteristics of Thai elections in the 1980s and 1990s indicate problems as well as development in the electoral process of the country. The problems highlight why restructuring the electoral system was one of the main objectives of the political reformists.

The New Parliamentary and Electoral Systems

The corruption, lack of transparency and accountability, and the insulation of politicians, which in the end undermined the legitimacy of the popularly elected Chatichai government and led to its downfall in February 1991, can be in part traced back to flaws in the constitutional and electoral processes. Although the results of Anand Panyarachun's prime ministership were most desirable, its source of power was not quite legitimate. Furthermore, it was strongly believed that there must be a system that could prevent a takeover by the military. The new constitution has three aims: to break up the monopoly of politicians and allow for more meaningful participation of the people; to ensure stronger political legitimacy for political and bureaucratic systems by creating a more effective system of checks and balances; and to put in place a system that ensures stronger prime ministership and government stability (Borwornsak 1998, 50–52).

Certainly, the new electoral system is expected to be a crucial mechanism to achieve good government. The electoral process hopefully will be capable not only of screening out incompetent, corrupt, rascal politicians from Parliament, but also of recruiting well-qualified, visionary, and honest candidates into the chamber. In the words of Anand Panyarachun, chairman of the drafting committee of the new constitution: "[The past] electoral system did not help in nurturing democracy in Thailand. On the contrary, [it] encouraged money-dumping, corruption and frauds" (Anand 1998, 47).

While the new constitution retains the bicameral system, both houses are now very different from the past. The House of Representatives, the Lower House, has two types of members—100 elected using a party list system, and 400 others elected from single-member constituencies in the country's seventy-six provinces. The 200 members of the Senate, the Upper House, are now directly elected for the first time, using the simple majority system.

The House of Representatives

One dominant feature of the Thai electoral system has been the multimember constituency, where the number of votes each person has was determined by the number of representatives in the constituency: a voter had three votes in a three–member constituency, and so forth. The number of MPs varied according to population, with 150,000 people per elected member. On this basis, the number of parliamentarians had increased over the years as the number of the eligible voters increased. Most recently, Parliament had 393 members. For the first time, the Constitution fixed the lower house at 500 members. At the drafting stage, the issue of using a single-member constituency system was quite contentious. Proponents of the system argued that it was consistent with universal democratic principle that one person should have one vote; that compared to the usual three-member constituency, the single-member constituency would be much smaller, making it easier for the MP to look after constituent interests; and that smaller geographical areas would require less money for electioneering, thus allowing poorer, but good-quality candidates, to contest seats (Somkid 1999, 43).

For Uthai Pimchaichon (1998, 25–28), the chairman of the Constitution Drafting Assembly, a system of one person, one vote, single-member constituencies would get rid of patronage electoral politics. According to Uthai, a veteran politician who is known for his stance against military dictatorship, the larger three-member constituency system made it impossible for candidates to canvass in person effectively. Candidates relied heavily on their client-canvassers, who often turned out to be *chao phor*, local "influential" people. Under this system, money is the main source of getting electoral support. Furthermore, in turn, these local influentials retained strong bargaining power with the politicians for whom they delivered votes. And in the event that the candidate became a minister, he or she would often feel obliged to serve the interests of those rascals whose very influence was shady, if not outright illegal. This sense of obligation has been a source of corruption, nepotism, and abuses of power by politicians.

Alternatively, in a smaller constituency, it was felt, candidates would not have to rely on money or local influential people and therefore would not be held hostage by them (Uthai 1998, 25–28). If a candidate were well known and had a good track record, he or she could run for a seat and win free of corrupting influences. This system should, therefore, be able to prevent the damaging effects of vote-buying, which undermines the legitimacy of electoral politics. Of course, if the voters demand money, money-dumping could be even more rampant in a smaller constituency.

As mentioned above, the party list system to select 100 members was introduced for the first time in Thailand, and the system has yet to be electorally tested. Under the system, each party can nominate a maximum of 100 candidates for Parliament; their election is determined by the percentage of the vote that that party attracts nationwide. For example, a party that gets 30 percent of the vote nationwide would theoretically receive 30 seats. Parties that attract less than 5 percent of the total vote nationwide are automatically eliminated, so large parties hypothetically could receive a higher proportion of the 100 seats than their total proportion of the votes cast.

The rationale for the list system is that it allows the electorate to express their preference along party lines—or simply put, the party they prefer to form the government. To attract voters, political parties must include in their list better known—or, so to speak, more qualified—people. Furthermore, the new constitution provides that a member of Parliament relinquish his/her parliamentary seat if appointed minister. This makes it easier, and less risky, for a political party to appoint a minister from the list because that party needs only to move a new name up on the list. This can be contrasted to the appointment of an MP elected from a constituency as a minister. In that case, a by-election would need to be held in which all the parties would compete.

Some argue that the party list system, in effect, provides a more direct role to the people in choosing a prime minister. According to Uwanno Borwornsak (1998), the system would enable electors to vote for a party led by a person they want to be prime minister. It is also expected that the list system may attract high-quality candidates. Since candidates running on the list theoretically do not have to campaign personally, it is believed that more qualified individuals who were unwilling to campaign for a seat might be encouraged to have their names placed on the list. For instance, this route to office might be attractive to a successful businessman, academic, or retired government official who lacked public speaking skills or energy or simply could not stand Thai-style "mud-slinging" politics. The system has implied to some that list MPs are better individuals and as such will stand a better chance to be selected as cabinet ministers. In such a scenario, the list system could create two classes of MPs and tension within political parties.

The new constitution also requires a bachelor's degree as the minimum educational level to be eligible to run for a parliamentary seat (Article 107). (This requirement also exists for holding a ministerial appointment.) It might seem odd that a political reform that rode on a wave of democratic values would discriminate against prospective parliamentarians on the basis of their education. Even more odd was the fact that the academics among the 99 constitution drafters opposed the provision but were voted down by the nonacademic members of the drafting assembly. Again, this has to be viewed within social, political, and historical context. One of the factors perceived to be obstructing democratic development in Thailand has been the entrance into Parliament of local tycoons whose sources of wealth have been questionable. These rascal politicians often did not have higher education or any education at all. Through their involvement in shady businesses, however, they were able to amass wealth, and with wealth, they were able to win parliamentary seats through vote-buying and other intimidation. Although in reality MPs without a degree historically constituted a small number, several managed to hold influential portfolios. The assumption here is that to require a degree as part of the qualification for political offices is to prevent rascal politicians. Furthermore, the drafting assembly believed that people with formal educational qualifications would be more likely to pay attention to policy issues and be able to formulate policy while *chao phor* would be generally more interested in using political power to further enhance their influence. The result has been that several members of Parliament and many aspirants have sought either real or concocted degrees to meet the requirement.

Under the new electoral system, it is also envisaged that the House of Representatives will be a mature, second deliberative body independent of the Senate. In the past, the unstated presumption was that the Lower House could be a bit sloppy since the historically appointed Upper House, composed of many well-educated bureaucrats, would more closely scrutinize legislation. Now the House is expected to be as well-versed in public affairs and legislative requirements as the Senate.

The Senate

In the past, the Senate was appointed by the prime minister of the day, so its role as a legislative goal-keeper was to favor the government. Under the new constitutional system, the elected Senate has added to its traditional legislative scrutinizing role more powers of control to ensure government honesty, transparency, and accountability. The unprecedented powers of the Senate include selecting, appointing, advising, or endorsing the following appointments: the Election Commission, the Ombudsman, the National Human Rights Commission, the Constitutional Court, the members of the Justice Commission, the Administrative Court, the National Counter-Corruption Commission, the National Broadcasting and Telecommunications Commission, and the auditor-general. All of these agencies are either newly created or existing ones modified by the Constitution of 1997. These agencies "supervised" by the Senate are collectively designed to ensure government transparency, accountability, and honesty.

Moreover, for the first time, the Senate is empowered to dismiss (with petition of not less than 50,000 eligible voters and through a due process) the prime minister, ministers, members of Parliament, members of the Senate, the Chief Justice of the Supreme Court, members of the Constitutional Court, Chief of the Administrative Court, the attorney general, members of the Election Commission, the Ombudsman, members of the auditor-general's office, and justices, prosecutors, and other top government officials.

The mandate of the new 200-member, nonpartisan, directly elected Senate is to be an umpire rather than a goal-keeper. The term of the senators is six years (Article 130), and Senators are not allowed to run for two consecutive terms (Article 126 [3]). This is a major shift from the appointed Senate of the past whose role was to support the government. The change is politically significant and consistent with the political reforms designed to allow for greater public control or direct democracy. The significance lies in the notion that Senators are the "real" representatives of the people by virtue of being elected and nonpartisan. This means in the end they are, if all else fails, the final check in the event that politics has run wild.

The desire to have the Senate as umpire is also demonstrated by the way Senators are elected. Senators are not allowed to be members of any political party. Former party members must wait one year before they are eligible to run for a Senate seat. Senate candidates are not permitted to campaign in any form, except to publish self-introduction leaflets. A discussion of policy issues or political stance is not allowed. Instead, the state is required to publicize backgrounds of the candidates for the benefit of voters. In addition, the state is required to provide candidates with air time and public venues so that they can introduce themselves and their backgrounds. The underpinning assumption here is that senators must be honest, well-educated with known expertise, and free from control of vested interests. In short, they are to be "nonpoliticians."

Compulsory Voting

Another "first" established by the new Constitution is compulsory voting, making voting a duty and not a right of the people (Article 68). This is an attempt to address what many believe is the lack of a strong sense of possession or ownership of their democracy among the Thai, which may have inhibited the country's democratic development. Because voting is now a duty, one may lose certain political rights if found neglecting to vote without sufficient reasons, although it is not clear what penalties would be applied. To further facilitate this compulsory voting, a number of new provisions have also been stipulated. They include advance voting for those who cannot be in their registered constituencies on the voting day and voting at Thai embassies and consular offices for those abroad.

The Administration of Elections

Another breakthrough is in the administration of elections by an independent organization, the Election Commission (EC), appointed by the Senate. In the past, the administration of elections was under the purview of the Ministry of the Interior, which gave an incumbent government an advantage. The Minister of the Interior could influence provincial governors and other officials in the ministry—whom the minister appoints—to influence election outcomes in favor of the government. This power to administer elections is now completely out of the hands of Interior Ministry officials.

This administrative change also allows for greater participation by the citizenry through the Election Commission, which, in a way, evolved from PollWatch. Members of this election watchdog have now been largely absorbed by the Election Commission, particularly at the provincial level. One of the members of the five-member commission, Gothom Arya, was secretary-general of PollWatch. Nevertheless, PollWatch continues to play an independent monitoring role in elections. Members of the Election Commission are responsible not only for overseeing the election but also for disseminating information about elections, educating the electorate, and preventing vote-buying and other abuses.

Vote-Buying and Other Abuses

One of the major concerns of the reformists was the prevention of vote-buying and abuses of power by both bureaucrats and capitalist-cum-politicians. A number of provisions have been made to prevent or minimize such abuses:

1. Stricter control is exerted over expenditure by candidates. The Election of the House of Representatives and Senators of 1998, an organic law of the new constitution, requires political parties to set up election accounts under supervision of a qualified accountant detailing how the money is received and spent with accounts submitted to the Election Commission within ninety days after the election results are announced (Article 43). The Election Commission is to audit the accounts and make them public (Article 43, [2]). These regulations are supported further by a provision of the Political Party Act of 1998 on donations to political parties. For the first time in Thai parliamentary history,

political parties are required to detail donations including the names of donors and amounts they donate (Articles 45, 48). Furthermore, the Political Party Act of 1998 requires the state for the first time to provide financial support to political parties (Articles 56–64).

2. Giving promises of rewards to woo voters is prohibited. Article 44 of the same law prohibits candidates from proposing rewards in any form, to either individuals or organizations, and from intimidating voters.

3. Vote counting will be done at one location, such as a district office (there are about 850 districts in the seventy-six provinces of Thailand), instead of at polling stations—at the village level as previously done. This measure under Article 69 of the 1998 election law is designed to try to prevent vote-buying. By previously counting votes at polling stations, which cover a small area, vote-buyers could more or less verify whether citizens were actually voting as instructed. In the event that the latter did not, some form of retribution could then be applied. Under the new system, it is expected that there will be no way to check whether the canvassers actually delivered what they promised because all the ballots will be mixed together.

Political Parties, the Civil Society, and the Military

As mentioned earlier, the political party system is much less chaotic today than twenty years ago. During the 1990s, about ten parties were on the political scene, but the major parties have been the Democrat, New Aspiration, Chart Thai, Chart Pattana, Social Action, Prachakorn Thai, and Palang Dharma Parties. In 1998, the Thai Rak Thai Party emerged with considerable support. No party in Thailand has enjoyed the good fortune of dominating for very long. Over the years, each has had an equal share of ups and downs. Chart Thai and the Democrat emerged out of the "semidemocratic" period of the 1980s somewhat stronger than others, which enabled them to be major players in the late 1980s and the 1990s. In 1988, with the reemergence of democracy, Chart Thai took advantage of having the largest number of parliamentary seats to form a coalition government. The party was then under the leadership of Chatichai Choonhavan. But the party suffered a setback following the "Black May" of 1992, when a splinter group formed the Chart Pattana (National Development) Party. The splinter group feared that Chart Thai was too closely associated with the hated military regime. Despite the defection, Chart Thai remained very strong and emerged as the largest party with ninety-two seats in the 1995 elections, which enabled it to form a coalition government with its leader, Banharn Silpa-archa, as prime minister. The party suffered another major breakup in 1996 when an influential faction joined the New Aspiration Party. The faction, led by Sanoh Tienthong, was disappointed with the allocation of ministerial portfolios, particularly Sanoh himself, who had earlier hoped to be appointed to the most sought-after ministry, the Ministry of Interior. The defection weakened Chart Thai considerably, and it was able to win only thirty-nine seats in the 1996 elections. The party now is the third largest party in the Democrat-led coalition, and it is unlikely in the near future that Chart Thai will win as many seats as it did before 1996. Nevertheless, the party will continue to be a significant force on the Thai political stage for years to come.

Established in 1946, the Democrat is the oldest and, arguably, the most institutionalized party. Over the past fifty years, the party has experienced ups and downs, but it has stood the test of time and is currently the largest party. The Democrat emerged on the political scene as a fighter against the military dictatorship. During years of authoritarianism, the Democrat served as a comfort home for prodemocracy people, particularly the young intellectuals who despised the military rule; it was the hope for a democratic change right from the beginning. When military regimes during the 1960s and early 1970s allowed elections and Parliament, the party was seen as providing a voice for antiauthoritarians. It was no accident therefore that in the 1975 election, the first following the downfall of a military regime led by Field Marshall Thanom Kittikachorn, the Democrat won the largest number of seats in the Parliament—72 of 269. The Democrat formed a minority government that collapsed less than a month later, lacking support from other parties. In the 1976 elections, it again won the most seats—114 of 279—and formed a coalition government with the Chart Thai Party as its major partner.

Thailand in the mid-1970s was very volatile politically. The country was divided clearly along left-right ideological lines. Perceived as a progressive party, the rise of the Democrat in the mid-1970s caused great concern among the conservatives led by the military-bureaucracy alliance. The Democrat Party was readily put on the left, which, given the heightened threat of communist Indochina at the time, was seen as potentially detrimental to the security of the Thai state. The Democrat became a target of attack by the rightists, and the military coup of 1976 ended the political ascendance of the party in the 1970s.

In the 1980s, the Democrat was again brought back into the political limelight by Prime Minister Prem Tinsulanonda, then concurrently the Army Commander-in-Chief, a moderate who was more understanding of the democratic forces. Prem saw in the Democrat, which had more technocrats than other parties, quality politicians. Furthermore, because key people in the Democrat came from academic backgrounds or had never held high positions in either the military or businesses linked to the old establishment, the party was relatively untainted. This, of course, seemed to go well with Prem's impeccable background as a "rural soldier" known for his honesty, competence, dedication, and incorruptibility. He recruited technocrats to serve on his advisory teams and in key ministries. He proved to be very effective and helped stabilize the country in the early

1980s after the turmoil of the 1970s. He was a popular prime minister—though he was not elected and not known for his tolerance of parliamentary scrutiny. Because of their mutual admiration, Prem's popularity seemed to have helped the Democrat electorally. And in the 1986 elections, the Democrat again won the largest number of seats, 100 out of 347.

With the exception of the March 1992 election, when it won just 44 seats, the Democrat has grown in popularity in the 1990s. In the September 1992 election, following "Black May"—the military's violent suppression of mass demonstrations opposed to its attempt to take control of government—the party again won the largest number of seats, 79 out of 360. This victory allowed Democrat to form a coalition government, with its leader, Chuan Leekpai, as prime minister. The Chuan-led government lasted for more than three years before it collapsed as a result of a land reform scandal involving a Democrat minister. The 1995 election saw Democrat running second with 86 seats. Chart Thai ran first with 92 seats in the 360-seat House of Representatives. Following the 1996 elections, the Democrat, second in the polls, sat in the opposition camp. When the New Aspiration Party, led by Chavalit Yongchaiyudh, collapsed under the weight of the economic crash of July 1997, the Democrat once again took over government, with Chuan Leekpai, the party leader, as prime minister. So long as Chuan, best known for his honesty, incorruptibility, and, not least, political mastery—something he has been able to maintain for more than thirty years in the political arena—remains party leader, the Democrat will most likely go into the next election with considerable strength.

The New Aspiration Party, established in 1990 by former chief of the army General Chavalit Youngchaiyudh, started with great fanfare with many "star recruits," and it performed relatively handsomely in its first electoral test in March 1992, winning 72 seats. The fact that it came only third, however—which meant there was no chance for its leader to be prime minister—was a big disappointment given the high expectation it had prior to the election. The fortune of NAP rose only when a big faction in Chart Thai broke away and joined it in the 1996 elections, making it the largest party in Parliament. Chavalit was made Prime Minister but a year later was forced out of office because of the financial crisis in July 1997. NAP has suffered an image problem of having "old style" politicians dominating the party. In 1999, it tried to correct that image by anointing a young intellectual, Chaturon Chaisaeng, as its secretary-general, the second most powerful position next to the party leader. Unfortunately, Chaturon did not last long as the party's secretary-general, and only about a year later NAP gave the position back to a veteran politician. Internal bickering is threatening a breakup of the party. While it is unlikely that NAP will win big in the next election, however, it will continue to be a force to reckon with as it is likely to continue to dominate the largest region of the country, the Northeast.

Chart Pattana Party, a splinter of Chart Thai, essentially shares the same base of support as Chart Thai. Its big advantage is its strong support in the Northeast, second only to the New Aspiration Party. But its strength will be limited by its inability to expand nationwide, largely because the party no longer has a political heavyweight such as Chatichai Choonhavan to lead it. Chatichai's death in 1999 blunted the party's hope to expand its base. The best that could happen to Chart Pattana would be to win enough seats to be a critical member of a coalition government. Beyond that, there is very little chance that it will lead a government.

The Social Action Party has passed its heyday following the death of its leader Kukrit Pramoj, a highly regarded scholar dubbed a "renaissance man" and a "pillar" of Thai democracy. What the Social Action Party had hoped for was to be part of a government—any government! This party likely will have difficulty going forward and may be prepared to merge with a bigger party in the near future.

Prachakorn Thai (Thai Citizens), which had never been able to expand its electoral appeal beyond the capital city of Bangkok, has not done well enough recently to be a significant force in the next election. The party was cut in half in 1997 when a faction defected to the Democrat-led government. The decision of its leader, Samak Sundaravej, to run as governor of Bangkok in mid-2000 is likely to weaken further the party as a national player.

Palang Dharma (Moral Force), formed in 1986 and considered an alternative political force in the late 1980s and early 1990s, lost its support when it did not live up to the public's expectations. It performed miserably as a coalition partner. In the 1996 election, the party had only one member of Parliament, who has since defected to Thai Rak Thai Party. Since the charismatic party leader, Chamlong Srimuang, resigned from the party in 1997, Palang Dharma's popularity has consistently declined. It is now fast sinking into oblivion.

Thai Rak Thai, formed in 1998, has at the moment excited the public. A number of factors explain the rising popularity of the party. First, it is simply the excitement of an arrival of a new kid on the block. In a situation where the incumbent parties, both in the government and in the opposition, have to deal with the realities of day-to-day administration and balancing government respectively, which at times fumble, the Thai Rak Thai, as an outsider, can easily portray itself as an alternative. Second, the party's leader, Thaksin Shinawatra, occupies an envious position in the political landscape of Thailand; he is well educated (he has a doctoral degree), still young (in his early fifties), has many friends (through his background as a student of the armed forces' cadet school) who are rising up through the ranks in the military and policy force, and is a well-respected business entrepreneur. Third, Thaksin is attractive and popular simply because of his money; he is a billionaire, and his ever expanding business empire seems to be bringing in even more money all the time! Most importantly, unlike other tycoon-cum-politicians, whose wealth has often been under suspicion, Thaksin's money-making has been seen as above board—although his business empire is essentially based on state concessions. The public impression is that Thaksin's money has attracted a large number of MPs from rival parties and other personalities with high electability. With a huge amount of money and a score of well-known figures joining it, Thai Rak Thai will go in the next election as a formidable force.

In terms of political parties, by and large, the primary groups remaining are the Democrat, New Aspiration, Chart Thai, Chart Pattana, and certainly Thai Rak Thai. In fact, the real battle in the next election may well be between the Democrat and the Thai Rak Thai. The competing forces will be basically Chuan's mastery and Thaksin's money.

The military will watch the political situation with keen eyes, and it will be very reluctant to be seen as an active player for some time, having suffered politically as a result of its suppression of the demonstrators in May 1992. Although over the years it has become more acceptable to parliamentary politics, it still perceives itself as a "guardian" of the state, and it would probably intervene if and when parliamentary institutions lose their legitimacy, or if "national security" is threatened. At the same time, the civil society will be able to maintain its strength and will be ready to flex it muscles when things go wrong. Given the rising strength of the civil society, political parties as well as the military will be, to very considerable degree, constantly counterbalanced. The civil society will continue to play a very significant role in ensuring that elections are transparent and clean.

THE SENATE ELECTION 2000:
IS THE NEW ELECTORAL SYSTEM VIABLE?

On Saturday, 4 March 2000, a new chapter of Thai political history was written—the first senatorial election ever was held. Up to 70 percent of the electorate voted to pick 200 senators out of 1,526 candidates nationwide. The turnout was the highest in the history of Thai elections. Almost 70,000 members of the nongovernmental organizations helped to conduct the polls—the first time such a direct role was allowed to civil society groups. Despite the new laws to rid the polls of frauds, vote-buying and other uses of electoral influences continued, which resulted in a disqualification of 78 of the 200 winners. The electoral violations forced a new round of elections to replace those not permitted to serve. The Election Commission held the second round on 29 April 2000 in thirty-five provinces. In this round (the first by-election), another 66 were endorsed, while 12 others were suspended on fraud charges. This necessitated a third round, which was held on 4 June 2000. Eight of the 12 winners were endorsed in this round. The fourth round took place on 18 June 2000 for the remaining four senators in four provinces.

Although the Senate election has not yet produced final results, indications are that the Upper House will be dominated by former bureaucrats—including former police and military officers—and former politicians or those who have strong connections with politicians; they comprise about 75 percent of the 200-seat Senate. In other words, the overwhelming majority of senators are well-known public figures or are allied with political parties or interests. For the former public servants, a good track record was as crucial as their bureaucratic network and influence in winning their seats. As for the former politicians or relatives and friends of politicians, their access to the network of political parties with whom they have connections was a deciding factor in their victories. However discreet the use of these networks and influence may be, in effect the rule that prohibits senators from being members of political parties was circumvented. The senators who won the race purely on their popularity are small in numbers; only Bangkok voters elected most of their eighteen senators on this basis.

Whatever the case, the result that "old faces" dominate the Upper House was a direct result of the new Constitution, which prevents campaigning and electioneering. In practice, it means those who are not well known—or not "on the scene" long enough, so to speak—before the election would have very little chance to emerge winners. While the new provisions have, to some degree, discouraged electoral frauds, they also allowed an advantage to the well known, well connected, or well networked. Undoubtedly, however, the large majority of elected senators are well educated, highly experienced, and well known in their respective professions—which, by the way, is not very different from the previously appointed Upper House, this being one of the rationales for the existence of the appointed Senate. But whether such "qualities" will translate into an impartial Senate that can help rid Thailand of dirty politics remains to be seen. One thing is certain, though—because of the strong presence of the "old faces" in the Senate, it is predictably conservative in orientation.

The Thais greeted the election with enthusiasm and excitement and waited for its outcomes with great perplexity. One influential newspaper, *The Nation*, splashed its headline "Money politics vs. People Power" with the subtitle "Silent majority's vote may defeat corruption" (4 March 2000, p. 1). The daily suggested that a new political era had begun. More crucially, this election for the first time had tested new electoral measures, including compulsory voting, administration by an independent Election Commission, advance voting, and one person, one vote suffrage. The EC received a great deal of public attention. The public was quite apprehensive about the effectiveness of the EC in administering the election and ensuring a clean poll. The lack of funds and insufficient manpower were the two biggest problems for the five-member Election Commission. For example, commission members were worried almost up to the day of the election that they did not have enough wooden boxes for ballots. They were also concerned that a great deal of hostility was shown by the incumbent parliamentarians who approve the EC's budget because the independent agency would undermine the latter's ability to manipulate elections. But the most significant incident that led the public to doubt the credibility of the commission was its "too dogmatic, too legalistic" interpretation of the Constitution, which resulted in a disqualification of some forty candidates. The most problematic provision of the Constitution banned "other government officials" from running for Senate seats (Article 109 [11]). To the commission, any person who was appointed to serve on a specialized government body was in the "other government officials" category and therefore was ineligible to run for a seat. These people included university councillors, members of government-appointed religious bodies, chairpersons of Law Society. While the EC may have been correct, this was not the intention of the charter. The highest law of the land meant to bar such state employees as village headmen, who do have direct electoral influence. As one of the drafters of the Constitution, Amorn Raksasat, argued: "the Election Commission's subsequent interpretation of the 'other government officials' was so broad it covered many positions beyond the original intention" (*The Nation*, 5 February 2000, p.6). The decision was successfully challenged in court, and disqualified candidates were eventually reinstated.

The 2000 Senate elections exposed a number of flaws in the new electoral system. When the election laws were written, no one had thought clearly about the implications of suspending suspected winners. While it is sensible to hold new rounds of elections to screen out dishonest candidates, electors have clearly shown "election fatigue" in the second and third rounds of the polls, with voter turnout going down from 70 percent in the first round to 52 and 41 percent in the second and third rounds respectively. Besides, administering elections costs money, time, and manpower. The EC maintains, however, that under the current law, it must hold by-elections to replace the disqualified candidates and cannot do otherwise. Suggestions have been made to move up the candidate next on the list to replace the disqualified one in order to save time and money, and more importantly to prevent public electoral boredom and cynicism.

The second problem relates to the Constitution's provision allowing the Senate to convene only if all the required 200 seats are filled. This has caused a lot of anxiety, and it could, as some have argued, result in political uncertainty in future elections. For example, a new session of the current Parliament was scheduled to be convened on 24 June 2000, by which time, under the law, the Senate must already be in place. Three months after the general elections for the Senate took place in March, the Upper House was yet to be convened. Nevertheless, the EC was eventually able to fill the Senate before the scheduled 24 June parliamentary session. But what about future elections, especially for the House of Representatives, which is essentially a selection of a new government and a new set of policies? If the Senate election is any guide, there will certainly be suspensions of some winners for the Lower House on fraud charges. In such case, if there is no amendment to the law, by-elections will have to be held, possibly requiring several rounds over several months. In that situation, the House of Representatives could not be convened, and a government could not be formed within a reasonably short time as has been the practice. This could, furthermore, mean that the country would have to be under a caretaker government, which does have a mandate. Such a situation could have serious implications on the country's economy, security, and foreign relations.

Third, the election law did not put in place arrangements to enhance the compulsory voting rule. Electors are allowed to vote in advance, if they plan to be traveling out of their registered constituencies on the election day. But it is still a hassle for people who live or work outside of their registered areas. For example, during the first round of the Senate election, it proved very inconvenient and costly for Thai migrant workers and those who live outside of their home provinces to vote, as the law required that the casting of ballots only be done in their respective registered constituencies. In Thailand, migrant workers leave their home provinces to work in different places without registering their temporary residences or places of employment. During the March election of the Senate, a large number of voters, the majority of whom were migrant workers, had to endure the ordeal of long journey back to their home provinces—which could take up to two days each way—in order to cast their votes. The EC is now considering a change to this provision.

Fourth, the rule allowing Thai expatriates to vote—another first—did not work well. The government spent 75 million baht organizing polling for 700,000 Thais living in fifty-six countries during the two rounds of the Senate election. In the first round, only about 10,000 voted, and less than 5,000 voted in the second round. The main cause of the low turnout overseas was that electors were allowed to vote only in person at Thai embassies or consular offices, which in most cases are located in a few big cities in each country. This proves to be impractical. Since then, a committee chaired by the Minister of Foreign Affairs, Surin Pitsuwan, has called for the EC to allow postal votes for expatriates. The committee argued that postal votes are already allowed under the Articles 84 and 85 of the electoral law, but so far the EC has not issued regulations on the practice. The EC, however, is receptive to the proposal.

Despite the apparent flaws, overall, the new system seemed to have passed the first test. Clearly, the shortcomings have to be addressed. In fact, the Election Commission has responded positively to public suggestions for changes in the electoral laws. In early June 2000, the EC held a seminar among some 150 politicians, academics, former Constitution drafters, and legal experts to sort out their ideas on appropriate amendments to the laws. By and large, it is believed that a strong foundation has been laid for a new era of politics in Thailand. Although electoral cheats continue, legal mechanisms are now in place to deal with the wrongdoings more effectively. And as the suspended victories in the 2000 Senate election demonstrated, substantiated wrongdoings received immediate and severe punishment.

Conclusion

Thailand has reached yet another juncture in its parliamentary history. During the first five decades, from the 1930s through the 1970s, the country's electoral politics was interrupted by long periods of military takeovers. That became less frequent as time passed, and attempts by the military to stem electoral politics were resisted more strongly in the 1980s and 1990s. From the mid-1990s on, parliamentary politics has taken its course without intervention from the military. But while the voice for the virtues of democratic parliamentary politics was getting louder, abuses, vote-buying, and election of rascal politicians have obstructed the path to democratic politics. The civil society fought hard—literally with blood and tears—during the 1990s to launch a political reform. The result is the 1997 Constitution, which paid special attention to the country's election system and electioneering, and which found ways to clean up "dirty, old-style" politics. Although the new Constitution has introduced a new electoral system and a host of new provisions for governing future elections, and the historic Senate election results have shown positive democratic development for the country, further successes of the system will depend considerably on the attitudes of both politicians and the electorate and their commitment to abide by the rules. Plenty of room remains for those who want to commit wrongdoings. Vote-buying and other electoral frauds are likely to remain a part of the Thai election landscape for a long time yet. The old habits will die hard, but hope is very much alive that electoral politics will only get better in the future.

References

Anand, Panyarachun. 1998. "An Overview of the New Constitution" [in Thai]. In *Key Points in the People's Constitution*, edited by Boonlert Kachayuthadej. Bangkok: Matichon Publisher.

Anek, Laothamatas. 1993. *The Mobile Telephone Mob: The Middle Class and the Businesspeople and Their Role in the Development of Democracy* [in Thai]. Bangkok: Matichon Publishing.

———. 1996. "A Tale of Two Democracies: Conflicting Perceptions of Election and Democracy in Thailand." In *The Politics of Elections in Southeast Asia*, edited by R.H. Taylor. Washington, D.C.: Woodrow Wilson Center Press.

Borwornsak, Uwanno. 1998. "An Overview of the New Constitution" [in Thai]. In *Key Points in the People's Constitution*, edited by Boonlert Kachayuthadej. Bangkok: Matichon Publisher.

Chai-Anan, Samudavanija. 1990. "Thailand: A Stable Semidemocracy." In *Politics in Developing Countries: Comparing Experiences with Democracy*, edited by L. Diamond, J. Linz, and S.M. Lipset. Boulder, Colo.: Lynne Rienner Publishers.

Constitutional Drafting Assembly, Public Relations Subcommittee. 1997. *Constitution for the Kingdom of Thailand: People's Version* (Draft). Bangkok: Bangchak Plc.

Prasarn, Maruekkapitak, et al. 1999. *Anand Panyarachun: Life, Thoughts, and Achievements of the Twice Prime Minister* [in Thai]. 4th ed. Bangkok: Amarin Press.

Riggs, Fred W. 1966. *Thailand: The Modernization of a Bureaucratic Polity*. Honolulu: East-West Center Press.

Somkid, Lertpaiboon. 1999. *The Election Act as Required by the Present Constitution* [in Thai]. Bangkok: Winyuchon Publication House.

Surin, Maisrikrod. 1992. *Thailand's Two General Elections in 1992: Democracy Sustained*. Singapore: Institute of Southeast Asian Studies.

Surin, Maisrikrod, and D. McCargo. 1997. "Electoral Politics: Commercialisation and Exclusion." In *Political Change in Thailand: Democracy and Participation*, edited by Kevin Hewison. London: Routledge.

Uthai, Pimchaichon. 1998. "The People's Constitution: A New Dimension for the Thai Society" [in Thai]. In *Key Points in the People's Constitution*, edited by Boonlert Kachayuthadej. Bangkok: Matichon Publisher.

CHAPTER 10

Malaysia: The Barisan National Supremacy

by James Ung-Ho Chin

MALAYSIA IS A FEDERATION of thirteen states and two federal territories. The federation was formed in 1963, linking up the territories of Malaya, the island of Singapore, and the states of Sabah and Sarawak located on Borneo island. In 1965, however, Singapore was thrown out of the federation and became a separate entity. The most important political distinction in Malaysia is the bumiputera/nonbumiputera dichotomy. *Bumiputera* (literally "son of the soil") is a legal term meaning that the state recognizes the indigenous status of a Malaysian. *Nonbumiputera* signifies the opposite, that is, the citizen is not indigenous. According to the Constitution, the bumiputera category consists of the Malay race and other indigenous tribal groups in the peninsula and the many indigenous tribal groupings in Sabah and Sarawak. All other ethnic groups are classified as nonbumiputera. The two largest nonbumiputera ethnic groups are the Chinese and the Indians. Collectively, the bumiputera make up approximately 60 percent of Malaysia's 22 million population, the Chinese 27 percent, and Indians 9 percent, with minor groups such as Eurasians making up the rest.

The bumiputera/nonbumiputera dichotomy has important legal, economic, and political implications. Under the Constitution, a bumiputera is entitled to "Special Rights" due to his/her indigenous status. These special rights were not spelled out in detail other than the general meaning that the government may make special provisions to protect the economic, social, and cultural interests of the bumiputera. Under the New Economic Policy (NEP), which ran from 1971 to 1990, and its successor, the New Development Policy (NDP), bumiputera were given a host of economic benefits. Quotas were set aside in both the private and public sectors for the direct benefit of bumiputera. Public universities were required to enroll a certain percentage of bumiputera students, special bumiputera-only institutions such as the MARA Technical Colleges were established, special bumiputera scholarships were set up, and bumiputera-only business loans were made compulsory for financial institutions operating in Malaysia. Certain government tenders, contracts, and licenses could only be awarded to bumiputera companies and individuals. Private companies with a certain paid-up capital were required to maintain 30 percent bumiputera shareholdings. The straightforward discriminatory system was justified on the grounds that the nonbumiputera (read Chinese) were more commercially advanced than the bumiputera. The argument was that the wealth gap between the bumiputera (read Malay) and the nonbumiputera would lead to political instability especially in light of the May 1969 incident.[1] In recent years, the government has used the anti-Chinese riots in Indonesia in 1998 as the justification for the continuation of the discriminatory policies to prevent "racial problems."

ELECTORAL SYSTEM

Due to its colonial heritage, Malaysia follows the Westminster parliamentary system of government, and its political system reflects this. Malaysia uses the plurality, first-past-the-post system based on single-member constituencies with voters coming from a common roll. The two houses of Parliament are the Dewan Rakyat (House of Representatives) and the Dewan Negara (the Senate). All the seats in the Dewan Rakyat are elected directly from single-member constituencies, while members of the Dewan Negara are all nominated. Senators are selected through a complex system: some are chosen by the prime minister, others by the *Agong* (king), and the remainder by the thirteen state legislative assemblies. Each senatorial term lasts three years. The Dewan Negara is often regarded as a "rubber stamp" hardly ever rejecting any bills from the Dewan Rakyat. The former is often used as a tool for political patronage—senior politicians who lose their seats in elections are often appointed senators to allow them to take up cabinet posts. Others are appointed as a political reward. Sometimes smaller Barisan Nasional (BN or National Front) parties in Sabah are given senatorial posts in exchange for not fielding candidates or as part of the seat allocation process. In Sarawak, the Sarawak United People's Party (SUPP) gave the senator's post to its most important financial benefactor. This chapter, however, concentrates on the Dewan Rakyat.

Both parliamentary and state-level elections must be held once every five years, or earlier, if the prime minister or the individual state *menteri besar* (chief minister) decides that a more favorable time exists. The prime minister is chosen from the party or coalition that commands the majority in the Dewan Rakyat. State legislatures mirror the federal Parliament with one important exception; all thirteen state legislatures are unicameral. With the exception of Sabah and Sarawak, which are discussed separately below, state elections are held concurrently with the parliamentary elections.

State elections in general are not deemed as important as federal or parliamentary elections due to the dominant role played by the federal government. The states rely on the federal government for the bulk of their development expenditure, and this allows the federal government a high degree of political control over state politics (Shafruddin 1987). Withholding development funds is a favorite ploy by the federal government against renegade state politicians or state governments under opposition control.

The first "real" elections were held in 1955 for local government officials in selected settlements in Malaya, and subsequently this franchise was extended throughout the peninsula. Self-government was realized in Malaya in 1957, and the first nationwide election using single-member constituencies was held in 1959.

The electoral system is run by the Suruhanjaya Pilihan Raya Malaysia (SPR or Malaysian Election Commission). The members of the SPR are appointed by the *Agong* upon the recommendation of the government, and the commission is supposed to be an independent body. In practice, many believe that the government manipulates the workings of the commission, especially in the areas of boundary delineation and voter registration. The government's close hold on the commission was evident when its long-serving chairman announced in May 1999 that he would retire. The opposition requested that it be consulted on the appointment of the next chairman, and the government responded that it was "none of the opposition's business" (*The Star*, 16 June 1999). Some evidence suggests that the SPR is biased. Prior to the 1974 election, more than 400,000 eligible voters were removed from the voter registration list. It was widely believed that many of these were non-Malays (Sothi 1980, 265). Many opposition parties report that the ruling BN have "special" access to the commission, resulting in opposition supporters being removed from the voter registration list or being moved to another constituency without their knowledge. In Sabah, there is credible evidence that the voter registration list contains up to 300,000 illegal voters, mainly ineligible Muslims from the Southern Philippines and Indonesia who are known to vote for the BN (Chin 1994).

Another instance of bias was the number of opposition candidates who had their candidacies rejected for minor technical details on nomination day. In past elections, many opposition candidates were disqualified on frivolous or technical grounds such as typographical errors. While some BN candidates were also rejected on such grounds, many more opposition candidates were disallowed (Crouch 1996, 60; Sothi 1993, 124–35). The electoral commissioner has recently said that he will instruct the returning officers to be more helpful and allow candidates to correct simple mistakes on their forms.

In 1990, the government amended the Elections Act to allow vote-counting to be conducted at polling centers where the votes were cast. Hitherto, ballot boxes were taken to a central counting center in each constituency. Under the new system, a high degree of anonymity was lost as the government (and the opposition) would immediately know how particular areas voted. This is significant, as the ruling BN has a long history of retaliation against areas and communities that vote against it. In many rural areas where the major source of development and livelihood is directly dependent on government money, the fear generated by the knowledge that the government may retaliate against opposition areas deterred some voters.

All Malaysian citizens over the age of twenty-one are eligible to stand for Parliament as independents or as representatives of a registered political party.[2] For state seats, candidates must be a residents of the state. The nomination must be seconded by two persons living in the contested constituency. An electoral deposit (to discourage frivolous candidates) must be paid (in 1995, it was M$5,000 for a parliamentary seat and M$3,000 for a state seat), though it is refunded if the candidate gets at least one-eighth of the votes in the constituency contested. Voters must be citizens over the age of twenty-one, and voting is not compulsory. One is only eligible to vote when one is registered with the SPR and one's name appears on the common roll.

One oddity is that the SPR does not control the registration of political parties. This function is performed by the Home Ministry through the Registrar of Societies (ROS). Since the Home Minister is invariably a United Malays National Organisation (UMNO) nominee (Prime Minister Mahathir was also Home Minister for more than half of his tenure), the government may delay or reject the registration of opposition parties. Parties that are friendly to the government can be registered in a day or two while opposition parties can take up to three years to register, if they are not rejected. The Sabah Progressive Party (SAPP), a breakaway group from the opposition Parti Bersatu Sabah (PBS or Sabah Unity Party) was registered in less than two days when its founder let it be known that he intended it to become a component party of the BN. In contrast, the Socialist Party of Malaysia's application to register was rejected by ROS after more than a year (*The Star*, 9 February 1999). Parties can hold any persuasion or espouse any cause with the exception of communism, which is still legally banned.

The power of ROS goes beyond simply approving or rejecting the registration of political parties. All political parties are required to submit annual reports to the ROS; all party holders must have their positions confirmed by the ROS; and the ROS is empowered to direct political parties to change or amend their constitutions. Failure to submit annual reports to the ROS or other breaches can constitute grounds for the ROS to deregister a political party.

Several key features distinguish the Malaysian electoral system. The first is the uneven distribution of voters in each constituency. The 1957 Constitution provided that the disparity between the number of voters in an urban seat (high density) and a rural seat (low density) should not be more than 15 percent. In 1962, the law was amended to allow rural constituencies to be as much as half the size of urban constituencies. In 1973, such ratios were removed completely. This deliberate gerrymandering was to consolidate Malay dominance of the system. Since the bulk of the Malay voters live in rural areas, power immediately shifted to those areas, where more than two-thirds of the constituencies were located. The non-Malays, living mostly in urban areas, were thus grossly underrepresented (Sothi 1993). For example, in the 1995 parliamentary election, 85,954 registered voters were in the urban Chinese constituency of Ampang Jaya, while only 28,105 voters were in the rural Malay seat of Gua Musang, a disparity of more than 2.5 times. The situation is even worse in some constituencies in East Malaysia. Hulu Rajang constituency in Sarawak only has 15,849 voters—compared to Ampang Jaya, this is a disparity of more than 5 times.

In the 1978 election, 79 of 114 peninsula constituencies were Malay-majority seats (69 percent). In the 1986 election, 92 of 132 (70 percent) constituencies were Malay-majority, and in the 1995 election, 101 of 144 (70 percent) seats in the peninsula were Malay-majority (Crouch 1996, 59). In other words, to capture power, one had to win the Malay vote. With the bias toward rural seats and Malay-majority seats, and voting along ethnic lines, this meant that a nonbumiputera electoral victory was impossible.

Under current laws, delineation exercises can be carried out only once every eight years. An amendment to the Election Act in 1962 redefined the role of the SPR in delineation exercises to an advisory one in which the SPR could only recommend changes that the government could then accept or reject. Thus the government could prevent any unfavorable electoral boundary changes.

The second feature is that the first-past-the-post system allows the ruling BN to be overrepresented in Parliament at the expense of the opposition. Opposition parties regularly get about 40 percent of the total votes cast, but they rarely end up with more than 20 percent of the seats.

The third is consistent manipulation of constituency boundaries to favor the ruling BN during the various delineation exercises. In almost every delineation exercise undertaken by the SPR since independence, two trends can be clearly observed. The first is the distribution of new constituencies—many of these new constituencies are invariably Malay or Muslim majority seats, thus reinforcing the Malay dominance of the electoral system at the expense of the nonbumiputera. The second is the shifting of "BN-friendly" voters into constituencies deemed opposition strongholds. This is done by redrawing constituency boundaries in such a way that BN-friendly voters from a neighboring constituency are relocated into opposition strongholds.

The fourth feature is the continuous decline in the number of nonbumiputera voters in every election. This corresponds with a sharp increase in the number of bumiputera voters in every election. The major cause of this is the declining nonbumiputera population in Malaysia while the bumiputera population is increasing at a rapid rate. The number of bumiputera voters is also boosted by an influx of Indonesian migrants, numbering about 1 million, who are registered to vote. These Indonesians are allowed to settle in Malaysia largely because they are Muslims and are culturally quite similar.

The fifth feature is the short campaign period. Under Article 55 (4) of the Constitution, a general election shall be held within sixty days of the dissolution of Parliament. The law states that the campaigning period must not be less than seven days, with no mention of the maximum period. The four general elections under Dr. Mahathir had the shortest election campaign periods in Malaysian history: fifteen days in 1982, nine days in 1986, and ten days in 1990 and 1995.

The short campaign period severely disadvantages the opposition parties, as they can campaign openly only during the official campaign period. For the ruling BN, the campaign often starts earlier in the guise of "government business" such as ministerial visits and opening of major projects. Prime Minister Mahathir is known for going on nationwide "meet the people" public rallies before calling for elections. Although the opposition parties also start their campaigns earlier than the formal period, this has to be done on a very low-key basis, compared to the BN.

Party System

Although in theory Malaysia's political party system can be classified as multiparty, in reality, the opposition parties are so weak and their activities curtailed to such an extent that the system could easily be classified as one-party dominant. Since independence, the BN coalition and its predecessor, the Malayan Alliance, have been in power. With the exception of the 1969 elections, the BN has always won the general elections with more than two-thirds of the seats in the federal Parliament. The two-thirds majority is crucial because it allows the ruling coalition to amend the Malaysian Constitution and electoral and other laws at will. On average, the Malaysian Constitution has been amended at least twice every year.

Malaysian politics centers on ethnicity and religion. The BN is thus made up of a coalition of ethnic political parties (Mauzy 1983). Throughout the years, the number of parties in the BN coalition has gone up and down, from about ten in the 1980s to fourteen today. The core of the BN consists of four parties: UMNO, the Malaysian Chinese Association (MCA), the Malaysian Indian Congress (MIC), and Gerakan. UMNO unashamedly stands for Malay and Islam dominance, while MCA and MIC, as the names suggest, seek to represent the Chinese and Indian communities. The official philosophy of Gerakan is "multiracial" politics, but with more than 90 percent of its members being ethnic Chinese, it is essentially a Chinese interest party.

Although the BN claims to be a multiethnic coalition representing all the major races in Malaysia, in reality UMNO holds the governing position in the coalition. UMNO accounts for more than half of all seats won by the coalition, and it is widely acknowledged that if it wished, UMNO could take power alone with a simple majority in the Dewan Rakyat. The leader of UMNO and his deputy automatically become the prime minister and deputy prime minister, respectively. UMNO dominates at the state level as well. With the exception of opposition-held states Penang and Sarawak, the state *menteri besar* are all UMNO nominees. All the key cabinet positions such as Finance, Defense, and Education are held by UMNO.

UMNO was established in 1946 as a communal party with the Malay race and Islam as its raison d'être. In its initial years, UMNO was led mostly by civil servants (who came from aristocratic backgrounds), with rural schoolteachers making up its most influential supporters and vote-getters. UMNO played the key role in negotiations with the British to gain independence and was an instigator in the creation of the federation of Malaysia (Funston 1980). Since the mid-1980s, and as a result of the NEP and NDP, UMNO has been led mostly by professionals and businessmen and has adopted a political culture of "money politics." To reach the top echelons of the party requires vote-buying of party delegates, and it is not uncommon for an ambitious UMNO politician to spend millions to win a coveted seat in the UMNO Majlis Tertinggi (Supreme Council)—the party's top decision-making body. Membership of this body often leads to selection as a UMNO candidate in general elections, cabinet or other senior government posts, or lucrative government-related business contracts.

Although UMNO officially champions Islam, the party leadership under Mahathir firmly stands for the "modern" secular brand of Islam (Khoo 1998). UMNO's support among the Malay community lies largely in its extensive patronage-dispensing network, so much so that the standard joke among the Malay community was that one had to be a "UMNOputera" instead of merely a bumiputera in order to get the preferential benefits under the NEP and NDP. Many bumiputera joined UMNO simply as an "investment" to benefit financially. At present, UMNO has a membership of more than 2.7 million, making it the largest party in the country. It also boasts of an extensive branch network that reaches every constituency in peninsular Malaysia.

MCA was founded in 1949 as a welfare organization but eventually moved into the political arena as UMNO's Chinese partner in the Malayan Alliance and later the BN (Heng 1988). Since its inception, it has been led by the Chinese business elite and English-educated Chinese professionals. The MCA's main claim is to be the Chinese "voice" in the ruling coalition. It seeks to represent and protect Chinese business and cultural interests through discreet negotiations with UMNO. MCA leaders often claimed that its discreet style allows its to get concessions from UMNO, and that without it "things would be much worse for the Chinese." Under the leadership of Ling Liong Sik beginning in the mid-1980s, the MCA leadership has accepted the notion that it is not in a position to challenge UMNO nor Malay political supremacy and that the Chinese community in Malaysia must realize that it is a minority and, as such, must behave as a minority (Ling 1995). Consistent with this, Ling has opened the membership of MCA to anyone with a "single drop" of Chinese blood. This significant shift in position, from being a Chinese party to a Chinese-minority party, has led to an erosion of its support within the Chinese community. Many Chinese regard the MCA as "sellouts" and racial traitors. Despite this, MCA attracts some votes from the Chinese community, especially from petty traders and small Chinese businessmen who require the assistance and protection of the MCA.

Parti Gerakan Rakyat Malaysia (Malaysian People's Solidarity Movement) was founded mainly by MCA dissidents in 1968 (Lee 1987, 78). The power base of Gerakan has always been in Penang, where the party founder, Lim Chong Eu, ruled as chief minister for more than two decades. By tradition, its nominee holds the post of chief minister in Penang. The party has little influence outside the island. Although it claims to be multiracial and membership is open to all races, deference to UMNO means that the party is reluctant to accept Malay members. With 90 percent of its membership Chinese, it is just another Chinese party in the BN.

MIC was founded in 1946 on the premise that the Indian community needed a "voice" in the political arena. Its support base came largely from lower-class Indian plantation laborers and the urban Indian working class. It has no real clout in the BN, as there are no Indian-majority seats in the country and all MIC-BN candidates rely on Malay votes to get elected. Nevertheless, MIC has always been given one federal cabinet post. Internal party politics have been marked by physical fights, threats, and the use of thugs and gangsters to enforce discipline and get votes. The current party leader's tenure has been marked by erratic behavior and the need to control every facet of the party. He has been known to sack party officials on the spot and appoint incompetent but loyal (to him personally) party members.

The parties in the BN are marked by three key features: "money politics," concentration of power in the hands of the party leader, and long tenure of the incumbent. "Money politics" refers to the extensive use of financial and other rewards to secure party support for leadership positions. The magnitude of "money politics" in the individual BN coalition parties correlates directly with the power they yield in the government. UMNO, as the most powerful party, thus suffers most acutely from money politics within its ranks. Despite measures introduced to curb money politics in all the BN parties, money politics is now deep rooted and will be difficult to wipe out. Practitioners know that their chances of being appointed to posts in the government equate more or less directly to the party pecking order. The money they spend on winning party positions can easily be recouped once they are elected as MPs or state assemblymen, or appointed to posts in government or state-owned enterprises.

Money politics also stretches to the political parties themselves. In the 1980s and early 1990s, many of the key BN parties such as UMNO and MCA began to get directly involved in business in order to secure more permanent sources of finance. These political parties selected nominees, usually young successful entrepreneurs, to manage business opportunities flowing from huge government projects such as highway construction or from privatization efforts undertaken by the government (Gomez 1994).

Party constitutions tend to concentrate power in the hands of the party president, along with all the related powers of patronage. Once a party leader is installed, it is virtually impossible to remove the incumbent. Barring unforeseen circumstances, party leaders can look forward to long tenures. Mahathir Mohamad has been UMNO president/prime minister since 1981, Ling Liong Sik (MCA president) since 1986, Samy Vellu (MIC) since 1979, and Lim Kheng Yaik (Gerakan) since 1980. In other words, all the current leaders have been in power for close to two decades.

The Opposition

The opposition parties, like the BN parties, are organized by ethnicity and religion. Although there are more than three dozen registered opposition parties, most are small and inactive except during elections. The two most important opposition parties are the Democratic Action Party (DAP) and Party Islam Malaysia (PAS). Both have had electoral success and have been represented in Parliament since independence.

The DAP is a Chinese-based party with some support from the Indian community. Its establishment can be traced back to the separation of Singapore from Malaysia in 1963 (Lee 1987, 76). The Malayan wing of the People's Action Party (PAP) was reconstituted as the DAP with the old Malayan PAP leaders assuming the leadership. The political philosophy of the DAP, "Malaysian Malaysia," was similar to the old PAP slogan. Essentially this means that the DAP fights for the abolition of the bumiputera/nonbumiputera dichotomy and all the discriminatory policies against the nonbumiputera, and strives to make Malaysia a meritocracy. Many of the issues championed by the DAP, such as Chinese education, more places for non-Malays in public universities, recognition of Chinese culture, more air time for Chinese programs on radio and television, more rights for non-Islamic religions, less corruption in government, and human rights have endeared the DAP to the non-Malay communities who bear the brunt of the state's discriminatory policies. The stand also means that the DAP finds it difficult to recruit the Malays, the beneficiaries of the discriminatory system. Most of DAP's membership and electoral support comes from the Chinese and Indian communities. The party's numbers in Parliament fluctuate from around ten to a high of twenty-four in the 1986 elections.

In recent years, the party has suffered an image problem largely due to its long-serving leader and parliamentary opposition leader, Lim Kit Siang. Lim has been secretary-general of the DAP since October 1969 (he was elected while he was under detention) and is widely perceived to harbor plans for his son, Lim Guan Eng, to take over the party. This has led to charges of nepotism and cronyism against the elder Lim. The younger Lim, also an MP, was jailed in 1998 for printing a pamphlet condemning the government's decision not to press statutory-rape charges against a former UMNO *menteri besar*. The other accusation against Lim is that he is as dictatorial as his main opponent, Mahathir (Kua 1996). In 1998, the party was perilously divided over these two issues, with more than a few thousand members deserting the party. Although Lim was defeated in the 1999 general elections, the public perception is that he still controls the party from his new post as chairman of the party. The biggest problem facing the DAP is the dwindling Chinese population that will translate into fewer seats for the DAP in the coming years.

While the DAP attracts support from the nonbumiputera population, PAS's support comes mainly from Muslim bumiputera. PAS started off as the Pan Malayan Islamic Party (PMIP) in 1951. Most of its members were former UMNO members who were unhappy with UMNO's secular outlook. Unlike DAP, which has never captured any governments, PAS has been successful in capturing two states (Alias 1994). In the 1959 election, PAS managed to win the states of Kelantan and Terengganu, both overwhelmingly Malay states populated by religiously conservative voters. Two years later, however, UMNO managed to take back Terengganu when it enticed several key PAS legislators to defect. In 1973, PAS was persuaded to join the BN but was thrown out of the coalition in 1977. In the 1978 election, PAS lost control of the Kelantan state government to UMNO. PAS was out of power until 1990 when it teamed up with an UMNO splinter party, Parti Semangat 46 (Spirit of 46 [S46]), led by former UMNO strongman Tengku Razaleigh Hamzah, and won all thirty-nine seats in the Kelantanese state assembly. In the 1995 elections, the PAS-S46 alliance managed to retain Kelantan although UMNO was able to win seven state seats. UMNO's position in Kelantan was boosted when S46 was dissolved after the elections and its members rejoined UMNO. PAS's stronghold on Kelantan can be explained in part by the parochial nature of the Kelantanese voters who see themselves as different from other peninsular Malays (Kessler 1978; Chin Ung Ho 1997)

PAS's avowed aim is to turn Malaysia into an Islamic state, and because of this, its appeal outside the Malay community is constricted. PAS's support comes mainly from the four northern Malay states (Perlis, Kedah, Terengganu, and Kelantan) where the population is overwhelmingly Malay and mostly peasants. Even within the Malay community, PAS suffers difficulties in attracting mainstream support as many Malay (especially the urban-based, Western-educated middle class) fear the imposition of lifestyle restrictions should PAS come into power and turn Malaysia into an Islamic state. The non-Muslim community absolutely rejects PAS, knowing full well the consequences of an Islamic state.

The most significant opposition party to establish itself in recent years is the Parti KeADILan Nasional (National Justice Party). It was set up by supporters of Anwar Ibrahim, the former deputy prime minister and one-time successor to Mahathir. In the 1999 general election, KeADILan won five parliamentary seats, but this was due mainly to its electoral pact with PAS and the DAP. Although KeADILan has attracted some support from the urban middle class and the younger Malay community with its "reformasi" platform, the general consensus is that KeADILan's political future depends on Anwar. As long as Anwar is incarcerated, KeADILan's future is limited.

Several attempts have been made to cross the ethnic divide and form multiethnic parties, but most failed in less than a decade (Vasil 1971). While Gerakan and DAP claim to be multiracial, their memberships are overwhelmingly Chinese and they take up mostly Chinese issues. The public perceives these two parties as Chinese parties and acts accordingly.

The most enduring of the genuine multiracial parties appears to be Parti Rakyat Malaysia (People's Party [PRM]). Originating as Parti Socialis Rakyat Malaysia (PSRM) with a socialist platform, it became home to many left-wing intellectuals, especially among the urban university class and the Malay left wing who rejected racial and Islamic politics. In 1993, PRM dropped the word *socialis* when it became clear that on a global scene, socialism and communism were in retreat. The Malaysian polity, moreover, did not cherish the idea of a socialist state, and neither PRM nor its predecessor PSRM was ever able to win a seat. In the early 1990s, PRM came under the control of a university anthropologist, Syed Husin Ali.

In sum, the party system reinforces racial and religious divide within the polity. Attempts to cross politically the ethnic and religious divide have failed and have deterred further efforts.

Campaign Issues and Strategies

Since independence, the key campaign issues (economic, education, cultural, and religious) have generally been related to ethnicity—bumiputera and nonbumiputera being the main division.

Economic issues center on government subsidies and preferential economic policies designed to aid the bumiputera. These economic policies are widely perceived as detrimental to the development of Chinese businesses and employment opportunities for the nonbumiputera. Many Chinese businessmen resent such discriminatory policies as preferences in contracting or access to credit. Big Chinese business resents the government for imposing ownership structure rules. Under the NEP and its successor, the NDP, nonbumiputera companies over a certain size and all public-listed companies have to set aside and maintain 30 percent of their shares in bumiputera hands. In many cases, these shares have had to be sold at below market prices to fulfill government regulations.

Education issues focus on access to tertiary education and the plight of vernacular education. A quota system has severely restricted the entry of nonbumiputera into local universities. Thus every year, thousands of Chinese and Indian students are denied a place in the universities solely on the basis of their ethnicity. To add insult to injury, many less academically qualified Malay students are accepted to the universities to fulfill the quota. Officially, the quota for local universities is set at 55 percent bumiputera and 45 percent nonbumiputera, but in reality, bumiputera students make up more than 70 percent in government institutions of higher education. This situation has forced thousands of nonbumiputera (mostly Chinese) students to go overseas for their college education, creating further resentment due to the high costs involved. Throughout the 1970s and 1980s, the numbers of Malaysian students consistently ranked in the top five of international students in the United States, Australia, and the United Kingdom. Often the prohibitive costs of overseas higher education meant that a typical Chinese family could afford to send only one sibling.

Since the large-scale arrival of Chinese and Indian immigrants during the colonial era, these two communities have established schools to serve the needs of their children. Over the years, the Chinese community, and the Indian community to a lesser extent, have build up an extensive network of vernacular schools throughout the country (Kua 1990; Tan 1996). After independence, for political reasons, the Malay language, renamed Bahasa Malaysia (Malaysian language), was made the official tongue. This change meant that certificates from the Chinese and Indian secondary schools were not officially recognized by the government. In practice, these graduates could not apply to public universities or vocational institutions, and they could not apply for employment with the public service, statutory bodies, and other state-owned enterprises. More importantly, these vernacular schools were not eligible for any form of government funding, and their existence depended totally on community support. Nevertheless, the vernacular schools, especially the Chinese ones, managed to survive and thrive because the Chinese community equated the survival of Chinese language and culture with the survival of these schools. The government, however, sees these schools as a hindrance to national unity and assimilation. Today, many of these independent Chinese schools teach a dual curriculum to prepare their students for the government public examinations as well as examinations sanctioned by the Dong Jiao Dong, an umbrella group of Chinese educators.

Culturally and religiously, the big divide is again between the bumiputera and nonbumiputera and between Muslims and non-Muslims. Islam is the official religion, and the national cultural policy refers to Malay and Islam as the starting and ending points. The culture and traditional beliefs of the Chinese, Indians, and indigenous tribes of Borneo do not have a place in the national cultural policy. The government rigorously supports an Islamization program aimed to make Malaysia a "modern and model" Muslim, nonorthodox Islamic state. This policy includes vastly increasing the number and hours of Islamic programs on television (while non-Islamic religions are denied any air time), inculcating Islamic values into the public service, rapidly expanding state-funded religious primary and secondary schools, establishing an Islamic university and Islamic banking system, building mosques throughout the country, and funding proselytizing campaigns to convert the non-Muslim population. All these policy goals have created uneasiness and fear in the non-Muslim communities. Since becoming a Muslim in Malaysia also requires one to give up one's culture and adopt the Malay culture, the non-Muslims in Malaysia see the Islamization program as a blatant attempt at assimilation on the government's terms. In recent years, there were many reports of overzealous religious authorities ordering the demolition of Christian churches and Hindu temples, refusing permits for the building of non-Islamic places of worship, and applying pressure on non-Muslims in schools and universities to convert. The Christian churches appeared to be the main target of the Islamization policy and lived under a siege mentality.

The government's push for Islamization is largely due to pressures exerted by UMNO's main rival, PAS. PAS's main campaign theme is that a pious Muslim's duty is to vote for an Islamic state. Other issues raised by PAS include UMNO's "unIslamic" ways such as allowing the existence of legalized gambling, the sale of alcohol, the westernization of society, and the promotion of material culture. UMNO's reply is that PAS's brand of orthodox Islam is regressive, paying more attention to rituals than substance, and that turning Malaysia into an Islamic state is simply unrealistic given that close to half of the country's population is non-Muslim.

Generally, campaigns in Malaysia center on parties, with the party leaders given prominent positions. This is especially true of the UMNO leader and the prime minister. It would not be wrong to say that in most general elections, the prime minister symbolizes the entire ruling BN and represents all its component parties. Typically, the BN campaigns on a platform of political stability and continuity, with subtle threats that an opposition victory may lead to race riots and chaos.

The opposition campaign can be divided into two main types: the non-Muslim parties and the Islamic parties. The main non-Muslim party, DAP, campaigns against the discriminatory policies of the government, while the main bumiputera opposition party, PAS, campaigns on the need to set up an Islamic state.

Electoral campaigns in Malaysia cannot be described as fair. The ruling BN has so many advantages that the opposition parties are often severely handicapped even before the campaign starts. The problems faced by the opposition include inadequate resources (especially financial), limitations on access to mass media, and campaign restrictions. These are discussed below.

Electoral campaigns in Malaysia are expensive, especially in rural areas where voters expect to be rewarded. Since the late 1980s, it has not been uncommon for the ruling parties to spend more than 2 million ringgit to win a parliamentary constituency and half that amount to win a state constituency—sometimes spending 50 times the amount spent by the opposition.

Direct vote-buying has been the standard practice among rural voters in Sabah and Sarawak since the first elections in the 1960s. This practice was extended to the northern peninsula states in the 1980s and has escalated throughout the peninsula in recent years. UMNO discovered that cash incentives were very effective in the PAS strongholds of Kelantan and Terengganu following UMNO's defeat in 1990. On top of overt vote-buying, the incumbent BN makes full use of government facilities to campaign. These include the sudden approval of development projects worth millions just prior to polling day, "on the spot" government grants for all sorts of projects and activities,[3] the use of civil servants, and the use of such government resources as helicopters to access remote areas. All these can be justified on the grounds that the ministers are on "government business." The total commitments made during the campaign period by the government for infrastructure development often amounts to billions of ringgit. For rural areas with limited services and growth, the amount promised makes it hard for the people to turn against the ruling BN. In general, the use of development and infrastructure funds to solicit votes is more effective in rural areas than in urban areas where such services are taken for granted. Threats by the government often do not work in urban areas.

The mainstream mass media in Malaysia are tightly controlled by the ruling coalition through ownership structures and legislation. The two biggest media groups, the Utusan Malaysia Group and the New Straits Times Publications Group (NST), are both owned by UMNO-related interests. Utusan and NST account for all the major nationwide Malay and English newspapers and more than 70 percent of all popular publications. All three private television stations are also owned by UMNO-related interests. The two government-owned television stations, Radio Television Malaysia (RTM) 1 and RTM 2, together with several RTM radio channels, have nationwide audiences. These stations are widely seen by the educated public as instruments for government propaganda. The information minister has publicly admitted that the state television's role is to promote the ruling coalition (*New Straits Times*, 18 June 1999). In the rural areas such as the interiors of Sabah and Sarawak, however, RTM is often the only source of news and an effective tool for swinging votes to the BN.

Newspapers and other publications not owned by UMNO- or BN-related interests are controlled by legislation, including the Printing Presses and Publications Act. Among other things, this law requires annual permits to operate a newspaper or a periodical. It offers the government the option of not renewing the permit of a publication it deems to have misbehaved. In 1987, it closed three newspapers after they were judged to have overstepped the bounds of acceptable criticism. Journalists contend that the act forces newsrooms to self-censor. Other restrictive laws include the Sedition Act, the Official Secrets Act, and the Internal Security Act.

The cumulative effect of this legislation, plus the close links between the media owners and the ruling parties, is that the opposition is negatively portrayed as racial chauvinist (DAP) or religious extremist (PAS) or is not covered during the campaign period (Commonwealth Observer Group 1990). In contrast, the BN is constantly portrayed as the only guarantor of political stability in a diverse multiethnic and multireligious society. This blatant message is reinforced by massive advertising campaigns reminding voters that economic gains made since independence and continued economic growth are dependent on a BN victory. During the campaign period, it is common to read stories and see pictures of ministers attending various official functions.

Since the late 1990s, the government's grip on the media has loosened with the growth of the Internet. By 1999, Internet subscribers in Malaysia numbered more than half a million, and web users were estimated to be more than 1 million. The opposition found, for the first time, that it could reach the public directly through the web. The majority of Internet users tend to be professional, middle-class people living in urban areas. This group is becoming increasingly critical of the government, especially after the sacking and jailing of Anwar Ibrahim, the deputy prime minister. Anwar's supporters have waged a war against the BN mainly through the Internet. In the coming years, with the Internet penetrating the rural areas, the BN's control over the flow of information likely will be severely challenged by alternative sources of information.

In the 1960s, one of the key strategies of the opposition was to stage public rallies where key speakers would publicly chastise the government. These rallies typically attracted large crowds and were effective tools for both political communication and recruitment. After the 1974 election, the BN moved to restrict public rallies. Open-air public rallies were completely banned, and only indoor *ceremahs* (political talk in an enclosed room) were allowed. Even then, a police permit was required to hold an indoor *ceremah*. The permitting process allowed the police to reject applications, impose conditions that made it difficult for the opposition to hold rallies, or cancel permits at the last minute (*The Star*, 20 June 1999).

The short campaign period, usually ten days, also favored incumbents. This short period generally limited the opposition's ability to mount an effective campaign. Moreover, the government, taking advantage of the power of incumbency, made use of official helicopters in the rugged interior of Sabah and Sarawak—a prohibitively expensive option for the opposition.

Electoral Behavior and Voter Trends

While weather, polling location, and the date of the election are important variables, turnout in Malaysian elections generally hovers around the 60 percent mark. In hotly contested seats or in seats where the candidates are well known or controversial, this figure can rise to about 80 percent. The Electoral Commission usually schedules elections on weekends to increase turnout.

Voting in Malaysia is clearly along racial and religious lines. In other words, it is almost impossible for an ethnic Malay to win in a constituency that is overwhelmingly populated by ethnic Chinese voters, and vice versa. Ethnic voting is strongest among the Malay population, which explains why many of the non-Malay party leaders in BN parties such as Gerakan, MCA, and MIC represent constituencies that are heavily populated by Malay voters. These voters, mostly UMNO members, are expected to vote en-bloc for the BN candidate, in this case a non-Malay. These UMNO members know that although their representative may not be a Malay, real power in the system lies in the hands of UMNO, and that these non-Malay BN candidates are needed to provide the façade of a multiethnic coalition. The leaders of Gerakan, MCA, and MIC prefer to stand in Malay-majority constituencies because they know that they cannot depend on the ethnic groups they claim to represent, while with solid UMNO support, they are secure in their constituencies.

In the Malay heartland states of Perlis, Kelantan, Kedah, and Terengganu, where the contest is essentially between UMNO and PAS, religion is the deciding factor in how people vote. The choice is essentially between a secular, modernist Islam espoused by UMNO or the more orthodox, radical brand of Islam promoted by PAS. Interestingly enough, in these constituencies, the minority Chinese and Indian voters cast the crucial vote. Often the Malay voters are split evenly between UMNO and PAS supporters—thus the non-Malay voters cast the deciding vote. With PAS's avowed aim of creating an Islamic state once it is in power, the non-Malays in these seats usually vote for UMNO, allowing the party to win by a slight margin.

With a few exceptions, party identification is always more important than the individual candidate. In most constituencies, a key criterion for winning is the backing of a strong party and its electoral machine. Party identification is strongest in urban areas where the voters are more sophisticated and better educated, and weakest in the rural areas where personality often counts more. This trend is slowly breaking down, however, as the party machinery penetrates the rural areas. The distinction between the urban and rural voters is also important in ethnic voting. The bulk of the non-Malay population live in urban areas, so this is where the nonbumiputera opposition is strongest. The bulk of the Malay population live in rural areas, and this is where PAS contests UMNO.

Voters in Malaysia appear to be consistent in their votes for the BN (Crouch 1996, 74). The BN share of the vote between 1974 and 1986 was between 57 and 60 percent (see table 10.1, p. 226). In 1990, the BN share of the vote went down largely because of the emergence of Semangat 46, noted above. In 1995, BN's share went up to 65 percent largely because of the booming economy and the swing in Chinese votes toward the BN (Chin 1996a). In the 1999 election, despite inroads made by the opposition PAS in traditional UMNO areas, the BN still managed to get 56 percent of the vote.

The opposition's share of the vote is consistently around 35 to 40 percent. Due to the first-past-the-post system, however, this ratio is never reflected in Parliament. The BN normally holds between 70 and 85 percent of the seats in Parliament, but as mentioned above, they get only 57 to 60 percent of the votes.

The opposition vote is divided unevenly among the two major opposition parties, the DAP and PAS, and is largely dependent on the number of candidates each puts up for election. Unlike the BN, which fields candidates in all constituencies, DAP tends to field candidates in Chinese and urban areas while PAS concentrates on the Malay and rural constituencies. Normally, DAP garners about 20 percent of the vote while PAS receives about 15 percent.

Table 10.1 Malaysian Parliamentary Election Results, 1974–99

Party	Seats Won (Percentage of Vote Share)						
	1974	1978	1982	1986	1990	1995	1999
BN	135 (60.7)	131 (57.2)	132 (60.5)	148 (57.3)	127 (53.4)	162 (65.1)	148 (56.5)
PAS[a]		5 (15.5)	5 (14.5)	1 (15.5)	7 (6.7)	7 (7.3)	27 (15.0)
DAP	9 (18.3)	16 (19.9)	9 (19.6)	24 (21.1)	20 (17.6)	9 (12.1)	10 (13.6)
S46[b]					8 (15.1)	6 (10.2)	
SNAP[c]	9 (5.5)						
PBS[d]					14 (2.3)	8 (3.3)	3 (2.1)
KeADILan[e]							5 (11.5)
Others[f]	1 (15.5)	2 (6.9)	8 (5.4)	4 (6.1)	4 (4.9)	0 (2.0)	0 (1.3)
Total	154	154	154	177	180	192	193

Sources: Election Commission Reports, various years; Crouch 1996, 75.
a. PAS was in the BN coalition in the 1974 election but was expelled in 1977.
b. Semangat 46, an UMNO splinter group, was founded in 1987. It dissolved in 1998 when its members rejoined UMNO.
c. The Sarawak National Party joined the BN in 1976.
d. Parti Bersatu Sabah was formed in 1985, joined the BN coalition for the 1986 election, but left the coalition in 1990.
e. KeADILan or National Justice Party was established in 1999 by Anwar Ibrahim's supporters.
f. These four "independents" elected in 1990 were in fact Parti Bansa Dayak Sarawak (PBDS) members and therefore voted with the BN.

PAS normally receives the bulk of its votes in the Malay heartland (Perlis, Kedah, Terengganu, Kelantan), where the mostly peasant population is attracted to its Islamic message. In 1995, PAS won seven parliamentary and thirty-three state seats. Of these, six parliamentary seats and twenty-four state seats were won in Kelantan. The other parliamentary seat was won in Terengganu, while the rest of the state seats were won in Kedah (two) and Terengganu (seven). In 1990 and 1995, the total vote share for PAS dropped significantly because of its alliance with S46; PAS was obliged to let S46 compete in some of its constituencies. In

1999, the Anwar-sacking affair helped PAS to make major inroads into the Malay heartland. PAS was able to capture the Terenggnau state government as well as retain control of Kelantan. It was able to more than triple its seats in Parliament to twenty-seven from a mere eight won in 1995. PAS also doubled its share of the popular vote to 15.07 percent from 7.3 percent in 1995.

The DAP normally wins roughly 70 percent of the Chinese vote. Past results have shown a strong correlation between DAP's success and the number of Chinese voters in any single constituency. The DAP usually wins in constituencies where 60 percent or more of the voters are ethnic Chinese (Crouch 1996, 71). Clearly the DAP attracts considerable support from Indian voters as well. The strong support for the DAP among non-Malay voters suggests that the constituencies won by non-Malay-based BN parties such as MCA, MIC, and Gerakan are based largely on Malay UMNO supporters. The DAP lost the support of the Chinese vote in the 1995 election when the country was experiencing record economic growth—growth that allowed the government to grant significant concessions to the Chinese community in the education, economic, and cultural areas (Chin 1996a). They also lost some support of the Chinese community in the 1999 election when the DAP formed an alliance with the Islamic PAS. Many Chinese voters voted against the DAP as a protest against the alliance. Chinese voters were angry that the DAP would enter into a formal coalition with a party that propounded the establishment of an Islamic state with no rights for non-Muslims (Chin 2000).

Sabah and Sarawak

Important differences exist between elections in peninsular Malaysia and the eastern Malaysian states of Sabah and Sarawak. The differences lie mainly in the political parties and issues.

The departure point for understanding East Malaysian politics is the differing political development of these two states. Sabah was ruled for most of the twentieth century by a trading company, the British North Borneo Company, while Sarawak was ruled for more than 100 years by the Brooke family as a personal kingdom. Thus these two territories lagged behind the peninsula in terms of both physical and political development. Sabah and Sarawak helped form the federation in 1963, but only after both states were granted special political autonomy known as the "Twenty Points." The key provisions were the following: (1) Islam's status as a national religion was not applicable to Sarawak and Sabah; (2) immigration control was vested in the state governments of Sabah and Sarawak; (3) the civil service was Borneanized, and English could be used as the official language of both states; (4) no amendments or modification of any specific safeguards granted under the Twenty Points could be made by the federal government without the agreement of the Sabah and Sarawak state governments; and (5) there would be no right to secede from the federation.

Since then, one of the key political debates in Sabah and Sarawak has been the extent to which the federal government has honored the Twenty Points. The federal government and UMNO's position has been that these constitutional guarantees were transitional in nature and would shrink in the face of pressures for national integration (Chin 1997). Many East Malaysian critics argue that these rights were vested in the peoples of Sabah and Sarawak and not open to redefinition by the federal government. Critics in both states have argued that the federal government has circumvented many of the guarantees, especially in areas of religion and Borneanization of the civil service. Islam was made the official religion of Sarawak and Sabah despite the guarantee. Many senior officers in government departments in Sabah and Sarawak have been posted from peninsular Malaysia despite the explicit promise to give first preference to local civil servants under the Borneanization pledge. A strong regional sentiment is felt among the voters in Sabah and Sarawak, and local parties that fight for state rights or are believed to be protecting the state from federal incursion usually win the support of the people.

State Politics

Politics in East Malaysia are complicated by the demography of both states. Unlike the peninsula, which essentially has three ethnic groups, Sabah and Sarawak each have more than thirty ethnic groups, all competing for political power. Thus there is constant maneuvering among the groups as alliances change and shift according to circumstances and the political climate. The most important difference is that the Malay and Muslims are minorities in both states. In Sabah, the largest ethnic/political grouping is the Kadazan-Dusun, who constitute about 40 percent of the state's 1.8 million population. In Sarawak, the largest ethnic/political grouping is the Iban-Dayak, who make up about 40 percent of the state's 2.1 million population. Both of these groups are non-Muslims—the Kadazan-Dusuns are mainly Roman Catholics while the Iban-Dayaks are mainly Christians and animists. The emphasis on Islam and bumiputerism by the federal government has meant that the political lines are increasingly drawn as follows: Muslim bumiputera (MB), non-Muslim bumiputera (NMB), and Chinese.

The two main features of Sabah politics have been political patronage and shifting loyalties. Those in power commonly use the state's natural resources, especially the awarding of timber concessions and business opportunities to loyal supporters and financial backers, to cement political ties. Another feature has been the rapid shifting of electoral loyalty. The ruling party in Sabah usually holds office for roughly ten years. In the 1970s, Sabah politics was dominated by Tun Mustapha Harun and his party, the United Sabah National Organisation (USNO). Mustapha ruled Sabah from 1967 to 1975 before he was thrown out by the electorate in favor of Parti Bersatu Rakyat Jelata Sabah (Berjaya, or Peoples Racially-United Front of Sabah). Berjaya's rule lasted until 1985, when it was dislodged by PBS. The PBS government lasted until 1994, when defections caused its downfall. Since then, Sabah has been ruled by a UMNO-led BN coalition (Chin 1994; 1999).

In Sarawak, political patronage through timber concessions and business opportunities plays a key role as well. Compared to the climate in Sabah, state politics in Sarawak is relatively uneventful. Since 1970, politics has been dominated by a small elite of Melanau-Muslims and Foochow-Chinese though their respective parties—Pesaka Bumiputera Bersatu (PBB) and SUPP (Chin 1996b; 1996c; Chin Ung Ho 1997). Together with the Sarawak National Party (SNAP) and Parti Bansa Dayak Sarawak (PBDS, or Dayak Peoples' Party), these four parties constitute the Sarawak Barisan Nasional (SBN), the state-level equivalent of the federal BN. The main opposition parties in Sabah and Sarawak tend to be locally based and generally represent a single ethnic group. The only exception is the Chinese-based DAP, which has active branches throughout Sabah and Sarawak. The DAP has been quite successful in capturing the opposition Chinese vote in Sarawak, consistently winning several parliamentary seats since 1982 and two state seats in 1996 (Chin Ung Ho 1997). The DAP's performance in Sabah has been erratic due to the fluidity of Sabah politics. The DAP won at parliamentary level in Sabah but has never won a state seat. Like its counterpart in the peninsula, the DAP was successful only in Chinese-majority constituencies.

Political parties in both states are less ethnicity-based than those on the peninsula. The demography forces them to seek support from other ethnic groups. The usual pattern for political parties is to anchor support in one particular ethnic group and seek additional backing from as many outside groups as possible. Almost all the successful political parties in East Malaysia claim to be multiracial and have open membership. Two examples are PBS in Sabah and PBB in Sarawak. PBS won the previous Sabah state elections chiefly because it has been able to attract considerable electoral support from the Chinese and Muslim communities in addition to its anchor, the Kadazan-Dusun community. PBB, though led by a Melanau Muslim with its base in the Muslim community, has been able to attract significant support from the non-Muslim Iban-Dayak community. One-fifth of PBB's state seats come from non-Muslim constituencies.

Campaigns and Issues

Elections in Sabah and Sarawak are marked by extensive vote-buying. It would be fair to say that parties and individuals get elected primarily due to their financial resources and their ability to buy votes. Vote-buying is done openly and blatantly. In one instance, money was thrown from a helicopter to voters below (*Far Eastern Economic Review*, 3 March 1994). In 1997, the High Court nullified an election result won by the BN component PBDS in Sarawak due to "extensive bribery" (*Sarawak Tribune*, 14 February 1997). Incredibly, the PBDS vice president claimed that PBDS had no reason to be ashamed (*Sarawak Tribune*, 14 February 1997), noting that vote-buying was normal practice. More incredible, in the by-election that followed the court's decision, the same PBDS candidate implicated in the vote-buying scandal was reelected. Since both states are relatively underdeveloped, the use of government infrastructure projects to entice voters works effectively, especially in the rural interiors where such basic necessities as running water and electricity are still nonexistent (Chin 1996b).

Since state elections are usually held on different dates than parliamentary elections, the issues differ. Nationwide and federal-state relations tend to dominate parliamentary elections, while local issues tend to dominate state-level elections. The major reason that DAP found it hard to win state seats previously was that the voters in East Malaysia made a distinction between parliamentary and state issues. They were willing to support DAP in parliamentary elections but voted for local BN parties at state elections because they wanted representation at both government and opposition levels. In recent years, however, the issues have been merging and there has been less separation of parliamentary and state election issues.

Three issues tend to dominate elections in East Malaysia. The first is the condition of federal-state relations. This thorny topic is the mainstay of Sabah election issues since independence. Parties such as PBS that champion states' rights tend to do well, and in fact, PBS won four consecutive state elections (in 1985, 1986, 1990, and 1994) on a states' rights platform. Federal-state relations in Sabah is a potent issue given the historically bad relations between the MB community, the NMB community, and the various federal government/UMNO interventions to support local Muslim parties (Chin 1999; Chin Ung Ho 1999). The large number of illegal immigrants from the Southern Philippines and Indonesia has also heightened federal-state tensions.

In Sarawak, federal-state relations lurk in the background, although this has never been a central campaign issue as in Sabah. The reason for its relative lack of prominence is that the state has always been under the control of the Sarawak BN, and the federal government has largely taken a "hands-off" approach to local politics.

The second issue that dominates elections is ethnic solidarity. Since most political parties in both states represent one or two particular ethnic/religious groups, calls for voting along ethnic/religious lines is common and effective. With no ethnic/religious group in a clear majority in either state, the call for ethnic/religious solidarity is often portrayed as a vote for the future survival of the entire ethnic/religious community (Chin 1996b; 1996c; Chin Ung Ho 1999).

Finally, the third issue is a cluster of local concerns such as development, access to public utilities, business and educational opportunities, and corruption and malpractice.

Conclusion

Malaysia is one of the few countries in Southeast Asia to hold elections regularly without widespread reports of fraud or ballot-box stuffing. The results of the elections are generally accepted by the political parties and the people. Despite this, the electoral process in Malaysian elections clearly cannot be described as fair and equitable. The ruling BN often wins even before the first ballot is cast, as the structural arrangements make it virtually impossible for the BN to be defeated. The unfair distribution of seats, rural bias, and Malay-majority seats ensure that the only outcome of any nationwide poll is either an all-Malay government or a coalition government with a Malay party in the center (Crouch 1996, 57). Victory for the opposition has been construed as denying the BN a two-thirds majority, which is widely seen by both the ruling BN and the opposition as the benchmark of the government's popularity and mandate.

Since the current system does not allow for the victory of a non-Malay party, the chance for reform is remote. The current system suits the BN well, and any change to the system may cause it to lose its all-important two-thirds majority. If any changes were to be made to the system, it would likely be fine-tuning to ensure the continued dominance of UMNO and BN.

The opposition would of course like to see a proportional representation (PR) system put in place. This would ensure that it receives at least 30 percent of the seats in Parliament. The opposition would also like to see the voting age lowered to eighteen, in the belief that young voters are more supportive of its positions.

In the future, the increasing use of "money politics" to buy votes will perpetuate and exacerbate the uneven playing field. The BN's massive financial resources will ensure that the opposition is kept at bay. The BN's "3M" (Money, Media, and Machinery) also ensures that it will remain almost unbeatable at the federal level. Elections in Malaysia will be more open, however, as the government's hold on the information flow is broken by the process of globalization and the rise of the information age through applications such as the Internet and publications on the World Wide Web. Regardless, elections will continue to play a central role in Malaysian politics as both the opposition and the government accept the notion that part of their political legitimacy is derived from the ballot box.

NOTES

1. In May 1969, racial riots broke out between Chinese and Malay youths in downtown Kuala Lumpur, the capital. Several hundred people died in the riots before the army assumed control. The Constitution was temporary suspended, and the whole nation was placed under emergency rule. The official version of the cause of the riots was that the Malays feared that the Chinese dominance of the economy was so complete that the Malays would never be able to catch up or be on par with the Chinese economically. Thus the NEP and the NDP were brought in to address the imbalance. See National Operations Council 1969 for the official view. See Von Vorys 1975 and Vasil 1972 for alternative perspectives.
2. Exceptions to this rule include undischarged bankrupts, holders of "public office" or "office of profit," and those recently convicted of crimes.
3. All BN MPs and state assemblymen have access to a slash fund called the Minor Rural Projects Fund, which amounts to about M$300,000 a year to an MP and M$150,000 to a state assemblyman. These funds can be used for any project approved by the member.

References

Alias, Mohammad. 1994. *PAS' Platform: Development and Change 1951–1986*. Petaling Jaya: Gateway.
Chin, James. 1994. "Sabah State Election of 1994: End of Kadazan Unity." *Asian Survey* 34:904–15.
———. 1996a. "The 1995 Malaysian General Election: Mahathir's Last Triumph?" *Asian Survey* 36:392–409.
———. 1996b. "PBDS and Ethnicity in Sarawak Politics." *Journal of Contemporary Asia* 26:512–26.
———. 1996c. "Sarawak's 1991 Election: Continuity of Ethnic Politics." *South East Asia Research* 4, no. 1:21–40.
———. 1997. "Politics of Federal Intervention in Malaysia, With Reference to Kelantan, Sarawak And Sabah." *Journal of Commonwealth and Comparative Politics* 35:96–120.
———. 1999. "Going East: Umno's Entry into Sabah Politics." *Asian Journal of Political Science* 7, no. 1:20–40.
———. 2000. "A New Balance: The Chinese Vote in the 1999 Malaysian General Election." *South East Asia Reseach* 8, no. 3:281–99
Chin, Ung-Ho. 1997. *Chinese Politics in Sarawak: A Study of the Sarawak United People's Party*. Kuala Lumpur, Malaysia: Oxford University Press.
———. 1999. "Kataks', Kadazan-Dusun Nationalism and Development: The 1999 Sabah State Election." Regime Change and Regime Maintenance in Asia and the Pacific Monograph Series, Department of Political and Social Change, Research School of Pacific and Asian Studies. Canberra: Australian National University.
Commonwealth Observer Group. 1990. *General Elections in Malaysia, 20–21 October 1990: The Report of the Commonwealth Observer Group*. London: Commonwealth Secretariat.
Crouch, Harold. 1996. *Government and Society in Malaysia*. Sydney, Australia: Allen and Unwin.
Election Commission Malaysia. Election Reports. Various years.
Funston, John. 1980. *Malay Politics in Malaysia: A Study of the United Malay National Organisation and Party Islam*. Kuala Lumpur, Malaysia: Heinemann.
Gomez, Edmund 1994. *Political Business: Corporate Investment of Malaysian Political Parties*. Townsville, Australia: Center for South-East Asian Studies, James Cook University.
Heng, Pek Koon. 1988. *Chinese Politics in Malaysia: A History of the Malaysian Chinese Association*. Singapore: Oxford University Press.
Kessler, Clive. 1978. *Islam and Politics in a Malay State: Kelantan 1838–1969*. Ithaca, N.Y.: Cornell University Press.
Khong, Kim Hong. 1991. *Malaysia's General Election of 1990: Continuity, Change and Ethnic Politics*. Singapore: Institute of South East Asian Studies.
Khoo, Boo Teik. 1998. *Paradoxes of Mahthirism: An Intellectual Biography of Mahathir Mohamad*. Kuala Lumpur, Malaysia: Oxford University Press.
Kua, Kia Soong. 1990. *A Protean Saga: The Chinese Schools of Malaysia*. Kuala Lumpur, Malaysia: Selangor Chinese Assembly Hall.
———. 1996. *Inside the DAP: 1990–1995*. Kuala Lumpur, Malaysia: Oriengroup.
Lee, Kam Heng. 1987. "Three Approaches in Peninsular Malaysian Chinese Politics: The MCA, The DAP and The Gerakan." In *Government and Politics of Malaysia*, edited by Zakaria Haji Ahmad. Singapore: Oxford University Press.
Ling, Liong Sik. 1995. *The Malaysian Chinese towards Vision 2020*. Petaling Jaya: Pelanduk Publications.
Mauzy, Diane. 1983. *Barisan Nasional: Coalition Government in Malaysia*. Kuala Lumpur, Malaysia: Marican Publications.
Means, Gordon. 1991. *Malaysian Politics: The Second Generation*. Singapore: Oxford University Press.
National Operations Council. 1969. *The May 13 Tragedy*. Kuala Lumpur, Malaysia: Government Printer.
Shafruddin, B.F. 1987. *The Federal Factor in the Government and Politics of Peninsular Malaysia*. Singapore: Oxford University Press.
Sothi, Rachagan. 1980. "The Development of the Electoral System." In *Malaysian Politics and the 1978 Election*, edited by Harold Crouch, Harold Lee Kam Hing, and Michael Ong. Kuala Lumpur, Malaysia: Oxford University Press.

———. 1993. *Law and the Electoral Process in Malaysia.* Kuala Lumpur, Malaysia: University Malaya Press.
Strauch, Judith. 1981. *Chinese Village Politics in the Malaysian State.* Cambridge, Mass.: Harvard University Press.
Tan, Liok Ee. 1996. *The Politics of Chinese Education in Malaya, 1945–1961.* Kuala Lumpur, Malaysia: Oxford University Press.
Vasil, R.K. 1971. *Politics in a Plural Society: A Study of Non-communal Political Parties in West Malaysia.* Kuala Lumpur, Malaysia: Oxford University Press.
———. 1972. *The Malaysian General Election of 1969.* Singapore: Oxford University Press.
Von Vorys, Karl. 1975. *Democracy without Consensus.* Princeton, N.J.: Princeton University Press.

CHAPTER 11

Electoral Innovation and One-Party Dominance in Singapore

by Diane K. Mauzy

SINGAPORE IS A SMALL, tropical island state located at the tip of peninsular Malaysia, with a population of just less than 4 million. It has always been strategically and commercially important because it guards the narrow Straits of Malacca, linking the Indian Ocean to the South China Sea. Singapore is a moderately "democratic" state that features a parliamentary system and an elected president, regular elections, and a dominant-party system. Singapore has been remarkably successful economically, and its citizens enjoy one of the highest standards of living in Asia—indeed, in the world.

Until the early nineteenth century, Singapore was sparsely populated by Malay fishermen, petty traders and pirates, and a few Chinese pepper growers. In 1819, however, Stamford Raffles of the British East India Company (EIC), recognizing the value of the island's location, signed treaties with the territorial chief of Singapore and the Sultan of Johor that allowed him to establish a settlement and trading post. Five years later, the Sultan ceded the entire island and surrounding islands to the EIC. In 1826, Singapore was joined administratively with the EIC's peninsular outposts of Penang and Malacca as the Straits Settlements. Already Singapore was prospering as a transshipment center, and its multiethnic but Chinese-majority population was growing rapidly. In 1867, the Straits Settlements, with a population exceeding 80,000, became a British crown colony.

Singapore was occupied by the Japanese during World War II, and after the war, it was made a separate British crown colony, because of the ethnic complications presented by its large Chinese population and its continuing strategic value, while Penang and Malacca were joined to the Malay-dominated Federation of Malaya. Its ethnic composition was similar to today's: 76 percent Chinese, 15 percent Malays, 7 percent Indians, and 2 percent others. The Chinese were divided into a number of dialect and clan groups originating from southern maritime China, with the Hokkien being the largest at 22 percent. The important political division that was emerging in Singapore, however, was between the English-educated of all ethnic groups and the Chinese-educated Chinese of all dialects. It was believed that many of the Chinese-educated were susceptible to the influence of the Communists, who had penetrated the Chinese middle schools and trade unions, and this concern increased when a violent Communist insurrection broke out in Malaya in 1948.

Electoral History

The political divisions in Singapore took on more salience when the British, in accordance with the Labour government's policy of encouraging eventual self-government throughout its colonial empire, agreed to hold elections. At first, however, the franchise was very limited because of literacy qualifications (Milne and Mauzy 1990, 46). The first election was held in 1948 for a minority of the Legislative Council seats. The six successful candidates were all pro-British, English-speaking lawyers and political moderates. Similar results were recorded for nine elected seats in 1951.

A new constitution providing for an elected legislative majority and some self-rule, with a considerably expanded electorate, made the 1955 election Singapore's first important one. In preparation, several new parties were formed, among them the moderately left-wing Labour Front and the radical anticolonial People's Action Party (PAP). The Labour Front won the most seats and formed a minority government. The PAP, established by a group of British-educated intellectuals who then joined in an uneasy "united front" with the "pro-Communists" (a term widely used in Singapore for believers in communism who were not under party discipline), won three of the four seats it contested. One of its successful candidates was a recent Cambridge University graduate (with double first-class honors and a star of distinction) and practicing lawyer, Lee Kuan Yew.

It was a period of turbulence: Communist agitation, mass strikes, and violent riots occurred. The trade unions and Chinese middle school students were virtually out of control. The economy was in a mess, and the Labour Front disintegrated. Constitutional progress was slow because of the difficult internal security situation.

A new constitution providing for nearly full self-rule came into force in late 1958, however, and it provided, among other things, for a Singapore citizenship to those born on the island or residing there for eight years. Further, voter registration was made automatic and voting compulsory (Milne and Mauzy 1990, 51). This had the result that nearly half of the electors were new voters for the May 1959 Legislative Assembly elections.

The PAP seriously contested the 1959 elections, with candidates in every constituency. The pro-Communists backed the PAP, giving the party an army of volunteer workers from the trade unions and Chinese schools (Pang 1971, 3). This support was given despite the fact that the PAP campaigned for "independence

Table 11.1 The 1959 Election in Singapore: Seats Won

Party	Number of Seats
PAP	43
Singapore People's Alliance	4
Alliance	3
Worker's Party	0
Liberal Socialists	0
Independents	1
Total	51

Source: Milne and Mauzy 1990, 51.

through merger" with Malaya, something that the Communists opposed because of Malaya's much tougher internal security laws. (Malaya, however, was showing little interest in the idea.) The election results, with about 90 percent of the electorate voting, gave the PAP a majority with forty-three of the fifty-one seats and slightly more than 53 percent of the popular vote against a handful of parties (see table 11.1). The PAP won the Chinese-educated vote, but according to Lee Kuan Yew, it lost much of the English-educated and Malay vote (Lee 1998, 309–13).

When the PAP took power, with Lee Kuan Yew as prime minister, the party moderates running the government realized that it was just a matter of time before there would be a showdown with the Communists, inside and outside the party (Bloodworth 1986, 158 and passim). They knew they had to retain the Chinese working-class vote while attracting more of the English-educated and Malay electorate. Merger was a popular issue, but effective government performance, especially to improve the economy and provide more jobs, was the key. One of the first moves made by the new government was to abolish the city council and the office of mayor as unnecessary expenses, thereby reducing elections in Singapore to a single national legislative tier.

Clearly the PAP pro-Communists controlled most of the party branches and party bureaucracy, as well as most secondary organizations in Singapore. To counter this, the PAP government built new grassroots organizations, including more than 100 community centers and various People's Associations (Lee 1998, 324), and then used these parapolitical organizations as a substitute for party machinery to reach the grassroots.

The years 1961 and 1962 saw political struggle characterized by mass strikes, boycotts, and civil violence. Records show that 153 strikes occurred between July 1961 and September 1962 (Lee 1998, 389). The PAP lost two by-elections in 1961. The first loss, to a populist politician in a poor, mainly Hokkien constituency with a high percentage of illiteracy, taught the PAP that if "the ground is not with you, no amount of organization can turn the tide" (Fong 1979, 93). The second loss directly resulted from the Communists withdrawing their support for the PAP to show the moderates that they could not win without them. The event that precipitated the crisis was a surprise speech by the prime minister of the Federation of Malaya suggesting the formation of Malaysia—a merger of Malaya with Singapore and the Borneo territories then under the control or protection of the British.

When the PAP pushed for a "yes" vote on merger in the assembly, the party split. Thirteen members of the assembly, along with most the PAP party bureaucracy and thirty-five of the fifty-one branch committees defected and formed a new political party, the *Barisan Sosialis* (Socialist Front) to oppose the merger. With a precarious hold on power, the PAP decided on a bold strategy—to hold a national referendum on the merger in September 1962. Referenda can be influenced by the way propositions or questions are worded, or by the options allowed. This referendum was no exception. It offered a choice of three alternative sets of terms (A to C) *for* merger, and it was explicitly stated that blank ballots would be interpreted as the voter wishing to leave the choice to the assembly. No option was provided for opposing the merger. The PAP conducted an intensive political campaign, including a series of twelve radio talks by Lee Kuan Yew, each given by him in three languages, to explain the benefits of the merger and why the PAP had split. When the votes were counted, the PAP could claim a major victory. Its alternative (A) had won 71 percent of the valid votes cast. After this, preparations for the formation of Malaysia proceeded apace.

The PAP, however, still had to survive the next election—the most critical one in Singapore's history—with the Chinese-educated composing 63 percent of the electorate and the PAP's ability to attract their votes compromised. The government was helped when the *Barisan Sosialis* publicly supported a violent revolt that had broken out in Brunei in late 1962. When more than 100 pro-Communists, including some of the most effective leaders of the *Barisan Sosialis*, were arrested for abetting an illegal insurrection in February 1963, no protests or riots were staged on their behalf, and no curfew was needed (Lee 1998, 472). The government scheduled the election for 23 September 1963, giving the minimal legal notice of five days and the minimal campaign period of nine days (and even this was interrupted by the birth of Malaysia celebrations on 16 September). With the opposition unprepared and some of the *Barisan Sosialis'* most persuasive campaigners in jail, the PAP was able to focus on its record, emphasizing stability and prosperity and the success of its merger into the new entity of Malaysia. The PAP won thirty-seven of the fifty-one seats but gained only 47 percent of the total vote, while the *Barisan Sosialis* won thirteen seats and 33 percent of the vote (the remaining popular vote was spread across four other parties and sixteen independents, and the remaining seat was won by the United People's Party).

After twenty-three months of turbulence, tension, and political and economic misunderstandings, as well as two serious race riots in Singapore in 1964, Singapore was expelled from Malaysia in August 1965 (Milne 1966). Interestingly, two elections provided much of the tension and rancor. During the 1963 Singapore general election, the Tunku and some other United Malays National Organization (UMNO) members from the Malaysian peninsula spoke at rallies of the Singapore Alliance Party (SAP), which was contesting forty-two seats. To Lee and the PAP, this breached a verbal agreement and sullied trust. To Kuala Lumpur, the SAP's loss of all forty-two seats, including some in heavily Malay-populated constituencies, was humiliating. In the 1964 Malaysian federal election, the PAP surprised the federal Alliance government by contesting eleven parliamentary seats in the peninsula against the Alliance. In the end, only one PAP candidate was elected, but the intrusion angered the Tunku and soured relations between Singapore and Kuala Lumpur. The next year, Singapore, unwillingly and with very little time for preparation, had independence thrust upon it.

Singapore's first election as an independent state was held in 1968, but it was a very tame election, unlike the previous ones. One reason was that in 1966 the *Barisan Sosialis* quit participating in parliamentary politics, having decided instead on a "back to the streets" strategy of mass political agitation (Milne and Mauzy 1990, 65). The *Barisan Sosialis* did not compete in an election again until 1972, and it never again won a seat. In 1968, the PAP won all fifty-eight seats, fifty-one of which were uncontested. For the seven contests in which votes were cast, none of the PAP candidates won less than 82 percent of the popular vote. The PAP also won every seat in the general elections of 1972, 1976, and 1980, gaining between 69 percent and 75 percent of the popular vote against a handful of opposition parties. The PAP did not start out as a dominant party, but it emerged as one with the 1968 election sweep (Bellows 1970; Chan 1976).

The PAP's monopoly was ended (but its dominance hardly dented) in October 1981, when the PAP lost a by-election in troublesome Anson, a largely Chinese working-class constituency, to the leader of the Workers' Party, J.B. Jeyaretnam. This victory seems to have invigorated the opposition and to have ignited a public interest in "having an opposition."

The 1984 general election was held amidst extensive preparations for political transition and on the heels of some unpopular policies. It is quite often viewed as a watershed event signaling "the return of the opposition" (Cotton 1993, 5; Singh 1992, 15). For the seventy-nine seats, only thirty PAP candidates were returned unopposed; eight opposition parties contested the other forty-nine seats. The PAP won seventy-seven seats, losing to Jeyaretnam again and to the head of the Social Democratic Party, Chiam See Tong, in the middle-class constituency of Potong Pasir. What really shocked the PAP, however, was the nearly 13 percent swing (to 63 percent) in the popular vote against the government.

Despite a number of constitutional adjustments and innovations made to the system to provide "ballast" (thought to be needed in the absence of a weighted conservative rural vote in highly urbanized Singapore), which pundits believed would make the next election less competitive, the PAP was challenged in 1988 by seven opposition parties and four independents in seventy of the eighty-one seats. The PAP won eighty of the seats, losing only to Chiam. It did not reverse the decline in its popular vote, however, and in fact, the PAP dropped another percentage point (to 62 percent). The opposition was excited, "sensing a permanent shift of voter allegiance that put it on the brink of a significant breakthrough against PAP dominance" (Milne and Mauzy 1990, 74). The trend continued in the 1991 election, called two years early by the new prime minister, Goh Chok Tong, who sought a "solid endorsement" for his more consultative style and marginally more politically liberal government. On nomination day, a majority of forty-one PAP candidates were returned unopposed as part of a coordinated opposition strategy (which is discussed below). Five opposition parties and seven independents competed against the PAP for the remaining forty seats. Prime Minister Goh and the PAP were clearly disappointed when the PAP won only seventy-seven of eighty-one seats and slightly more than 61 percent of the popular vote. Although the rate of decline in the popular vote was slowing, the decline was persisting—now through three general elections. It was getting very near the threshold where the opposition, in a first-past-the-post electoral system without exaggerated gerrymandering, begins seeing its accumulation of popular votes translate into many more seats won. A number of observers wondered if the PAP's days as a dominant party were numbered (Singh 1992; Mutalib 1992).

The 1997 general election results reversed the trend against the PAP's dominance, however, and showed that earlier reports of its imminent demise had been greatly exaggerated. The opposition followed its previous strategy of allowing a majority of PAP candidates to be returned unopposed, in this case forty-seven out of eighty-three, so that there would not be an issue of "who" would form the government. Four opposition parties and one independent contested thirty-six seats against the PAP. The revived PAP won eighty-one seats and more than 65 percent of the popular vote in seats contested (where the PAP was presumably weakest), thus reasserting its dominance at the end of the millennium.

Independent Singapore has always had a president as ceremonial head of state. Since August 1993, Singapore has had an elected president with some powers as a guardian against the government concerning the use of foreign reserves and key civil service appointments. Two contests have been held for the post, a national election in 1993 and a walkover in 1999.

THE ELECTORAL SYSTEM

Elections, if conducted freely and honestly, are an important component of democracy. They contribute to the legitimacy of a government and the political system, which in turn is vital for political stability. Elections allow the citizenry to participate directly, and in the process, they further political education and acceptance of the institutions and principles guiding the state. They also reinforce the notion of governmental accountability and provide feedback for those in charge. Elections in many parts of the world are also at times destabilizing, because of violence arising from campaign rhetoric and heightened emotions, compounded often by ethnic group perceptions of a "zero-sum" situation. Consequently, in many of these states, political competition needs to be constrained in terms of duration and nature of electoral campaigns and in terms of what candidates can say. Singapore's early elections were competitive but were held against a background of street agitation and social unrest. Since the late 1960s, when the PAP emerged as a dominant party, elections have been peaceful and orderly, but less competitive.

Types of Elections

Singapore holds regular parliamentary elections with a five-year legal term limit for single- and (since 1988) multiple-member constituencies, and, since 1993, a nationwide election for president every six years. Singapore has a first-past-the-post electoral system (the candidate or team with the most votes wins) as opposed to any of the variants of proportional representation. No local elections are held in Singapore. Provisions exist for by-elections to fill vacancies, but it is not required that the government do so. Singapore has universal adult suffrage. Voting registration is automatic and voting is compulsory (an average of 95 percent of those eligible to vote cast ballots). Those who do not vote may be fined and deregistered, although reregistration is easy. No ballot rigging, intimidation of voters, or tinkering with the voter rolls occurs. Elections are considered to be free and honest, if not absolutely fair (given a controlled media and other obstacles facing the opposition). The U.S. State Department characterizes elections in Singapore as follows: "The voting and vote-counting systems are fair, accurate and free from tampering" (U.S. Department of State 1999, 10).

Singapore has continued with the type of parliamentary election instituted by the British in the last years of colonial rule, although the PAP government did eliminate city government and hence elections for the city council and mayor, officially to save money, but also to eliminate what was perceived as a breeding ground for the opposition and communally charged tensions. A presidential election was inaugurated in 1993, replacing an appointed ceremonial president (who had replaced the British governor), to give the elected president the legitimacy to accompany his new executive powers.

Grievances Concerning the Electoral System

The types of elections held in Singapore and the procedures for them are quite well accepted. A rather widespread perception is that the PAP purposely handicaps, and indeed hamstrings, the opposition, but there remains little demand for procedural change. In at least four areas the opposition articulates some grievances about the system. The first grievance is that the counterfoil on the ballot is numbered. This was a minor issue in the early 1970s, but it does not seem to be of much concern nowadays (DaCunha 1997, 64; *Straits Times Weekly Edition* [*STWE*], 25 January 1997) since there apparently has been no government abuse of the serial numbers. The opposition contends, however, that it does not matter that the government apparently has not checked numbers with names and votes, because just having numbers on the back of the ballots worries voters.

The second grievance has to do with the provision making by-elections optional instead of mandatory for the government. The opposition contends that the PAP has been fearful of by-elections ever since it lost one in 1981, because voters can register a protest vote in a by-election without having to consider broader implications such as the government losing power. During the 1991 election campaign, veteran Workers' Party campaigner J.B. Jeyaretnam complained that the general election was held early to prevent him from contesting (he was barred at the time as a result of a legal conviction). Prime Minister Goh promised to hold a by-election when Jeyaretnam was eligible. A by-election was held in December 1992 in the prime minister's own multimember constituency. The Workers' Party failed to file nomination papers, and the PAP won 73 percent of the vote against three other opposition parties (Vasil 1993). On other occasions where vacancies have arisen, however, the government has chosen not to hold by-elections, including for a recent vacancy (*Straits Times*, 6 and 9 June 1999).

A third grievance arose in 1997 when the government revealed, just before polling day, that the counting of votes would be at the "precinct" level, an area of about twenty blocks including approximately 5,000 voters (*STWE*, 18 and 25 January 1997). The opposition contends that not only did this practice intimidate voters, but it also provided information to the government to allow it to gerrymander boundaries in order to disperse opposition support (*STWE*, 1 February 1997).

The fourth grievance, as in a number of countries, concerns the first-past-the-post or plurality electoral system. In Singapore, this system has led to a marked discrepancy between the votes cast for an opposition party and the number of seats it obtains in Parliament. Over the last four general elections, the opposition has gained an average of 30 percent of the vote in contested seats, but this has led to only between 1.2 percent and 4.9 percent of the parliamentary seats (Gomez 1997; Ooi 1998). It should be remembered, however, that no votes are cast in the uncontested constituencies won by the PAP, and these tend to be where the PAP is the strongest.

Another grievance concerns the stringent candidacy qualifications governing eligibility for the presidency that severely limits choice. To become a candidate, the nominee must be approved by a three-person Presidential Elections Committee. To qualify, beyond possessing good character and being at least forty-five years of age, the nominee must have at least three years' experience in one of the following positions: cabinet minister, chief justice, speaker of Parliament, attorney general, auditor-general, chairman of the public service commission, permanent secretary in the civil service, or the chair of a company with paid-up capital of at least S$100 million (Singh 1994, 275). The nominee must also not be in the government or a current member of a political party. This has meant that in 1993, two nominees, from the opposition, were rejected, while two were approved—one a former PAP deputy prime minister and the other a former auditor-general (and reluctant candidate). In 1999, only one was approved (a former high-ranking public servant, diplomat, and corporate chair), who thereby won by a walkover (*Business Times* [*BT*], 13 August 1999).

Clearly, the PAP government benefits from parliamentary election rules and procedures that tend to favor the majority party. In parliamentary systems, the government party has the advantages of election timing and of being able to exert control over the redrawing of electoral boundaries. The first-past-the-post electoral system tends to benefit the major party (or parties), and automatic registration and compulsory voting—given a relatively apathetic electorate in a dominant party setting such as Singapore's—must surely benefit the government. Small opposition parties tend to prosper in strict proportional representation (PR) voting systems that directly translate votes into seats, and in settings where political activists are more likely to register and vote than the average citizen.

Election Reforms and Innovations

The government party also benefits from being in a position to effect electoral changes, reforms, and innovations, which may or may not be "voter neutral." After the electoral setback in 1984, the PAP government in Singapore began adding "ballast" to the system by making selective changes that would provide some cushion against sudden voting fluctuations (in the absence of a stable, conservative rural electorate) (Milne and Mauzy 1990, 96). These innovative reforms include changing the electoral system by creating some multiple-member constituencies; providing more non-PAP voices in Parliament; creating an elected president as a guardian with some blocking powers; and linking decentralization to MPs.

Perhaps the most important change was the creation in 1988 of some multiple-member constituencies, called Group Representation Constituencies (GRCs), for the stated purpose of enlarging minority representation in Parliament. At first, thirteen GRCs with three members each (for a total of thirty-nine seats) and forty-two single-member constituencies were created (Milne and Mauzy 1990, 71). Each party contesting a GRC was required to put up a three-person team that included a designated minority (Malay, Indian, or Eurasian). For the GRCs, members would be elected by a bloc vote; in other words, the party receiving the most votes would elect all of its team. From this cautious beginning, in late 1996 an amendment was passed enlarging the GRCs to a maximum of six-member teams. Also, the required minimum for single-member constituencies was reduced to eight (Ganesan 1998, 230). In the 1997 election, for the eighty-three seats, only nine single-member constituencies remained. The rest of the seats were divided into four GRCs with six-member teams; six GRCs with five-member teams; and five GRCs with four-member teams. In a decade, Singapore's electoral system went from entirely single-member constituencies to a preponderance of multiple-member constituencies.

The second innovation was the introduction of Non-Constituency Members of Parliament (NCMPs) and later Nominated Members of Parliament (NMPs). To satisfy the desire of many Singaporeans for some opposition in Parliament and to defuse the issue by making an elected opposition seem unnecessary, the government devised two schemes to add diversity to the legislature. In 1984, Parliament passed an act providing for the appointment of up to three NCMPs, to bring the opposition in Parliament to a minimum of three, allocated to those opposition candidates with the highest losing percentage of votes. The NCMP can speak in Parliament and can take part in debates and vote except on no-confidence motions, constitutional amendments, and budget and financial bills. In 1984, one NCMP seat was offered (the opposition had won two seats) but was rejected as a second-class seat and a ploy to provide a "toothless alternative" to genuine opposition. In 1988, two NCMP seats were offered, and one of the defeated Workers' Party candidates, Lee Siew Choh, previously head of the *Barisan Sosialis*, accepted. He was able to speak at length about abolishing the Internal Security Act (ISA) and about the need for electoral reform to a fairer PR system, and thus lent some credibility to the position. In 1997, one seat was offered and it was accepted by J.B. Jeyaretnam. The Workers' Party said it would be an injustice to the voters who wanted an opposition if the party rejected the seat.

The NMP scheme was passed by Parliament in 1990, beginning with two nominated members, to contribute to parliamentary debate as outstanding citizens and nonpartisan members with independent voices. NMPs are nominated by the public and chosen by a parliamentary Special Select Committee. NMPs are able to speak on motions, debate, raise questions, but not vote. Usually, elsewhere, such nominees serve in a second or upper house, to expand representation, but in Singapore, the NMPs are inside a unicameral lower house. The number of NMPs was first expanded to six, and then nine in 1997 (*STWE*, 7 June 1999). Also, functional groups, as well as the general public, will now formally nominate individuals.

Another change was the legislation to create an elected president as a custodian with some blocking powers over the use of the reserves (estimated at US$75 billion) and a veto over high civil service appointments that, in the president's view, were not merited. Some see this as an effort by Lee Kuan Yew to preserve his legacy through institutionalization after the 13 percent drop in popular vote in 1984 (Cotton 1993, 7–8). The legislation for an elected president had a long gestation period, and it has been misunderstood and controversial from the beginning. Many believed initially that the position was being tailored for Lee Kuan Yew himself. The first public mention of an elected president came in 1984. The scheme reemerged in 1988, was debated in Parliament, and became an election issue. In November 1991, the final constitutional product was passed, and the first direct election for a six-year term was held in August 1993 after the term of the appointed president ended.

The first elected president, Ong Teng Cheong, a former PAP deputy prime minister, completed his term in August 1999. He was succeeded by S.R. Nathan, who was uncontested for the position (*BT*, 13 August 1999). The government and the first elected president engaged in a long process of trying to devise a "common understanding" of the role of the president. This resulted in a forty-six-page White Paper released in July 1999 that attempts to spell out the parameters and procedures regarding the presidency, and the relationship between the president and the government (Chua 1999). After that, however, Ong held a press conference in which he spoke of the obstacles, frustrations, and the "long list" of problems he had encountered in his attempt to test his authority as guardian of the reserves (Hamilton 1999b; Seah 1999). This generated more public debate and extensive media attention about how "independent" a president should be, leading Lee Kuan Yew to address it in an interview. Lee said that the elected president was never intended to be an executive office. Unless an irresponsible government takes power, the president's duties are basically ceremonial. The president has no executive powers to initiate anything nor to stop the government from doing anything other than spending the reserves or making inappropriate civil service appointments (Ibrahim 1999). He continued to explain that the president's powers are quite specific and delimited, and even then the president must have the support of a majority of the six-member council of presidential advisers (two are appointed by the president, two by the prime minister, one by the chief justice, and one by the head of the public service commission) (Ibrahim 1999).

Finally, legislation was passed in June 1988 for another innovation, which was linked to the GRC scheme, for the establishment of town councillors to manage the large complexes of government housing estates. As this represented a step towards decentralization, the move was approved in principle by the opposition. There was a catch, however: members of Parliament would become the town councillors. This meant that "voters would have to live with their choice of MPs," not merely as national representatives but also "as town councillors making local decisions directly affecting the lives of constituents" (Milne and Mauzy

1990, 70). The government noted further that badly run councils would not be bailed out. In 1997, the town councils' boundaries were altered as a result of new electoral boundaries, leaving sixteen town councils, two of which were run by opposition MPs (*STWE*, 18 January 1997). Also in 1997, a new layer of administration was added with the creation of Community Development Councils (CDCs) to coordinate and lead the various existing parapolitical grassroots organizations. The CDCs incorporate a combination of GRCs and single-member constituencies and will be headed by nonelected mayors (DaCunha 1997, 9).

Reactions to the Innovations

The opposition and at least some of the public believe that the legislative innovations in the last decade were instituted primarily to handicap the opposition and improve the electoral performance of the PAP (*STWE*, 22 February 1997). All four opposition MPs voted against the November 1996 legislation to enlarge the size and increase the percentage of GRCs, saying the changes were designed to move the "goal posts back" again (Mauzy 1997, 266). For the opposition, the GRCs dilute the force of personality of party leaders and also present the problem of fielding competent teams with minority representatives. The GRCs have also allowed the government to abolish the more vulnerable single-member seats, although the government was careful not to do away with the single-member constituencies held by the opposition, and in 1997, it even created a new single-member constituency, as requested by the leader of one of the main opposition parties. For the PAP, the GRCs shield new candidates behind a team led by a minister, and results have shown that there are voting advantages for the PAP to larger-sized constituencies, namely, that the vote "will generally reflect the size of the popular vote accorded to the party that gets an overall majority nationwide" (DaCunha 1997, 15).

As for the legislative innovations, the opposition initially rejected the NCMP seats as leading to "second-class MPs," as mentioned earlier. More recently, the seats have been filled, and complaints about the concept have died down. The NMPs are popular with the public, because of the high quality of the nominees and the range of interests they represent (*STWE*, 7 June 1997). They are disliked, however, by the opposition and some academics. The opposition believes— correctly—that it tends to be overshadowed by the NMPs in Parliament. Further, the opposition believes the exercise represents a prime example of PAP cooptation. Some academics and constitutional lawyers criticize the scheme as an aberration of the parliamentary model that they believe erodes democracy.

The elected presidency has been controversial from the beginning, when many Singaporeans believed that a powerful post was being especially created for Lee Kuan Yew, and it is clear that the purpose and parameters (and limitations) of the position remain somewhat misunderstood (*BT*, 13 August 1999). The chief criticism of the elected presidency, however, is directed towards the strict candidacy requirements that severely limit the choice of candidates. Some opposition candidates would like to contest but cannot get their nominations approved. Clearly the position was not created as a new avenue of competitive oppositional politics.

Finally, reactions to the town councils have been twofold. On the whole, the opposition approves of decentralization. It believes, however—probably correctly—that making MPs the town councillors discourages voting for the opposition because it makes such a vote "risky." The opposition also believes that this is a way of having local government without having local elections—a venue often favorable to the opposition (Mauzy 1997, 266).

THE PARTY SYSTEM

Given a limited franchise initially, Singapore started out as a multiparty system with competing conservative parties. As the franchise was extended to include the majority of Chinese-speaking voters, several left-wing parties were formed and soon eclipsed the older conservative parties. Typically, five or six parties contest each election, although more than twenty parties are registered. Only one party has been banned, and that is the Communist Party of Malaya.

The PAP participated in a competitive multiparty system in 1955, 1959, and 1963. It emerged as a dominant party in 1968, however, winning every seat (Bellows 1970; Chan 1976). The PAP repeated this feat in the next three general elections. Since then, in the four following general elections, the opposition has won a few seats and between 25 percent and 39 percent of the vote in contested seats, but the PAP remains a dominant party. The percentage of the vote won by the opposition is somewhat misleading. Typically, the PAP's strongest candidates are returned unopposed (a majority of them in the past two general elections). It is reasonable to expect that if there were contests for these seats, the PAP's overall percentage of the popular vote would be higher. The characteristic of a dominant-party system is that although several or many parties legally compete, the same party is expected to win every time. The PAP dominates but does not completely control the political process; it is somewhat responsive to societal demands. In fact, the PAP fits the paternalistic "responsive-repressive" mold described by Harold Crouch for UMNO in Malaysia (Crouch 1996, 236–47).

The PAP is an odd dominant party in many ways. It came to power as a left-wing mass mobilizing party, and it has remained in power despite the fact that it is no longer left-wing. Some of its policies are typical of a social democratic party—it has built schools, clinics, hospitals, and public housing—yet it abhors welfare and the "welfare state." It stands for law and order, stability, and family values, and it is probusiness—yet it is not a conservative party. It is a cadre party that has borrowed some of its organizational methods from the Communists, and yet the PAP parliamentary wing largely ignores the party bureaucracy and branches between elections (as amplified below). It recruits candidates from the ranks of the civil service and professions rather than from the party workers and activists. It is a party dominated by the almost-larger-than-life presence of Lee Kuan Yew, yet the party is institutionalized and has proven itself capable of forcing out the old guard and renewing itself.

The PAP is basically a nonideological "catchall" party that occupies most of the political space in the middle and co-opts and recruits the best political talent. It is widely viewed as a pragmatic party, and ultimately it is flexible, but the leaders "will not bend easily or very far, or for long, on policies they deem to be essential" (Milne and Mauzy 1990, 112).

Race, Religion, Class

The PAP is a multiethnic party and tries to project a multiethnic image. Several Indian and Malay ministers are in the government, some with important portfolios, and the new president is an Indian, but the Chinese dominate the very top positions in the party and government. The party is nonreligious but is very alert to protecting the religious rights of the minorities, particularly the ever-sensitive Malay Muslims. In terms of class, the party is elitist and adheres to the Confucian ethos that holds that rule should be by the "best and the brightest." This translates into a high moral tone in government (and *very* little official corruption) and a system of meritocracy for society and the promotion of Asian values. It has also meant that the PAP regularly has cabinets containing individuals with higher educational qualifications per capita than any other cabinets in the world.

Cleavages

The PAP is in many ways a product of its history of struggle against the pro-Communists inside the party. The English-educated moderate faction narrowly prevailed over the pro-Communist faction (Bloodworth 1986, 87, 330, and passim; Drysdale 1984, 272, 311), and "the need for cohesion in the 1950s and early 1960s forged a remarkable solidarity of PAP leadership in later years" (Turnbull 1977, 299). The successor generation has been thoroughly groomed to work as a team and to avoid factionalism—probably the most common reason for the demise of dominant parties. No one in the PAP cabinet will admit to *any* factionalism in the party. Unsubstantiated rumors used to surface occasionally about "hard-line" and "political liberalization" factions, but since the 1991 election when prime minister Goh was finally convinced that liberalization had no political payoff, the factional rumors have focused more on followers/supporters of two individuals: prime minister Goh and the person already designated by Goh as the next prime minister, B.G. Lee Hsien Loong (who is, incidentally, the eldest son of Lee Kuan Yew). No indication or evidence suggests that factionalism will become a problem for the PAP.

Personalized Party or Institutionalized Party?

The PAP may seem superficially to be a "party of personality" given the towering presence of Lee Kuan Yew—prime minister for thirty-one years and credited with being the founder of modern Singapore—and the fact that the PAP party bureaucracy is small and weak. Raj Vasil describes the PAP as having little direct influence on government; no officials outside the parliamentary wing; no strong bureaucracy; and no effective institutions for mobilization or recruitment (Vasil 1988, 27–56).

Clearly, the PAP has been indelibly marked by Lee's leadership, however, it is institutionalized in a sense despite a weak party apparatus. Here, again, the PAP has been influenced by its struggle against the pro-Communists. The PAP moderates lost control of most of the party apparatus to the pro-Communists, so it set up a number of parapolitical grassroots organizations as a substitute: the People's Associations and Citizens' Consultative Committees, in 1960 the Community Centres, and later the Residents' Committees (Hill and Lian 1995, 163; Seah 1985). The PAP controlled mobilization and channeled participation through these ancillary organizations (Milne and Mauzy 1990, 100–101), and many credit the PAP's long political dominance to these government-sponsored and PAP-identified grassroots organizations (Hill and Lian 1995, 175–76). Therefore, many of the roles one would expect a major party to perform are in fact conducted by government organizations, and the line between party and government has been substantially blurred.

The Opposition

In many electoral systems, the opposition parties have some hope each election of winning power. In dominant-party systems, the opposition has little hope of coming to power in the short term. Parties in such systems are sometimes labeled "parties of pressure" because their efforts can compel the dominant party to adjust its policies and practices in order to protect its dominance.

In Singapore, the opposition parties are only marginally successful as parties of pressure, because the PAP successfully resists that kind of influence. Most of the parties are multiethnic, especially since the establishment of GRCs has made including minority candidates mandatory. Some have a quasi-class base (e.g., the Workers' Party), and some a moderate ideological position (such as the democratic socialism espoused by the Social Democracy Party). As is quite typical in such a system, however, they tend primarily to be parties of personality. The opposition on the whole is poorly organized, is thin on substantive policy proposals, does not have access to the parapolitical organizations (the exception being the two town councils run by the opposition), and cannot attract many qualified candidates; some of the parties have been wracked by internal dissension. They tend to be defensive and to focus their efforts on opposing particular PAP policies and government arrogance and intrusiveness.

The Impact of the Electoral System on the Party System

The first-past-the-post electoral system has the effect of reducing the number of parties that compete, and it tends to penalize the opposition by not translating votes into seats proportionately. The multimember GRCs further disadvantage small parties that have difficulties fielding competent teams, and they discourage the formation of new parties. Also, the large size of the GRCs tends to eliminate ethnic concentrations or socioeconomic blocs, which could perhaps be targeted by the opposition. Finally, the absence of elections below the national parliamentary level deprives the opposition of the opportunity of using local elections as a stepping stone to power.

ELECTION CAMPAIGNS

It might be expected that electoral campaigns in one-party-dominant systems would offer little of interest. This is not the case in Singapore these days, however. Considerable attention is given to the question of whether or not the PAP is in decline, given recent trends and the generally large attendance at opposition campaign rallies.

The PAP typically tries to convince voters that their choices have consequences. In the 1980s, the PAP campaigns focused on the idea that voting against the PAP as a protest against some feature of PAP rule (while actually wanting a PAP government) could lead to a "freak" election result that inadvertently knocked the PAP from power. This strategy seemed to have some success. The opposition countered in the 1991 and 1997 elections by employing a so-called "by-election" strategy of contesting fewer than half of the seats, thus eliminating the chance of the PAP losing power and allowing voters to support the opposition "risk free" in seats contested. This strategy enjoyed some success in 1991, but in 1997, the PAP countered by forcing voters to concentrate on constituency-level issues where the competency of the MP would be crucial, and by threatening to tie votes to housing upgrading (Mauzy 1997, 265). The implication was that housing estates in constituencies won by the PAP would have first priority for upgrading paid for by the government while opposition-held constituencies would go to the "back of the queue" (Mauzy 1997, 269; Ganesan 1998, 232). Although this strategy caused unease, and even anger, among some Singaporeans it seemed to work (*STWE*, 25 January 25 and 1 February 1997).

The PAP is not an ideological party in a narrow sense of the term (in a broad sense, it could be said that the PAP has elitism, neo-Confucianism, and pragmatism as its ideological strains). Lee Kuan Yew's personal views, expressed in a 1999 interview, parallel the modus operandi of the PAP: "I'm an empiricist. I'm not an ideologue. I don't believe in theories. I read about theories. I'm interested in them. But when I have a problem, I'll just solve it" (*New York Times*, 22 February 1999). The PAP typically focuses on "bread-and-butter" issues during an election year, and then during the campaign, it spells out its performance record and its plans for the future.

Since the 1990s, however, the PAP has been caught up in class and ethnic issues. The PAP believes it erred in 1991 in focusing on the perceived demands of the primarily English-speaking middle classes, in the process neglecting the concerns of the poorer, mainly Chinese-speaking working classes. This resentment led to a voter backlash by the working classes (Rodan 1993, 59–64), and the results subsequently allowed Lee Kuan Yew's views concerning liberalization and PAP electoral strategy to prevail over Goh Chok Tong's (Cotton 1993, 10). The 1997 campaign concentrated on wooing back the working classes through "asset-enhancing investments and subsidies"—an elaborate redistribution policy designed to reduce the gap between rich and poor without negatively impacting on business and investment. Some of the asset enhancement concerned plans to upgrade the older housing estates, and the PAP tied the priority given to various estates to voting results, as mentioned above.

The opposition is not very ideological either, although most claim to be moderately to the left of the PAP and to stand for social democracy and social justice (*STWE*, 27 December 1997). The opposition tends to be on the defensive and to react to PAP moves (DaCunha 1997, 64). Instead of offering itself as an alternative to the PAP (which it cannot do with its by-election strategy), the opposition limits its focus to criticizing the government.

The votes-for-upgrades campaign strategy sounds like a beginning of pork-barrel politics in Singapore. Beside this, however, there is virtually no official corruption and, unusually for Southeast Asia, no vote-buying. The opposition is nonetheless handicapped in other ways. Campaigns are short—normally nine days—and because only the government knows when the election is going to be called, it is prepared while the opposition often is not. In 1996, for example, the opposition was in a state of election readiness for almost the entire year and seemed exhausted when the election finally was called in late December.

Another opposition disadvantage is that the media are not politically neutral. The opposition is not seen much on government-controlled television during the campaign, and while the opposition is given considerable coverage in the print media, the news slant is not always presented in a favorable light. No pro-opposition newspapers exist. The Internet allows for a range of views and political commentary in technologically advanced Singapore, however, this activity appears to be limited at the moment to a group of young, educated English-speakers (DaCunha 1997, 86, 96). Also, unlike most of the other Southeast Asian countries, the government still has some control—or at least is perceived as having such—over electronic mail and the Internet. A ban remains on political parties making political films or videos to distribute during election campaigns (*STWE*, 7 March 1998). These handicaps have no doubt contributed to the curiosity of the public that has led to large turnouts at opposition rallies. Finally, the opposition faces the ever-present threat of being sued for libel by any PAP member if they misspeak during the campaign and cannot back up their words with evidence.

Singapore has also had one presidential campaign and election, in 1993. It was not much of a campaign, since the anointed candidate, former PAP deputy prime minister Ong Teng Cheong, faced a reluctant candidate, former auditor-general Chua Kim Yeow, who no doubt had his arm twisted to stand so there could be an election (unlike the situation in 1999). Chua emerged as a sympathetic figure, however, who struck a chord when he said that "the PAP dominates the government and dominates the legislature. Do you want the PAP to dominate the presidency too?" Further, the "by-election effect" came fully into play: voters could oppose the PAP with no risk (Singh 1994, 276). The result was a bit embarrassing for the PAP; Ong collected only 58.7 percent of the vote.

VOTING BEHAVIOR

Voting is compulsory in Singapore, and in 1997, some 95.9 percent of eligible voters (slightly more than 700,000) cast their ballots in the contested-seat elections (*STWE*, 25 January 1997). More than one million eligible citizens did not have an opportunity to vote in the seats where the PAP won uncontested. No intimidation of voters occurs at the polls in Singapore, and unlike much of Southeast Asia, for decades no violence or deaths have been associated with election campaigns or polling.

Singapore is a multiethnic, multireligious, multilingual state, and these factors have a bearing on voting behavior. To analyze voting behavior, however, one needs quantitative data breaking down the vote in each precinct or constituency into such categories as race, primary language, religion, occupation, gender, age, education, and income group. Unfortunately, such data are not *publicly* available. While there have been some systematic analyses of elections, no formal voter surveys or exit polls are available in Singapore. The total votes in each constituency are available, however, and it is possible to categorize constituencies generally as to class and race, thus allowing some voting behavior analysis.

Singapore's 76 percent Chinese population can be divided into four categories: older Chinese-educated intellectuals; older, less educated or uneducated Chinese-speakers—the so-called "Chinese ground"; mostly younger bilingual Chinese; and English-educated Chinese of all age groups. The PAP is dominated by English-educated and mostly bilingual Chinese (although Indians and some Malays are well represented in the party hierarchy). The PAP faces the challenge of managing the "Chinese ground." The 1990 census revealed that there were still almost 500,000 older Chinese Singaporeans with no formal education, and another 400,000 with only primary or incomplete secondary education (*STWE*, 18 January 1997). These constitute the bulk of the lower-income working classes, and politically they are susceptible to being stirred up by the Chinese-educated intellectuals, many of whom harbor resentments about being bypassed in the 1970s when English education was being emphasized and rewarded. In many ways, this is a continuation of an old struggle.

In 1997, the hardest fought, "no-holds-barred" contest of the election reflected the struggle for the "Chinese ground." This was the contest between the

PAP and the Workers' Party, led by old campaigner J.B. Jeyaretnam and Chinese-language advocate Tang Liang Hong in the multimember GRC of Cheng San, an area of factories and low-income, mainly Chinese-speaking residents. In the campaign, the PAP became alarmed when Tang hit a responsive chord in raising sensitive language and religious issues. Tang said that English-educated Christians were overrepresented in Parliament and the Cabinet. Further, he reportedly made the point, in a more incendiary fashion, that Chinese speakers were a majority, and asked why then they were the ones "carrying the sedan chair" when they should be the ones sitting on it? The PAP focused its considerable arsenal against Tang, branding him a dangerous radical and a Chinese-language chauvinist who must be defeated. The prime minister and both deputy prime ministers joined the campaign, and on the last day, Prime Minister Goh said it was "a contest between me and him" (*Far Eastern Economic Review* [*FEER*], 17 January 1997, p. 17) and warned the voters in Cheng San that either they "win big" or they "lose big" (DaCunha 1997, 39). The PAP won the contest, with less than 55 percent of the votes, and then several PAP leaders sued Tang for defamation, and he fled the country. One Western diplomat commented afterwards on the PAP's hardball campaign, saying, "the election has shown that the kinder, gentler approach loses four seats," referring to the 1991 election. "The tough-guy approach loses only two seats. Their tactics are vindicated. Why go soft?" (*FEER*, 16 January 1997, p. 17).

In Singapore there is a stable, hard-core opposition to the government of nearly 30 percent, and "floating voters" fluctuate between 10 and 20 percent. The PAP wins between 60 and 70 percent of the vote, depending on the floating voters. The two opposition members elected in 1997, incumbents Chiam See Tong, now of the Singapore People's Party, and Low Thia Khiang of the Workers' Party won because they were both "effective grassroots organizers who avoided highly publicized clashes with the PAP" (*FEER*, 16 January 1997, p. 16). Chiam won in a largely middle-class constituency, and Low won in a predominantly working-class constituency. By contrast, Chee Soon Juan, leader of the Social Democratic Party, chose a strategy of high-profile confrontations with the PAP. He won only 35 percent of the vote in his constituency (*STWE*, 8 February 1997). One analyst wrote that "Singaporeans who want opposition voices in Parliament usually want the opposition to represent someone else's constituency (DaCunha 1997, 65), and another, Bilveer Singh, concluded that Singaporeans vote pragmatically for whomever offers the best package: "Its got nothing to do with ideology, political space or having a civil society" (*STWE*, 27 December 1997).

Conclusions: An Assessment of Elections in Singapore

Elections, voting, and the vote-counting system in Singapore are free and honest (U.S. Department of State 1999, 10). Elections are fair in a legal sense, but the methods used by the PAP to disadvantage the opposition, such as announcing constituency boundary changes only three months before the election and the intimidation inherent in the threat (sometimes carried out) of libel suits, leave the impression that the process is less than scrupulously fair. The PAP is unlikely to change its methods. Lee Kuan Yew once said that it was not his job to build an opposition, only to make an opposition possible (*FEER*, 8 January 1987, p. 63). That is the case in Singapore: An opposition exists, but it is weak and divided, and the government is not giving it any breaks.

Singapore seems to defy the theory that economic growth, especially growth with equity, facilitates democracy. "Since 1959, when the PAP came to power, Singapore has been among the world's most successful countries 'by any measure' [*Economist*, 28 May 1994, p. 9] at improving its citizens' welfare" (Mauzy 1997, 264). But democratic development has not played a part in the process. Now, in moving with the times—and particularly in facing up to the fact that before the new millennium, every home in Singapore was connected to a cable providing television, advanced telecommunications, and high-speed Internet access—the government has signaled a readiness in its "cautious way" to allow "the boundaries of control to be pushed back" (*Economist*, 29 May 29 and 4 June 1999).

The improved communications infrastructure may contribute to a growth of civil society (there is a dearth of social action–oriented or politically oriented NGOs in Singapore at the moment). One observer believes that with the evolution of civil society, in the future the primary political competition will be between the PAP and the demands of civil society, rather than within the political party system (Tay 1998, 257). Yet there is not really a very strong demand for more democracy, greater civil society, or a stronger opposition. Surveys regularly show that a strong majority of Singaporeans are reasonably well satisfied with their government. As was noted in *Asiaweek*, "citizens appear to offer little support for the opposition or sympathy for its travails" (Hamilton 1999a).

Dominant parties often do decline eventually—because of internal factions, because people eventually simply want a change, or because young voters think they are missing some excitement. Until the 1997 election, the data seemed to indicate that the PAP was slowly losing its dominance and Singapore was heading towards a semicompetitive "one-and-a-half-party system" with a sizable opposition (Mutalib 1992, 102–4). In the 1997 election, the PAP reversed the trend. The PAP has brought the country through the Asian economic crisis in spectacular fashion, it has learned a few new "dirty tricks" to throw at the opposition, and it shows no signs of weakening or splitting. Likewise, Singaporeans continue to vote pragmatically. As one Singaporean said: "They may be an arrogant lot, but they know how to govern."

References

Bellows, Thomas. 1970. *The People's Action Party of Singapore: Emergence of a Dominant Party.* New Haven, Conn.: Yale University Southeast Asia Series.

Bloodworth, Dennis. 1986. *The Tiger and the Trojan Horse.* Singapore: Times Books International.

Chan, Heng Chee. 1976. *The Dynamics of One Party Dominance: The PAP at the Grass-Roots.* Singapore: Singapore University Press.

Chua, Lee Hoong. 1999. "The Presidency: Striking a Tricky Balance." *Straits Times*, 7 August.

Cotton, James. 1993. "Political Innovation in Singapore: The Presidency, the Leadership and the Party." In *Singapore Changes Guard,* edited by Garry Rodan. Melbourne, Australia: Longman Cheshire.

Crouch, Harold. 1996. *Government and Society in Malaysia.* Ithaca, N.Y.: Cornell University Press.

DaCunha, Derek. 1997. *The Price of Victory: The 1997 Singapore General Election and Beyond.* Singapore: Institute of Southeast Asian Studies.

Drysdale, John. 1984. *Singapore: Struggle for Success.* Singapore: Times Books International.

Fong Sip Chee. 1979. *The PAP Story—The Pioneer Years.* Singapore: Times Periodicals.

Ganesan, N. 1998. "Singapore: Entrenching a City-State's Dominant Party System." In *Southeast Asian Affairs 1998.* Singapore: Institute of Southeast Asian Studies.

Gomez, James. 1997. "Proportionalising Political Representation in Singapore." *Commentary* 14:118–31.

Hamilton, Andrea. 1999a. "Down and Possibly Out." *Asiaweek*, 22 January.

———. 1999b. "The President Speaks Out." *Asiaweek*, 30 July.

Hill, Michael, and Lian Kwen Fee. 1995. *The Politics of Nation Building and Citizenship in Singapore.* London: Routledge.

Ibrahim, Zuraidah. 1999. "Largely Ceremonial." *Straits Times Interactive*, 11 August.

Lee Kuan Yew. 1998. *The Singapore Story: Memoirs of Lee Kuan Yew.* Singapore: Prentice Hall.

Mauzy, Diane K. 1997. "Singapore's Dilemma: Coping with the Paradoxes of Success." In *Southeast Asian Affairs 1997.* Singapore: Institute of Southeast Asian Affairs.

Milne, R.S. 1966. "Singapore's Exit from Malaysia: The Consequences of Ambiguity." *Asian Survey* 6:175–84.

Milne, R.S., and Diane K. Mauzy. 1990. *Singapore: The Legacy of Lee Kuan Yew.* Boulder, Colo.: Westview Press.

Mutalib, Hussin. 1992. "Domestic Politics." In *IPS Year in Review,* edited by Lee Tsao Yuan. Singapore: Institute of Policy Studies and Times Academic Press.

Ooi, Can Seng. 1998. "Singapore." In *Political Party Systems and Democratic Development in East and Southeast Asia,* edited by Wolfgang Sachsenroder and Ulrike Frings. Singapore: Ashgate Publishing Ltd.

Pang, Cheng Lian. 1971. *Singapore People's Action Party: Its History, Organization and Leadership.* Singapore: Oxford University Press.

Rodan, Garry. 1993. "The Growth of Singapore's Middle Class and Its Political Significance." In *Singapore Changes Guard,* edited by Garry Rodan. Melbourne, Australia: Longman Cheshire.

Safire, William. 1999. "Interview with Singapore's Senior Minister Lee Kuan Yew." *New York Times,* 22 February.

Seah, Cheang Nee. 1999. "Suspicions Linger after Executive Spat." *The Star* (Malaysia), August 22, 1999.

Seah Chee Meow. 1985. "Parapolitical Institutions." In *Government and Politics in Singapore,* edited by Jon S.T. Quah et al. Singapore: Oxford University Press.

Singh, Bilveer. 1992. *Whither PAP's Dominance: An Analysis of Singapore's 1991 General Election.* Petaling Jaya: Pelanduk.

———. 1994. "Singapore: Change amidst Continuity." In *Southeast Asian Affairs 1994.* Singapore: Institute of Southeast Asian Studies.

Tay, Simon S.C. 1998. "Towards Singaporean Civil Society." In *Southeast Asian Affairs 1998.* Singapore: Institute of Southeast Asian Studies.

Turnbull, C.M. 1977. *A History of Singapore, 1819–1975.* Kuala Lumpur, Malaysia: Oxford University Press.

U.S. Department of State. 1999. *Country Reports on Human Rights Practices for 1998.* http://www.state.gov/www/global/human_rights/1999_hrp_report/singapor.html.

Vasil, Raj. 1988. *Governing Singapore.* Rev. ed. Singapore: Times Books International.

———. 1993. "Singapore 1992: Continuity and Change." In *Southeast Asian Affairs 1993.* Singapore: Institute of Southeast Asian Studies.

CHAPTER 12

Indonesia: Electoral Politics in a Newly Emerging Democracy

by Donald E. Weatherbee

ON 7 JUNE 1999, 112 million Indonesian voters went to more than 320,000 polling stations scattered over the vast archipelago nation to cast votes in the eighth general election in the country's fifty-five-year history. The turnout was more than 90 percent of 118 million eligible voters, and more than 105 million valid votes were counted. The voters selected from a ballot carrying the names and logos of forty-eight contesting political parties. Rather than the usually prescribed five-year interval, the 1999 election took place only two years after the 29 May 1997 poll. In the intervening period, the government of six-term president Suharto had collapsed, a victim of Asia's economic crisis, regime political incapacity, and democratic opposition. A new election in the country of more than 200 million people with the world's largest Muslim population was considered crucial to the efforts to simultaneously democratize and stabilize the post-Suharto political system. It was hoped that the elections would be a positive first step towards forming a new government with a popular mandate to attack Indonesia's economic crisis and to stop the process of social disintegration.

In Indonesian language, the general election is the *pemilihan umum*, abbreviated in Indonesian style to *pemilu*. Although always called "democratic festivals," the 1999 *pemilu* was the first since 1955 that met Samuel Huntington's (1991,7) minimalist definition of democracy being based on representative government elected by universal franchise in a free, fair, and open electoral process in which the voters have choices of parties and candidates. To its opponents, the Suharto regime had been characterized by corruption, collusion, and nepotism, sloganized as KKN (*korupsi, kolusi, nepotisme*), and its electoral system was designed to legitimate a "soft authoritarian" rule behind the facade of representative democracy. The 1999 *pemilu* was the first test of a new commitment to democratic reform in the political system, one in which the military and heavy-handed government would stay in the background. The public demanded an honest (*jujur*) and fair (*adil*) election, *jurdil* in the Indonesian penchant for acronyms. It had been feared that mounting social and ethnic conflict would spill over into the electoral campaigns.[1] In fact, the process was relatively peaceful and violence free. Suspicion that the government would intimidate the voters and rig the outcome was not justified. The legion of domestic and foreign election observers and monitors agreed that the goal of free and fair elections was largely achieved.[2]

The voters elected 462 of the 500 members of Indonesia's Parliament, the *Dewan Perwakilan Rakyat* (DPR) that began its five-year term in October 1999. The other 38 DPR seats are filled by appointed members of the Indonesian Armed Forces, *Angkatan Bersenjata Republik Indonesia* (ABRI). In addition, the voters elected 1,455 representatives to provincial assemblies (DPRD-I) and 11,785 members of district legislatures (DPRD-II). As soon as they were sworn in, the 500 DPR members joined 135 DPRD-I delegates and 65 appointed representatives of "functional groups" in the 700-seat Peoples Consultative Assembly, the *Majelis Permusyawaratan Rakyat* (MPR). The MPR is Indonesia's highest constitutional body, and it meets every five years to elect a president and vice president. The *pemilu*, therefore, was connected only indirectly to the election of the president. The outcome of that election depended on the distribution of political power in the MPR among the competing parties at the national and provincial representative levels and the institutional preferences represented by the ABRI and "functional groups'" delegates.

Hopes for democracy soared with the success of the *pemilu*. The experience of a dysfunctional multiparty parliamentary period in the first years of independence, however, was a reminder that a *pemilu jurdil* did not guarantee a government capable of managing the country's economic and social crises, let alone bridging with public policy the deep social, cultural, and ethnic cleavages threatening to rip the country asunder. The result of the 1999 election was sobering in that regard. Six large parties with different social, cultural, and political agendas emerged as significant parliamentary actors among the twenty-one parties gaining at least one DPR seat. No one party obtained close to a majority. Coalition building would be necessary for governing, but stalemate could only be avoided by agreement in the MPR on who from Indonesia's post-Suharto leadership rivals would become president to lead the country into the new millennium. In some respects, the parties, issues, and outcome of the 1999 election were déjà vu 1955, Indonesia's first and the only previous national election that even began to approximate the *jurdil* ideal. That election, however, took place in a different constitutional and political setting.

INDONESIA'S ELECTORAL HISTORY

The Republic of Indonesia was proclaimed on 17 August 1945. Dutch efforts after World War II to restore sovereignty in the former Netherlands East Indies were met with armed resistance in the national revolution. Under great international pressure, the Dutch government finally came to terms with the Indonesian nationalists, and sovereignty was formally transferred to the Republic of the United States of Indonesia (RUSI) on 27 December 1949. The RUSI consisted of the Java-centered Republic of Indonesia and fifteen states created by the Dutch. The process of absorption of the weaker RUSI states into the Republic began immediately. On 14 August 1950, the RUSI legislature ratified a provisional constitution making Indonesia a unitary state. Its initial 232-seat nonelected Parliament was made up of members of the legislature of the dissolved federal republic divided almost evenly between members from the original Republic of Indonesia and the other component states of the old federation (Feith 1962, 128, table 1). In April 1953, an election law was passed for a new Parliament and Constituent Assembly. The law provided for universal adult suffrage and elective seats to be allotted on a basis of proportional representation spread through sixteen electoral districts following the old RUSI state lines.

Parliamentary Democracy and Sukarno's "Guided Democracy"

Indonesia's first election took place in September 1955. About 39 million Indonesians, more than 90 percent of those registered, went to the polls to elect 257 of 5,000 candidates on 120 lists. The organization and conduct of the elections were generally considered in large measure free and fair (van Marle 1956; Feith 1957). Indeed, according to Benedict Anderson (1996, 29), it could be argued that the 1955 polling "was the most open and participatory election held anywhere in Southeast Asia since World War II." From the ballot choices representing a complex diversity of political, cultural, and interregional divisions, four parties of the twenty-eight that won seats emerged dominant with among them 78 percent of the vote, and capturing 198 (77 percent) of the parliamentary seats (see table 12.1, p. 258). The largest vote-getter with more than 22 percent of the total was the secular Indonesian Nationalist Party (PNI), the party of Indonesia's President Sukarno. The modernist Muslim Masyumi Party had nearly 21 percent. Masyumi made the strongest showing of all the parties outside of Java. East Java–based Nahdlatul Ulama (NU), a traditionalist Islamic party, had more than 18 percent of the vote.[3] The Indonesian Communist Party (PKI) won more than 16 percent. The Indonesian Islamic Association Party (PSII) garnered nearly 3 percent. The two Christian parties, one Protestant (Parkindo) and one Catholic (Partai Katolik), each received 2 percent. The Indonesian Socialist Party (PSI), the closest in ideology to a Western democratic socialist party, also had 2 percent. Only two other parties had more than 1 percent: the League of Upholders of Indonesian Independence (IPKI) and Perti, a Sumatran Islamic party.

The election's outcome clearly delineated the basic cleavages in Indonesian politics that persist to the present: relations between Islam and the state, schisms inside the Islamic community, and the political demands of regionalism, class, and ethnicity. The instability of the political party system led to six different

Table 12.1 Results of the 1955 Indonesian General Election

Party	Percentage of Vote	Number of Seats Won	Seats in Provisional Parliament
PNI	22.3	57	42
Masyumi	20.9	57	44
NU	18.4	45	8
PKI	16.4	39	17
PSII	2.9	8	4
Parkindo	2.6	8	5
Partai Katolik	2.0	6	8
PSI	2.0	5	14
IPKI	1.4	4	—
Perti	1.3	4	1
18 other parties with at least one seat	6.9	24	44
Other parties and candidates	2.7	—	46
Total	100.0	257	233

Source: Adapted from Feith 1957, table 2, 434–35.

cabinets between 1950 and 1957. As one historian puts it: "The elections had produced no solutions and thereby represented a further step in discrediting the whole parliamentary system" (Ricklefs 1981, 238). The distribution of party strength was confirmed in the December 1955 Constituent Assembly elections. The four big parties together won nearly 80 percent of the vote: PNI, 23.5 percent; Masyumi, 20.2 percent; NU, 18.2 percent; and PKI, 16.2 percent (based on Feith 1957, 65, table 2). The resulting membership was split between the secular parties with 285 seats and the Islamic parties with 230 seats (Lev 1966, 124). The process of drafting a constitution was stalemated because each article required a two-thirds majority vote for adoption. A final, locally limited electoral test of relative party strength took place in the summer of 1957 with provincial elections in East, Central, and West Java, Jakarta, and South Sumatra. The cumulative total showed the PKI with 30.9 percent, NU 25.1 percent, PNI 24.8 percent, and Masyumi 19 percent (Lev 1966, 97).

The deadlocked political party system led to parliamentary stalemate in the face of regional challenges to Jakarta's authority and President Sukarno's scorn for the parties. Sukarno chafed in his weak constitutional role. His contempt for parliamentary government was shared by the senior military, but for different reasons.[4] On 14 March 1957, the last parliamentary cabinet resigned.

Sukarno, backed by the army, declared martial law, and parliamentary democracy in Indonesia was dead. Sukarno dissolved the Constituent Assembly and by decree reinstated the 1945 Constitution of the original Republic of Indonesia. Although it too was originally conceived as a temporary document, the 1945 Constitution remains the legal underpinning of the Indonesian political system today. It provides for a strong executive and weak legislature. The Masyumi and PSI were banned as complicit in the regional rebellions, and in April 1961, all but ten of the remaining parties were dissolved. Those left were the PNI, NU, PKI, Murba (Trotskyite), Parkindo, Partai Katolik, PSII, Perti, IPKI, and Partindo (splintered from the PNI in 1958). The parties as such held fewer than half the seats in a rubber-stamp 283-member appointive Gotong-Royong ("Mutual Cooperation") DPR and a 616-member "Provisional" MPR. In addition, a mass-mobilizing National Front was created.

As the economy collapsed and the government stridently distanced itself from the liberal democratic, noncommunist world, the growing influence of the PKI stoked the tensions that led to the 1965 abortive PKI-aided coup, military countercoup, and collapse of the Sukarno regime. Between October 1965 and March 1966, anti-Sukarno forces led by the army under General Suharto extinguished the PKI and dismantled Sukarno's "Guided Democracy." In March 1966, Sukarno was forced to give de facto presidential authority to Suharto. In March 1967, the Provisional MPR revoked Sukarno's presidential mandate and named Suharto acting president. In the orderly and technically constitutional sequence of events, a year later, the Provisional MPR elected Suharto president, officially inaugurating Indonesia's New Order government.

Parties and Elections in the New Order

The old multiparty parliamentary system had been completely tarnished in the eyes of the military and civilian technocratic architects of the New Order. Yet for both domestic and international reasons, they could not simply abandon the forms of representative democracy and abolish the parties. The task then was how to bring the party system into the framework of governance without actually sharing power through the DPR. The most important government initiative, one that defined electoral politics for the following three decades, was to mobilize a nonparty electoral alternative to the old political parties. This was the Golongan Karya or Golkar (Functional Groups). Golkar was designed to unite all organizations and interest groups for the common goal of stability and development. Golkar became the quinquennial electoral machine of the Suharto regime. Backed by ABRI, the organizational cement of Golkar was the government bureaucracy. In an increasingly corporative state framework, all functional groupings were to be brought under the Golkar umbrella.

In November 1969, a new General Elections Act was enacted. Under this act, proportional representation was maintained. The new electoral law divided the country into twenty-six provincial electoral districts with a fixed number of seats to be filled by each province. As a result, Java's voting strength was diluted. Two-thirds of the voters came from the Javanese provinces, but they could only choose 182 of the 360 elected members (van Marle 1974, 40). The electoral arrangements were firmly in the hands of the government. The General Elections Institute, *Lembaga Pemilihan Umum* (LPU), headed by the Minister of Home Affairs, was placed in charge. The military agency for domestic security screened candidates and verified voter eligibility. The campaign was a primer for future elections. The full power and resources of the government, especially ABRI, backed Golkar. All government employees and their families were expected to be Golkar adherents. No criticism of government, policy, or officials was permitted in the short span of time the parties had to campaign; the media was controlled. Psychological and in some cases physical intimidation were employed. The outcome was never in doubt.

On 5 July 1971, nearly 55 million voters went to the polls to elect 351 representatives to the DPR. Nine parties were allowed to compete. Eight had been represented in the 1955 elections: PNI, NU, Parkindo, Partai Katolik, PSII, Perti, IPKI, and Murba. The ninth party was Parmusi, which was viewed as the successor to the still-banned Masyumi. Filling out the list was Golkar. The turnout was nearly 95 percent of the registered voters. In light of the constraints on the campaign and the government's support of Golkar, its win was expected, but its nearly 63 percent of the votes was surprising (see table 12.2). Golkar had an absolute majority in twenty-three provinces, falling short but still far outdistancing any opposition in Aceh, Jakarta, and Maluku (van Marle 1974, 54–55, table 2). The margin of Golkar's victory came at the expense of the PNI, which finished third with less than 7 percent of the vote compared to its more than 22 percent in 1955. Traditional PNI constituencies defected to the government-sponsored Golkar juggernaut. The NU maintained its core Islamic support and emerged as the strongest traditional party. The new Parmusi, a modernist Muslim party with less than 6 percent of the vote, obviously did not have the same appeal as its Masyumi predecessor. In the new 460-seat DPR, the traditional political parties held only 124 seats. In addition to the 236 elected Golkar legislators, the government ranks were filled with 100 appointed members, 75 from ABRI and 25 nonmilitary.[5] The DPR's constitutional function of being the principal legislative organ of the state was subordinated to comply with the government's will. This was also the case in the new 920-seat MPR, with half its members coming from the DPR and the rest either appointed by the government or delegated from the Golkar-dominated provincial legislatures.

The Golkar steamroller crushed any politically meaningful role for the parties. The government continued to press for simplification and fusion. In 1973, the nine parties were forced to federate into two umbrella parties. The four Islamic parties were joined in the Development Unity Party (Partai Persatuan Pembangunan [PPP]). The two Christian and three secular nationalist parties

Table 12.2 New Order Election Results in Indonesia: Party Percentage of Vote and DPR Seats Won

Year	Golkar Percentage of Vote	Golkar Number of Seats	PPP Percentage of Vote	PPP Number of Seats	PDI Percentage of Vote	PDI Number of Seats
1971	62.6	236	27.2[a]	94	10.0[a]	30
1977	62.1	232	29.3	99	8.6	29
1982	64.1	242	28.0	94	7.9	24
1987	73.0	299	16.0	61	11.0	40
1992	68.1	282	17.0	62	14.9	56
1997	74.5	325	22.4	89	3.1	11

Sources: Adapted from King 1992, 160, 166; Baker 1997.

a. The 1971 totals represent the aggregates of the four Muslim parties later grouped in the PPP and the five non-Muslim parties later grouped in the PDI.

were uneasily linked under the heading Indonesian Democratic Party (Partai Demokrasi Indonesia [PDI]). No other parties were legal, nor was there a place for independents. The parties were forced to adopt the government's Pancasila ideology as their sole principle.[6] In between the five-year election cycles, the population was a "floating mass" not to be mobilized, organized, or recruited by politicians. Golkar, however, with its backbone of the army and civil service, reached right down to the village. The explicit goal was to "depoliticize" politics.

After 1971, the succeeding *pemilus*—1977, 1982, 1987, 1992, and 1997—continued to produce huge Golkar majorities (see table 12.2). In 1987, the DPR was enlarged to 500 members—400 elective and 100 ABRI. In 1997, the ABRI faction was reduced to 75 and there were 425 elected seats. Each of the elections was followed the succeeding year by an MPR session in which Suharto was re-elected president by consensual unanimity, with Golkar, PPP, and PDI declaring themselves for Suharto well in advance of the meeting. The system worked in the sense that the elections allowed a degree of popular participation and controlled public access to the political system without threatening regime "stability." In addition to being a well-oiled government election machine, Golkar's success was due in part to an instrumental legitimacy given the regime in terms of real economic progress; what R. William Liddle (1996, 42) called "developmental legitimacy" as opposed to democratic legitimacy. The elections were relatively clean. Liddle (1996, 45) asserts that in the context of the developing world, or even the Southeast Asian experience, with few exceptions, ballots were cast and counted honestly. Given the great advantage that Golkar had in organization and campaigning, ballot box stuffing or dishonest counts were not necessary to rig favorable outcomes. The major undemocratic feature of New Order elections was that they did not provide real choice to the voters. The PPP and PDI were not "opposition parties"; they could not offer alternative visions of the state or government. They were prohibited from raising issues that might be sensitive in terms of race, ethnicity, religion, or class. The parties had been forcibly co-opted, to be complementary to Golkar in mobilizing popular support for Suharto's "Pancasila Democracy," not to influence policy.

Often overlooked is the fact that despite Golkar's backing by the government, upwards of one-third or more of the electorate voted for either the PPP or PDI (see table 12.2). The question is whether this vote can be considered an "opposition" vote. The PPP provided a mainstream "home" for Muslims who might reject the secularism of Golkar or the PDI but who did not have to move to fundamentalist rejection of the Pancasila state to keep their religious identity in politics. The drop in the PPP's share of the vote after 1982 is partially explained by NU's decision to quit the party system. The PDI was useful to the government because it provided a legally confined base for old Sukarno-era PNI types, younger but yet to be emboldened "liberals" willing to work within the system in hope of changing it, and individuals who found the corporative structure of Golkar stultifying. The government "managed" the PPP and PDI through overt and covert intervention into party affairs.

Adding to the problem of defining opposition in the New Order's electoral system is the question of the strength of the so-called Golongan Putih, the "White Group" or *golput*. This term is used to describe a kind of protest vote whereby someone deliberately casts an invalid ballot or boycotts the polls. Voting is not compulsory, but more than 90 percent of the registered voters go to the polls. It is hard to measure the *golput*. For example, in the 1992 *pemilu*, 90.9 percent of the registered voters cast valid ballots. Obviously, some voters had died between registration and voting day. Others for various reasons never made it to the polls. Some invalidated their ballots by accident. How many of the 9.1 percent of the voters who did not cast valid ballots were acting in protest? Blair A. King (1992, 163) estimates that perhaps 1 percent of the missing votes in New Order elections are true *golput*, mainly cast by university students.

Despite its better than two-thirds majority in the 1992 vote, the government perceived the outcome as a setback given its 73 percent of the vote in 1987 (see table 12.2). It was particularly dismayed by the swing of nearly 4 percent to the PDI. In addition to first-time voters, it appeared that NU voters had become the real "floating mass." Also in 1992, direct ABRI intervention in support of Golkar was not as apparent (MacIntyre 1993, 209). Golkar was intent in 1997 on reversing the trend, setting a goal for itself of 70.25 percent of the vote. In the event, it exceeded its target, winning 74.5 percent of the votes cast on 30 May, an increase of more than 6 percent. LPU statistics showed Golkar with more than 60 percent majorities in every province; with more than 80 percent in eighteen provinces; and with more than 90 percent in nine. The results gave Golkar 325 or three-quarters of the elected DPR seats. The PPP too increased its share of the vote with 22.4 percent compared with its 1992 share of 17 percent. It won 89 seats, an increase of 27. The PDI was crushed with barely 3 percent of the vote. At first count it appeared that the PDI had won only 10 seats. This would have disqualified it from representation in the DPR because the legal minimum was 11 for representation on each of the 11 DPR committees. It was suggested that Golkar might transfer some of its remainder votes to the PDI for the 11th seat, but this was rejected by the PPP as illegal. The additional seat for the PDI was found by some last-minute recalculations of the vote count in North Sumatra.

Golkar's stronger performance can be explained in part by more visible and vigorous ABRI support. The official campaign was only four weeks long, although beginning in 1995, the public was fed a steady Golkar diet. In the run-up to the elections, there was a wave of arrests and intimidation of opposition activists. The rules for campaigning were much more rigid. All in all, Golkar and the government put on a full-court press to make sure that the 1997 election was a ringing endorsement of Golkar's "single majority." At the same time, the campaign was the most violent of any of the previous New Order elections. The campaign violence mirrored the growing ethnic and social discontent that sparked a wave of mob clashes and rioting around the country in 1997. Golkar's intensity had less to do with the DPR than with preparing the ground for the 1998 MPR at which Suharto was expected to stand for his seventh five-year term. Golkar wanted a "mandate" for that and a preemption of any possible party dissent from the traditional consensus.

The threat came from the PDI's chair, Megawati Sukarnoputri, daughter of Sukarno. In December 1993, over the government's objection, the PDI's national congress elected her party chair for a five-year term. The government blatantly tried to undermine her from within by sponsoring party dissidence, throwing up the red scare, and barring her from party functions. Its campaign against Megawati climaxed in mid-1996 when it masterminded a party coup stripping her from office. She did not go quietly. She launched a barrage of lawsuits, and her supporters took to the streets and occupied PDI headquarters in Jakarta. Events took a violent turn, presaging the greater violence of 1998. An ABRI-inspired gang forcibly ejected Megawati supporters from the PDI Jakarta headquarters building on 27 July 1996, provoking bloody street clashes seen around the world on CNN. The government and ABRI viewed the PDI under Megawati as a potential source of real opposition. The regime's political managers were especially concerned about mutually supportive links between Megawati and Abdurrahman Wahid, the respected leader of NU, Indonesia's largest Muslim organization. Megawati supporters continued the political battle under the banner of the "Struggle PDI" (PDI-Perjuangan [PDI-P]). It was not a recognized party and could not legally take part in the 1997 campaign. By pushing Megawati's faction out of legal politics, even the remote possibility that legislators might break step at the 1998 MPR session was obviated. The split within the PDI, popular disgust at the government's heavy-handed treatment of Megawati, and the perception that the official PDI was a government puppet all contributed to the PDI's electoral eclipse.

THE ROAD TO THE 1999 ELECTIONS

The Southeast Asian economic bubble burst on 2 July 1997. By January 1998, Indonesia had fallen into a financial abyss comparable to the economic chaos of the late Sukarno period. The Suharto government resisted implementation of IMF-sponsored measures for recovery, seemingly unwilling and unable to attack the vested interests of the New Order. Even as the economy spiraled downward out of control, Suharto kept a tight political grip on the country. Mounting protest and political challenge was met with intimidation and force. It was becoming increasingly evident that the regime's "development legitimacy" was rapidly eroding, as the real economic gains of three decades were lost. As long as the political machine of Golkar continued to run and ABRI stood fast, however, Suharto and his closest family advisers appeared to believe that his presidency could outlast the economic crisis.

In early 1998, political attention was focused on Suharto's decision to run for a seventh term. Opposition voices challenged his decision. In addition to Megawati and Abdurrahman Wahid, Amien Rais, charismatic leader of Muhammadiyah, called for Suharto to retire.[7] The Suharto forces were still fully in political command. When the MPR met on 10 March 1998, there was no doubt about the outcome—the 76-year-old Suharto was reelected by acclamation. The surprise, to many a shock, was his selection of vice president, Dr. B.J. Habibie. Habibie was best known as Indonesia's technology czar, under whose direction an extravagant, high-priced, and noncompetitive aircraft industry was built. His political strength was unfailing loyalty to Suharto.

If anything, Suharto's reelection galvanized opposition forces, with university and high-school students the shock troops. They insisted on an end to KKN. Growing numbers of influential members of the establishment elite echoed their battle cry—*reformasi*. Suharto's political support base began to melt away. The turning point came on 12 May when military Special Forces killed four students, triggering massive rioting that turned into a savage anti-Chinese rampage with hundreds killed. The hard-pressed military were confronted with the real possibility of facing a massive student march on Jakarta in support of those who had occupied the Parliament building. Visions of Tiananmen Square were in the air. The calls for Suharto to step down reached a political crescendo. Most members of his newly appointed cabinet resigned. The Golkar leadership distanced itself. ABRI chief General Wiranto promised to protect him in retirement, and on 21 May, Suharto resigned. Power was constitutionally transferred to Vice President Habibie.

President Habibie was thought to be a transitional figure; he was not expected to serve out Suharto's five-year term. Radical student groups and NGO activists demanded that Habibie step down immediately. They saw him as a Suharto clone and defender of the status quo. In particular, they were angered that his government did not aggressively move against Suharto and his family members for corruption. In an atmosphere of new political excitement and freedoms, political parties of all stripes began springing up. The Habibie government resisted the counsels of urgency. It committed itself to an orderly constitutional process leading to free and fair elections for a new DPR in June 1999 to be followed by a sitting of a new MPR to elect a new president and vice president before 2000.

A special session of the incumbent MPR called in November 1998 took the first legislative steps. This was essentially the same MPR that ten months earlier had reelected Suharto without a dissenting voice. Outside the building, raging students denounced the MPR as illegitimate and besieged the session. In the rioting, eight more students were killed by security forces. In the four-day session, 10–14 November, the legislators, keenly aware of the national mood and looking to their own political futures, adopted twelve decrees that went beyond simply adopting the government's proposal for a new general election.[8] This they agreed would take place no later than June 1999. In addition, they limited the president to two five-year terms. They revoked the emergency powers that had been given to Suharto in March and demanded a corruption-free government. They affirmed the importance of human rights in Indonesia. In addition, the legislators called for referendums on constitutional amendments, supported greater regional autonomy, and terminated compulsory Pancasila ideological indoctrination.

The task of turning MPR decrees into law lay with the DPR, which met from November 1998 through January 1999. Even though the composition of the DPR was that produced by the 1997 *pemilu*, political reform was the agenda, albeit cautious and compromising. Three political bills were passed and signed into law by President Habibie on 1 February 1999: Law No. 2/1999 Concerning Political Parties; Law No. 3/1999 Concerning General Elections; and Law No. 4/1999 Concerning the Composition and Membership of the MPR, DPR, and DPRDs.[9] One of the most contentious issues was the number of DPR seats to be reserved for ABRI. Democracy activists had wanted to slash ABRI's seventy-five seats to zero. The MPR had left the number open. The government with ABRI concurrence proposed a reduction of the number of seats to fifty-five, but this still did not satisfy the reformists. The DPR compromise contained in Law No. 4/1999, Article 11, was thirty-eight appointed ABRI parliamentarians, half the number in the previous DPR.

Another holdover from the Suharto years that had to be addressed was the political role of the more than 5 million Indonesian civil servants. Under Suharto, they acted as the agents and electoral backbone of Golkar. By Government Regulation No. 5/1999, henceforth civil servants would have to resign from the bureaucracy in order to take an active part in politics. The goal was to ensure the neutrality of the government. Always looming in the background was the presence of ABRI. General Wiranto promised that ABRI would respect the will of the people and as an institution would stand above politics. ABRI did have vested interests in the outcome.

THE 1999 GENERAL ELECTION

With the passage of the political bills, the stage was set for the 1999 election. Law No. 3/1999 created an election system that according to the National Democratic Institute is "without exact precedent or parallel anywhere else in the world" (NDI 1999a, 2). Prior to the DPR sessions, seven-member team of academics appointed by the Minister of Home Affairs had prepared a draft election law that called for single-member districts in which the voter would cast a ballot for a candidate, not a party. This was purposefully designed to weaken the hold of the parties and make legislators more accountable to their constituents. Not surprisingly, the main features of the Team of Seven draft was rejected by all of the political factions in the DPR who opted to retain proportional representation with elements of a district system.

At the national level, the electoral district was the province. The number of DPR seats in each province was based on population with a national average of one seat per 500,000 persons and one seat per 255,000 registered voters with the stipulation that each provincial district should have at least one seat. The latter requirement meant that greater weight was attached to votes in the lesser-populated provinces than to those in the Javanese provinces. The provincial allocation of seats is shown in table 12.3. Essentially there were twenty-seven separate elections with the seats allocated to winning parties based on the results of the overall vote in the province (Law No. 3/1999, Article 67, 3). The parties could nominate twice as many candidates as there were seats, but each candidate had to stand in a district (Article 41, 6a). The importance of competition at the district level was emphasized by the rule that the winning candidates would be based on the largest number of votes won in the districts by the political parties (Article 68, 3). If implemented, this would have of diminished the authority of the party leaders to name the elected DPR member from the priorities of their candidate list. By later regulation, however, this provision was negated, leaving the naming of the winning candidates to the parties. The allocation of winning seats in Indonesian's proportional representation was by quota and largest remainder. The quota for a seat was determined by dividing the total number of valid ballots by the number of seats in the province. Seats to be filled by less than full quotas, the largest remainders, were allocated by plurality in the order of largest party vote. Provision was made for vote-sharing agreements (*stembus akkords*) among parties, in which case the seats would be allocated to the parties with the *stembus akkord* based on largest remainders. The interpretation of this provision later led to a major dispute.

The Organization of the Election

Even though Indonesia has a long history of organizing and conducting national elections, the 1999 contests presented special challenges. The popular demand for free and fair elections, the conditionality of continuing economic assistance on

Table 12.3 Provincial Representation in the 1999 Indonesian General Election

Province	DPR Seats	Registered Voters	Voters per Seat
Aceh	12	1,486,294	123,858
North Sumatra	24	5,831,247	242,968
West Sumatra	14	2,364,404	168,886
Riau	10	2,543,575	254,357
Jambi	6	1,372,710	228,785
South Sumatra	15	4,071,504	271,434
Bengkulu	4	808,604	202,151
Lampung	15	3,676,301	245,087
Jakarta	18	5,072,249	281,792
West Java	82	25,333,464	308,944
Central Java	60	18,720,597	312,010
Yogyakara	6	1,929,404	321,567
East Java	68	21,811,625	320,759
West Kalimantan	9	2,074,557	230,506
Central Kalimantan	6	997,409	166,235
East Kalimantan	7	1,335,342	190,763
South Kalimantan	11	1,745,113	158,647
Bali	9	2,040,162	226,685
West Nusa Tenggara	8	2,082,267	260,283
East Nusa Tenggara	13	2,001,790	153,984
East Timor	7	420,096	60,013
South Sulawesi	24	4,229,606	176,234
Central Sulawesi	5	1,202,792	240,558
North Sulawesi	7	1,738,421	248,346
Southeast Sulawesi	5	900,831	180,166
Maluku	6	1,025,728	170,955
Irian Jaya	13	1,001,853	77,066
Total	462	117,817,645	255,016

Sources: KPU and PPI.

regaining political stability, and the unprecedented presence of domestic and foreign official and unofficial election monitors all required procedural transparency.[10] Since the impartiality of the existing government electoral machinery was suspect, new structures had to be put in place. Article 8 of the electoral law gave the president ultimate responsibility for holding general elections. It placed the implementation of the elections in the hands of a General Election Commission, the *Komisi Pemilhan Umum* (KPU), which replaced the former LPU. The KPU was made up of representatives of the forty-eight political parties certified to contest the elections and five government-appointed members responsible to the president.

From the KPU's formation, a critical question was whether it could fairly and independently organize and supervise the elections. The most contentious aspect of its tasks was to give by decree political substance to the bare-bones framework of a loosely drawn and often ambiguous electoral law. To give credence to the suspicion that the government might try to stack the KPU, a purported list of politically controversial government candidates was leaked to the public. The government gave way to pressure with the actual appointment of credible and respected nominees, including two of the most vocal and ardent reformers in the civil community: human rights lawyer Adnan Buyung Nasution and Team of Seven gadfly Andi Mallarangeng.[11] The rules called for the KPU chair to be elected by the members of the commission. Buyung Nasution was the majority choice but stepped aside for runner-up retiree General Rudini, a former Minister of Home Affairs and head of the small MKGR party, a Golkar splinter. This was apparently part of the bargain leading to the appointment of real reformers to the KPU (Masters 1999, 21). The voting arrangement in the KPU was balanced equally between the five government members and forty-eight party members. The fear was that the five government members plus Golkar would be an automatic 50 percent plus one majority. In fact, the KPU strove for consensus. When consensus could not be achieved in some crucial questions, the government members and the representatives of the large parties found themselves at odds with the smaller parties whose parochial interests and future survival were at stake. In fact, for the small parties, membership on the KPU was the only political leverage they had, lacking real ballot strength.

The authority of the KPU was tested early on. Although it decided to allow its own members who were from political parties to campaign and be candidates, the KPU barred senior government officials, including cabinet officers, from the campaign. This was directed against Golkar ministerial incumbents. President Habibie challenged this decision, and it was referred to the Supreme Court. The court tossed it back to the president with a ruling that confirmed the electoral law statement that the president had final responsibility. The affected officials claimed that they were not part of the bureaucracy covered by Government Regulation 5/1999, but were political appointments. The issue was compromised by the affected ministers taking leaves of absence during the campaign period. The KPU was in a difficult position. Political party critics accused it of abuse of authority and dictatorial practices when its interpretations and rulings went against their interests. Reformist critics chafed at the KPU's willingness to compromise for the sake of consensus. The KPU had also had the special task of appointing the sixty-five representatives to the MPR from society's functional groups. This was politically sensitive because this number was more than 9 percent of the total membership of MPR that would elect the next president.[12]

An Indonesian Electoral Committee, the *Panitia Pemilihan Indonesia* (PPI) was formed under the KPU's direction and was responsible for actually conducting and coordinating the elections. It operated from the center through electoral committees and at all levels through the provinces, districts, subdistricts, villages, and local polling stations—six bureaucratic levels in all. Representation on the PPI paralleled that of the KPU. This split government/political party committee system was replicated at each level of the electoral bureaucracy. The work of the KPU, PPI, and lower-level committees was facilitated by a secretariat backstopped by the bureaucracy of the Ministry of Home Affairs. Oversight or supervisory committees *(Panitia Pengawas [Panwas]*) were formed down to the subdistrict level; committee members were supposed to be independent of the political competition. Their tasks under judicial mandate included resolving electoral disputes. The complex electoral structure involved overlapping and competitive lines of authority among the KPU, Ministry of Home Affairs, and the judiciary. A great deal depended on the ability and fairness of a bureaucracy socialized to the practices of New Order elections. Ultimately, more than 3 million Indonesians were directly involved from the polling sites to the KPU in the administration and oversight of the elections.

The Political Parties

In the political euphoria attending the collapse of Suharto's "Pancasila Democracy," new political parties flourished. The actual programs and goals represented the spectrum of values and interests in the Indonesian political culture that had existed from the foundation of the state. These had been suppressed in Sukarno's "Guided Democracy" and the Golkar-PDI-PPP straitjacket of Suharto's New Order. Some of the parties found their inspiration in the democratic opposition to Suharto. A newly energized political Islam flexed its muscles. Religious and ethnic minorities sought refuge in political parties. The liberal left, and from ABRI's vantage point even the hard left, reemerged to articulate class economic and social interests. Finally there was a constellation of parties huddled around Golkar that sought to protect the vested interests of an incumbent elite. A hundred flowers began to bloom.

Being a legal political party did not guarantee party access to the newly established electoral system. A ballot competition with a list of 154 parties that was still growing would be unmanageable and unlikely to provide the stable government necessary for Indonesia's political and economic recovery. The principal condition for participation was a demonstration of a nationally representative organizational network and membership basis. For the 1999 election, this meant a party had to have an organizational structure in at least nine of Indonesia's twenty-seven provinces and in at least half of the districts of those provinces (Law No. 3/1999, Article 82).[13] Before the KPU was in place, the Minister of Home Affairs had set up an Election Commission Formation Preparation Committee, the *Panitia Persiapan Pembentukan KPU* [P3KPU]), popularly known as the Team of Eleven. Led by Nurcholish Madjid, a highly respected Islamic scholar, the group of distinguished academics and intellectuals was charged with determining which parties were eligible to compete. It had been expected that twenty-five to thirty parties would meet the criteria. To public surprise, the Team of Eleven certified forty-eight parties. The parties are listed in table 12.4 (p. 272–73) according to their order on the ballot as drawn by lot. Naturally, some of the parties that did not make the cut bitterly protested the legality of the Team of Eleven, but the nonpartisan eminence of the group undercut political attacks against it.

Only a handful of the parties listed on the ballot had the constituencies, organization, financing, and leadership to mount national campaigns. Overall, the parties proposed nearly 14,000 candidates for the 462 seats in the DPR, although only fourteen parties nominated candidates in all twenty-seven provinces. All forty-eight parties were on the ballot in only five provinces.[14] The strongest party in terms of national support was Megawati's Struggle PDI. The PDI-P inherited the mantle of the old PNI that was symbolized by Megawati's lineage to Sukarno. A secular nationalist party with a strong attraction to minorities, the PDI-P's support was inclusive of all religions and groups in Indonesia. Although in the forefront of the opposition to Suharto, the PDI-P under Megawati was in many respects the most politically conservative of the major parties. It did not endorse major constitutional change and had good relations with the military. Megawati herself played an enigmatic role, speaking only in very general terms, letting her advisers publicly flesh out a platform.

Despite its history of association with Suharto, Golkar remained formidable. The new, "reformed" Golkar admitted its past failings. It had the advantage of incumbency, was well financed, and was organizationally sound. It had modified its secular image by reaching out to modernist Muslims. Even though the civil servants had been cut free from Golkar and ABRI was neutral, Golkar was expected to run well especially outside of Java. A Golkar splinter party, the Justice and Unity Party (PKP), shadowed Golkar. It was led by retired general Edi Sudradjat, who had been defeated by Akbar Tanjung in the July 1998 election for Golkar chair,. The PKP hoped to draw support from retired military and civil servants as well as from Golkar members alienated by President Habibie.

Two traditionalist Muslim parties, the PKB and the PPP, competed for the old NU voters. The National Awakening Party (PKB) had the advantage of the sponsorship of Abdurrahman Wahid, NU's national leader. Wahid is popularly known in Indonesia as Gus Dur, a sobriquet of affectionate respect.[15] He had long been Indonesia's most eloquent spokesman for religious tolerance and pluralistic democracy. Although NU's homeland was in Central and East Java, Wahid was a national figure. He also had been politically sympathetic to Megawati. The National Development Party (PPP) in the Suharto regime had been the Islamic umbrella party. Like Golkar, it had good organization and voter recognition. In the transition period, it had been a major voice for reform. Its leader, Hamzah Haz, a NU member, was an effective politician and was a member of Habibie's cabinet.

Three modernist Muslim parties were major contenders. Amien Rais, the most vocal spokesman for real reform for Indonesia, led the National Mandate Party (PAN). Rais resigned his position of chair of the 28-million-member modernist Muslim social organization the Muhammadiyah to become a full-time political activist. His Islamic and economic nationalist agenda was toned down over time to give PAN broader electoral appeal. At the bottom, PAN may have been Islamic, but at the top, it looked more like the old PSI with its modern, urban, democratic intellectuals. Muhammadiyah-types not attracted to PAN's increasingly pluralist appeal could turn to the Crescent Moon and Star Party (PBB), which (among others) claimed to be the legitimate successor to the old Masyumi. The PBB called for a state based on Islamic principles and was supported by more militant Islamic organizations. The Justice Party (PK) was another conservative modernist Islamic party with significant presence. Its roots were in university mosques, and its leaders were relatively young and well educated.

Categorizing the parties on the basis of ideology or platforms does not capture the diversity and complexity of the Indonesian electoral landscape in 1999. The PDI-P and PAN, for example, sought to frame the election in terms of reformist versus status-quo parties. In fact, all of the major parties were reformist in the sense of democratization and the elimination of KKN. The secular-Islamic division also is misleading. In Indonesia, the major support for the so-called secular parties—the old PNI and the new PDI-P—came from Muslim voters. No uniform Islamic political agenda existed for the Muslim parties. In fact, the parties with greatest national appeal tried to be culturally inclusive. Some real policy issues also distinguished the parties: coping with the economic crisis; attitudes toward constitutional reform, including a parliamentary system; greater regional autonomy or even federalism; ABRI's appropriate political and social role.

The official campaign was limited to the period 19 May–4 June, with the two days before the 7 June election being quiet days. An official calendar and schedule tracked party activities, and no more than ten parties were allowed to have rallies on the same day. The goal was to reduce the prospects of party clashes and violence. The crowds were enthusiastic and sometimes rowdy but generally peaceful. Radio and television were the major media for reaching the voters.[16] All of the parties had essentially the same basic message—change. For the voters, the question seemed to be which party and leader they trusted to best steer the country towards economic recovery and reform.

The Outcome of the 1999 Election

In many ways, the success of the June 1999 elections was an impressive feat. In a relatively limited time frame, after forty years of undemocratic rule, in a daunting geographic, logistic, and administrative environment, 112 million Indonesian citizens were able to make free political choices without the feared violence or widespread fraud. From early on in the official count and the parallel unofficial

Table 12.4 Parties Contesting the 1999 Indonesian Election (Listed in Order They Appear on the Ballot)

	Party	Party Name (English Translation)
1	PIB	P. Indonesia Baru (New Indonesia)
2	KRISNA	P. Kristen Nasional Indonesia (Indonesian National Christian)
3	PNI	P. Nasional Indonesia (Indonesian Nationalist)
4	PADI	P. Aliansi Demokrat Indonesia (Indonesian Democratic Alliance)
5	KAMI	P. Kebangkitan Muslim Indonesia (Indonesian Muslim Awakening)
6	PUI	P. Ummat Islam (Islamic Community)
7	PKU	P. Kebangkitan Bangsa Ummat (Community National Awakening)
8	PMB	P. Masyumi Baru (New Masyumi)[a]
9	PPP	P. Persatuan Pembangunan (United Development)
10	PSII	P. Syarikat Islam Indonesia (Indonesian Islamic Union)
11	PDI-P	P. Demokrasi Indonesian –Perjuangan (Indonesian Democratic-Struggle)
12	PAY	P. Abdul Yatama (Aceh Orphans Foundation)
13	PKM	P. Kebangsaan Merdeka (National Freedom)
14	PDKB	P. Demokrasi Kasih Bangsa (National Gift of Demcracy)
15	PAN	P. Amanat Nasional (National Mandate)
16	PRD	P. Rakyat Demokratic (Democratic People's)
17	PSII 1905	P. Syarikat Islam Indonesia 1905 (Indonesian Islamic Union 1905)
18	PKD	P. Katolik Demokrat (Democratic Catholic)
19	PILAR	P. Pilihan Rakyat (People's Choice)
20	PARI	P. Rakyat Indonesia (Indonesian People's)
21	PPIIM	P. Politik Islam Indonesia Masyumi (Indonesian Islamic Politics Masyumi)[a]
22	PBB	P. Bulan Bintang (Crescent Moon and Star)
23	PSP	P. Solidaritas Perkerja (Workers Solidarity)
24	PK	P. Keadilan (Justice)
25	PNU	P. Nahdlatul Ummat (Community Awakening)
26	PNI-FM	P. Nasional Indonesia—Front Marhaenis (Indonesian Nationalist—Marhaenist Front)[b]
27	IPKI	P. Ikatan Pendukung Kemerdekaan Indonesia (League of Supporters of Indonesian Independence)
28	PR	P. Republik (Republic)
29	PID	P. Islam Demokrat (Democratic Islam Party)
30	PNI-MM	P. Nasional Indonesia – Massa Marhaen (Indonesian Nationalist—Marhaen Masses)[b]

Table 12.4 — Continued

	Party	Party Name (English Translation)
31	MURBA	P. Musyawarah Rakyat Banyak (Many People's Consultative)
32	PDI	P. Demokrasi Indonesia (Indonesian Democratic)
33	GOLKAR	P. Golongan Karya (Functional Groups)
34	PP	P. Persatuan (Unity)
35	PKB	P. Kebangkitan Bangsa (National Awakening)
36	PUDI	P. Uni Demokrasi Indonesia (Indonesian Democratic Union)
37	PBN	P. Buruh Nasional (National Labor)
38	MKGR	P. Musyawarah Kekeluargaan Gotong Royong (Mutual Self-Help and Familial Consultation)
38	PDR	P. Daulat Rakyat (People's Sovereignty)
40	PCD	P. Cinta Damai (Love and Peace)
41	PKP	P. Keadilan dan Persatuan (Unity and Justice)
42	SPSI	P. Solidaritas Pekerja Seluruh Indonesia (All-Indonesia Worker's Solidarity)
43	PNBI	P. Nasional Bangsa Indonesia (Indonesian People's Nationalist)
44	PBI	P. Bhinneka Tungga Ika Indonesia (Unity in Diversity)[c]
45	SUNI	P. Solidaritas Uni Nasional Indonesia (Indonesian National Union Solidarity)
46	PND	P. Nasional Demokrat (National Democratic)
47	PUMI	P. Ummat Muslimin Indonesia (Indonesian Muslim Community)
48	PPI	P. Pekerja Indonesia (Indonesian Workers)

a. Masyumi (Majlis Syuro Muslimin Indonesia), Council of Indonesian Muslim Associations.
b. Marhaen, the (fictional?) name of a poor peasant claimed by Sukarno as inspiration for his brand of democratic socialism.
c. Bhinneka Tunggul Ika ("Unity in Diversity") is Indonesia's official national motto.

counts, five parties clearly far outdistanced the rest of the field in both aggregate popular votes and seats won: PDI-P, Golkar, PKB, PPP, and PAN (see table 12.5, p. 275). The results could not be confirmed, however, until the official vote tabulation was completed. This was an agonizingly slow process, and the KPU missed several self-announced deadlines for finalizing the election results. More than two months after the elections the results finally became official. The slowness of the official count became a matter of concern with allegations of manipulation. In part, the delay was simply a question of the complexity of the system, with the votes being tallied at every level of the electoral bureaucracy. The checks and balances built into the organization of the election braked the processing of the results. One KPU member quipped that "the tabulation of the count is going slowly because this time we actually have to count the votes" (as cited in USINDO 1999, 8). In addition, the smaller parties tried to use the forums of the KPU and PPI to obtain what the voters had denied them, a share of political power.

Once the votes were counted, two issues held up the certification of the outcome and the official allocation of DPR seats to the winning parties: 342 DPR seats had been won by full quotas; 120 seats were to be determined by the largest remainder system, and most of them would go to the largest parties through assignment to the largest plurality. The parliamentary future and even survival of the small parties were at stake. Article 39 of Law No. 3/1999 states that in order for a party to participate in the next (2004) general election, it must have won at least 2 percent of the DPR seats or 3 percent of the seats in DPRD-I or DPRD-II (province or district) assemblies spread over at least half the provinces and half the districts in the country. This was a deliberately high threshold: 2 percent of the DPR seats is 10; 3 percent of the DPRD-I seats is 44; and 3 percent of DPRD-II seats is 354. The fact that the DPRD-I and DPRD-II seats have to be scattered over half the provinces or districts discourages regional or ethnic parties. It was hoped that this would rationalize the party system by either eliminating or forcing the merger of minor parties. Contrary to democratic theory, however, barring the parties that did not meet the threshold from the next election means that not all political forces in the regions will be able to freely express themselves. The fact that a party did poorly in 1999 does not itself prove possible lack of support five years later. Natural selection seems a more democratic way to prune the party list than arbitrary and high eligibility requirements. Arguments in future DPRs will certainly favor amendments to Article 39 of Law No. 3/1999.

Only six of the forty-eight parties participating in the 1999 election reached the threshold for eligibility for future elections (see table 12.5). Fewer than half the parties even have seats in the new DPR. In the KPU, it had been decided that a two-thirds vote of the KPU would be required to certify the elections. The small parties sought to use their leverage to force their way into the DPR and nullify Article 39 of Law No. 3/1999. The parties that had won more than 93 percent of the vote quickly ratified the outcome, but the smaller parties held out in a vote that was twenty-two for ratification, including the government representatives, and twenty-seven against, with four abstentions. The smaller parties used allegations of irregularities in the count as the justification for their refusal to sign off on the elections. Their actual agenda was to postpone until at least 2009 implementation of Article 39, and to ensure that distribution of the 120 DPR seats would be determined by largest remainder votes so that every party would have at least one parliamentarian. In late July, an exasperated KPU leadership passed the problem on to President Habibie, who gave the small parties a week to plead their case to the Election Supervisory Committee (*Panwas*). The

Table 12.5 1999 Indonesian National Election Results

Party	Ballot Number	Number of Votes	Percentage of Vote	DPR Seats
PDI-P	11	35,689,073	33.7	153
GOLKAR	33	23,741,758	22.4	120
PKB	35	13,336,982	12.6	51
PPP	9	11,329,905	10.7	58
PAN	15	7,528,956	7.1	34
PBB	22	2,049,708	1.9	13
PK	24	1,436,565	1.4	7
PKP	41	1,065,686	1.1	4
PNU	25	658,069	0.6	5
PDI	32	655,049	0.6	2
PDKB	14	550,851	0.5	5
PP	34	550,808	0.5	1
PPIIM	21	456,718	0.4	1
PDR	39	429,854	0.4	1
PSII	10	375,920	0.3	1
PNI-FM	26	363,397	0.3	1
PBI	44	354,292	0.3	1
PNI-MM	30	345,720	0.3	1
IPKI	27	327,301	0.3	1
PKU	7	300,064	0.3	1
PKD	18	216,675	0.2	1
27 other parties		4,023,355	3.8	0
Total		105,786,638	100.0	462

Sources: KPU and PPI.

Panwas rejected the complaints, and finally, on 4 August, the president issued Presidential Decision No. 92/99, legally confirming the results of the general election at all levels: DPR, DPRD-I, and DPRD-II. He based this on Article 8 of Law No. 3/1999, which have him final authority over the election, while noting that the inability of the KPU act in a timely matter was a cause of public unrest (*Kompas*, 4 August 1999).

Next, the final allocation of seats was held up by a paralyzing KPU dispute over the formula to be used for allocating seats to the eight Muslim parties that had made a *stembus akkord*: PPP, PBB, PNU, PKU, PSII-1905, PUI, and PPIM. The parties claimed to be entitled to fifty-eight seats while the PPI calculated the seats at thirty-nine.[17] Ironically, according to the PPI, without the *stembus akkord*, the group would have had forty-eight seats. The other smaller parties used this new dispute to press once again their demand that every party should be entitled to at least one seat. A special KPU Team of Eight could not break the deadlock. The large parties would not agree to sacrifice seats they had fairly won to placate the smaller parties in the name of consensus. Passions ran high, and it was even proposed that those parties who had not met the 2-percent threshold be immediately expelled from the KPU. Finally, on 30 August, after missing another deadline, the KPU cut the Gordian knot by nullifying the *stembus akkord* and accepted the PPI's division of the seats determined by largest remainders (see table 12.5). The eight Muslim parties appealed to the president, who supported the KPU. The final allocation gave ten of the twenty-one qualified parties only one seat each. A senior election official wryly noted that if the eight Muslim parties had had their way, only sixteen, not twenty-one, parties would be represented in the new DPR. With the Muslim parties threatening legal action, the winning parties were officially notified and were requested to present the names of their legislative nominees. The list of members of the new DPR to be sworn in 1 October 1999 was not finalized until 11 September, three months after the election.

THE PRESIDENTIAL ELECTION

The Indonesian people had spoken, but the message was unclear.[18] The PDI-P with its nearly 34 percent of the popular vote and one-third of the elected DPR members naturally claimed a mandate for the presidency of its leader Megawati Sukarnoputri. It had the largest plurality in twelve provinces. Its greatest number of votes was from Java, with its rich harvest of seats. A desperate last-minute exhortation by ultra-Muslim clerics that a vote for the PDI-P was a vote against Islam seemed to have had little impact and may have been counterproductive. Golkar, too, did very well, but its main strength was outside Java. It led in eleven provinces, including every one east of Bali. Habibie is originally from South Sulawesi. The PKB edged out the PDI-P in the NU heartland of East Java. The PKB's good showing kept alive the hopes that Gus Dur could be a compromise presidential candidate. Even though its total vote count was higher than the PPP, the proportional representation system rewarded the PPP with seven more seats than the PKB. The PPP became the other Muslim party of choice, with a strong showing in Islamic constituencies across the archipelago. Its vote total was four times that of the combined vote of PBB and PK, the only two parties with avowedly Islamist agendas to win more than one seat. The smaller Muslim parties, particularly those with an extreme exclusivist demand for an Islamic state, fared poorly. They were marginalized with less than 5 percent of the vote. PAN had had high expectations and was disappointed to have finished fifth, behind the PPP in popular vote. Amien Rais's high profile as an opponent of the regime could not be translated into the vote totals necessary to make him a viable presidential candidate. Yet he still had a major role to play in the maneuverings in the selection of the president. Some analysts compared PAN to the old Indonesian Socialist Party (PSI): a party with high ideals, intellectual leadership, and commitment, but without a mass base. Finally, the specter of a significant political left lurking in the wings waiting to replace the old PKI was laid to rest. The PRD, the "reddest" of the radical parties, received far fewer than 100,000 votes.

The 462 elected DPR members composed only 66 percent of the membership of the MPR that met in October to elect the president of Indonesia. Megawati's PDI-P legislators were only 22 percent of the MPR membership. Assemblies that broadly resembled the DPR's seat distribution selected the 135 representatives from the DPRD-I legislatures. Rather than act to represent their provincial interests, the DPRD-I MPR representatives were simply assimilated to the party factions. The exercise in coalition building to establish a majority was not open and transparent. The behind-the-scene dealings were in full sway even before the votes were counted. Former American ambassador to Indonesia Paul Wolfowitz commented that "if you were trying to design a system that would make it as difficult as possible to translate a popular vote into a popular mandate for the presidency and as easy as possible to introduce dirty back room deals into that process," you could not find a better model than Indonesia (USINDO 1999, 34). Talk of money and promises of cabinet posts were common.

Given the PDI-P, PKB, and PAN's (Megawati, Gus Dur, Amien Rais) shared opposition to Golkar and Habibie, it would have seemed that this was a natural coalition. The problem was a Megawati presidency. Her claim to a popular mandate was not uncontested. Rather than the 33.7 percent of the vote she received, her opponents pointed to the 66.3 percent of the votes that went to the other parties. As soon as the votes were in, die-hard Muslim clerics raised the gender issue and the fact that large numbers of non-Muslims were on the PDI-P's candidate slate and among her advisers.[19] Responsible Islamic leaders decried the ad hominem and ethnic-baiting attacks, yet the issues raised made them cautious. In contrast, Megawati supporters threatened violence if the "people's will" was thwarted. By mid-September, Habibie's government was unraveling in the wreckage of first the Bank Bali scandal[20]—a diversion of funds to Golkar—and then the terror and tragedy following the 30 August independence referendum in East Timor.[21] Megawati appeared to remain aloof and withdrawn from the politics preceding the MPR session, seemingly unwilling to take part in the bargaining process necessary for coalition building. Perhaps she believed that "people power" would carry her to the presidency.

Amien Rais reentered the maneuverings as the driving force behind the creation of a "Middle Axis" based on the PBB, PBK, and PAN as well as smaller moderate Islamic parties. Rais occupied a strategic position as the elected chairman of the MPR. The goal was for the moderate Muslims to unite behind Gus Dur.[22] Finally abandoning his on again–off again support of Megawati, Wahid indicated he would be available. Unlike Megawati and Rais, he had not been a candidate for office but was a nominated member of the MPR as a representative of the religious functional group.

Going into the MPR session, none of the proposed presidential candidates or coalitions seemed to have enough votes to guarantee election. The situation was clarified after President Habibie presented his report to the MPR on 17 October accounting for his 512 days in office. The MPR on 19 October rejected it by a vote of 355-322. Habibie withdrew his candidacy, leaving Gus Dur and Megawati to face off. On 20 October, ignoring the high-tech electronic voting equipment installed on their desks, the MPR members filed into a voting booth and used paper ballots to vote 373-313 with 5 abstentions to elect Abdurrahman Wahid Indonesia's fourth president. Golkar legislators and the ABRI faction were crucial to his 60-vote margin, joining the Muslim parties to give victory to the candidate of a party, the PKB, that had won only 12.6 percent of the popular vote in June over the choice of 33.7 percent of the voters.

Enraged Megawati supporters took to the streets in angry and violent demonstrations. In the MPR on 21 October, the immediate effort was to achieve unity by making Megawati vice president. This was not uncontested. The Golkar faction nominated Akbar Tanjung. General Wiranto was nominated by United Ummat Sovereignty faction (a nine-member small-party parliamentary coalition), and the PPP nominated Hamzah Haz. Megawati's name was placed in nomination by Gus Dur's PKB. Both the new president and Amien Rais worked behind the scenes to ensure Megawati's election. Stressing the need for unity, Akbar withdrew just before the election. Then Amien Rais read a letter from Wiranto stating that he was not a candidate. Hamzah, candidate of the anti-Megawati Muslims and die-hard Habibie loyalists, could not be prevailed upon to withdraw. Megawati handily won the ensuing vote, 396–284. The new post-Suharto leadership team was in place. The politics of the presidential election was completed on 26 October with the announcement of a thirty-five-member "National Unity Cabinet" drawn from the PKB, PAN, PPP, PDI-P, Golkar, and ABRI.

Sri Bintang Pamungkas, the leader of the liberal Indonesian Democratic Union Party (PUDI) and a KPU member, in the midst of the strife over DPR seat allocations remarked that the 1999 polls "were grand political laboratories where political experiments took place." He added, "unfortunately not all experiments were successful and prone to deadlocks" (*Jakarta Post*, 24 August 1999). Clearly, in a first-past-the-post, winner-take-all district system, the PDI-P would have been swept into power and Megawati would be Indonesia's president. In a country as culturally and ethnically complex as Indonesia and in the absence of a democratic political culture, however, it is doubtful that a president with only a one-third plurality and whose political commitment to Islam was suspect could unite the country. The arguments against proportional representation have to be evaluated in the Indonesian context of a country that always has the potential of unraveling. With the indirect election of Gus Dur, Megawati, and at the MPR, Amien Rais, the forces of reform won the outward struggle against the status quo. Whether this can be translated into policy and action remains to be seen.

The 1999 election was not the culmination of a process of democratization but an important first step. Before the next election, the MPR will have considered constitutional amendments that could fundamentally alter the way Indonesia is governed. Some Indonesians argue for direct popular election of the president. Others would return to a parliamentary system. Structural changes in the state itself may occur, with some form of a federal system a real possibility. If the 1999 electoral process was the first of the post-Suharto era, it may have been the last of the 1945 Constitution era. Whatever choices the MPR makes, at minimum it would seem that the next elections will take in a system of greater representational accountability to the Indonesian public.

Notes

1. As late as 12 May 1999, a senior adviser to the National Democratic Institute told a congressional committee: "Political or election-related violence, however, poses an even more immediate and direct threat to the quality of the elections" (Cowen 1999, 4).
2. The cover letter of the 15 July 1999 "Post-Election Statement No. 3" of the National Democratic Institute and Carter Center election observation mission notes the "extraordinary commitment to democracy shown by the Indonesian people on June 7" and the "impressive effort" of the election administration, party agents, and observers. It concluded that no evidence had been provided "to support allegations of widespread or significant fraud or tampering designed to benefit a particular party or parties."
3. The basis of the political distinction between "modernist" and "traditionalist" Muslim political parties is their attitudes toward the state. The "modernists" would infuse the state with Islamic values although not necessarily demand the creation of an Islamic state. The Masyumi and successor modernist parties found their greatest strengths in urban areas and the outer islands. In the social, cultural, and educational sphere, modernist Islam was represented in the Muhammadiyah organization. Modernist Muslims give weight to individual interpretation of Islam while the traditionalists rely on the *ulamas*, the clerical teachers. The traditionalist Nahdlatul Ulama had its strength in the rural areas of Central and East Java with a leadership based on the Islamic boarding school (*pesantran*). The traditionalist politicians are more relaxed in a pluralist state.
4. Sukarno's political vision, charisma, and ego were frustrated in a constitutional order that was weighted to the Parliament. The military had two major concerns: local military commander-backed regional revolts in Sumatra and East Indonesia and the growing strength of the PKI. Lev 1966 is the most detailed study of this period.
5. The rationale for ABRI legislative seats is that ABRI is officially recognized as a national social force and as such it should be functionally represented in the DPR. Since active duty ABRI members can neither vote nor run for office, however, its representation has to be nonelective.
6. The Pancasila is the basis of state ideology and consists of five principles enunciated by Sukarno in 1945: belief in God; humanitarianism; unitary nationalism; consultative democracy; and social justice. It is culturally neutral and was designed to promote the values of an ethnically plural society. The most complete discussion of the political use of Pancasila ideology is in Ramage 1995.
7. Amien Rais was a professor of political science at Gajah Mada University and has a University of Chicago Ph.D.. He was the youngest leader of Muhammadiyah, Indonesia's second largest Muslim association.
8. The full texts of the relevant MPR decrees as cited here are as published (in Bahasa Indonesia) on the Internet: http://www.detik.com/berita/tapmpr98.
9. The full texts and elucidations of the three political laws cited here are as published (in Bahasa Indonesian) by the Department of Foreign Affairs at its web site: http://www.dfa-deplu.go.id.

10. Indonesian domestic election monitors numbered 300,000 from a variety of NGOs, and more than 500 members of foreign groups plus a host of unaccredited individuals were at polling stations.
11. The other government representatives were former Supreme Court justice Adi Andojo Soetjipto, former DPR member and Ministry of Justice official Oka Mahendra, and university political scientist Afan Gaffar.
12. The membership of 65 representatives from "functional groups" is specified in Article 2:2c of Law No. 4/1999. These are drawn from religion (20), veterans (5), weak economic groups (9), women (5), intellectuals, scientists, artists, journalists (5), NGOs and youth (5), civil servants (5), ethnic minorities (5), and the physically handicapped (2). When it came time to actually nominate individuals, the KPU became embroiled in disputes involving KPU "political" appointments and the desires of organizations representing the various categories.
13. This is one of the "transitional" provisions of the law. In the next (2004) election, the requirement is increased to more than half the provinces or fourteen (Law No. 3/1999, Article 39).
14. West Sumatra, West Java, Jakarta, Central Java, East Java (NDI 1999b, 11).
15. "Gus" is a Javanese honorific given to young men of good birth, and "Dur" is a diminutive of his given name. Gus Dur was the third generation of one of East Java's most distinguished Islamic clerical families. His grandfather had been a founder of NU, and his father was Indonesia's first Minister of Religion in 1945.
16. A 1999 survey showed that for the voter, the most acceptable sources of information about the election are television (78 percent) and radio (61 percent). Television reached 64 percent of the electorate every day and radio 37 percent (Asia Foundation 1999).
17. The heart of the issue was how the remainder votes of the parties to the *stembus akkord* should be treated and what divisor should be used in calculating seats. Its technical roots were in the ambiguities of the law and KPU regulations.
18. A major postelection survey is being conducted by Prof. William Liddle of Ohio State University and counterparts at the University of Indonesia. This study explores voter behavior, focusing on such variables as religion, ethnicity, regionalism, social class, role of leaders, and patron-clientage. Its results will eventually be published.
19. More than one-third, fifty-seven, of the PDI-P elected parliamentarians were non-Muslim, a far higher percentage than in the general population.
20. It was alleged and an independent audit confirms that millions of dollars were illegally funneled through the Bank Bali to Golkar and Habibie's campaign as well as into the pockets of cronies. An attempted cover-up was thwarted when the IMF made release of the audit a condition of renewed financial assistance.
21. Habibie was criticized for announcing the referendum without bureaucratic and political preparation and then was held responsible by Indonesian nationalists for the conditions that forced Indonesia to allow Australian-led foreign military intervention in East Timor in September to restore peace and order in the troubled territory.
22. PDI supporters castigated Rais for his maneuverings against Megawati in collaboration with Golkar, whose leader, Akbar Tanjung, became Speaker of the DPR. In a biting profile, an anonymous *Jakarta Post* writer characterized him as basically "unreliable and inconsistent" and his political behavior as "shameful."

References

Anderson, B.R. 1996. "Elections and Participation in Three Southeast Countries." In *The Politics of Elections in Southeast Asia*, edited by R.H. Taylor. Washington, D.C.: Woodrow Wilson Center Press.

Asia Foundation. 1999. *Indonesia National Voter Education Survey: Report Summary*. Produced by Charney Research and ACNielsen.

Baker, R.W. 1997. "Indonesia's Evolving Politics: Implications of the 1997–1998 Elections." *USINDO Report* I.

Cowan, G. 1999. *Statement by Glenn Cowan, Senior Advisor National Democratic Institute for International Affairs before the Subcommittee on Asia and the Pacific of the House Committee on International Relations, May 12, 1999.*

Ecklof, S. 1997. "The 1997 General Election in Indonesia. "*Asian Survey* 37:1181–96.

Feith, H. 1957. *The Indonesian Elections of 1955.* Ithaca, N.Y.: Interim Report Series. Cornell Modern Indonesian Project.

———. 1962. *The Decline of Constitutional Democracy in Indonesia.* Ithaca, N.Y.: Cornell University Press.

Huntington, Samuel. 1991. *The Third Wave.* Norman: University of Oklahoma Press.

King, B.A. 1992. "The 1992 General Election and Indonesia's Political Landscape." *Contemporary Southeast Asia* 14:154–73.

Lev, Daniel S. 1966. *The Transition to Guided Democracy: Indonesian Politics, 1957–1959.* Ithaca, N.Y.: Cornell Modern Indonesian Project.

Liddle, R. William 1996. "A Useful Fiction: Democratic Legitimation in New Order Indonesia." In *The Politics of Elections in Southeast Asia*, edited by R.H. Taylor. Washington, D.C.: Woodrow Wilson Center Press.

MacIntryre, Andrew. 1993. "Indonesia in 1992: Coming to Terms with the Outside World." *Asian Survey* 32, no. 2 (February): 204–10.

Masters, E. 1999. *Indonesia's 1999 Elections: A Second Chance for Democracy.* New York: Asia Society, Asian Update.

NDI. 1999a. *The New Legal Framework for Elections in Indonesia.* Washington, D.C.: National Democratic Institute for International Affairs.

———. 1999b. *The Prospects for Democratic Elections in Indonesia: Pre-Election Report.* Washington, D.C.: National Democratic Institute for International Affairs.

Oey Hong Lee, ed. 1974. *Indonesia after the 1971 Elections.* London: Oxford University Press, Hull Monographs on South-East Asia No. 5.

Ramage, D. 1995. *Politics in Indonesia: Democracy, Islam and the Ideology of Tolerance.* London: Routledge.

Ricklefs, M. 1981. *A History of Modern Indonesia.* London: Macmillan Press.

Taylor, R.H. 1996. *The Politics of Elections in Southeast Asia.* Washington, D.C.: Woodrow Wilson Center Press.

USINDO. 1999. *Parliamentary Elections In Indonesia: Consensus, Coalition, or Confusion?* Washington, D.C.: The United States–Indonesia Society.

van Marle, A. 1956. "The First Indonesian Parliamentary Elections." *Indonesie* 9:257–64.

———. 1974. "Indonesian Electoral Geography under Orla and Orba." In *Indonesia after the 1971 Elections*, edited by Oey Hong Lee. London: Oxford University Press, Hull Monographs on South-East Asia No. 5.

Index

Abanse Pinay (Phil.), 152
Alliance for a Prosperous Macau, 86
Alliance for Entertainment Associations (Macau), 84
Amien Rais, 264, 271, 276–78
Amity Association (Macau), 82, 87
Anand Panyarachun, 193–95
Angkatan Bersenjata Republik Indonesia (ABRI), 256, 259–65, 271, 278
Appointments, 54, 76–79, 196–98, 211, 243, 245, 260
Association for the Defense of the Interests of Macau (ADIM), 76
Association for the Promotion of Macau's Economy and Livelihood, 86
Association in Promotion of Democracy and Livelihood (Macau), 82, 87

Barisan Nasional (BN; Malay.), 211–18, 222–25, 228, 230
Barisan Sosialis (Sing.), 237–38, 243
Basic Law (HK.), 53–54, 64, 66–67, 72
Basic Law (Macau), 78, 80
Buddhist Liberal Democratic Party (BLDP; Camb.), 168, 174
Bumiputera/nonbumiputera dichotomy, 210–11, 213–14, 218, 220–22, 228–29
Bureaucracy, in politics, 51, 169, 188, 190, 204–5, 227, 259–65, 268
Business, 68, 77
  and elections, 56, 84–89, 96, 103–4, 126, 136, 217–18
  See also Constituencies, functional
By-elections, 207–8, 236, 238–41, 249, 251

Cambodia, 165–86
  campaigning in, 167–69, 172–78, 181
  democracy assessment, 182–85
  electoral system, 167, 171–73, 184
  party system, 165, 167–68, 174–75, 183–84
  transfer of power, 179–82

voter behavior, 165, 178–79, 181–82
Cambodian People's Party (CPP), 165–72, 174–84
Campaign finance
  government resources for, 178, 229, 249–50, 259–65, 268
  public funding, 92, 96, 138, 144, 200
  rules, 92, 96, 103–4, 138–39, 199
  spending, 84, 87, 89–90, 102–3, 138–39, 145, 161, 191, 199, 222
Campaign issues
  corruption, 93, 102–3, 136, 158, 175, 193–94
  cultural, 220–21, 230, 249, 252, 277
  economic, 38, 41–42, 44, 105, 112–15, 134–35, 143–44, 174–75, 220, 237, 249–50
  environment, 44, 113
  federal/state power, 227, 229–30, 271
  leadership/regime, 133–36, 139, 143
  national defense, 41, 105
  national identity/reunification, 38–40, 42, 44–47, 133, 136, 174
  policy, 38–41, 44, 56–58, 106–7, 121, 134–35, 152
  pro-democracy *vs.* pro-China, 56–58, 61, 64–65, 68–69, 81
  reform *vs.* stability, 38, 40–42, 94, 121, 133–35, 143, 222, 224, 237, 271
  religious, 219, 221–22, 225–28, 252, 276
  See also under country name
Campaign restrictions, 14, 95–96, 103, 137–39, 161, 198, 205, 215, 224, 250, 263, 271
Campaign strategies, 9–10
  advertising, 156, 161, 191
  by-election strategy, 239, 249, 251
  candidate-centered, 9–10, 46, 113, 136, 139, 142, 158–59, 161, 175
  canvassing, 1–3, 95, 103, 137–38, 144, 196
  debates, 139, 144
  party-centered, 9–10, 103, 137, 222
  personalized, 46, 104, 113, 136, 139, 142, 145, 155–56

policy-based, 102, 105, 111–14
rallies, 137, 139, 224–25, 250, 271
responsibility zone (RZ) system, 45
voter mobilization, 86, 140, 145
See also Intimidation; Media; Patronage; Violence; Vote-buying
Candidates
  civil servants as, 265, 268
  criteria for, 14, 67–68, 76, 102, 197, 204–6, 212–13, 242, 245–47
  nomination of, 19, 26, 45, 73, 243
  number of, 19, 22, 59, 71, 148, 157, 196
  party switching, 104, 121, 126, 153–55, 159, 191–92
  recruitment of, 191, 195, 246
Centre Democratico de Macau (CDM), 76
Chart Pattana (Thai.), 192, 200, 203–4
Chart Thai, 189, 192, 200–204
Chatichai Choonhavan, 189, 193, 203
Chavalit Yongchaiyudh, 192, 202
China, People's Republic of (PRC), 18–30, 41
  democracy assessment, 24–30
  electoral system, 21–24
  and Hong Kong, 50, 53–54, 58–59, 65–69, 71–72
  and Macau, 77–78
  party system, 27–29, 35–36, 44
  township elections, 29–30
Chinese, 234, 247, 251, 264
  in Macau, 76–77, 81–82, 84–85, 89
  in Malaysia, 210–11, 216–21, 225–26, 228
Chinese Communist Party (CCP)
  China, 18, 21, 27–29
  Hong Kong, 56
Chun Doo Hwan, 118, 134, 141
Chung Ju Yung, 126, 134–36, 138
Citizens' Alliance for the 2000 General Elections (Korea), 135–36
Citizens Party (HK.), 55–56
Civic Force (HK.), 55
Civil society, 170–71, 177–78, 184–85, 189–94, 204, 208, 253, 264
Class, 175, 247, 249–50, 257
  middle-class, 55, 69, 157, 163, 189, 192–94, 224, 250
  voting, 158, 162–63, 192–93
  working-class, 55, 82, 86, 235–36, 238, 250–51
Coalition for Free and Fair Elections (COFFEL; Camb.), 177
Commission on Elections (COMELEC; Phil.), 150, 152–53, 155, 161
Committee for Free and Fair Elections (COMFREL; Camb.), 177, 182
Communist Party of Malaya, 246
Communist Party of Thailand, 188

Confederation of Trade Unions (CTU; HK.), 56, 65
Conservative Party (NCP; Japan), 98–100, 112
Constituencies
  functional, 14, 52–53, 55, 59, 61, 64–66, 68–71, 77, 256, 259, 264–65, 268–70, 273, 276–78
  geographical, 14, 59, 61–62, 64, 68, 71
  See also Electoral systems; Gerrymandering
Constitutions, 20, 33–35, 119, 210, 215, 235, 257, 259
  Cambodia, 169, 172, 180
  Thailand, 187, 190–91, 194–95, 205–8
Corruption, 43, 76, 156, 161
  election fraud, 151, 153, 161, 165, 168–69, 180–82, 191, 204, 208
  as election issue, 102–3, 158
  in elections, 46, 84–91, 102–3, 134, 137–39, 144
  in government, 20, 88, 93, 112–15, 134–36, 175, 189–91, 255, 264, 271
  See also Vote-buying
Crescent Moon and Star Party (PBB; Indon.), 271, 275–77
"Cronyism," 189–91

D'Assumpcao, Carlos, 81–83, 89
The "Decision" (HK.), 53, 65–66
Democracy, definition of, 32–33
Democratic Action Party (DAP; Malay.), 218–20, 222–23, 226, 228–29
Democratic Alliance for the Betterment of Hong Kong (DAB), 55–56, 64–65, 67, 69
123 Democratic Alliance (HK.), 56, 65
Democratic Alliance (Taiwan), 43
Democratic Justice Party (DJP; Korea), 120–21, 127, 141
Democratic Liberal Party (DLP; Korea), 119–21, 126, 130, 134, 138, 142
Democratic Party (DP)
  Hong Kong, 55–56, 59, 65
  Japan (DPJ), 98, 100–102, 104–5, 108–9, 112
  Korea, 119–20, 126, 130–31, 135, 142
  Thailand, 192, 200–204
Democratic People's Party (DPP; Korea), 127
Democratic Progressive Party (DPP; Taiwan), 32, 42–43, 45–47
Democratic Republican Party (Korea), 121
Democratic Socialist Party (DSP; Japan), 96–98, 107–8
Development Union (Macau), 82–83, 86
Dewan Perwakilan Rakyat (DPR; Indon.), 256, 259–61, 263, 265–66, 274–76
D'Hondt rule, 81–82, 87, 89, 172
Dong Jiao Dong (Malay.), 221
Duverger's theories, 36

Education, 197, 220–21, 235–37
Election administration, 25–26, 138
  ballots, 19, 23, 88, 150, 152–53, 160, 241
  Cambodia, 166–69, 171–73, 177, 180
  Hong Kong, 65, 68–70
  Indonesia, 151–152274–276, 260, 262, 266–70, 273–76
  Macau, 87–90
  Malaysia, 212–14
  monitoring, 160–61, 163, 166–68, 173–74, 176–78, 180–82, 184, 193, 199, 267
  Philippines, 150, 152–53, 155, 161
  security, 168, 173
  Thailand, 193, 199, 204–7
  timing, 22–23, 110, 113, 148–50, 224, 237, 242
  vote counting, 14, 147, 150, 200, 212–13, 241, 273
Elections
  direct, 59, 68, 72–73, 76, 78, 80–84, 119, 127, 195
  general, 24, 255–56, 266–76
  indirect, 64, 79
  for legitimacy, 151, 165
  local and state, 18–30, 34, 104, 111–13, 121, 126, 147, 150, 160–62, 211–12, 227–30, 240, 256
Electoral colleges, 52–53, 71, 79
Electoral systems, 3–7, 59
  chairmanship method, 23–24
  manipulation of, 127–28, 241, 245
  mixed, 92, 127–33
  multimember districts, 127, 195–96, 242–46, 248–49
  "one person, one vote," 65, 70, 195–96
  one-vote, 127–33
  party-list proportional representation, 9, 95, 105, 108, 111, 127, 129, 131, 152, 167, 195–97
  plurality (first-past-the-post), 5, 9, 35–36, 43–44, 46, 59, 69, 71, 127, 129–33, 151–52, 211, 214, 239–42, 248
  reforms, 61, 64, 92–96, 114, 138–39, 242–46, 269–70, 273–76
  rule changing, 71–73
  runoffs, 66
  simple majority, 195
  single-member districts (SMDs), 9, 35–36, 43–44, 46, 64, 92, 95, 97–98, 100–105, 112, 129, 131–33, 151–52, 195–96, 211, 242, 266
  single nontransferable vote (SNTV), 6, 9, 35–36, 44–46, 92, 94–95, 102–3, 112–13, 127, 131
  single transferable vote (STV), 6, 9, 69
  transferable vote (TV) method, 22–23, 69
  two-vote, 131

  See also Constituencies; country names; Proportional representation systems; Seat allocation methods
Electoral Union (Macau), 81–83
Estrada, Joseph E., 152, 154–56, 158–59, 162–63
Ethnicity, 257
  balance, 78, 242–43
  as campaign issue, 220–22
  ethnic conflict, 174, 179–80, 211, 238, 264
  ethnic voting, 157, 224–25, 230
  in Malaysia, 210–11, 217–22, 224–30
  and parties, 215–20, 247, 251, 269
  in Singapore, 234, 247, 249–51
  See also Bumiputera; Islam; Religion; individual groups
Executive branches, 33–35, 51–52, 79, 93, 152, 196–97
  chief executives, 54, 65–66, 72, 78–79
  See also Presidential systems

Federation of Trade Unions (FTU)
  Hong Kong, 56, 65
  Macau, 82
Flower of Friendship and Development of Macau, 81
Frontier Party (HK.), 55–56
Functional groups. *See* Constituencies, functional; Golongan Karya

Gender, 93, 152, 277
Germany, 95–96, 111, 131–32
Gerrymandering, 14, 71, 109, 212–14, 241–42, 253
Gifts. *See* Patronage system
Goh Chok Tong, 239, 241, 247, 250, 252
Golongan Karya (Golkar; Indon.), 256, 259, 264–65, 268–70, 273, 276–78
Governors, 51–52
Grand National Party (GNP; Korea), 119, 126–27, 135, 143
Great Britain, 50–54, 67, 71–72, 131–32, 234–35, 237
Group Representation Constituencies (GRCs), 242–46, 248–49
"Guided democracy," 257–59, 269
Gus Dur. *See* Wahid, Abdurrahman

Habibie, B.J., 264–65, 268, 270, 274, 276–78
Hata, Tsutomu, 94, 106, 108
Hong Kong, 50–75
  campaigning in, 56–59, 61, 64–65
  democracy assessment, 70, 72–73
  electoral system, 52, 58–71
  Macau, influence on, 78–79, 89–91
  party system, 54–58, 68
  voter behavior, 56–58, 61, 68–69

Hong Kong Association for Democracy and People's Livelihood (ADPL), 55, 65
Hong Kong Progressive Alliance (HKPA), 55, 69
Hong Kong Special Administrative Region (HKSAR). *See* Hong Kong
Hosokawa, Morihiro, 94–96
Human rights, 170, 175–77, 265
Hun Sen, 169–71, 173–75, 179–80

Iban-Dayak community, 227, 229
Incumbency advantage, 14, 102–3, 175–78, 224, 241–42, 245, 252–53
Independents, 36–37, 55, 59, 61, 64–65, 69, 239
Indians, 210, 217–18, 220–21, 225–26, 234, 238, 242–43, 247, 251
Indigenous people. *See* Bumiputera; Ethnicity
Indonesia, 255–81
 campaigning in, 29–30, 260, 263, 270–71, 276–77
 democracy assessment, 255–56, 261–62, 279
 electoral system, 257, 259–61, 265–70, 273–76
 general election (1999), 255–56, 266–76
 party system, 256–66, 268–73, 276–78
 presidential election (1999), 276–78
 voter behavior, 255, 260, 262–64
Indonesian Communist Party (PKI), 257–59
Indonesian Democratic Union Party (PUDI), 278
Indonesian Islamic Communist Party (PSII), 257–60, 275
Indonesian Nationalist Party (PNI), 257–60
Indonesians, in Malaysia, 212, 214, 229
Indonesian Socialist Party (PSI), 257–59
Interest groups, 54, 69, 77–79, 81, 113
International community, 166–68, 170–71, 173–74, 176–77, 184, 188
International Monetary Fund (IMF), 135, 143, 264, 266–67
Internet, 136, 224, 230, 250, 253
Intimidation, 88–89, 167, 169, 172–73, 176–77, 181, 197, 253, 260, 263
Islam, 247
 in Indonesia, 257–60, 269–71, 275–76
 in Malaysia, 212, 215–16, 219–23, 225–29

Japan, 92–117, 131–32
 campaigning in, 93–94, 102–5
 democracy assessment, 101, 113–15
 electoral system, 92–96, 111–13
 party system, 93, 96–109, 114–15
 voter behavior, 109–11
Japan Communist Party (JCP), 94, 96, 98, 100–102, 105, 107, 109
Japan New Party, 94

Japan Socialist Party (JSP), 93, 95–96, 98–100, 104, 107
Jeyaretnam, J.B., 238, 241, 243, 252
Joint Declaration (HK.), 54, 71
Joint International Observer Group, 181
Justice and Unity Party (PKP; Indon.), 270
Justice Party (PK; Indon.), 271, 276

Kadazan-Dusun community, 227–28
Khmer Nation Party (Camb.), 174–75, 178–80
Khmer People's National Liberation Front (KPNLF; Camb.), 166, 168
Khmer Rouge (Camb.), 166–67, 169–70, 175–77, 179, 182
Kim Dae Jung, 119–21, 126–29, 133–37, 141–44
Kim Jong Pil, 120–21, 126–27, 135–36, 141–42
Kim Young Sam, 119–21, 126, 128, 133–38, 141–42
Komeito, New (Japan), 108–9, 112, 114
Komeito (CGP; Japan), 95–98, 100, 104, 107
Komisi Pemilhan Umum (KPU; Indon.), 267–69, 273–76
Korea, Republic of, 118–46
 campaigning in, 133–39, 144–45
 democracy assessment, 144–45
 electoral system, 127–33, 144
 party system, 119–27, 131–33, 136
 voter behavior, 139–45
Kuomintang (KMT; Hong Kong), 56
Kuomintang (KMT; Taiwan), 32, 34–49

Labour Front (Sing.), 235
Labour Solidarity (Macau), 82
LAKAS (Phil.), 154–55
LAMP (Phil.), 155
Language, 157, 221, 227, 237, 252
League of Upholders of Indonesian Independence (IPKI), 257–60
Lee Hoi Chang, 119, 126–27, 143
Lee Kuan Yew, 235–38, 244–50, 253
Legislative branches, 195, 211
 Constituent Assembly
  Cambodia, 165, 167
  Korea, 119
 Consultative Assembly (MPR; Indon.), 256, 259–61, 263–65, 268, 277–78
 DPR (Indon.), 256, 260–61, 263, 265–66, 274–76
 House of Councillors (Japan), 93, 100, 110–12
 House of Representatives
  Japan, 92–111, 131
  Malaysia, 211, 215
  Philippines, 151–52, 154–55
  Thailand, 195–97, 206–7
 Legislative Assembly (Macau), 76–89

INDEX **287**

Legislative Council (Legco; HK.), 51–53, 58–65, 67–72
National Assembly
  Cambodia, 165, 167, 169–72, 179
  Korea, 119–21, 126–33, 145
  Philippines, 144
  Taiwan, 33–36, 43
Provisional Legislature (HK.), 66–69
Senate
  Malaysia, 211
  Philippines, 152
  Thailand, 187, 195, 197–98, 204, 206
  state and local, 26, 211
  See also Parliamentary systems
Legitimacy, 133, 151, 165, 175, 194–95, 261, 264
Lembaga Pemilihan Umum (LPU; Indon.), 260, 262
Liberal Democratic Party (LDP; Japan), 92–94, 96, 99–109, 112–14
Liberal Party (LP)
  Hong Kong, 55–56, 61, 64–65, 69
  Japan, 98–100, 105, 109
  Philippines, 153, 155
List system. *See under* Electoral systems
Local government, 20–21, 24–29, 80, 244–46

Macanese, 76–77, 81–82, 89
Macau, 76–91
  campaigning in, 82–84, 86–89
  electoral system, 76–82, 87, 89
  electoral systems, 81–82
  and Hong Kong, 78–79, 89–91
  parties and groups, 80–87
  voter behavior, 80–81, 84, 86, 88–91
Macau Special Administrative Region (MSAR). *See* Macau
Mahathir Mohamad, 213, 215–16, 218–19
Majelis Permusyawaratan Rakyat (MPR; Indon.), 256, 259–61, 263–65, 268, 277–78
Malays, in Singapore, 234, 247, 251
Malaysia, 210–33, 237
  campaigning in, 220–24, 229–30
  democracy assessment, 230
  East Malaysia, 226–30
  electoral system, 211–15
  party system, 215–20, 228
  and Singapore, 235–38
  voter behavior, 224–26
Malaysian Chinese Association (MCA), 215–18, 225–26
Malaysian Indian Congress (MIC), 215, 217–18, 225–26
Marcos, Ferdinand, 147, 150–51, 153, 155, 157, 161
Masyumi Party (Indon.), 257–60
Media
  access to, 168, 173, 178, 222–24

advertising, 95, 103, 105, 139, 144, 156, 161, 191, 271
election coverage, 38, 82, 139, 144, 156, 167–68, 170, 173, 178, 223–24, 250, 260
television, 95, 139, 144, 156, 191, 221, 223
Meeting Point (HK.), 59, 61
Megawati Sukarnoputri, 263–64, 270, 276–78
Military, 118, 133, 141, 151, 170, 187–89, 193–94, 202, 204, 208
See also Angkatan Bersenjata Republik Indonesia (ABRI)
Millennium Democratic Party (MDP; Korea), 120, 127, 135
MKGR party (Indon.), 268
"Money politics," 191, 193, 205, 217–18, 230
Muhammadiyah (Indon.), 264
Municipal councils, 51, 53, 71, 77, 79–80
Murba Party (Indon.), 259–60

Nacionalista Party (Phil.), 153, 155
Nahdlatul Ulama (NU; Indon.), 257–60, 262–63, 270, 275
National Alliance for Democracy and Unification (Korea), 136
National Awakening Party (PKB; Indon.), 270, 272–73, 276–78
National Citizens' Movement for Free Elections (NAMFREL; Phil.), 160–61, 163
National Congress for New Politics (NCNP; Korea), 119, 126–27, 135, 142
National Development Party (PPP; Indon.), 270, 273, 275–76, 278
National Front (Indon.), 259
National Mandate Party (PAN; Indon.), 271, 273, 276–78
National People's Congress (China), 21, 53, 65–69, 73
National United Front for an Independent, Neutral, Peaceful and Cooperative Cambodia (FUNCINPEC), 166, 168–72, 174–75, 178–80, 182
Neutral Independent Committee for Free Elections in Cambodia (NICFEC), 177
New Aspiration Party (NAP; Thai.), 192, 200, 202, 204
New Democratic Macau, 82, 87
New Democratic Republican Party (NDRP; Korea), 120–21, 128, 130, 142
New Frontier Party (NFP; Japan), 97–98, 100, 104, 108
New Hong Kong Alliance (NHKA), 56
New Korea Party (NKP), 120, 135, 142
New Nation Association (NNA; Taiwan), 37, 40, 43, 45
New Order (Indon.), 259–65, 269
New Party by the People (Korea), 126–27

New Party Harbinger (Japan), 96
New Party (NP) (Taiwan), 37, 39–40, 43, 45–46
New Politics Party (Korea), 130
Nominated Members of Parliament (NMPs), 243, 245
Nomination authority, 19, 73, 243, 245
Non-Constituency Members of Parliament (NCMPs), 243, 245
Nongovernmental organizations (NGOs), 170–71, 177–78, 184, 204, 264

Organic Law of the Village Committees, 19–21, 24, 26, 29
Organic Statute (Macau), 76–78
Ozawa, Ichiro, 94, 98, 108

Palang Dharma Parties (Thai.), 200, 203
"Pancasila Democracy," 261–62, 265, 269
Panitia Pemilihan Indonesia (PPI), 269, 274–76
Panitia Pengawas (*Panwas*; Indon.), 269
Panitia Persiapan Pembentukan KPU (P3KPU, Team of Eleven; Indon.), 269–70
Pan Malayan Islamic Party (PMIP), 219
Parapolitical organizations, 236, 245, 248
Parish-Pastoral Council for Responsible Voting (PPCRV; Indon.), 161
Parkindo (Indon.), 257–60
Parliamentary systems, 33, 211
  Indonesia, 256–61, 263, 265–66, 274–76
  Japan, 92–94, 111
  Korea, 118, 135
  Singapore, 234, 240, 243, 245
  Thailand, 188–90, 194–98
  See also Legislative branches
Parmusi (Indon.), 260
Partai Demokrasi Indonesia (PDI), 261–63
Partai Katolik (Indon.), 257–60
Partai Persatuan Pembangunan (PPP; Indon.), 260–64
Parti Bansa Dayak Sarawak (PBDS; Malay.), 228–29
Parti Bersatu Rakyat Jelata Sabah (Berjaya; Malay.), 228
Parti Bersatu Sabah (PBS; Malay.), 213, 228
Parti Gerakan Rakyat Malaysia (Gerakan), 215, 217–18, 220, 225–26
Parti KeADILan Nasional (KeADILan; Malay.), 219–20
Partindo (Indon.), 259
Parti Rakyat Malaysia (PRM), 220
Parti Semangat 46 (S46; Malay.), 219, 226
Parti Socialis Rakyat Malaysia (PSRM), 220
Party for Peace and Democracy (PPD; Korea), 120–21, 126, 128–30, 142
Party Islam Malaysia (PAS), 218–20, 222–23, 225–26

Patronage systems
  Cambodia, 167, 176–77
  Indonesia, 259–65, 268
  Japan, 102–7, 111–14
  Korea, 137
  Macau, 88, 90–91
  Malaysia, 211, 216–18, 228–30
  Philippines, 155–57, 161
  Singapore, 249–50
  Thailand, 189–93, 195–97, 205
  See also Incumbency advantage
Patten, Christopher, 61, 64, 72
Patten Reforms, 61, 64
People First Party (PFP; Taiwan), 37, 40
People's Action Party (PAP; Sing.), 218, 235–39, 241, 245–49, 251–53
People's Republic of Kampuchea (PRK), 166, 175
Personalization
  of campaigns, 46, 113, 136, 139, 142, 145, 155–56
  of parties, 121, 247–48
  of support groups, 102, 105–7, 112–14
Perti (Indon.), 257–60
Pesaka Bumiputera Bersatu (PBB; Malay.), 228–29
Philippines, 147–64
  campaigning in, 155–56
  democracy assessment, 159–63
  electoral system, 145, 151–53
  party system, 153–55
  voter behavior, 147–50, 156–61
Philippinos, in Malaysia, 212, 229
PKU (Indon.), 272, 275
PNU. *See Nahdlatul Ulama*
Policy-specialization schemes, 102, 111
Political culture, 140, 142, 182–83, 187
Political party systems, 8–9
  business and, 56, 103–4, 126, 136, 217–18
  Cambodia, 165, 167–68, 174–75, 183–84
  dominant parties, 14, 121, 176–78, 215–20, 234, 241–42, 245–49, 252–53
  electoral system effects on, 35–36, 44, 68, 101–9, 131–33, 248–49
  eligibility, 213, 269–70, 274
  factions/fragmentation, 32, 37, 43–45, 47, 97, 104, 107, 113–15, 247–48
  institutionalization of, 247–48
  multiparty, 36–37, 44–45, 97, 120, 126, 169, 191–92, 215, 246
  Muslim parties, 212, 219–20, 222–23, 225–26, 229, 257–60, 270–71, 275
  opposition parties, 107–9, 113, 218–20, 222, 226, 228, 238–39, 243, 245, 248, 262–63
  organization, 105–7, 155, 183–84, 218, 246, 248
  party-centered campaigning, 9–10, 137

party identification, 10, 55–58, 109–10, 143, 154, 225–26
party switching, 104, 121, 126, 153–55, 157, 159, 191–92
personalized, 121, 247–48
platforms, 103–5, 222, 224, 237
three-party, 126
two-party, 35–36, 97, 121, 126
women's party, 152
See also Campaign strategies; Interest groups; Parapolitical organizations; individual parties
Polling, 159, 162
Poll Watch (Thai.), 192–93, 199
PPIM (Indon.), 275
Prachakorn Thai, 200, 203
PRD (Indon.), 277
Prem Tinsulanonda, 188–89, 201–2
Presidential systems, 33, 35, 37, 118–19, 126–27, 144, 148, 151–52, 161, 234, 239–46, 250–51, 256, 261, 264–65, 268, 276–78
PROMDI (Phil.), 155, 159
Proportional representation (PR) systems, 9, 35–36, 68, 71, 230, 242
Cambodia, 167, 171
Indonesia, 257, 259, 266, 276, 278
Japan, 92, 95, 97–103, 111–12
Korea, 127–33
PUI (Indon.), 275

Ramos, Fidel, 154, 156–59
Ranariddh, Norodom, 169–71, 173, 175–76, 179–80
Referenda, 237, 265
Reform
Hong Kong, 55, 61, 64
Indonesia, 264–66, 269–76
Japan, 92–96, 114
Korea, 138–39
Macau, 78, 87, 89
political parties under, 266, 268–73
Singapore, 242–46
vs. stability, 38, 40–42, 143, 158, 175, 222, 224, 271
Thailand, 188–93
Religion
as campaign issue, 219–22, 225–28, 252, 276–77
and parties, 215–20, 247, 260, 262, 269–71
and voting behavior, 158–59, 225, 227–28, 230, 276
See also Islam
Rengo (Japan), 105
REPORMA (Phil.), 155
Reunification Democratic Party (RDP; Korea), 120–21, 128, 130, 142
Rhee, Syngman, 118–19

Roh Tae Woo, 118–21, 129, 133–34, 138, 141–42
Royalty, 174, 211–12

Sabah Progressive Party (SAPP; Malay.), 213
Sabah (state), 211, 222, 226–30
Sam Rainsy Party, 174–75, 178–80
Sarawak Barisan Nasional (SBN; Malay.), 228–29
Sarawak National Party (SNAP; Malay.), 228
Sarawak (state), 211, 222, 226–30
Sarawak United People's Party (SUPP; Malay.), 211, 228
Seat allocation methods, 129–33, 266, 274–76
Balinski/Young, 173, 180
bloc voting, 69
"highest average," 172
Jefferson/d'Hondt rule, 81–82, 87, 89, 172
"largest remainder," 129, 167, 172, 266, 274–76
quota, 266
seat-vote ratios, 130, 241
vote share, 112, 225–26
Sihanouk, Norodom, 166, 174, 180, 182
Singapore, 210, 234–54
campaigning in, 239, 241, 249–51
democracy assessment, 240, 252–53
electoral system, 240–46
and Malaysia, 235–38
party system, 246–49
voter behavior, 251–52
Singapore Alliance Party (SAP), 238
Singapore People's Party, 252
Sino-Portuguese Joint Declaration of Macau, 77, 89
Social Action Party (Thai.), 200, 203
Social Democratic League (Japan), 107
Social Democratic Party (Sing.), 238, 248, 252
Socialist Party of Malaysia, 213
Social Weather Stations, 149, 159
State's rights, 227, 229, 271
"Struggle PDI" (PDI-P; Indon.), 263, 270–71, 273, 276–78
Students, 235, 262, 264–65
Suharto, 255, 259, 261–64, 269
Sukarno, 257–59, 269

Taiwan, 34–49
campaigning and voting behavior, 45–47
democracy assessment, 32–34
electoral system, 35–36
party system, 35–45
Taiwan Independence Party (TAIP), 37, 40, 43, 45
Tangwai/DPP, 36–37, 42
Team of Seven, 266, 268

Term of office, 119, 198, 240, 265
Thailand, 187–209
  campaigning in, 191–94, 196–97
  democracy assessment, 204–8
  electoral system, 187, 194–200, 204–7
  party system, 191–92, 199–205
  reform movement, 188–91
  voter behavior, 187, 189, 192–94, 198–99, 204–5
Thai Rak Thai Party, 192, 200, 203–4
Three Unions (Macau), 82
Tiananmen Square incident, 50, 53, 61
Tong Chi Kin, 79, 86
Towns, 29–30, 244–46
Transfer of power, 150–51, 169, 179–82
Tung Chee-hwa, 65–66, 71
"Turncoatism," 153
"Twenty Points," 227

Unification National Party (UNP) (Korea), 120, 126, 130, 134, 138, 143
Union for the Construction of Macau, 84, 86
Union for the Promotion of Progress (Macau), 82–83, 86
Unions, 56, 65, 82, 105, 107, 235–36
United Ants (HK.), 55
United Democrats (HK.), 59
United Liberal Democrats (ULD; Korea), 120, 126–27, 135, 142
United Malays National Organisation (UMNO), 213, 215–19, 222–23, 225–26, 228–30, 238, 246
United Nations, 170, 176
United Nations Transitional Authority in Cambodia (UNTAC), 166–68, 178
United People's Party (Sing.), 237
United Sabah National Organisation (USNO; Malay.), 228
Venecia, Jose de, 154–56, 159
Vietnamese, 166–67, 174–75, 179–80
Villages, 18–28, 151
Violence, 137–38, 144, 165, 167, 173, 176, 211, 238, 263–64

Vote-buying, 14, 84–91, 138, 144, 168, 177, 181, 191, 196–97, 199–200, 208, 222–23, 229–30, 250
Voter behavior, 9
  attitude on elections, 25–26, 30, 147–50, 159–61, 163, 181–84, 194, 205
  candidate image voting, 10, 142, 158–59, 161
  class voting, 158, 162–63, 192–93
  "election fatigue," 206
  electoral rule confusion, 109–10
  ethnic voting, 157, 224–25, 230
  government or opposition voting, 143
  issue voting, 10, 56–58, 143–44
  name recognition and recall, 152
  party identification, 10, 55–58, 109–10, 143, 154, 225–26
  protest vote, 262
  regional voting, 121, 139–44, 179, 192–94, 225, 257
  and religion, 158–59, 225, 230, 276
  "sentimental votes," 88
  social cohesion and, 110–11, 140
  turnout, 61, 69, 80–81, 109, 113, 140, 147, 150, 152, 168–69, 178, 187, 204, 206, 224, 251, 255, 260, 262
  See also under country name
Voter education, 173, 177–78, 184, 199
Voter restrictions, 52–53, 77
  registration, 61, 69, 86, 167–68, 173, 181, 212–13, 235, 240, 242
Vote sharing agreements, 266, 275–76
Voting
  in advance, 199, 205
  compulsory, 198–99, 205, 207, 235, 240, 242
  by expatriates, 199, 207
  franchise, 54, 64, 66, 69–71, 80, 89, 93, 150, 205, 213, 240, 246, 257
  by mail, 207
  secret ballots, 19, 88, 241

Wahid, Abdurrahman ("Gus Dur"), 263–64, 270, 276–78
Workers' Party (Sing.), 238, 241, 243, 248, 252

About the Contributors

JAMES UNG-HO CHIN is associate dean of the School of Humanities and Social Sciences, University of Papua New Guinea. He has published widely on Malaysian, especially Sabah and Sarawak, politics. His most recent publications include *Chinese Politics in Sarawak* (1997) and *The Chinese of Southeast Asia* (2000).

JEFFREY C. GALLUP is a member of the Board of the Cambodian Institute of Human Rights in Phnom Penh. A former American diplomat and Visiting Fellow at the National Endowment for Democracy's International Forum for Democratic Studies, he has written on human rights and democratization for various journals. He is working on a book-length study of the 1998 Cambodian elections.

JOHN FUH-SHENG HSIEH is professor of government and international studies and director of the Center for Asian Studies at the University of South Carolina. He received his Ph.D. in political science from the University of Rochester and has written extensively on constitutional choice, electoral systems, electoral behavior, political parties, democratization, and foreign policy.

LO SHIU HING is associate professor in the Department of Politics and Public Administration at the University of Hong Kong. He is the author of *The Politics of Democratization in Hong Kong* (1997) and *Political Development in Macau* (1995).

SURIN MAISRIKROD, formerly a journalist based in Bangkok, received his Ph.D. in political science from the University of Hawaii. He is currently a senior lecturer in the politics program at James Cook University, Queensland, Australia. Before moving to Australia in 1995, he was a researcher at the Institute of Southeast Asian Studies (ISEAS) in Singapore.

DIANE MAUZY is professor of political science at the University of British Columbia, Vancouver, Canada. She has authored five books and edited one, and has written numerous articles. She is the former president of the Canadian Council of Southeast Asian Studies and served on the Southeast Asian Council of the Association for Asian Studies.

DAVID NEWMAN is associate professor of public policy at the National University of Singapore. He received his Ph.D. in political science from the University of Rochester. He is coauthor (with Bruce Bueno de Mesquita and Alvin Rabushka) of *Forecasting Political Events: The Future of Hong Kong* (1985) and *Red Flag over Hong Kong* (1996).

EMERSON M.S. NIOU is associate professor of political science and director of the Center for Chinese Electoral Studies and the Program in Asian Security Studies at Duke University. He is coauthor of *The Balance of Power* (1989) and numerous articles in the fields of international relations, East Asian politics, and electoral affairs.

CHAN WOOK PARK is professor of political science at Seoul National University. He received his Ph.D. in political science from the University of Iowa and has taught at Franklin and Marshall College and Duke University. His articles have appeared in *Legislative Studies Quarterly, Journal of Legislative Studies, Asian Survey,* and other scholarly publications.

STEVEN ROOD is the Country Representative to the Philippines for the Asia Foundation. He received his Ph.D. in political science from Boston University and previously was professor of political science at the University of the Philippines College Baguio, where his research focused on local governance, community development, and Philippine politics and society.

MICHAEL F. THIES is assistant professor of political science at the University of California, Los Angeles, and 1999–2000 National Fellow at the Hoover Institution, Stanford University. He has published extensively on Japanese elections, with articles appearing in the *American Journal of Political Science, British Journal of Political Science, World Politics,* and *Comparative Political Studies*. His current research focuses on interparty delegation in coalition governments and on the electoral foundations of legislative organization.

DONALD E. WEATHERBEE is the Donald S. Russell Professor Emeritus of Contemporary Foreign Policy at the University of South Carolina. He specializes in the politics and foreign policy of Southeast Asia, with special interest in Indonesian affairs.